Leadership in Leisure Services:
Making a Difference

Debra J. Jordan, Re.D.

University of Northern Iowa

Leadership in Leisure Services:
Making a Difference

Debra J. Jordan, Re.D.

University of Northern Iowa

Venture Publishing, Inc.
1999 Cato Avenue, State College, PA 16801

Copyright © 1996
Venture Publishing, Inc.

1999 Cato Avenue
State College, PA 16801
Phone (814) 234-4561; FAX (814) 234-1651

Photographs used in this book are courtesy of the following:

The American Red Cross, Waterloo, Iowa
The Black Hawk County Community Playhouse, Waterloo, Iowa
Cedar Falls Lutheran Home, Cedar Falls, Iowa
Conestoga Council of Girl Scouts, Waterloo, Iowa
Family YMCA of Black Hawk County, Waterloo, Iowa
Harmony House, Waterloo, Iowa
Hartman Nature Reserve, Waterloo, Iowa
The University of Northern Iowa Public Relations Department, Cedar Falls, Iowa
Western Home, Cedar Falls, Iowa
YWCA of Black Hawk County, Waterloo, Iowa

Production Supervisor: Richard Yocum
Manuscript Editing: Michele L. Barbin and Diane K. Bierly
Layout, Design and Graphics: Michele L. Barbin
Cover Designed and Illustrated by Sandra Sikorski, Sikorski Design

Library of Congress Catalogue Card Number 96-60762
ISBN 0-910251-83-5

For Zu—Thank you for making a difference.

TABLE OF CONTENTS

Section III
Synergy in Leadership:
Pulling It All Together 303

PREFACE

All of us have been influenced by great leaders in some way or another. It might have been through our admiration of their work—their ability to get the job done, the smoothness with which they handled diverse situations, or the way they seemed to do good things for people in spite of inevitable difficulties. In addition, we have been influenced by people important to us who exhibited a variety of leadership and followership skills. We have also learned from our own struggles with leadership and followership throughout our lives, although we might not have recognized it at the time.

This text is an outgrowth of my own journey through leadership, and it is but a step in the process. I have learned that leadership is something one does not *do*, but *is*. Being something requires time, focused energy, and a commitment to continuous learning. It requires a willingness to take risks, to stand up for what one believes, and the strength and courage to pick oneself up after unsuccessful attempts. In learning to become a leader, then, one must first come to accept that notion that not all leadership experiences will be successful. In fact, we can often learn more from unsuccessful efforts than those that required no real challenge or reflection.

Leadership is a difficult concept to thoroughly understand. However, we do use the term in everyday language, "Danielle is going to be an excellent leader!" or, "Boy, his leadership was not very effective, was it?" There is some shared meaning in these exchanges, although just what exactly was meant is not easily known. Although leadership as a construct might be difficult to grasp, many believe that leadership is the crux of the recreation, parks, leisure services, and tourism field. Because we are a people-oriented discipline, leadership is a common element of all aspects of the profession, no matter the setting, through which one provides leisure services to participants. This text is an attempt to capture some of the elements of leadership which are specific to the breadth of the field of leisure services, and to provide a starting (or continuation) point from which developing leaders may learn.

To aid in putting the pieces together, this text is divided into three sections: a foundation, the skills needed in working with people, and capstone material. In Section I, The Foundation: Developing the Underlying Construct, information is provided to help place later information into perspective. This section offers insight into expectations of a leader and is intended to assist readers in seeing themselves in relation to leadership. The very nature of our profession dictates that we learn about people—information in this first section will provide a basis upon which to develop specific skills. Through learning about how people perceive leadership, ways of looking at and conceptualizing leadership, and through learning about human development as it relates to leisure services, leaders will be best prepared for a variety of situations.

Section II, Working with People: Essential Skills of Leadership, begins to delve into the specific skill areas required of successful and effective leisure services leaders. Technical skills, conceptual skills, and human relations skills constitute necessary competencies of leisure services leadership. The material in this section is comprised of information and knowledge needed and utilized by leaders and followers alike, and in a variety of settings. To be either an effective follower or an effective leader, skills in working with others are absolutely critical. Group dynamics, communication skills, approaches and techniques for managing difficulties, and managing and motivating participant behaviors are all necessary to effective leadership in leisure services.

The purpose of Section III, Synergy: Pulling it All Together, is to pull the foundational material and the information about specific skills and techniques together in a cohesive blend of leadership knowledge. Issues such as diversity, leader values and ethics, and risk management are presented for consideration and implementation with direct leadership techniques. In addition to knowing and practicing basic skills, leisure services leaders need to stay abreast of social and professional issues as they arise. This requires ongoing education and a commitment to lifelong learning.

One intent of this text is for readers to learn the material and then practice it—with friends, family, and in work and school situations. Reading about leadership will aid in cognitive knowledge about leadership; however, becoming a better leader can only be achieved with practice. Therefore, readers are encouraged to use this book as a guide in their own leadership development—to reflect, practice, receive feedback, and practice some more.

In addition to acknowledging those participants and students who have helped me to learn and hone my own leadership skills, appreciation and acknowledgment are also expressed to those who have impacted my professional life and encouraged my study of leadership. I have considered these individuals to be personal mentors and leaders in their fields of study and owe them each a great deal of gratitude. Heartfelt thank-yous go out to Chris Cashel, Roger Guthrie, Karla Henderson, Michal Anne Lord, Frank Lupton, John and Nancy Peterson, Paul Petzoldt, Ruth Russell, Sherril York, my colleagues at UNI, and my family for their support, challenges, and an overall willingness to provide me what I needed throughout my own development. In addition, a special note of appreciation is extended to the people who helped in the review of this manuscript: Jeff Ashby, Victoria DeFrancisco, Don DeGraaf, and Kathy DeGraaf. Chris Cashel served as the primary reviewer and her comments and insights were greatly appreciated.

Just as these individual leaders have made a difference in my life I suspect that in some form, leadership has also made a difference in your life. My hope is that as a developing leader in the field of leisure services, you will make a difference in the lives of others, as well.

—DJJ, 1996

Section I

The Foundation:
Developing the Underlying Construct

Leadership is a complex process which is not yet fully understood, yet through study (and practice) information can be learned to aid in the understanding of what leadership is and how to use it effectively. To help in the study of the various elements of leadership this text is divided into three sections, all of which are inextricably intertwined. Successful leadership requires more than technical skills (which could make one an excellent technician). It also requires an understanding of why one is doing what, and an understanding of how the practice of leadership influences the people with whom we work.

In this section of the text, the foundation is laid—information is provided to help place later materials into perspective and to provide a context for learning more specific skills. Basic definitional information, theories and models of leadership, and material about human development are presented as the frame around which other leadership skills are built.

By examining and understanding the evolution of how leadership has been defined and illustrated one can better view leadership as a process. This is important because without this material it can be difficult to understand the *why* of leadership. Therefore (while perhaps a bit drier than other material), material about definitions; leader competencies, traits, and qualities; and how leaders are identified is provided early on.

In addition, as a basis for developing one's own leadership style preferences, it is important to have a sense of what leadership looks like. Thus, several alternative ways of looking at leadership are presented in this section as theories and models of leadership. It is hoped that out of these alternative views, one or more will feel like they fit. It often is easier to integrate book and practical knowledge into one's own experience base if a model or representation of a phenomenon feels like it makes sense.

Once exposed to background information about leadership, it is just as important to have a solid knowledge base about people—people, after all, are what defines a leader. The people whom we call clients, guests, customers, participants, users, players and by other titles are the individuals who make leisure services exciting, challenging, and highly rewarding. Thus, information about physical, socioemotional, intellectual, and moral development across the life span and how cultural differences affect that development is presented.

This first section of this text provides a basis for understanding—a foundation for—leadership. It may be a section that is read and discussed early in one's leadership education as well as a place to return after learning and practicing specific leadership skills. In this manner, a model (or philosophy) of leadership that provides guidance in a wide variety of leadership opportunities can be further developed.

Chapter One
Learning Opportunities

Through studying this chapter students will have the opportunity to:

- define leadership and followership;
- explore common leadership skills and competencies;
- identify qualities and traits of successful leaders;
- examine three classes of leadership; and
- explain how leaders are identified from within groups.

Photo courtesy of the University of Northern Iowa Public Relations Department

CHAPTER

(1)

Understanding Leadership

Recreation and leisure services is an exciting field! Practitioners work with all types of people in a variety of settings. Leisure services professionals help women and men, the elderly and children, those with disabilities and those without, people with low incomes and people with very high incomes to achieve a high quality of life. We do this through recreation and leisure activities in the out-of-doors, in hospitals, in recreation centers, in eldercare facilities, at tourist destinations, and in military settings. As you might imagine, being a leader of recreation and leisure services can be a demanding yet highly enjoyable task.

In various ways the field of recreation and leisure services directly impacts the health and well-being of all individuals. People use leisure time and engage in recreation activities for many reasons including to learn new skills, as a means to refresh themselves, and to share in fellowship with friends and family. For most people, recreation and leisure services are important elements of their lives. They engage in self-initiated activities as well as those provided by leisure service practitioners.

In the delivery of leisure services, recreation and leisure service practitioners interact with participants in ways that may enhance or detract from the leisure experience. A quality recreation experience commonly results in positive feelings and mental well-being, and in physical, social, and spiritual benefits. On the other hand, a poor recreation experience may leave a participant with negative feelings and a desire to avoid other similar leisure opportunities.

Quite often the difference between quality and poor leisure or recreation experiences can be traced back to the people involved. In particular, the leadership provided at an event has a tremendous influence on its success or failure. Because leadership is an inherent factor in structured recreation experiences, it is a skill needed by *all* leisure service professionals. Examples of leadership in recreation and leisure services surround us: a youth sports coach directs the team to prepare for practice; a lifeguard provides feedback about a swimmer's stroke; an executive director makes a presentation to the board. In all of these instances, someone engages in certain behaviors and exudes certain qualities that results in others identifying her or him as a leader.

This chapter will explore the basic concepts related to leadership. As you will quickly learn, leadership is a composite of many concepts, theories, and practical skills. This chapter will provide the foundation for the remainder of the text. First, discussions will revolve around defining terms, then leadership qualities and competencies will be addressed. Finally, classes of leadership and how leaders are identified will be presented.

Definitions

Before getting too far into the text it is important to discuss definitions of terms used throughout the book, such as *leisure* and *recreation*. There are many varied definitions of leisure and recreation used in the field today. It appears, however, that to laypeople (i.e., nonleisure services professionals), the terms recreation and leisure generally mean the same thing. Frequently, these terms are used interchangeably and seem to refer to nonwork activities engaged in during one's free time. This text takes a similarly loose (layperson) approach to defining leisure and recreation.

Therefore, throughout this text leisure and recreation are used interchangeably and refer to those nonwork activities in which people engage during their free time. By this definition, then, leisure and recreation might include such things as arts and crafts, game-like activities undertaken during physical rehabilitation, reading, exercise routines, sports, music, board games, camping, and others. In addition to coming to an agreement on the definitions of recreation and leisure, it is also important to define leadership.

On the face of it, leadership may seem to be an easy term to define. After all, most everyone reading this text has been in some type of leadership position at some time in her or his life. And, it is a safe bet that everyone reading this text has been a follower to someone else's leadership. If each person in a leisure services leadership class was asked to define leadership, however, the answers would certainly be varied, and most likely ambiguous and difficult to "get a handle on." Because individual experiences influence one's view of concepts, defining leadership is not as easy as it might first seem.

A well-phrased definition helps in coming to a basic understanding of a term, in this case, leadership; it is also important to clearly state the definition of leadership used for this text so that the meaning of the term throughout the book is understood. Prior to defining leadership, however, it is wise to appreciate the difficulty people have had over the years in agreeing on a single definition of leadership. While not covered in depth here, those studying leadership should know that over the years leadership has been defined as:

- a group process;
- the personality of the leader;
- the inducement of compliance in followers;
- the exercise of influence by one person (designated as the leader);
- the behaviors one exhibits (e.g., planning, organizing, directing);
- a power relationship between an individual and others;
- an effect of interaction (When certain people come together, one emerges as the leader.);
- a differentiated role (e.g., leader, follower);
- the initiation of structure (e.g., taking initiative, getting a task started);
- both as art and skill; and
- a combination of two or more of the above definitions (Bass, 1990).

These definitions evolved from interpretations of observations and studies of various groups and leaders. The definitions are fluid; that is, based on one person's perceptions, leadership is one thing and in another person's eyes leadership is something different. In the following chapter, which deals with leadership theories, these definitions are based on the models and theories which people developed in an attempt to understand leadership better.

A definition, then, is a starting point for understanding leadership. Once a construct or term is understood, it is much easier to integrate it into one's own style of working with people. It is also easier to use the information to grow and improve in the use of leadership techniques.

Defining Leadership

It is critical to gain an appreciation for how the term leadership is used throughout this text so that everyone operates from a common basis of understanding. Remember, defining leadership is no easy task and definitions have changed and evolved over many years of study. It makes sense to define leadership as a combination of many elements. Throughout this text, leadership is viewed as:

> a dynamic process of interactions between two or more members of a group which involves recognition and acceptance of leader-follower roles by group members within a certain situation.

In the following chapter you will be exposed to various theories of leadership which will help to explain what is meant by this definition. In the meantime, examining each component of the definition would be helpful.

Leadership is a dynamic process...

Dynamic process refers to the fact that leadership changes constantly; it is never stagnant. In any group, leadership fluctuates based on internal and external factors affecting the group. In addition, as a process, leadership consists of a series of actions which evolve over time. In other words, a single act or behavior that might relate to leadership does not necessarily define a leader.

...of interactions between two or more members of a group...

The term *interaction* refers to reciprocal actions which occur between people. For instance, a reciprocal action would occur when one person says hello and another person nods her or his head in response. It is an action-response process. Typically, leadership interactions include verbal and nonverbal communication, a sharing of tasks, and the establishment of relationships. The term *group* refers to two or more people, who together, form a complete unit and share common goals. More will be said about groups later in the text.

> *...which involves recognition and acceptance of leader-follower roles by group members...*

In order to be a leader, one must first be recognized as a leader. If others do not see and accept that person as the leader, leadership does not exist (Geis, Boston & Hoffman, 1985). Leader-follower roles are differentiated from one another by intent (i.e., what one has her or his mind set to do), interpersonal skills (commonly called people skills), task orientation (i.e., good leaders must be able to get others involved in a task or job), and an understanding of how to work toward goal achievement (i.e., leaders take an active initiating approach, followers work cooperatively with the leader to make things happen). In the definition of leadership used for this text, leaders and followers fulfill different roles within a group, all necessary for effective group functioning.

> *...within a certain situation.*

This will be discussed in later chapters, but be aware that leadership tends to be situational. That is to say that in one situation one person may be a leader, yet in another situation she or he may not be the leader. Some of this is based on the skills and experience of the leader, some is based on the skills and experience of group members; yet other influences are elements such as time, weather, and safety issues. Whatever the reason, leadership roles change with the situation.

Followership

To discuss leadership without discussing followership would be missing half of the leadership equation. As mentioned previously, without followers there would be no leaders. Followers recognize, acknowledge, and accept one (or more) person as the leader. Despite this, the concept of followership has been receiving study and attention only recently. It is commonly believed that to be an effective leader (i.e., to use leader qualities effectively and efficiently) one must first be a good follower. Therefore, a good follower shares many traits with effective leaders (Bass, 1990; Chemers & Ayman, 1993; Foy, 1994).

Followership and leadership are interrelated and neither makes sense without the other (Bass, 1990). As processes, leadership and followership are mutual acts of influence and counterinfluence. That is, reinforcement of behaviors, attitudes and values goes both ways. Followers' expectations affect the performance of leaders (i.e., what followers expect leaders to do affects the way leaders behave, and vice versa). Furthermore, the followers' perceptions of the leader's motives and actions constrain what the leader can accomplish. For example, if followers perceive that leaders are being self-serving, they may block successful leadership. On the other hand, if followers perceive that a leader acts for the good of the group, they usually will work harder to help the leader accomplish the group goals. Leaders exert the same types of influence on followers.

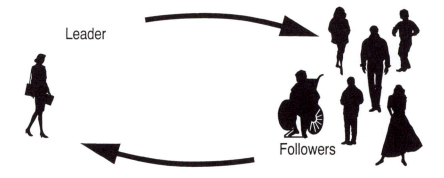

Figure 1.1   *Successful leadership requires reciprocal interactions between leaders and followers.*

Good followers are as important, if not more important, than good leaders. Therefore, a wise leader is one who practices good followership when appropriate. Capable followers use their skills to help "get the job done" and work cooperatively, putting pieces of a task together to achieve a shared goal. Followers work within groups in several ways. Examples in the leisure services profession include: to help a sports team to win; to successfully prepare for a special event; or to prepare a budget. Within the group the leader serves in the role of group guide, director, counselor, resource, authority, and other roles as needs dictate.

As mentioned earlier, capable leaders and followers share many traits, skills, and competencies. Leaders typically are stronger in initiative, relationship building, and conceptual skills than are followers because these are the ingredients that help groups to function well. In this next section of the text, the various types of skills that are typically associated with leadership, and which we now know also are associated with effective followership, will be discussed.

Leader Competencies/Skills

There are many areas in which successful leaders are highly skilled. Some of these skills might be seemingly innate (i.e., a person is born with the skills) while other skills seem to be learned. Whichever is the case, effective leaders continually work on their skills to become better at what they do. Three areas of skills have been identified which combine to make a skilled leader. They are *technical skills, human relation skills,* and *conceptual skills.*

Technical Skills

Technical skills are those that are specific to accomplishing tasks. They enable a person to do a particular job or task. Among other things, leaders plan, implement and evaluate programs and services (Chemers & Ayman, 1993; Phipps, 1987; Russell, 1986). Leaders also deal with logistics, safety and legal issues, and office tasks. Other technical skills that are used by leisure practitioners in direct leadership positions include leading songs, games, and activities in a variety of settings. Technical skills are readily taught to most leaders-to-be. It should be noted that a person who is successful at technical tasks may be an excellent technician, yet a poor leader. An effective leader also needs strong human relations and conceptual skills.

Human Relations Skills

Human relations skills (also called interpersonal skills) are those skills and leadership techniques that involve relationships with people (Chemers & Ayman, 1993; Phipps, 1987; Russell, 1986). Understanding group dynamics, facilitating cooperation and trust building among participants, and being a good communicator all fit within the human relations skills of leadership. Understanding and being able to resolve conflicts, making people feel welcomed, valued, and respected also fit within the human relations component. This component of leadership is required to be successful in the field of leisure services. It is difficult to be successful in a human services profession, such as leisure, and lack human relations skills. In addition to technical and human relations competencies, being able to "see the big picture" is another important skill for successful leadership.

Conceptual Skills

Conceptual skills include the ability to analyze, anticipate, and see the big picture and are a bit more esoteric than the others (Chemers & Ayman, 1993; Phipps, 1987; Russell, 1986). Critical thinking, problem solving, creativity, and being able to handle ambiguity are commonly considered conceptual skills. Being able to articulate a philosophy of recreation and how it guides one's use of leadership styles, contributing to the agency, and striving to better society are other competencies which fit within this skill group. In addition, following the organizational mission through one's actions and decisions, adhering to internal values, and understanding one's role in promoting the leisure services profession are also elements of conceptual skills. Without conceptual skills it would be difficult to integrate technical and human relations skills into leadership situations.

All three of the abovementioned leadership skill domains are critical to being successful in the field of leisure. Much study, practice, and experience are necessary to become proficient in the three areas. As with all concepts there is ongoing study and refinement of what skill domains characterize leadership.

Figure 1.2   The three functions of leadership are all needed for effective leadership.

Impacts of Sex, Race, and Age

The skills identified in the previous section have been identified as being critical to successful leadership. Research has shown that leaders, if they are to be effective, should be highly skilled in technical, human relations, and conceptual skills (in addition to other things) (Bass, 1990; Bolton, 1979; Chemers & Ayman, 1993; Johnson, 1993). Because early research about leadership primarily utilized white males as study subjects, much of it did not examine the influences of sex, ethnicity, or age on the effective use of the three types of skills. As these influences became more prominent in terms of the study of and concern about leadership, researchers began to investigate the impact on the delivery of leisure services.

Stereotypes people hold related to demographic variables, such as ethnicity, age and sex, influence the acceptance of leadership by followers (Chemers & Ayman, 1993). Ashmore and DelBoca (1979) defined a stereotype as "a structured set of beliefs about personal attributes of a group of people" (as cited in Chemers & Ayman, 1993). When individuals identify and acknowledge the leader, they mix expectations (i.e., stereotypes) of leadership with expectations about the group that person appears to represent (e.g., elderly, Asian Americans, disabled). If the expectations and stereotypes do not appear to be in "sync," group members will not follow that person, or will do so with some hesitation.

For instance, teenagers often are perceived (and therefore, expected) to be irresponsible, immature, unable to make sound decisions, and impatient. Leaders are expected to exhibit the opposite characteristics; therefore, the expectations of teens and leaders are perceived as incompatible. While the stereotype is not accurately applied to all teens, as a whole, teenagers would not be viewed as leaders. Obviously, this would eliminate leadership opportunities for many talented teens. Similar scenarios could be devised relating the influences of sex, ethnicity, and physical impairment on the perceived acceptance of leadership.

Generally, in the United States society prescribes roles for women and men, for old and young, and for whites and people of color. On the face of it, some of these roles would seem incompatible with the competencies identified as necessary for leadership. For instance, it has long been noted that in U.S. culture, women are expected and perceived to be better at human relations skills (i.e., better with relationships) than

Photo courtesy of the Cedar Falls Lutheran Home

Leisure services leaders are creative and have a sense of humor which they are not afraid to show.

men, and men are presumably better than women with technical and conceptual skills (i.e., better with doing and thinking) (Bass, 1990). In addition, there is a stereotype that men should be dominant over women. This might lead one to believe that men would make better leaders than women.

What has been found, however, is that in general, men have had more opportunities for formal leadership than have women; at the same time, women have garnered much experience in informal settings and in followership roles.

> Once they [women] are legitimized as leaders, the preponderance of research suggests that women actually do not behave differently from men in the same kinds of positions. (Bass, 1990, p. 725)

The expectations that followers hold for them may differ, but leadership capabilities are the same. Therefore, group expectations must be managed for a female (or elderly, or Black) leader to be truly effective.

To make a generalization that one sex, age group, or race is better at leadership than another is highly inaccurate. To be an *effective* leader, rather than a woman leader, elderly leader, or Native-American leader, one must be skilled in the three types of skills and have the ability to use those skills in appropriate fashions. An effective leader, therefore, might be anyone: a 10-year-old, a person of Hispanic heritage, an individual who is blind, a woman, or anyone else with the skills and initiative to fill a leadership role.

Leader Traits and Qualities

In addition to the three types of competencies/skills necessary for successful leadership, there are many qualities or traits that people have identified as being important to leadership. Generally, people believe that a leader is someone who has many positive qualities. Several studies have been conducted which report lists of desirable leadership qualities. Much of that information is reported under the following headings.

Creativity

According to Cohen (1990), a leader is one who is creative. Creativity involves thinking broadly and a willingness to try new ideas. It also includes not being afraid to look silly. Creative people can usually think in abstract terms and have an outlook on life that lets them see one thing from many different perspectives. Creative people color outside of the lines (and are proud of it), challenge others to think in a fluid fashion, and have a good sense of humor. Being creative is necessary whether one is leading an activity, solving a facility-related problem, or planning programs.

Positive Mental Attitude

Highly sought-after leaders are able to maintain a positive attitude in the midst of not-so-positive situations. A positive mental attitude (PMA) allows a leader to always see the bright side of situations. The ability to view a situation from the funny side is often the way that learning can occur. People with PMAs are fascinating people. They always seem upbeat and look for the good in others and in situations. People desire to be around others who have a positive attitude; leaders who can maintain this tend to be well-respected, and consequently, successful.

High Expectations

Effective and respected leaders are those with high expectations (Cohen, 1990). These leaders have high expectations of themselves as well as others. They expect quality, are willing to work for quality, and thereby achieve quality. High expectations carry over into all aspects of leadership—technical skills (e.g., striving for a perfect safety record), human relations skills (e.g., expecting positive and upbeat people skills), and conceptual skills (e.g., expecting to be able to find solutions to all dilemmas). The self-fulfilling prophecy suggests that as people expect, they receive. This means that a leader who expects a great deal and who has high standards commonly finds that followers meet these high expectations. At the same time, a leader with low standards and expectations of others may find that followers rise only as high as those expectations.

A Sense of Identity

An effective leader has a sense of identity; an understanding of who one is and who one is not (Hitt, 1993). A sense of self allows one to be in many different situations and remain true to oneself. Identity is based on a set of core values, the guiding beliefs in one's life, and is related to

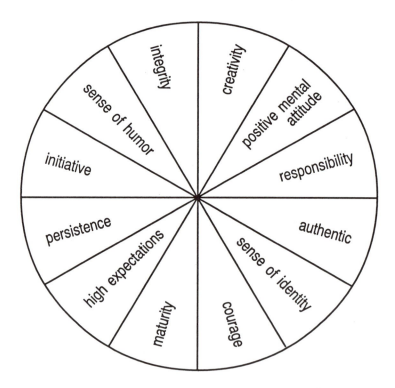

Figure 1.3   *Leaders are expected to have many positive qualities and traits.*

integrity. It is what allows a person to feel a sense of wholeness and integration within oneself. A leader with a strong sense of self exudes self-confidence and a sense of who she or he is no matter the situation. These leaders tend to be easy to follow because they are consistent in their leadership efforts.

Has Integrity

Every day people are faced with ethical choices. Respected and effective leaders have the integrity and courage to be honest with themselves and others. Integrity means doing what is right rather than what is the easiest. It is the basis for trust between people. If a group does not trust a leader, the leader will be ineffective in working with the group. Like a person with a strong sense of self, a leader with integrity has a solid core of values and ethical principles upon which she or he bases decisions, actions, and thoughts. These values are apparent to others and remain consistent across situations.

Accepts Responsibility

A successful leader willingly accepts responsibility for what occurs; she or he is accountable not only to others, but also to herself or himself. For effective leaders, responsibility comes from inside themselves rather than outside (from others). Responsibility comes from the awareness that one has the freedom to choose and the knowledge that all freedoms have corresponding responsibilities. Successful and effective leaders accept responsibility for their thoughts, attitudes, and actions and do not try to place that responsibility on others or on a situation.

Has Courage

An effective leader has courage to do what she or he believes is right, to stand up for her or his convictions, and to go against the grain when needed; she or he has the courage to take risks (Hitt, 1993). Courage involves the willingness to make and admit mistakes so that as much as possible can be learned from the situation. Courage, however, must be accompanied by consideration. Being considerate of others in the face of courage is necessary to achieve a balance in leadership.

Is Authentic

Authenticity is defined as "being for real" (Hitt, 1993). Being authentic addresses the need for a leader to be herself or himself while maintaining a sense of responsibility. An authentic leader is one who is not merely the job position she or he represents (e.g., building supervisor, aerobics instructor, naturalist), but who allows herself or himself to be fully human while being the leader. Authentic and successful leaders make mistakes, have good days and bad days, and are perceived as "down to earth" people.

Other research has reported desirable leader qualities to include honesty, competence, vision, inspiration, intelligence, fairness, tolerance, straightforwardness, imagination, and reliability (Kouzes & Posner, 1987). Bass (1990) identified additional items for the list of leader qualities: a sense of friendliness, self-motivation, supportive of group tasks, control over one's own emotions, dominance, great physical energy, a willingness to take risks, strong values, and maturity.

In discussing desired qualities of camp counselors (who are recreation leaders in an outdoor setting), Meier and Mitchell (1993) provide a self-assessment checklist of leadership qualities against which an individual could measure herself or himself to assess personal leadership potential. According to Meier and Mitchell desired qualities of leaders include the following:

• stamina	• persistence
• good health	• curiosity
• pleasing appearance	• good manners
• tact	• cooperation
• sense of humor	• positive attitude
• good communication skills	• warm personality
• adaptability	• initiative
• emotional maturity	• can follow as well as lead

Many other authors have discussed a variety of leader qualities; most resemble the list above (Bass, 1990; Chemers & Ayman, 1993; Foy, 1994; Hitt, 1993; Niepoth, 1983; Sessoms & Stevenson, 1981; Shivers, 1980). It is important to recognize that while particular qualities are important, one must have many skills and a knowledge base to be a truly effective and respected leader. In and of themselves, leadership qualities will not result in effective leadership.

Values

A solid core of values is one of the items identified by researchers and followers as being necessary for effective leadership. Discussions about values often arouse controversy with some believing that is it not right for any one person to assert her or his values on another while others believe this to be absolutely necessary. One belief position asserts that all values are equally good; another belief paradigm judges values by religious or philosophical tenets. It is common to question where (and by whom) values should be taught—the home, church, school, playground, or other institution.

The fact is that values are everywhere and none of us operates in a values vacuum (Edginton, Jordan, DeGraaf & Edginton, 1995). Everything we say and do reflects our values. The way we wear our hair, choice of clothing, even the language we use reflects our values. Therefore, it is very important that leaders in leisure services know and understand the values they promote covertly (subtly) as well as overtly (purposefully) through their work and chosen leadership styles.

In addition to values related to right and wrong, there are other values that effective and well-respected leaders exhibit in their work. These values tend to distinguish leaders from followers and cause certain individuals to stand out. Used appropriately, the following values or qualities indicate a commitment to positive leadership opportunities.

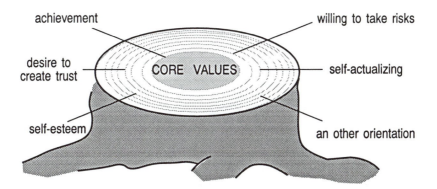

Figure 1.4 *A solid core of values is one of the items identified as necessary for effective leadership.*

An Achievement Orientation

Achievement orientation is a value which indicates a sense of initiative or taking action. A leader who exhibits an achievement orientation and focuses on achieving goals (i.e., societal, agency, or personal) tends to be well-respected. An achievement orientation can help a leader see a task through from beginning to end (including cleanup and evaluation). It involves staying focused on the task and working with people to insure that each individual's strengths are being utilized to achieve group goals.

An Other Orientation

In most leisure services situations, simply manifesting an achievement orientation is insufficient to be an effective and capable leader. In addition to being goal-focused an effective leader exhibits the value of being other oriented. This means that the needs of others are put ahead of the needs of the leader. For instance, if a special program were being conducted for which T-shirts were made and there were not enough T-shirts for everyone, the leader (not a participant) should be the first one to go without. Without compromising safety and fairness, others' needs should come before the leaders' needs.

A Willingness to Take Risks

Often when people think about risk taking and they envision an element of danger, they wonder why a capable leader would value risk-taking behaviors. As a value, risk taking is important because it enables and drives a leader to try new things; it keeps the leader from falling into a "rut" and being unwilling to change. It is critical, of course, that the risk taking be based on sound knowledge and good judgment. For example, a leader exhibits risk-taking behaviors when she or he decides to keep the center open until 4:00 a.m. so people working third-shift jobs can utilize the facility. If this decision is based on facts, the actual risk (of losing revenues due to low use) is minimized.

A Desire to Create Trustful Relationships

Trust is often perceived as the essence of leadership. Trust must be established between leaders and followers early in the relationship in order for leadership to be most effective. A person who values trust and believes in establishing trust with all participants will engender trust in others as well. Trust between group members often results in the entire experience being highly enjoyable and group goals easy to accomplish.

Self-Actualization

The fact that leaders lead by example and model behaviors is important to remember. Self-actualization is the belief deep inside a person that she or he can do anything to which she or he puts her or his mind. By living and modeling this type of value the leader helps others begin to believe in themselves as well. It is through self-actualization that people learn it is acceptable to fail; therefore, self-actualization is an important value of leaders in leisure services.

Self-Esteem

Self-esteem is evidenced by self-respect and tells a lot about how a person feels about herself or himself. High self-esteem means that a person likes and feels good about who she or he is. People with high self-esteem tend to take care of themselves, and to think through consequences before making decisions. Leaders who exhibit high self-esteem tend to be respectful, trusting, and have integrity; that is, we can believe that they will do what they say they will.

Leaders are people who fill a variety of complex roles. They have all of the qualifications and limitations of followers. They have good days and bad days. Some have leadership experience, and some do not. Those who strive to be the most effective in leadership work to develop the skills, competencies, and qualifications of leaders deemed by researchers as necessary to effective leadership. Leaders evolve over time and are continually improving their skills.

Classes of Leadership

So far, we have examined definitions of leadership, explained the types of skills needed for successful leadership, and identified leader qualities and traits which are important to followers and group members. There are many desirable traits and qualities of leaders. These traits and qualities are important whether one is the person leading a recreational activity or the leader developing the budget. These two very different tasks typically are the responsibility of individuals in different classes of leadership. Most commonly, people talk about the three classes of leadership that exist within an organization: *administrative, supervisory*, and *direct*.

Administrative Leadership

The administrative level of leadership also is referred to as the managerial or executive level. Administration typically includes the agency director and assistant directors, or president and vice presidents. If an organization is hierarchical in structure this would be the top layer; in a web or spoke-shaped organizational structure the administration may be at the center or the outer edge. In this class of leadership those tasks primarily concerned with what would be considered administrative matters such as the budget, organizational structure, establishment of a vision and agency philosophy, raising funds, and writing grants are found.

Typically, administrative leaders have responsibility for the entire (or a large part of an) organization. Thus, a solid knowledge of all aspects of an organization, including supervisory and direct leadership, is required for an administrative leader to be most effective. Good people skills and the ability to make sound decisions in the midst of much activity are needed traits for people in this class of leadership.

Supervisory Leadership

Supervisory leadership is commonly thought of as the middle layer or rung of leadership within an agency or organization. Supervisory leaders report to administrators and are expected to supervise, or help guide, those in direct leadership positions. Common titles for this class of leadership include program director, unit leader, district manager, and director of contract services.

Supervisory leaders typically have responsibility for a particular department, program area, or unit within an agency. Individuals in this type of leadership position make some decisions directly related to their particular unit and must be able to work with people and be good problem solvers. When needed, supervisory leaders will step into the role of direct leader. Therefore, a good foundation of direct leadership is necessary to be successful in the supervisory class.

Direct Leadership

In leisure service agencies and organizations the individuals in direct leadership roles are those who provide service directly to participants. If an agency conducts recreation programs, the direct leader is one who plans, prepares for, and implements the specific program. Common titles for people in direct leadership positions include recreation aide, recreation technician, activity leader, camp counselor, and instructor (e.g., martial arts, aerobics, canoe).

Direct leaders also are called face-to-face leaders because they interact on a one-to-one basis with participants. To be successful, direct leaders must have a solid knowledge of the activities which are appropriate to the position (i.e., swim instructors must know the techniques for swimming strokes), understand safety hazards and how to manage them, and practice excellent people skills. Direct leaders are considered front-line staff and, because they interact closely with participants, are considered vital to quality offerings. This text focuses on information and skills primarily needed by those involved in direct leadership.

Although the three basic classes of leadership are distinct, similar skills, values and traits are desirable for leaders in all classes. The skills will be utilized differently as required by the particular groups of followers for each class of leadership. While it is not a hard-and-fast rule, administrative leaders work directly with supervisors; supervisors work with direct leaders; and direct leaders work with participants. Within each of these classes, groups recognize different people as leaders through different mechanisms. There are situations whereby the same person fulfills all three leadership roles for one leisure services agency.

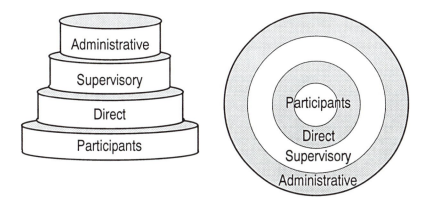

Figure 1.5   *Two ways of viewing the three classes of leadership.*

How Are Leaders Identified?

A person may have the title of leader and still not be accepted as such by the group she or he is to be leading. For instance, in a school classroom a substitute teacher may be the leader—in title. However, if the students do not accept and reinforce that role, the substitute teacher might not be perceived as the actual leader. In fact, when a substitute teacher is in the classroom it is not uncommon for a student in the class to be the true leader of her or his classmates. To be a leader, then, one must be recognized and accepted as such by the group. There are several ways that individuals become recognized and reinforced as leaders by the group. A leader might be *appointed*, she or he might *emerge* from the group, the leader may be *elected*, the person's *charisma* might cause others to follow, and leadership might be attributed to the *"halo effect."*

Appointment

A leader may be appointed to a certain position which identifies her or him as the leader. This may occur from the administrative level within an agency or from within a group. The agency director, for instance, may hire (appoint) a person to be a leader in a position of lifeguard. In another case the group might appoint a leader to facilitate completion of a task. Once appointed, it is up to that person to fulfill the roles and responsibilities of a leader, and to utilize leadership skills and tech-niques to the best of her or his ability. Appointed leaders often earn respect as a leader through their actions and attitudes related to the group goals.

Election

It is quite common in groups for leaders to be elected to leadership positions. In many sporting events, for instance, individuals may be elected leaders and given the title of "team captain." Team captains are expected to guide team members, set the tone for the team, and serve as a motivating force. Often, elected leaders are admired by those who follow; respect is given at first, but it must continue to be earned through leadership actions. It should be remembered that some people are elected to leadership positions due to their popularity, having the most money, or because others are afraid of them. Therefore, an elected leader is not necessarily the best person for the leadership role.

Emergence

In the early stages of group development there are times when a group has no clearly identifiable leader. No one has been appointed or elected, and initially, the group is somewhat adrift. Then, from within the group, one person emerges as the leader. In this situation as the task or group continues to exist, it becomes apparent that one person "rises to the top" in terms of leadership. That individual may be recognized as the leader by group members for her or his knowledge of an activity, her or his skills at mediating conflict, or having an understanding of what the group needs to accomplish. A leader who emerges from a group often has the respect of the group members because she or he is a group member who became the leader.

Charisma

Charisma is defined as personal magnetism or charm. A leader with charisma is usually able to induce group members to follow with ease, and has great influence over them. A charismatic leader arouses a great deal of enthusiasm and loyalty from within the group. In informal leisure settings, charismatic leaders seem to always draw group members to them, followers often work hard to be noticed by a charismatic leader, and followers tend to respect charismatic leaders out of a sense of loyalty. As with elected leaders people with charisma may be very positive role models and leaders (e.g., Jane Addams), or they may be individuals who use their personal charm to the detriment of others (e.g., Adolf Hitler). Care must be taken in the accolades given a leader who is selected based solely on personal charisma.

The Halo Effect

The halo effect refers to how certain attributes or thoughts about a person are carried over into other situations. For instance, if a youngster is a class clown in one classroom, she or he is often perceived to be a class clown in other classes—even if she or he does not engage in clowning behaviors. The same effect occurs in leadership situations. The halo effect describes a scenario whereby a person is a leader in one group or situation and others look to her or him to be the leader in other groups in which she or he is involved.

There are several avenues through which individuals may be identified as leaders. It is important to note that no matter how a person gained the position or title of leader, she or he may not be best suited for the needs of the group and situation. A skilled leader will constantly adapt and develop as situations warrant. In recreation and leisure settings, being aware of how one is perceived as a leader may help in guiding the use of leadership skills and techniques to move the group forward.

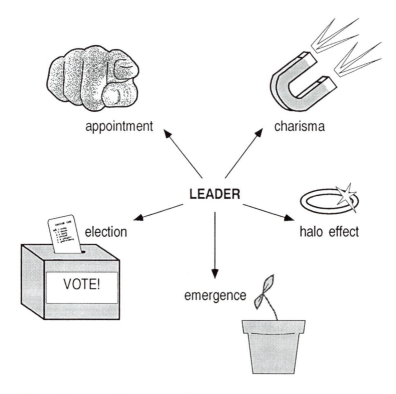

Figure 1.6   *Leaders emerge from within groups in a variety of ways.*

Summary

Leisure services practitioners interact with participants in many ways. These interactions may enhance or detract from the leisure experience. Because leadership is an inherent factor in structured recreation experiences, leadership is a skill needed by *all* leisure service professionals. Leadership can be defined as a dynamic process of interactions between two or more members of a group which involves recognition and acceptance of leader-follower roles by group members within a certain situation. It should be remembered that there are many definitions of leadership and some may find other definitions meaningful.

After establishing a definition of leadership for use in this text, this chapter presented information about necessary competencies and skills of leaders. Leadership skills fall into three categories: technical, human relations, and conceptual skills. Leader traits and qualities were reviewed as were the values of effective and successful leaders. Because it is not possible to live in a values vacuum, it is important for leaders to understand and appreciate the values they promote through action, attire, and attitude.

After examining traits and characteristics of successful leaders, the three classes of leadership were presented: administrative which interacts directly with supervisors; supervisory leaders who report to administrators and interact directly with face-to-face leaders; and direct leaders who also are considered face-to-face leaders because they interact directly with participants. Leaders in all classes of leadership may have a tremendous impact on a successful leisure experience; therefore, learning about leadership is vital for all who intend to work in the leisure services profession.

The Front Line

As women have moved into the ranks of leadership in all situations, research has begun to focus on the effects of gender on effective leadership. Some research shows that men are likely to emerge from groups as leaders because of their aggressiveness, activity, and dominance. It has been reported that female leaders typically show more socioemotional concern for followers than do males. Other research has shown that female leaders are challenged more often than males; men talk more than women in groups; female and male leaders do not differ from one another; and female and male leaders are different from one another. In other words, the research has been contradictory.

Communication is an integral aspect of leadership; therefore, Hawkins (1995) examined gender differences in communication content areas in an effort to predict emerged leadership. Subjects for the study included six mixed-sex groups of four or five individuals who attended a university. The group task was to produce a term paper over the course of the semester. All group meetings were observed and tape recorded, then the tapes were transcribed. The transcribed data were then coded into task-relevant comments (i.e., related to writing the term paper) and social-relevant comments (i.e., related to member feelings, fitting in, friendship). Emerged leadership was measured on an emerged leader scale (questionnaire).

Hawkins found that task-relevant communication was the sole predictor of emerged leadership. Social-relevant comments were not related to whether an individual emerged from within the group as a leader. In addition, females and males did not differ in terms of their communication contributions; and, there were no differences in emerged leadership based on the sex of group members.

Implications for Leaders

Those individuals who verbally contributed to the efforts related to accomplishment of the task were viewed as leaders within the group. In the many small groups found within the field of leisure services, then, it makes sense to keep things on track and on task—if one wishes to be viewed as a leader. As a caveat, however, while socially relevant comments were not relevant to emerged leadership in this study, other research about leadership indicates that attending to the socially relevant aspects of groups is highly important. Leaders who neglect this aspect of leadership may be viewed as ineffective.

Noting the lack of differences in the sex of an individual contributing to leadership may be viewed as positive. Both women and men have much to contribute to groups of all kinds, and those contributions and their interpretation need not be based on theories of dominance and aggression. Making task-relevant contributions helps to define emergent leadership, no matter the gender of the individual making the contribution.

References

Ashmore, R. and DelBoca, F. (1993). In M. Chemers and R. Ayman, Eds., *Leadership theory and research.* San Diego, CA: Academic Press, Inc.

Bass, B. (1990). *Bass and Stogdill's handbook of leadership* (3rd ed.). New York, NY: The Free Press.

Bolton, R. (1979). *People skills.* Englewood Cliffs, NJ: Prentice Hall.

Chemers, M. and Ayman, R. (Eds.). (1993). *Leadership theory and research.* San Diego, CA: Academic Press, Inc.

Cohen, W. (1990). *The art of the leader.* Englewood Cliffs, NJ: Prentice Hall.

Edginton, C., Jordan, D., DeGraaf, D., and Edginton, S. (1995). *Leisure and life satisfaction: Foundational perspectives.* Dubuque, IA: Brown and Benchmark.

Foy, N. (1994). *Empowering people at work.* Brookfield, VT: Gower Publishing Company.

Geis, F., Boston, M., and Hoffman, N. (1985). Sex of authority role models and achievement by men and women: Leadership performance and recognition. *Journal of Personality and Social Psychology, 49*(3), 636-653.

Hawkins, K. (1995). Effects of gender and communication content on leadership emergence in small task-oriented groups. *Small Group Research, 26*(2), 234-249.

Hitt, W. (1993). *The model leader.* Columbus, OH: Batelle Press.

Johnson, R. (1993). *TQM: Leadership for the quality transformation.* Milwaukee, WI: ASQC Quality Press.

Kouzes, J. and Posner, B. (1987). *The leadership challenge.* San Francisco, CA: Jossey-Bass.

Meier, J. F. and Mitchell, A. V. (1993). *Camp counseling: Leadership and programming for the organized camp* (7th ed.). Dubuque, IA: Brown and Benchmark.

Niepoth, E. W. (1983). *Leisure leadership.* Englewood Cliffs, NJ: Prentice Hall.

Phipps, M. (1987). Ethical decision making. Presentation at Fall Creek Falls State Park, TN.

Russell, R. V. (1986). *Leadership in recreation.* St. Louis, MO: Times Mirror/Mosby.

Sessoms, H. D. and Stevenson, J. (1981). *Leadership and group dynamics.* Boston, MA: Allyn & Bacon.

Shivers, J. S. (1980). *Recreational leadership.* Pennington, NJ: Princeton Book Company Publishers.

Chapter Two
Learning Opportunities

Through studying this chapter students will have the opportunity to:

- better understand how leadership has been viewed;

- examine several theories of leadership;

- understand the progression of thoughts related to leadership theory;

- relate leadership theory to their own life experiences; and

- begin to explore the impact of culture on leadership.

Photo courtesy of the Conestoga Council of Girl Scouts

CHAPTER

Leadership Theories and Styles

True comprehension of any new concept or idea only comes when a person knows and understands how and why something is the way it is. Knowing and understanding why something is the way it is begins with examining underlying thoughts, ideas, and theories about what makes it work. This is true of understanding how a car works, how birds fly, and the construct of leadership as well. In Chapter One we explored various definitions of leadership; we will now study leadership models and theories in an attempt to gain a solid foundation of leadership knowledge.

Since the beginning of humankind, in all cultures in all parts of the world, some people have led while others have followed. Some of those efforts and the leadership decisions were successful, others were not. Some efforts moved society forward, yet others interfered with social evolution. As people began to realize that this phenomenon of leading and following occurred in every group of people, the study of leadership began.

This chapter will examine early perspectives of leadership, what constitutes the construct of what leadership is and why it occurs. In addition, changes in thinking about leadership will be examined as theories and people's understanding of leadership have grown more sophisticated. Understanding leadership theories and models will enhance the usefulness of direct leadership techniques to be discussed in later chapters. Furthermore, making sense of theories helps individuals to make conscious and sound decisions related to leader-follower interactions.

A variety of theories are presented here in anticipation that one or more of them will help future leisure services leaders make sense of what they will do. Very often, individuals select various pieces of several theories or models to help in understanding this very complex phenomenon. No one theory or model is perfect in its representation of leadership, and individuals are encouraged to choose a model that makes the most sense based on one's past experiences and view of the world.

Early Theories

Early theories of leadership developed from observations of early leaders and their accomplishments; much was learned from leaders such as Attilla the Hun, Peter the Great, and Joan of Arc. As social movements emerged and researchers became increasingly sophisticated, the complexities and understandings of leadership deepened. Early leisure services theories include the great man theory, trait theories, attribution theory, behavioral theories, and the early study of leadership styles.

Great Man

The great man theory of leadership explained leadership by focusing on the greatness of the leader. Greatness was socially defined and used to describe a renowned individual who was usually a male and perceived as virtuous, magnanimous, industrious, and famous. It was theorized that leaders (great men) were born with specific characteristics that would result in their later emergence as highly effective leaders (Bass, 1990; Chemers & Ayman, 1993; Hunt, 1991).

According to the great man theory, a leader was predestined based on factors such as birthing order, family background (e.g., royalty, wealth), level and type of education, and overall upbringing. According to this model of leadership, if one were born into a good and virtuous family, received the best education, and was raised well (usually on the military model), one would become a great leader (Bass, 1990; Kraus, 1985).

Due to external factors working within this model (e.g., strict role expectations) and a European influence it was highly unusual for a female to be considered a leader. In some cultures, however, such as in the Native-American tradition, women were commonly socially defined and accepted as tribal leaders. In fitting with the great man theory, some of these women were tribal chiefs as a result of the characteristics they exhibited, their family lineage, and training.

Joan of Arc

Winston Churchill   **GREAT "MAN" THEORY**   Mao Tse-tung

Queen Elizabeth II

Harriet Tubman

Mohandas Karamchand
'"Mohatma" Ghandi

Figure 2.1   *According to the great man theory of leadership,*
successful leaders are born with innate leader
qualities.

Trait Theories

The trait theories of leadership advanced the great man theory another step. In exploring the trait theories, one sees that leadership was defined as a function of an individual's characteristics or traits (Bass, 1990; Brown, 1988; Hersey & Blanchard, 1982). Those characteristics might consist of physical, intellectual, or personality traits which were considered superior qualities that differentiated an individual from other group members.

It is important to bear in mind that what constitutes leader traits are culturally determined. This means that in some cultures valued traits of a leader might include creativity, superior intellect, and a petite physical stature. In yet another culture, highly valued traits might include a large physical stature, brute strength and the ability to be physically aggressive. According to the trait theory, in some cultures only men would be accepted as leaders, in others only women would be accepted as leaders, and in other cultures individuals of either sex might be perceived to have leadership traits.

The scientific evidence to support trait theories of leadership has been contradictory. It is interesting to note, however, that anecdotal evidence seems to support this theory in an informal setting. For instance, if one were to line up and observe the leaders of most technological nations one could develop a trait profile of a leader. The leaders of Canada, the United States, Japan, China, the former USSR, Germany, and most other European nations are male, tall (relative to their respective constituents), between 40 and 60 years old, light skinned, and somewhat fit looking. In addition, most of them probably would be considered extroverted, articulate, and charismatic.

While recognizing that many accept this theory of leadership on some level, it is critical to remember that this model of leadership has no scientific basis. Many nations are led by excellent leaders who are people of color, women, short, introverted, and lacking in charisma. Leadership is much more than the physical or personality traits one exhibits.

Attribution Theory

Similar to the trait theories, attribution theory explains leadership through the belief that leadership is attributed to one who looks and acts like a leader. Attribution theory also refers to how people (i.e., followers) tend to attribute "good" leadership to a leader of a group that has done something well regardless of the leader's actual impact. It is assumed that if the group did well, then it must have had a good leader. Conversely, if things are not going well in a group, the leader is attributed with poor leadership abilities regardless of her or his actual skill level (Chemers & Ayman, 1993).

It is important to understand attribution theory because these types of beliefs can impact the acceptance and success of a leader. Attributions are judgments or evaluations of another person. All people make judgments; for instance, we attribute kindness to some and stinginess to others. In group settings participants make judgments of the leader and the leader makes judgments of the participants. Sometimes the judgments or attributions are based on fact, other times judgments are based on perceptions and feelings. Attribution theory can be utilized to help explain why people attribute leadership to certain individuals based on overall perceptions, whether or not that person is actually the designated leader. Usually leadership is attributed to those with good relational skills (Chemers & Ayman, 1993).

Behavioral Theories

Behavioral theories encompass those ideas that describe leadership on the basis of behaviors exhibited by the leader (Bass, 1990; Russell, 1986). This belief about leadership suggests that an effective leader will manifest certain leadership behaviors at a particular time (Bass, 1990; Hersey & Blanchard, 1982). Recreation leader behaviors might include actions such as problem solving, teaching a song, or managing participant behaviors. If one believed in this explanation of leadership one would simply have to act like a leader to be perceived as one.

Many leadership theories encompass behavioral theories within them. It is generally accepted that in addition to *being* a leader, a leader *does* certain things. In discussing this model, Hitt (1993) identified the following tasks as leadership behaviors: planning, organizing, directing, and evaluating. These behaviors and functions of leadership are certainly integral to successful leadership, yet leadership goes beyond mere task completion.

Yukl (1989) developed a model of leadership typology that explained leadership through four primary leader tasks: making decisions, influencing people, building relationships, and giving-seeking information (see Figure 2.2, page 38). Within each of these four behavior categories specific behaviors were identified which essentially encompass task and human relations skills. Certainly in recreation settings, leaders engage in all of these behaviors at one time or another with both colleagues and participants.

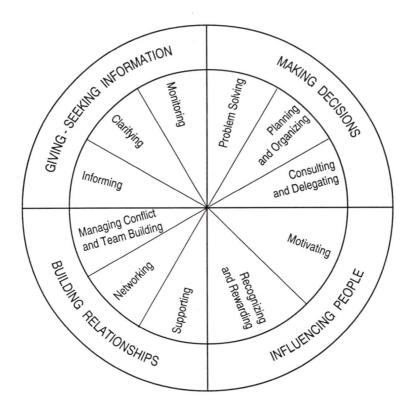

Figure 2.2 *Yukl (1989) suggested an integrative model of*
effective leadership behaviors. Reprinted with
permission of Gary Yukl.

The Influence of Stereotypes

While short-sighted in explaining leadership from a scientific perspective, the trait and behavioral theories carry some weight with laypeople, particularly in the early stages of developing leader-follower relationships. Because stereotypes often cloud the way people perceive others, both the trait and behavioral theories of leadership have implications for a variety of people in leadership roles.

In most cultures in the United States, leadership traits are attributed to men more often than women. For instance, women who exhibit the desirable leadership traits of assertiveness, being analytical, and task focused are often perceived as cold, aloof, and aggressive. Furthermore, women in direct leadership positions in recreation and leisure services find that they may not be as readily accepted as "voices of authority" because their voices are higher pitched than men's voices. In the predominant U.S. culture, authoritative voices are perceived as being low pitched, deep, and male. One only has to listen to the voice-overs on television commercials to recognize that male voices are perceived as having authority.

In addition, people of color and others who use styles of communication different than the socially prescribed Eurocentric style (e.g., street talk, jargon, thick accents) may not be perceived or accepted as leaders even if they hold legitimate leadership positions. As can be seen, leadership is very much culturally defined.

There are at least two approaches to dealing with the impacts of stereotypes on leadership. One would be to deal with the stereotypes as reality; that is, women would be advised to lower their voices when leading and those who might be inclined to use street jargon would be advised to use standard English and enunciation. Another approach is to educate others about leadership, what it means, and how it works. Of course, a third approach would be to combine the two mentioned tactics until all individuals with the necessary skills are perceived and accepted as effective leaders.

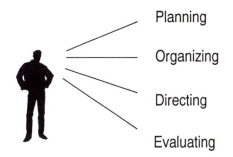

Planning

Organizing

Directing

Evaluating

Figure 2.3   *People who subscribe to behavioral models of leadership believe that certain behaviors define a leader.*

Leadership Styles

Early on as people looked for ways to understand the leadership phenomenon, it was observed that there were at least three primary types of leadership used by people in leadership positions: autocratic, democratic, and laissez faire. In 1939 Lewin, Lippitt, and White studied the impacts of those primary styles of leadership on group productivity (In: Bass, 1990; Chemers & Ayman, 1993; Stogdill, 1974).

Autocratic. Autocratic or authoritarian leadership is a style that may be perceived as based on the premise that "I'm okay, you're not okay." An autocratic leader directs, or orders participants to do various tasks, and does not allow input from group members. In this style, the leader does not reveal reasons behind her or his decision making or actions and believes that participants should do as they are told because she or he is the leader. This style is very unidirectional; the leader directs and followers are expected to follow those directions.

An autocratic leader takes on a role of determining all decisions, policies, and directions for the group. She or he usually has very little trust or faith in group members and expects them to react to directions as given. The leader promotes herself or himself as the authority figure, and as the only one with answers. In autocratic relationships group responsibility tends to be low, and people merely do what they are told. Often, when the leader is gone, participants 'cut loose' and act out.

While many perceive the autocratic style to be a negative style of influence and ineffective in the long run, there are times when an autocratic style of leadership or autocratic behaviors are appropriate. Safety situations are instances where autocratic decisions are best—a quick, sharp, immediate response from the group is required to protect someone or something from harm. In this type of setting, the leader is accepted by the group as having the necessary expertise and the group realizes that a delay might result in injury or damage. Ordering or directing an individual to do something would be appropriate in this type of instance.

After the safety issues have been resolved and things have calmed down a leader concerned with group affect and learning would share with the group information regarding the use of leadership styles, decision-making behaviors, and any other issues of concern related to the situation. Generally, participants of all ages appreciate being informed and treated with respect. By sharing the reasoning behind decisions and the use of autocratic techniques participants learn about leadership, safety issues, judgment, and responsibility.

Democratic. A democratic style of leadership is one where the leader and the group share in decision making. The message is "I'm okay, you're okay," and reasoning for any leader-made decisions is shared with group members. A democratic leader asks for and receives group input. Group members make decisions based on information supplied by the leader, and as a group, decide both the process and content of decisions. This is often accomplished by voting and accepting the majority opinion. In a democratic group, criticism and praise are given objectively and group members generally feel a sense of responsibility within the group in a democratic setting. A trust relationship between the leader and group members usually is well-developed, and a feeling of mutual respect is common.

Although in a democratic society there is a perception that a democratic leadership style is best, there are times when such a style is inappropriate. If a group is underskilled, immature or has little knowledge about a situation, using a leadership style that places decision making in the group's hands is not appropriate. In addition, if a democratic style of leadership were used and a "majority rules" attitude were followed to make decisions some people (i.e., the minority) would always be left out and their input would be nullified. Furthermore, because of the group input, a democratic style often takes more time than other approaches. If time is limited, it might be wise to avoid a democratic style.

Photo courtesy of the YWCA of Black Hawk County

The approach one takes toward leadership depends on the leader, the participants, and the situation.

Laissez faire. In French, laissez faire means to "let it be," to leave it alone. The message from the leader to group members is "I'm not okay, you're okay." In this style of leadership the leader tends to shy away from the group and decision-making responsibilities. Complete freedom is given to group members without any participation from the leader. The leader provides information or materials when asked, but otherwise stays out of the group process.

These behaviors may indicate a lack of confidence in oneself, and may leave a group feeling as though it has little or no direction. Because of this, following a laissez-faire style of leadership may result in low group morale; in addition, the leader of the group becomes whomever is willing to make decisions and do the work. Bass (1990) reported that "more activity by leaders, regardless of style, is usually associated with the greater satisfaction and effectiveness of their followers" (p. 551).

As might be imagined, laissez-faire leadership is often viewed as a weak form of leadership because of the low level of involvement by the leader. However, when used with a purpose, this style can be highly effective in helping a group to mature and grow in its decision-making abilities. In a positive approach to a laissez-faire style the leader is available to the group and shows interest in the group's needs. While she or he allows the group to struggle through decision making and task accomplishments, the leader is available to provide guidance and assistance when needed. Group dynamics can be extremely strong when facilitated with a laissez-faire approach to leadership.

Tannenbaum and Schmidt Continuum of Leader Behavior

Rather than taking an either/or approach, Tannenbaum and Schmidt placed leadership styles on a continuum from democratic to autocratic (Edginton & Ford, 1985; Hersey & Blanchard, 1982). On this continuum leader behaviors ranged from being very group-oriented (similar to a laissez-faire style) to very leader-oriented with the leader being very directive and authoritarian. Four elements influence the use of a particular style over others: leader values, leader confidence in the group, leader preferences, and the group's feelings of security about getting the job done.

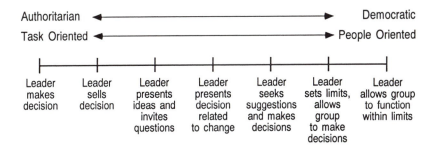

Figure 2.4   Tannenbaum and Schmidt perceived leadership as falling along a continuum of various behaviors.

Later Theories

Situational Theories

Situational theories are models of leadership that take into account the leader, followers, and the situation and explain leadership as emerging based on the situation. If the skills of an individual match the group task and fit within the structure of the group she or he will emerge as the leader. Simply put, a person emerges as the leader when a certain situation arises that draws her or him out. For example, if an Emergency Medical Technician (EMT) were taking an aerobics class, she or he would follow the lead of the aerobics instructor because the instructor, who is designated as such, has more knowledge, expertise and skills than the EMT in this situation (i.e., leading aerobics). The EMT would follow directions and suggestions based on these factors. During class, however, if one of the participants were to experience severe breathing or heart problems, the EMT would likely emerge as the leader *of that situation*. Others would defer to the EMT's directions and commands because, at that time, she or he would be the most appropriate leader.

Hersey and Blanchard (1982) presented a model of leadership that aligns task behaviors and follower (i.e., individual/group) maturity resulting in particular leadership behaviors (See Figure 2.5, page 44). If the task requires a great deal of focused activity and the group maturity is low, a telling or directing leadership style is required. On the other hand, if task needs are low and individual/group maturity is high, a participative leadership style is most appropriate. A leader would select a leadership style based on her or his own preferences, group maturity, and the demands of the task.

STYLE OF LEADER

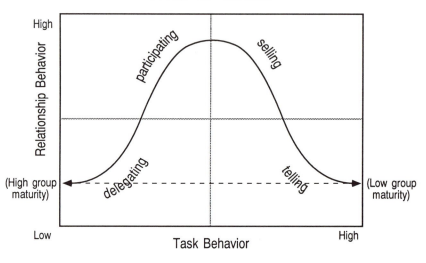

Figure 2.5   *Situational leadership involves relationship and task behaviors, the maturity of the group, and leadership style.*

Contingency Theory

Fiedler developed a *contingency theory* which explained leadership in terms of an individual's style of leadership and the response of the group she or he was leading (Bass, 1990; Fiedler, 1967; Yukl, 1989). The essence of this leadership theory is how the style of leadership used by a leader interfaces with the situation in which the group (leader and followers) finds itself. The style of leadership is contingent upon the situation and the relationship between the leader and the group.

Fiedler (1967) suggested that a leader is motivated from either a task or interpersonal perspective. That is, different leaders prefer and focus on either the job to be done or the people in the group. Three other elements help explain this theory:

> *the relationship between the leader and the group,* where the more liked a leader is by group members, the easier it is for her or him to exert influence;

the task structure, where the more clear the goals and tasks are, the easier it is for the leader to exert influence; and

the power of the leader, whereby the more powerful (e.g., having access to resources) the leader is, the easier it is for the leader to exert influence over the group.

According to this theory, leadership effectiveness depends upon, or is *contingent* upon, the appropriateness of the leader's style to the task (Chemers & Ayman, 1993; Russell, 1986). According to this theory a leader who is well-liked by participants, has clear goals for the session, and a leader who has power by virtue of her or his position would be highly effective using most any style of leadership with the group.

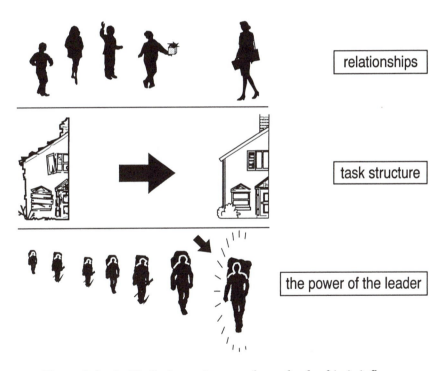

relationships

task structure

the power of the leader

Figure 2.6   *In Fiedler's contingency theory leadership is influenced by the interaction of three different elements.*

Managerial Grid

Blake and Mouton's managerial grid provides yet another look at leadership. In this model, leadership consists of two elements: a concern for task and a concern for people (the group) (Bass, 1990; Chemers & Ayman, 1993). The horizontal axis of the grid represents a concern for task, and the vertical axis represents a concern for people. The concern for task is related to getting a job done and producing outcomes and products. The concern for people is related to developing trust relationships, establishing a friendly atmosphere, and being concerned for the well-being of others.

Using this grid a person could be rated as to her or his degree of concern for people and concern for task. Through this process leadership strengths and weaknesses may be identified. A leader overly concerned with people might never complete a task, yet a leader overly concerned with task might alienate participants. Most people strive for a balance of the two concerns.

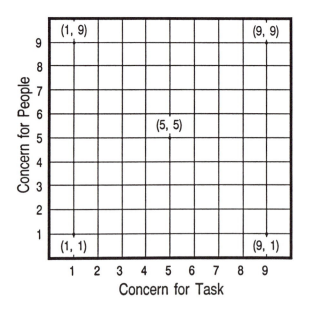

Figure 2.7 *Blake and Mouton's managerial grid explains leadership as the intersection of two foci—a concern for people and a concern for task.*

Contemporary Understandings of Leadership

Likert's System of Management

Stogdill (1974) presented a view of leadership which places leadership on a continuum from autocratic to fully participative. Called the Likert System of Management, this model allows for the notion that leaders behave in different ways, with different motivations, for a variety of reasons at different times.

Exploitive autocratic. On one extreme is a leadership style labeled exploitive autocratic where the message from the leader is, "You will do it." The motivation for leadership comes from within the leader and the results are designed to show the leader in the best possible light, even at the expense of others.

An example of this approach may be seen in the following (slightly exaggerated) scenario. A young, relatively inexperienced lifeguard sits on his stand, whistle at the ready. He is very proud of being a lifeguard and has heard all the myths about how girls respond to male lifeguards. He believes some of those myths and is feeling rather narcissistic; his tan is glowing and his muscles rippling. The young lifeguard gets it in his mind to impress the teenaged girls nearby. He sees two youngsters playing (within the rules) in the water and blows his whistle at them, shouting through the bullhorn to stop the horseplay because it is dangerous. He then sits back in his stand feeling all eyes on him imagining that the teenaged girls were impressed by his show of authority and power.

There was no real need for the whistle and horn, but the acts of using those tools and fulfilling his leadership role helped make the young lifeguard look larger than life. In exploiting his position of leadership and authority to get ahead he was exhibiting an exploitive autocratic leadership style.

Benevolent autocratic. Moving to the right on the Likert continuum, a leader moves into a benevolent autocratic mode; where a paternalistic attitude is evidenced through leadership acts. Here, the message from the leader to participants might be, "Do it, please." Some follower variance is allowed from the leader's directions, but participants know when the leader means business. Often, this style is used when a leader believes people should do something for their own good. The style is still directive, but the motivation is in the best interest of others, rather than self.

If, in the previous scenario, the young lifeguard simply asked the youngsters to ease up on the horseplay because someone might get hurt, he would have exhibited a benevolent autocratic style of leadership.

Consultive. At the consultive point along the continuum, the leader might ask for input, "How would you like to do it?" Yet the leader's decision is still final. Here, leaders allow group input and show some interest in group members, but still retain the decision-making power. A consultive style of leadership implies some level of trust between leader and group members. Participant knowledge and feelings are considered important and leaders sincerely try to make people feel included.

If the young lifeguard were to exhibit a consultive style of leadership with the playful youngsters, he might have asked them to get out of the water and talked with them about their perceptions of the danger of their play. In a consultive style the lifeguard would listen to the youth, then make a decision to either ask them to stop or let them return to their water play.

Participative. At the right extreme on the continuum is a leadership style labeled participative leadership where the leader not only seeks information from all participants, but actually includes group members in the decision-making process. The message from leader to participants is, "What do you think we should do?" This style allows for full group involvement throughout the leadership and decision-making processes.

A participative style of leadership is somewhat similar to a democratic style, yet the focus of decision making in Likert's System of Management is consensus-oriented rather than by vote. A consensus is garnered by involving all group members and coming to a decision that everyone can accept—it is typically quite time-consuming, but excellent for group development.

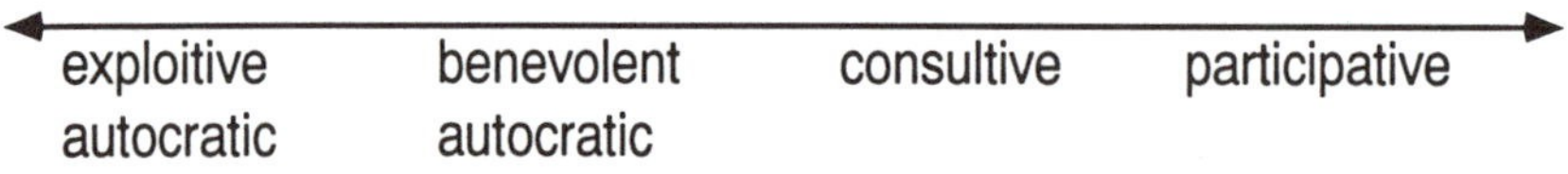

exploitive autocratic	benevolent autocratic	consultive	participative

Figure 2.8 *Likert's System of Management illustrates leadership as a continuum.*

Comprehensive View of Leadership

The comprehensive view of leadership is somewhat similar to situational leadership in that it identifies the interactions of the leader, followers, and the situation (Edginton & Ford, 1985; Ford & Blanchard, 1993; Jordan, 1988, 1989). It is the intersection of these three elements that results in the identification of an appropriate leadership style. In this model, one must bear in mind that the leader is a composite of her or his knowledge, skills and abilities, need disposition, experiences, motivation, personal style, history, personal "baggage" and sources of power.

Similarly, the group includes characteristics of each individual as well as the group as a distinct entity. These traits include knowledge, skills and abilities, experience, maturity, group goals, group methods and processes, and group norms. The situation encompasses all the external factors that influence a group: environment, time, temperature, external stresses, cultural attitudes, and the physical setting. As the elements of these three components interact, an appropriate leadership style is identified (e.g., autocratic, democratic, laissez faire, participative, consultive).

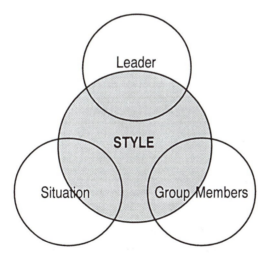

Figure 2.9 *The comprehensive view of leadership suggests leadership is a combination of leaders, followers, and the special circumstances of the situation.*

Comprehensive-Interaction-Expectation (C-I-E) Theory

To fully explain what occurs within the comprehensive model of leadership, the interactions and interpersonal relationships of people need to be further identified. Jordan (1988, 1989) proposed adding elements of interpersonal interaction and expectation into the leader-follower aspects of the comprehensive approach. It is common knowledge that interactions are dynamic; that is, people's relationships and interactions with one another change all the time. Whether it is due to individual moods, external forces, or a combination of factors, relationships and interactions continually ebb and flow.

Interaction-expectation theory. Those who agree with an interaction-expectation theory attribute leadership to group members (including the group leaders) as they interact, accept, and reinforce each person's role-oriented behaviors (Homans, 1950 as cited in Stogdill, 1974). Therefore, as activity leaders enact the leadership role group members must first accept and then reinforce that leader-role behavior if the leader is to be effective. It is imperative in any leadership situation that the group recognize and accept leadership behaviors in the designated leaders (Geis, Boston & Hoffman, 1985; Porter, Geis & Jennings, 1983). If that recognition and acceptance is accorded to another individual in the group, the legitimate leader(s) will be powerless.

The reinforcement of role-oriented behaviors engenders additional expectations among all group members. Followers continually expect leaders to accept leader responsibilities and to exhibit effective leadership skills. In turn, leaders expect followers to accord them the respect and deference they deserve due to their leadership status and skills. Each reinforced behavior and/or attitude sets up further expectations of each group member. The interactions and expectations tend to be both reciprocal and causal in nature.

Figure 2.10 illustrates the interaction-expectation theory of leadership. The level or amount of interaction may vary between and within group members. In this figure, level of interaction is viewed as the proximity of the leader-group member circles. Amount and reciprocity of recognition, acceptance, and reinforcement of role behaviors is illustrated as arrows that run between the leader-group member circles. As one can see, both the levels and amounts of interaction and acceptance of role behaviors may vary within any situation. A lack of interaction between leader and group members with recognition and

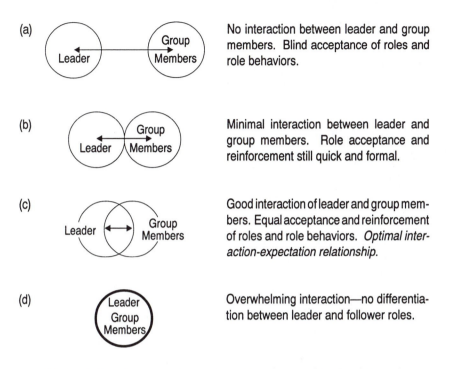

(a) No interaction between leader and group members. Blind acceptance of roles and role behaviors.

(b) Minimal interaction between leader and group members. Role acceptance and reinforcement still quick and formal.

(c) Good interaction of leader and group members. Equal acceptance and reinforcement of roles and role behaviors. *Optimal interaction-expectation relationship.*

(d) Overwhelming interaction—no differentiation between leader and follower roles.

Figure 2.10 *The interaction-expectation theory of leadership and the possible role relationships within the group.*

acceptance of role behaviors (or leadership title) will result in blind following. Group members who follow blindly lack the interpersonal relations necessary for a fulfilling recreation experience. This type of experience also may diminish the quality and effectiveness of the leadership process (see item a in Figure 2.10).

Minimal interaction allows for some exchange of recognition, acceptance, and reinforcement of role behaviors. In this situation, both the leader and participant make an effort to recognize and accept appropriate role behaviors. Due to the low level of interaction, however, there may be difficulties in the degree of leader effectiveness (see item b in Figure 2.10).

Optimal levels of interaction and recognition, acceptance, and reinforcement of role behaviors are illustrated in item c of Figure 2.10. There exists a reciprocity of components that tends to enhance the leadership experience. The balance in levels of interaction and acceptance of role behaviors continually strengthens and enhances leader and group effectiveness.

The fourth representation of the interaction-expectation theory illustrates an overwhelming amount of interaction that allows for no recognition of roles. This might occur when roles are confused, the leader has a weak personality, or the leader and group members become overly involved with one another's roles. Effective leadership is impossible in this situation and action must be taken to define roles more explicitly (see item d in Figure 2.10).

There also are instances when there is a total lack of recognition, acceptance, and/or reinforcement of role behaviors. This is illustrated through elimination of the connecting lines between the leader-group member circles. If a total lack of recognition were to occur, the legitimate leader would lack all authority within the group and be extremely ineffective in leadership situations.

Comprehensive-interaction-expectation view. To capitalize on the main components of the comprehensive and interaction-expectation leadership models, one must recognize that within all leadership theories, interactions are dynamic (Jordan, 1989). The movement illustrated within the combined comprehensive-interaction-expectation (C-I-E) model (Figure 2.11) allows one to view leadership as a dynamic, interactive process. Its effectiveness may be measured in the levels of

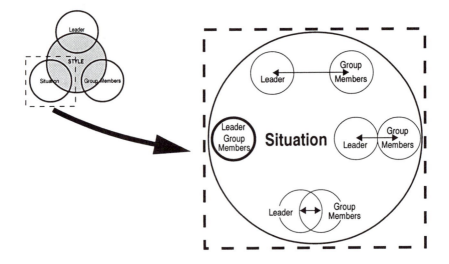

Figure 2.11 The comprehensive-interaction-expectation model of leadership combines the comprehensive theory with the interaction-expectation theory in examining role relationships within the specific situation.

recognition, acceptance, and reinforcement of leader-role behaviors within the scope of the leader–group-situation interactions.

Figure 2.11 illustrates the dynamic nature of the C-I-E theory of leadership. Within each unique situation (depicted as the enlargement from the situational component of the comprehensive model), individual group members interact with the leader. Each interaction within each situation is unique for each individual. The interaction acts as a causal agent and is reflected in the adoption of a particular leadership style at a particular moment. The interaction is not only through the leader's particular choice of style, but also through the levels of recognition, acceptance, and reinforcement of leader and group member role behaviors.

As an example of the C-I-E theory and its application to leisure settings, one might think of a common outdoor situation such as the establishment of a group campsite. If the leader and campers had no preestablished interactional relationship (as depicted in item a of Figure 2.10) the campers would consistently look to the leader for directions. The leader would tell the group members not only when to set up camp, but also how and where to set up camp. The expectation would be that the group members would comply merely because of the accepted role assignments. One might describe this leadership style as autocratic.

In the second instance (item b of Figure 2.10), the preestablished recognition and acceptance of role behaviors is strong, yet there is some interaction between the leader and the campers. If this were the case, the campers would still look to the leader for direction, but they may offer a modicum of unsolicited input. The leader might listen, but would still make the final decision. Due to the strong acceptance of role assignments, this decision would be readily accepted by the campers.

The optimal interaction-expectation relationship within the comprehensive model would result in the manifestation of leader behaviors that could be described as participative. The leader, or a camper, would suggest that camp be set up in a particular area. Further group input might be solicited, and discussion would most likely ensue. Because of the healthy recognition and acceptance of roles, the campers would expect that the leader would give them all of the information necessary to make a wise decision. The leader would in turn expect that group members would make the best decision their abilities would allow. Once a group decision was made, both the leader and campers would feel comfortable in carrying out the task of setting up camp.

The fourth type of interaction-expectation relationship within an outdoor leadership situation (illustrated in item d of Figure 2.10) is that of total role confusion. The overwhelming amount of leader-participant interaction does not allow for any recognition or expectation of roles or role behaviors. There is a total melding of leader-participant roles. The same probability would exist for any group member (including the leader) to suggest when and how to set up camp as any other member. With total role confusion (which may be thought of as a leader eclipse), the group would be directionless in its efforts to set up camp. This particular type of interactional relationship is different from a laissez-faire style of leadership in one important respect. A leader choosing a laissez-faire style of leadership would be *uninvolved* with the decision-making process, whereas a leader exhibiting role confusion would be *overinvolved* with the decision-making process.

Transactional Leadership

Transactional leadership theories are those that view leadership as a transaction or an exchange between two types of people, typically a leader and followers (Hunt, 1991). The theories and models presented up to this point are generally defined as transactional in nature. Within a given situation a leader uses particular leadership techniques while engaged in some type of interaction (exchange) with followers. This exchange is based on a subtle agreement between leaders and followers: if followers will acknowledge and validate the leader, the leader will give the followers recognition and status for their efforts.

McLean and Weitzel (1991) have identified three basic philosophies of transactional leaders: contingent reward, management by exception (active), and management by exception (passive). In the *contingent reward* philosophy, the leader and participants contract with one another for an exchange of rewards for efforts; in effect, participants accept the leader and the leader recognizes the accomplishments of participants. In the *management by exception (active)* approach, the leader watches and searches for deviations from rules and standards, she or he tries to catch people doing something wrong and then takes corrective action. And, in the *management by exception (passive)* approach, the leader only steps in if standards are not being met, the leader essentially abdicates or gives up responsibility and avoids making decisions. There is an alternative approach to leadership theories.

Figure 2.12 *Transactional leadership involves viewing leadership as an exchange of one set of goods for another—much like the purchasing of goods.*

Transformational Leadership

To transform means to change the nature, function, or condition of something. In terms of transformational leadership, the term describes a model of leadership that changes the nature or function of others in such a way that others become more concerned with collective (group) rather than personal (individual) interests (Bass, 1990; Chemers & Ayman, 1993; Hitt, 1993).

The definition provided at the beginning of this chapter has elements of transformational leadership in it. Where leaders strive to "elevate" followers to a higher good and to act in the best interest of the group's goals, followers are being *transformed* into moral agents (Hitt, 1993; Hunt, 1991). That is, followers are being changed into messengers for the leader; in this way followers help spread the leader's ideals, values, and convictions.

Transformational leadership has three components: leader charisma; individualized consideration where each follower is treated as an individual and is challenged to perform her or his best; and intellectual stimulation where the leader challenges old ways of thinking (Bass, 1990).

Leader charisma. Charisma is defined in the dictionary as a "rare personal quality attributed to leaders who arouse fervent popular devotion and enthusiasm," and as "personal magnetism or charm." As an element of transformational leadership, leader charisma serves as an outlet for visionary and inspirational abilities of the leader. A leader who is considered a visionary, who sees the big picture, who is not afraid to take risks, and who generates a great deal of enthusiasm, emotion, and confidence in her or his followers is considered a transformational leader. In recreation settings leaders with charisma seem to electrify the room. Everyone participates in activities, participant enthusiasm is high, and followers seem to gravitate toward the leader.

Individualized consideration. In a global sense, transformational leaders appeal to ideological values of followers. This means that what leaders say, what they do, and the values they espouse are well-liked by their followers. While appealing to these common values and ideals, transformational leadership allows for followers to be treated as individuals; a great deal of follower confidence is generated this way. Followers are held to relatively high standards and are given the message that the leader has confidence in their ability to meet those standards. In short, followers are empowered to engage in a variety of tasks. A recreation leader who allows for individual consideration makes each person genuinely feel special. Furthermore, the leader holds each person to high expectations and lets her or him know that she or he has great confidence in her or his ability to meet those challenges.

Intellectual stimulation. In addition to leader charisma and individualized consideration, the other element of transformational leadership is intellectual stimulation. A visionary and transforming leader is one who challenges existing thinking about the way things have been done. New ways of looking at things, innovative and cutting-edge thoughts are generated, and followers are given the opportunity to participate in the discoveries. This attribute tends to make a transforming leader one who is exciting to be around. A transforming leader, in leisure settings, challenges people to think differently than they are used to doing. Elements ranging from activity rules to social policy are challenged and the intellectual excitement is high.

Research has shown that leaders who engage in transformational behaviors are viewed as effective leaders, and have satisfied and highly motivated followers (Bass, 1990). It certainly would be easy to see how someone with charisma, who treats people as though they are each very special and challenges people to think, would be well-liked and well-respected. Transformational leaders use many leadership styles, and exhibit a transformational philosophy that influences both leadership tasks and people. Hitt (1988, 1993) talks about a transformational leader as one who is involved in several tasks: visioning, valuing, coaching, motivating, team building, and promoting quality.

Leadership and Culture

It was mentioned earlier that leadership is culturally defined. This means that within each culture leadership means different things. If we were to draw a picture of leadership, it would look different to various cultural groups. What is perceived as leadership to an aboriginal tribe is not the same as the leadership perceived by a highly technological society. The group roles are different, how a person becomes the leader is different, and how a leader acts (and is expected to act) is different.

It is important to recognize that within one country there are many cultures; therefore, within each country there are several definitions and models of leadership which are all valid. One way to look at the impact of cultures is to consider two different cultural philosophical positions: a collectivist perspective and an individualist perspective (Chemers & Ayman, 1993). Two examples of *collectivist cultures* in U.S. society include Native-American tribes and African-American culture.

Collectivists tend to look for similarities in people and consider the group to be more important than the individual. Cooperation, self-control, social order and group goals are important determinants of how groups and leaders function. A leader who puts the group before herself or himself, who works within a consensus model, and who is able to help the group achieve group goals would fit well within this philosophy. Collectivist values would permeate group structure. The group is the primary focus and the leader's role is to help the group reach its potential.

On the other hand, *individualists* look for differences in people and promote and value individual achievement over group accomplishments. Competition, personal exhibition, individual style differences, and achievement of personal goals form the foundation of this leader-group philosophy. Euramericans tend to favor this approach to working within a group. A leader who was an individualist would tend to promote competition within a group, encourage individuation, and look to put forth a group member as "the best."

Choosing the Appropriate Leadership Style

As can be seen from reading this chapter there are many ways to view leadership. Some theories have much in common with one another, while others are unique ways of looking at things. One thing is certain, there are many styles of leadership that people use in their roles as leaders. In addition, there are many subtle nuances to each of these styles. Most people feel more comfortable with one or two styles of leadership than others. For instance, one person may feel very comfortable using a participative style where group decisions are made through consensus. Another person may not feel comfortable with that much group involvement and would prefer to exert a bit more leader control. Just how can a person tell which leadership style is best?

Most people who study leadership believe that choosing a particular leadership style depends upon several factors including the leader, the group, and the situation (including the task). *Leader* maturity, knowledge, and skills will have a strong impact on which styles of leadership are within a person's repertoire. The maturity of the *group*, as well as group size, experience level, and other factors influence which styles of leadership will be effective in what situations. The *situation* includes the task to be done (activity), time constraints, the environment, equipment, temperature, and all the other external forces that influence a group.

With experience, a leader can tell which styles of leadership have potential to be effective and which styles do not. Take a close look at Table 2A for ideas on how to determine appropriate leadership styles to be most effective. Not all leadership styles are listed.

Table 2A *A Comparison of Leadership Styles*

Style	Leader	Group	Situation
exploitive autocratic	• strong • directive • total control • has no confidence in participants • immature • egotistical	• childlike • immature • low confidence • low skills and knowledge	• task oriented
benevolent autocratic	• skilled • experienced • mature • explains actions • maintains control	• low knowledge and skills • gives up control to leader • immature • needs much guidance	• safety hazard or crisis • shared people and task orientation
consultive	• mature • high in skills and knowledge • some trust in group	• mature • moderate skill and knowledge • trusts leader • wants to learn	• no crisis or time constraint • people oriented
participative	• mature • trusts group • confident in own and group abilities	• mature • involved • high skill and knowledge • cohesive • utilizes synergy	• consensus approach • no time constraints • relaxed • comfortable • people orientation
laissez faire	• mature • serves as resource • trust in group ability to work things out • leader gives up control	• mature • willing to work through group dynamics • trusts leader • takes initiative	• process focus within a task orientation
coaching	• mature • high skills and knowledge • group focused	• lacks confidence • needs assistance in putting skills and knowledge to work	• people orientation • just learning the tasks

Summary

Understanding leadership requires a thorough examination of how others have viewed what it is and how it functions. As may be seen from this chapter, leadership theories are models of the leadership construct that enable an understanding of the many aspects of human interactions. Leadership theories range from quite simplistic to very complex. They address a leader's physical traits (great man theory and trait theories), behaviors and actions (behavioral theories), and situations in which leaders find themselves (situational and contingency theories). Leadership has been viewed as situational, dynamic, and as relationships between leaders and followers.

Within each theory or model of leadership it is possible to exhibit a variety of leadership styles. These styles were identified to help explain how leaders and followers interact, and to allow for development of personal judgment related to use of leadership styles. Contemporary views of leadership generally support a transformational model where the leader uses her or his charisma to share ideologies, treat individuals as unique and important, and stimulate others to think and challenge the status quo. Research indicates that individuals who exhibit these characteristics are perceived as effective and competent. A variety of styles are used as followers and the situation warrant.

Choosing an appropriate leadership style is an ongoing concern for leisure services leaders. Each group, each situation, and each day are unique and require various responses by the leader. In choosing a style, leaders strive to match their own needs with those of the followers, the situation, and the environment. When safety or time is an issue of concern, or when participants are extremely young, an autocratic style of leadership may be appropriate. In another setting where the group is mature, committed to the task, and have some skill or knowledge, a consultive leadership style may be most appropriate. Time, experience, and practice will help leaders to determine which leadership style is best utilized in what circumstances.

The Front Line

One of the biggest challenges leaders face is to select an appropriate leadership style or technique based on the situation at hand. It may help if leaders become familiar with the various dimensions along which leadership situations vary and consider the choices among them.

First, it may be helpful to draw a continuum of leader styles or behaviors such as below:

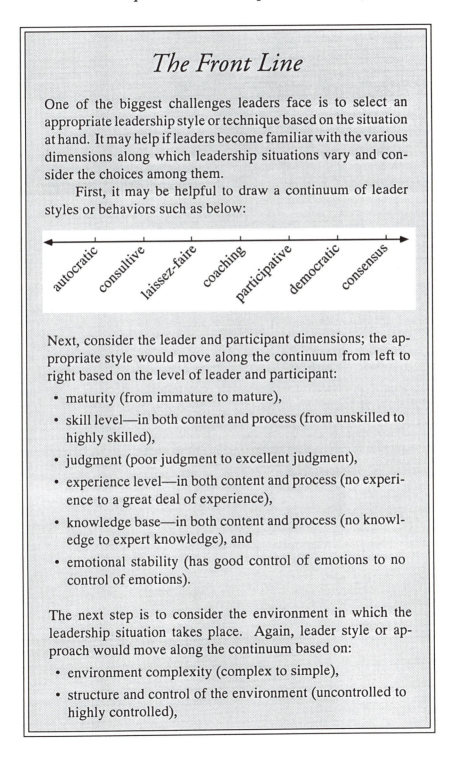

Next, consider the leader and participant dimensions; the appropriate style would move along the continuum from left to right based on the level of leader and participant:

- maturity (from immature to mature),
- skill level—in both content and process (from unskilled to highly skilled),
- judgment (poor judgment to excellent judgment),
- experience level—in both content and process (no experience to a great deal of experience),
- knowledge base—in both content and process (no knowledge to expert knowledge), and
- emotional stability (has good control of emotions to no control of emotions).

The next step is to consider the environment in which the leadership situation takes place. Again, leader style or approach would move along the continuum based on:

- environment complexity (complex to simple),
- structure and control of the environment (uncontrolled to highly controlled),

- concern over hazards (many potential hazards to few or no potential hazards),
- time constraints (from tight constraints to no time limits), and
- familiarity with the environment (totally unfamiliar environs to very familiar environs).

Finally, a leader would want to consider the activity dimension. Leader style or approach moves along the continuum from left to right based on how the activity varied:

- rule or strategy complexity (highly complex to very simple),
- level of importance (from activity is critical to group success to very low importance),
- level of structure to activity (no structure to activity to much structure), and
- degree of familiarity (totally new activity to a longtime favorite).

By considering one's own comfort level with various leadership styles and by attending to this checklist (of sorts), leisure services leaders may be helped to decide upon the most appropriate level of leader involvement in the leadership situation. Practice and much exposure to a variety of situations will also be extremely helpful.

References

Bass, B. (1990). *Bass and Stogdill's handbook of leadership* (3rd ed.). New York, NY: The Free Press.

Brown, R. (1988). *Group processes: Dynamics within and between groups.* New York, NY: Basil Blackwell, Inc.

Chemers, M. and Ayman, R. (Eds.). (1993). *Leadership theory and research.* San Diego, CA: Academic Press, Inc.

Edginton, C. and Ford, P. (1985). *Leadership in recreation and leisure services organizations.* New York, NY: John Wiley & Sons.

Fiedler, F. (1967). *A theory of leadership effectiveness.* New York, NY: McGraw-Hill.

Ford, P. and Blanchard, J. (1993). *Leadership and administration of outdoor pursuits,* (2nd ed.). State College, PA: Venture Publishing, Inc.

Geis, F., Boston, M., and Hoffman, N. (1985). Sex of authority role models and achievement by men and women: Leadership performance and recognition. *Journal of Personality and Social Psychology, 49*(3), 636-653.

Hersey, P. and Blanchard, K. (1982). *Management of organizational behavior.* Englewood Cliffs, NJ: Prentice Hall.

Hitt, W. (1993). *The model leader.* Columbus, OH: Batelle Press.

Hitt, W. (1988). *The leader-manager.* Columbus, OH: Batelle Press.

Hunt, J. (1991). *Leadership: A new synthesis.* Newbury Park, CA: Sage Publications, Inc.

Jordan, D. (1988). *An examination of gender differences in perceptions of outdoor leaders by Colorado Outward Bound preregistrants.* Unpublished dissertation, Indiana University, Bloomington, IN.

Jordan, D. (1989). A new vision for outdoor leadership theory. *Leisure Studies, 8,* 35-47.

Kraus, R. (1985). *Recreation leadership today.* Glenview, IL: Scott, Foresman & Company.

McLean, J. and Weitzel, W. (1991). *Leadership—Magic, myth or method?* New York, NY: AMACOM.

Porter, N., Geis, F., and Jennings, J. (1983). Are women invisible as leaders? *Sex Roles, 9*(10), 22-29.

Russell, R. V. (1986). *Leadership in recreation.* St. Louis, MO: Times Mirror/Mosby.

Stogdill, R. (1974). *Handbook of leadership: A survey of theory and research.* New York, NY: Macmillan Publishing Company.

Yukl, G. (1989). *Leadership in organizations.* Englewood Cliffs, NJ: Prentice Hall.

Chapter Three
Learning Opportunities

Through studying this chapter students will have the opportunity to:

- be exposed to major theories of human development;
- examine the role of environment in influencing human development;
- discover underlying reasons for cognition, actions, and affective behaviors;
- integrate knowledge of ages and stages of life into leadership concepts; and
- consider the implications of human development on leadership.

Photo courtesy of the YWCA of Black Hawk County

CHAPTER

3

Leadership and Human Development

Human development is a fascinating field of study! Learning about how people grow, mature, and develop across the life span helps leaders understand many things about the thoughts, behaviors, and choices of participants. For instance, a young child who refuses to share equipment does not necessarily do so out of selfishness. Rather, it is not until a certain stage of development that a child learns to share and cooperate with others. Development is a directional phenomenon, meaning that it occurs in one direction (we consider development forward in direction). What occurs during development is a result of the combined social, psychological, emotional, and physical evolution of individuals. Growth, a term often used in conjunction with development, results in new potential in specific areas of an individual's life. Due to its composite nature, many external factors influence human development including cultural mores, family experiences, and personal talents and liabilities (Bocknek, 1980).

While human development is a complex and extensive field, leaders who understand the basics have a foundation from which to draw when applying various leadership skills. Knowledge and understanding of general principles of human development is necessary to lead in a developmentally appropriate fashion. This is needed because at different stages of development, different techniques are effective with different participants. For instance, when dealing with a child who has not yet fully reached the concrete operations stage (according to Piaget) to be an effective leader, one must use concrete directions and instructions. Once a person develops the capability to understand literal language a leader may be a little more creative with her or his use of terms.   It should be noted that everyone does not move through developmental stages at the same time in life, and some people have arrested development in certain stages. Those people who are well above the chronological age most typical of a particular development stage (e.g., have slowed or stopped in development) are usually considered developmentally disabled.

The behaviors, skills, and abilities described within each developmental stage are simply more typical of one age group than another— they are not hard and fast rules of when every person should go through each stage or developmental phase. Therefore, while information about human development can be extremely helpful in understanding people, it cannot be used to predict individual behaviors or reasons behind individual behaviors. Knowledge of human development, however, is useful in matching leader expectations with participant capabilities, and leader actions with various groups. This is developmentally appropriate leadership.

This chapter is a summary of research about human development which will provide a basis for understanding people, and for making leadership decisions across the life span. There is much to understand about human development, yet only an overview is presented here. Therefore, leaders are encouraged to continue their study of human development outside of this material. This chapter sets the stage for understanding by first presenting an overview of popular development theories. The remainder of the chapter is designed to provide information and material related to various age groups and life stages. Implications for leadership are presented to help leaders make the best use of this information.

Theories of Human Development

People are the reason for the leisure services profession. To serve people best and to be the highest quality leader possible requires that leaders have some knowledge of human growth and development. If one has a basic knowledge of people, decisions and approaches to leadership have a sound basis for use. There are many different theories of human development and only a select few are mentioned here.

As mentioned in an earlier chapter, theories are the basis for understanding constructs or concepts. The information learned from theories allows leaders to put general knowledge about a topic into actual practice. The theories discussed here include Piaget's model of development which focuses on various cognitive abilities; Erikson's approach to development which involves dealing with various crises in life; Kohlberg's theory of moral development over the life span; and, a brief look at Gilligan's position on moral development.

Child Development According to Piaget

No matter how adult-like they may seem, children are not miniature grownups; they have different ways of learning and understanding than do adults. This difference is based on developmental stage and involves cognitive or mental abilities and limitations. Level of understanding and cognitive abilities evolve over time and impact the way an individual deals with others, approaches tasks, and makes decisions. According to Piaget, knowledge is constructed gradually through interactions with the environment. Responses to the environment depend upon how the individual understands the situation in which she or he finds herself or himself. Piaget theorized that four general stages of development exist through which people move as they age. They are the *sensorimotor intelligence stage, preoperational stage, concrete operations,* and *formal operations* (Beilin, 1992; Goode Vick, 1989; Howe, 1993; Sarafino & Armstrong, 1986; Schickedanz, Hansen & Forsyth, 1990).

Sensorimotor Intelligence Stage (Birth to 24 Months)

The sensorimotor stage occurs within the first two years of life. What occurs at this stage of development may not impact recreation leadership directly, but knowledge of this stage provides important foundational information for understanding people. The sensorimotor stage includes human learning through reflexes and exploration of the world (infants explore things through the five senses—taste, smell, touch, seeing, and hearing). It is through this type of exploration that babies recognize their own position in the world. As one might imagine, at this stage repetition is the primary method of learning. Through multiple exposures children learn object permanence (the knowledge that things do not cease to exist simply because they are hidden from view), physical causality (the knowledge that things do not happen at random), and that intentional acts are required to achieve a desired goal.

Photo courtesy of the YWCA of Black Hawk County

Infants learn about the environment through sensory exploration.

Preoperational Stage (2 to 6 Years)

The preoperational stage, as viewed by Piaget, is one that is achieved in early childhood. At this stage children learn how to use language, and are limited in understanding various constructs. For instance, a child in this stage believes that water poured from a short wide glass becomes more (in volume) when poured into a tall thin glass. The child becomes egocentric and is unable to distinguish her or his own perspective from other's—the child believes that everyone sees things the same way as she or he does.

   Knowing that young children are egocentric helps in modifying leader expectations about social capabilities (e.g., sharing) of young children. At this stage children also believe in animism, which is the belief that inanimate objects have feelings. Leaders would be wise to allow children in this stage this type of belief. In addition, at this stage children think they cause events of nature. For example, if in anger a child were to wish ill of someone and something bad were to happen, youngsters at this stage would believe that their wish caused the negative action to occur. Leaders who recognize this could be sensitive to a child's potential feelings of self-doubt.

Concrete Operations Stage (7 to 11 Years)

In middle childhood, according to Piaget, youngsters learn to classify and group objects, and begin to understand abstract notions and logical reasoning. At this stage, children are able to focus on more than one thing at a time and can handle multiple directions. In middle childhood, young people learn that general principles apply across a variety of situations, and that basic principles apply to everyone. They also learn how to retrace their thought processes and keep track of their thoughts. They begin to understand that merely changing the form of an object does not change the nature of it. Understanding what occurs developmentally during this stage helps leaders to communicate, assign tasks, and use increasingly sophisticated behavior management techniques. For instance, at this age children are able to understand what it means to play within activities rules. Prior to this stage children feel perfectly free to make up rules as they go along (usually to avoid failing).

Formal Operations Stage (11+ Years)

According to Piaget the development and acquisition of formal operations is gradual. While it generally begins around age 11, the skills acquired in this stage do not become consistent learning objectives until approximately age 16. The formal operations stage includes the development of problem-solving abilities and hypothesis testing (people have the ability to wonder, "what would happen if...?" and then test that notion). When moving through this stage young people learn best when confronted with novelty and a desire to understand. For example, as children develop the ability to solve problems, leaders might engage them in leadership decisions, conflict management, and the development of new games and activities.

In developing his four stage theory of development, Piaget studied boys as they moved from infancy into adolescence and noted that enough similarities existed to define the four stages of human development as described above. The primary foci of Piaget's model are how people learn, what they learn, and the beliefs they hold about their place in the world. While Piaget focused on cognitive learning and belief systems, Erikson began with the supposition that human development results from a series of crises which occur over the course of life. One's life course, then, is determined by how an individual reacts to each crisis as it occurs (Bee, 1992; Hughes & Noppe, 1985; King, Chipman & Cruz-Janzen, 1994; Sarafino & Armstrong, 1986; Schickedanz, Hansen, & Forsyth, 1990).

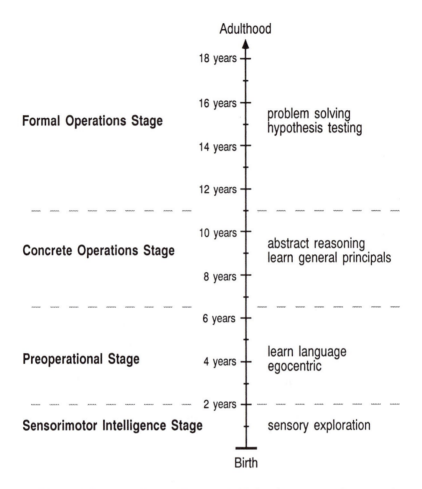

Figure 3.1 *According to Piaget, child development is directional and linear.*

Erikson's Life Stages

Erikson approached the understanding of life stages by articulating and considering several crises which people face over the course of development. One grows and matures in different directions based on how she or he deals with those crises. While Piaget believed that development was completed at young adulthood (formal operations are achieved around age 16), Erikson carried life-stage development through adulthood. An overview of each of the life crises and the potential results follows (Bee, 1992; Edginton, Jordan, DeGraaf, & Edginton, 1995; Schickedanz, Hansen, & Forsyth, 1990; Schuman & Olufs, 1995).

Trust vs. Mistrust (Birth to 18 Months)

Infants learn to trust that things are safe, predictable, and orderly (or not) from caregivers and the environment. A child learns that she or he is safe in the world, or that things are unpredictable and frightening. A baby who is fed when hungry, changed when wet, and comforted when frightened learns to trust others. An infant who does not have her or his needs met learns to distrust others. According to this theory this trust attitude is carried over into childhood and adulthood.

Autonomy vs. Shame or Doubt (18 Months to 3.5 Years)

In this stage, children develop motor skills and explore the environment as they learn independence. According to Erikson, if a child is overly criticized, she or he will learn shame or doubt; one who is allowed to explore will learn autonomy. The message from adults is that children can make choices and this leads to feelings of empowerment (or self-doubt).

Initiative vs. Guilt (3.5 to 6 Years)

Young children initiate activities out of curiosity and learn to use cognitive and language skills. Erikson suggested that at this developmental stage, the reaction to these developments by adults can lead to a sense of initiative or guilt. If successfully negotiated, children learn that they can accomplish tasks based on their own skills and support systems. For instance, a child who wants to show an adult her or his completed arts-and-crafts project will learn initiative if the adult reacts positively and comments on the effort. If the adult ignores, negates, or punishes the child's effort, however, the youngster may learn to feel guilty.

Industry vs. Inferiority (6 to 12 Years)

Through schooling and interactions with peers and adults children learn how to organize and develop rules. If these efforts are treated as silly, the child might develop feelings of inferiority. If the young child's efforts are treated as worthy she or he learns that working with others is good.

Identity vs. Role Confusion (Adolescence)

During adolescence teens begin to develop the ability to see perspectives other than their own. They also learn more about their own self-interests and goals. Erikson believed that teens must develop a sense of self as distinct from others or they will face role confusion later in adulthood.

Intimacy vs. Isolation (Young Adulthood)

Developing relationships with others may result in intimacy or isolation. If this crisis is handled well, intimacy occurs; if relationships are not developed in a positive fashion, isolation may occur. In young adulthood people learn that they can take risks with others and be accepted.

Generativity vs. Stagnation (Adulthood)

In adulthood, according to Erikson, a person faces the crisis of being concerned with humanity (self-propagation, society, others) or materialism. As individuals wrestle with this crisis, people learn to grow and regenerate their lives (or become stagnated and caught in the cycle of materialism). Those who engage in generativity seem to find a renewed purpose to life while others get caught up in the "rat race."

Integrity vs. Despair (Older Adulthood)

Erikson believed that as people age, they enter a time of reflection of their life. As a result of this they either feel a sense of integrity (wholeness) and acceptance about the life they have lived, or despair about what was missed.

As can be seen from this review of Erikson's theory of human development, Erikson developed a model which addresses major issues which occur over the course of life. Both Erikson and Piaget created theories which can be used as a foundation for understanding human development. They provide a framework for understanding how and why people develop, think, and behave the way they do. It is generally accepted that all people follow similar patterns of development across the life span although the actual age at which one reaches a particular stage varies.

Kohlberg's Theory of Moral Development

Through his research, Kohlberg attempted to understand how a sense of morality was developed over the course of one's life. Leaders understanding this information will better comprehend why people act the way they do and be in a position to intervene, if desired. It is generally thought that as people grow and mature, they move through various

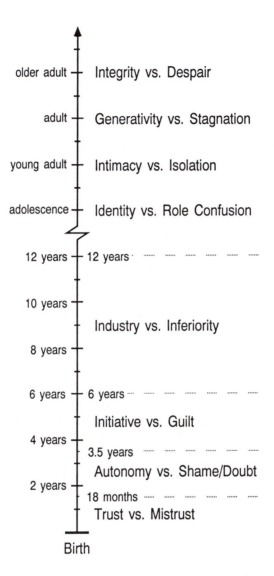

Figure 3.2 *Erikson viewed human development as a linear series of crises one would negotiate on the way through life.*

stages of moral development moving from an egotistical position ("me" orientation) to a more objective "other" orientation. As with other theories of development, it should be noted that all people do not move through all stages of moral development, and at times, individuals move in and out of various stages across the life span (Bee, 1992; Hughes & Noppe, 1985).

Stage 1 (Early Childhood)

In Stage 1, Kohlberg believes that moral decisions are based on a desire to avoid punishment. People in this stage of moral development decide not to violate social norms because they fear or want to avoid the consequences. For example, a child at this stage would behave as asked by a leader because she or he feared disapproval or punishment.

Stage 2 (Early/Middle Childhood)

In Stage 2, people make decisions based on a desire to obtain rewards. A person in this stage might resolve a question by determining what rewards would be gained by following instructions (and vice versa). Individuals in this stage of moral development would behave as expected if they believed they would be rewarded for doing so (e.g., the leader would pay them extra attention, the children might receive candy bars or prizes).

Stage 3 (Adolescence)

As people move through the stages of moral development, they move from making decisions based on a desire for tangible rewards to making decisions based on a desire to gain social approval. At this stage, people value trust, loyalty, and respect. The effects of peer pressure provide an example of individuals making decisions to gain social approval.

Stage 4 (Adolescence/Young Adulthood)

At this phase of development, morality is accepted as being determined by those in legitimate authority. What is legal is viewed as moral, what is illegal is considered immoral. A person at this stage would follow rules (because the leader said so) and act in legally appropriate ways because the law so dictated.

Stage 5 (Young/Middle Adulthood)

At Stage 5, morality is based on an assumption of the existence of an unwritten contract among members of society to behave in an acceptable and appropriate manner. The concern is not for the consequences of one's acts, but for the welfare of society. At this stage a person would make decisions and engage in behaviors which would be in the best interest of others. For instance if angry, an individual at this stage would prefer to talk out the issues as opposed to engaging in a fist fight.

Stage 6 (Adulthood)

As individuals achieve what Kohlberg viewed as the highest stage of moral development, decisions are based on self-chosen ethical principles which are directed toward the good of humanity. A consistent system of values and principles is apparent; a person at this stage is highly principled and has a great deal of integrity.

Kohlberg envisioned people's moral development as maturing over six stages across the life span. He viewed Stage 6 as the highest moral order and observed that many people never reach this stage of morality. Life stages, that is various age groups (cohorts), do not necessarily correlate to a particular moral development stage. It may be viewed however, that as one matures, one moves away from a fear-based morality to a moral viewpoint which focuses on the good of humanity.

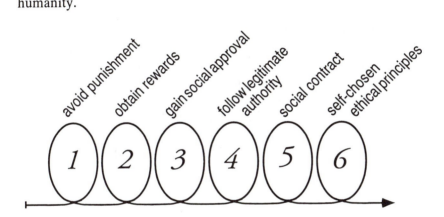

Figure 3.3 *Kohlberg postulated about moral development across the life span and viewed this development as directional, yet looped.*

Morality Based on an Ethic of Care

As with Piaget, Kohlberg studied males in his research, and out of those studies came the six-stage model just presented. In the past 10 to 15 years researchers have realized that females and males differ in their moral development. In response to that a body of knowledge has developed that attempts to explain the differences and similarities in moral development which exist between females and males. It has been discovered that girls and boys are not only different biologically, but they are also socialized differently; it is theorized that this results in varying opportunities, skills, and potentials for females and males.

As scientists studied the constructs of development created by Piaget, Erikson, and Kohlberg they discovered that in all three cases, only males were used as study subjects. This was common practice in early years of research, and still occurs today. As might be imagined, this raised questions related to the viability of the theories for girls and women. Concerned about the exclusion of females in the study related to moral development, Gilligan (1982) engaged in research to examine the moral development of girls.

In her research Gilligan found that girls and women are taught to value attachments to other people and remain connected to others (i.e., maintain relationships) while boys and men are taught to value independence and autonomy. Therefore, she surmised that girls and women might prefer and follow a moral code based on caring for and empathizing with others. She termed this an "ethic of care." In contrast, the moral development process presented by Kohlberg has been characterized as an "ethic of rights and justice." For example, a person believing in an ethic of rights and justice might not steal from someone because it was against the law, whereas a person following an ethic of care would not steal because it was the other person's property and she or he might be hurt by its loss.

In leisure services settings an individual in an adult sports league adhering to an ethic of rights and justice might not engage in an argument or fight with others because it was against the rules. On the other hand, an individual who subscribes to the ethic of care would avoid an altercation out of a concern for hurting the individual (emotionally and physically). It is difficult to know which model is more accurate or appropriate for females or males, and research has been inconclusive related to the differences found between the models presented by Kohlberg and Gilligan. Other issues related to the influences of gender on human development also exist.

Gender and Development

Cognitive, social, physical, and moral development is influenced both by the environment in which one is raised and by one's genetic predisposition. One of those elements of environment is gender (the notion of what is feminine and masculine). Children are taught what is

Figure 3.4 *As presented by Gilligan, the ethic of care requires a capacity to care and a concern for the well-being of others.*

feminine and what is masculine by the media, peers, parents, church, and through play; they come to understand their own gender by age three or four (Bee, 1992). This is to say that by age three or four children know the difference between girls and boys and are able to identify "girls games/toys" and "boys games/toys." Gender is one personality characteristic that is evidenced in all aspects of human development; girls and boys face different biological, psychological, and socioemotional changes across the life span.

Society has determined acceptable behaviors for girls and boys and from these expectations come stereotypes. Sex-based stereotypes are believed to lead to differences in behaviors based on sex. For example, boys are expected to show more aggression, dominance, and competitiveness than are girls. In addition, boys are expected to show more risk-taking behaviors (willing to try more on their own) than girls. On the other hand, girls face expectations to be more dependent on others than boys. Furthermore, girls are expected to be more nurturing, helping, and generous than are boys. In addition, girls are expected to show more sociability, be more compliant, and cry more than boys (Bee, 1992). Leaders should be careful, however, to avoid the traps of stereotyping others as labeling people tends to limit their potentials. In leisure services settings females and males are often victims of stereotypes and face social and structural constraints to full engagement in a variety of recreation and leisure services.

Life Stages and Age Groups

Life stages are rather broad in scope; that is, people of many ages may fall within each developmental stage. While it may not always be the

best approach, in fields such as education and leisure services participants are often separated by age. This is because, in general, people in
similar age groups tend to fall into similar stages of development. Thus,
people who are close in age tend to have similar mental, physical, social
and emotional capabilities (Goode Vick, 1989; Howe, 1993; Howe &
Strauss, 1993; Schickedanz, Hansen, & Forsyth, 1990).

So, with a foundation in the basics of human development, this text
next considers age groupings which are based on similar categories
found in the literature. Much of the information related to age groups
is based on extensive research which included interviews with school
teachers, parents, and youth; and observations of youth over extended
periods of time (Howe, 1993). Due to the fact that people are
composites of many aspects of themselves, within each age group
information related to physical, mental or cognitive, socioemotional,
and moral development is described.

Behavior results from a combination of physical, mental, socioemotional, and moral aspects of a person—it is a holistic process and a
product. Generally speaking, *physical development* includes energy
and growth, the acquisition of fine and gross motor skills; activity
preferences, and physical coordination. *Mental* or *cognitive development* includes the ability to think abstractly, academic achievement,
reasoning and logic, and limitations in mental abilities. *Socioemotional
development* consists of relationships with others (peers and adults),
fears, worries, and moods. The other element of development discussed
in this chapter is *moral development,* which involves how people make

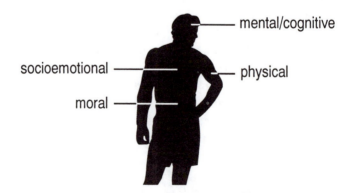

Figure 3.5   *Human development involves growth in all aspects of
a person: physical, mental/intellectual, socioemotional, and moral.*

decisions, and how they define what is good and right and what is bad and wrong.

These developmental elements will be helpful to a leader in terms of establishing expectations of participants, selecting effective leadership styles, and the use of appropriate leadership techniques (e.g., behavior management, communication, group dynamics). In addition, this knowledge will be useful in typical tasks for recreation and leisure practitioners such as programming, supervision, direct instruction, and the development of policies and procedures. It should be noted that as with all generalities about groups of people there are individuals who do not fall within the descriptions found below. Remember, this information can be helpful in many ways, but predicting *specific individual* behaviors is not possible.

Young Childhood (5 to 7 years)

Physical Development

In terms of physical development, children ages five to seven years have a large amount of energy which comes in spurts, and is often difficult to keep under control. As they continue to practice large motor skills, children at this age enjoy a great deal of running, hopping, skipping, climbing, and catching. In addition, chasing and being chased are favorite activities. Because children at this age struggle with fine motor control there may be frustration surrounding these efforts (such as tying shoes). The high level of physical activity is balanced by a similar need for rest as youngsters in this age group tend to tire easily.

Mental/Cognitive Development

Five-year-olds to seven-year-olds tend to be concrete thinkers and are very literal in interpreting meanings. At this age, children operate from perception and intuition rather than logic. It is difficult for young children to focus on more than one thing at a time and they only see things from their own perspective (they believe everyone sees things as they do, as well). Young children can accept and work with basic rules, but they will change rules when needed to avoid failure or losing a game. Due to the heavy reliance on concrete thinking, movement is often necessary for learning and understanding directions. At this age children have wonderful capabilities for fantasy and active imaginations.

Socioemotional Development

Young children do not have strong social skills (e.g., communication, conflict resolution, other orientation). They tend to be egoistic with everything centering on themselves. In this age group, children engage in some sharing, but do not necessarily seek out ways to share. In addition, there tends to be a separation of the sexes with boys and girls playing apart from one another. Children at this age generally are very honest; this is due in part to a lack of mastery over the nuances of lying. Organizational skills are not a strong suit for these young children and items are often lost or left lying about.

Youngsters at this stage of development (preoperational, according to Piaget; facing the initiative versus guilt crisis according to Erikson) can be overly sensitive to comments and actions of others (they may be very hurt if a child sticks out her or his tongue at them). If there is difficulty in understanding directions, youngsters of this age can be easily frustrated. They need a good deal of encouragement and support from adults and seem to crave adult affection. Children of this age are very impulsive and unable to control their emotions; they tend to use physical aggression to resolve problems, and start and stop crying quickly.

Moral Development

Generally, children between five and seven years of age are at the first and second stages of moral development. Decisions to do or not do as the leader asks or as the group expects are based on a fear of punishment and a desire for rewards. If a child fears punishment or desires rewards she or he will act in concomitant ways.

Implications for Leaders

Implications of human development for leaders may be considered from two perspectives. One is that knowledge of human development will provide a basis for understanding why people act the way they do. This is not meant to serve as an excuse for behaviors, however. One of the most fascinating things about humans is that we can learn. Thus, in addition to providing a leader a basis for understanding, this knowledge allows a leader to establish environments where people are challenged to grow and develop.

For instance, when working with a young child who becomes frustrated and hits another child, a leader first will be able to understand that this is not necessarily a purposeful act of aggression. Hitting among young children is often due to poor impulse control and the inability to reason through conflict. Once the inappropriate behavior is addressed (in a developmentally appropriate way), the leader can then begin to help the youngster develop control over her or his emotions through examples and practice.

Due to their physical nature, young children learn best by doing. Leaders would be wise then to present activity instructions in such a way as to incorporate physical engagement of the children. Bear in mind that activities need to be balanced with rest; youngsters tire easily. Both fatigue and a need to move may be underlying reasons for inappropriate behaviors; the leader will need to make a judgment based on her or his understanding of the entire situation. Logic and reasoning capabilities of young children are limited; therefore, extended lessons in reasoning will not be very effective when addressing various difficulties.

Preventative behavior management with this age group may be accomplished by much preparation—of the physical and social environments. At this age children have difficulty sharing, so being fully prepared with enough equipment to go around is important. Flexibility in adjusting activities based on physical capabilities (i.e., establishing environments for success), mental capabilities (i.e., providing opportunities for youth to show mastery in creative areas), socioemotional skills (i.e., structuring social interactions to address low levels of maturity),

Photo courtesy of the Conestoga Council of Girl Scouts

Young children need opportunities to practice fine motor skills.

and moral development will help set a tone for leader and participant success.

Relationships with adults are important to children in the five to seven age range. Often, dependent relationships on leaders are formed and youngsters will compete for leader attention. Leisure services leaders will need to be sensitive to this and aware of how they treat the attention-seeking youngsters. Youth at this stage are very literal thinkers and will follow directions literally rather than figuratively; therefore, explicit leader instructions are necessary.

Table 3A *Young Childhood (ages 5 to 7 years)*

Piaget's Theory of Cognitive Development: Preoperational Stage
Erikson's Theory of Human Development: Initiative vs. Guilt Crisis
Kohlberg's Moral Development Theory: Stage 1 and Stage 2

Characteristics	Description
Physical	Lots of energy balanced with need for rest.
	Struggle with fine motor skills, developing gross motor skills.
	Enjoy running, hopping, chasing, catching and climbing.
Cognitive	Concrete, literal thinkers.
	Children operate from perception and intuition; logic and reasoning abilities are limited.
	May change rules to avoid failure or losing; movement is necessary for learning.
	Creativity and imagination are active.
Socioemotional	Poor social skills; impulsive in emotional reactions.
	Tend to be egotistical; do not share well.
	Poor organizational skills; high need for adult love and affection
Moral	Decisions based on desire to avoid punishment or on hopes for rewards.

Leadership Implications
• Teach through physical demonstration; allow for practice of large motor skills; build in rest opportunities.
• Provide opportunities for success in social skills; give children a good deal of attention; lead simple activities with minimal and unsophisticated rules; be flexible.
• Take care to treat all youngsters with love and attention; be sensitive to their fragile emotional nature.
• Remember the power of words.

Middle Childhood (8 to 11 years)

Physical Development

As children move into middle childhood, physical coordination improves as do abilities in gross and fine motor skills. High energy levels are still apparent, although there is a reduced need for rest as children at this stage do not tire as easily as young children. While children at this age are able to be still for longer periods of time, active participation is still needed for optimum learning to occur. It is not uncommon for signs of preadolescence to occur in girls at ten or eleven years of age (e.g., onset of menstruation, change in body shape).

Mental/Cognitive Development

As youth move into the concrete operations stage (Piaget), logic and reasoning abilities begin to appear; in addition, the ability to effectively deal with abstractions develops. One of the characteristics of eight-year-olds to eleven-year-olds is that they ask a lot of 'why' questions as they begin to sort out and understand issues of cause and effect. Erikson would characterize this age group as facing the industry versus inferiority crisis; it is here that the development of self-concept begins to form. Youngsters in this age group tend to be easily motivated and are able to work within activity rules.

Children are now able to consider more than one aspect of a situation at once, and they understand general concepts better than when younger. Problem-solving skills are improving and at this age youngsters are able to work independently for short periods of time. When five to seven years of age, children often would give up if faced with frustration; at eight to eleven years of age, children tend to persevere longer—they begin to believe that they can make something happen if they try hard enough and long enough.

Socioemotional Development

As children move out of the egoistic phase (focused on self-interests) they become interested in their peer group. Because children are beginning to form attachments to groups, they become very concerned about fairness and equality. They share better, yet the sexes (for the most part) remain separate (girls/boys have "cooties"). Those children in this age group who are maturing more quickly than others may describe girlfriend/boyfriend relationships. As groups develop, so too, do relationship skills; youngsters at this age develop some tact, but are not always sensitive to others' needs. Adults remain important figures in the lives of these youth, although older children are beginning to test adults in their desire for independence.

It is important to remember that children between the ages of eight years old and eleven years old do not take criticism from peers or adults very well (they tend to be sensitive and defensive), and are easily embarrassed. An increased awareness of peers' and others' expectations impacts the development of self-esteem. This may be seen in an increase of girls "primping" and boys striving to look "cool." It has been documented that at about age ten or eleven years self-esteem in girls begins to drop (Howe, 1993; Sadker & Sadker, 1994).

Moral Development

Values are formulated and begin to be articulated by youth in this stage of development. Older youngsters in this age group begin to consider the consequences of their actions before acting. At the same time, youth

Middle childhood is a time of curiosity and high energy.

Photo courtesy of Hartman Nature Reserve

are striving to gain social approval and often base decisions of morality on peer or social approval.

Implications for Leaders

Leaders working with eight-year-olds to eleven-year-olds face young people at a time when many changes are occurring, particularly in social development. Physical coordination is improving, and children are beginning to understand reasoning and logic; therefore, leaders might experience increased success in using logic and reasoning when explaining activity directions or rules. These youngsters are not quite so literal as when younger and better understand leader meanings. Communication with adults seems to become easier as these abilities develop. The ability to work independently away from adult supervision often frees leaders to take care of other issues and allows youngsters to grow and develop.

In this age group, best friends come and go, and children may be sensitive to these changing relationships. Leaders who are aware of social development can help youth through the difficult times and help them practice new social skills. This may be accomplished by manipulating group membership and structuring activities for the practice and development of interpersonal skills.

Knowing that at this age youngsters test adult limits helps to lay the groundwork for the leader to understand that various testing behaviors are not personally directed and motivated out of malice, but out of learning to gain a sense of self and independence. Therefore, when it appears that preadolescents are acting to disrupt a leader's efforts, the leader should remember that there are many possible reasons for the behaviors. When working with all people, it is important to recognize the impact of leadership on the self-esteem of participants; this is particularly true at this age. Self-esteem issues for preadolescent girls are crucial. The values that leaders model in behaviors, words, and style of presentation also have a big impact on the development and esteem of young people. See Table 3B, page 88 for a summary of this developmental stage.

Table 3B *Middle Childhood (ages 8 to 11 years)*

Piaget's Theory of Cognitive Development: Concrete Operations Stage
Erikson's Theory of Human Development: Industry vs. Inferiority Crisis
Kohlberg's Moral Development Theory: Stage 2 and Stage 3

Characteristics	Description
Physical	Lots of energy balanced with reduced need for rest. Improved coordination skills. Active participation needed for learning. Early signs of preadolescence in girls.
Cognitive	Logic and reasoning abilities are being developed and practiced. Curiosity abounds; children ask a lot of "why" questions and are easily motivated. Youth learn to deal with abstractions and general concepts. Children begin to work independently.
Socioemotional	Social skills are improving; peer groups begin to become important. Friendships develop and change quickly; the focus on peer group results in easy embarrassment. Adults remain important figures. Self-esteem development becomes apparent.
Moral	Values development is initiated. Decisions are based on a desire for tangible rewards and social acceptance/approval.

Leadership Implications
- Provide opportunities to practice and achieve success with both gross and fine motor skills, as well as interpersonal skills.
- Be aware of frustration and impulsive acting out if things are not going well.
- Provide lots of opportunities for exploration and learning new things.
- Provide structured choices; engage youth in conflict resolution situations.

Young Adolescence (12 to 14 years)

Physical Development

In the early teen years youth experience a balance in their energy output; generally they have calmed down since early and middle childhood. The impulsivity of the previous years has lessened. At twelve to fourteen years of age most girls have experienced the onset of puberty and the development of secondary sex characteristics. There is great variation with boys; some boys have reached puberty, others are just beginning the sexual maturation process. For many young people in this age group, abilities related to coordination and fine and gross motor skills are well-developed.

Mental/Cognitive Development

Most teenage youth are in, and gaining experience in, the formal operational stage as described by Piaget. That is, logic, reasoning, and problem-solving skills are developing, and organizational skills and rules management are improved. Twelve-year-old to fourteen-year-old youth have the capabilities to understand multiple perspectives (e.g., they can see and begin to appreciate others' viewpoints) and to deal with abstractions. Teens begin to develop the ability to formulate and test hypotheses (e.g., "what if?" situations). In this period of early adolescence youth find themselves facing Kohlberg's identity versus role confusion crisis; they are beginning to develop a sense of self-identity. These are years of much exploration (e.g., drugs, sexuality, risk-taking behaviors) as this search for self ensues.

Socioemotional Development

Peers are a very important source of support for young teens as they strive to make the transition from family dependence to independence. This age group is easily influenced by its peer group and the need for belonging seems all-important. Sociosexual relationships (attractions to others based on sexuality) begin to develop, as does sexual exploration.

Emotions and moods can range widely as changes in hormones interfere with other cognitive, social, and physical changes. Self-esteem, particularly for girls, fluctuates tremendously in this age group. Research to determine why self-esteem for teenage girls drops so steeply is ongoing. Concerns with body image (as body shape changes with physical maturity) and embarrassment are important issues to this

Photo courtesy of the Conestoga Council of Girl Scouts

Young adolescents enjoy testing their skills through various projects.

age group of teens. Boys often work through determining a sense of self through being "cool" and engaging in between-boy competitions. That is, teenage boys often engage in showing off behaviors and spontaneous public competitions (e.g., basketball "jam" contests at the neighborhood court). Teen girls often subscribe to social images of what is beautiful and may experience negative effects on their own psyche (e.g., anorexia, bulimia).

Moral Development

At this age, teens understand intention and consequences; they have the ability to accept responsibility and blame for their own misbehaviors. As young people further develop their values and belief systems they often project a sense of absoluteness (black and white) in moral judgments. Social approval, loyalty, trust, and respect remain important in decision-making processes. Most youth at this age may be found in stage three or four of Kohlberg's moral development theory.

Implications for Leaders

Leaders should be very aware of issues surrounding body image for both girls and boys as embarrassment and acceptance of these changes can be difficult to deal with. It is during these years that teasing from peers based on differences occurs and teens can be very sensitive to this. As they work through breaking away from parents, teens often project this wrestling with independence on to other adults. Therefore, all adults may experience teens talking back and testing limits as the teens strive to identify how they define themselves.

Social opportunities and group opportunities are important to teens; therefore, leaders who address these issues will be more successful than those who do not. Teens recognize and are concerned with unfairness, inconsistency, jumping to conclusions, not being liked, and being criticized in front of others. Thus leaders will want to establish policies and develop leadership techniques to counteract these concerns.

Photo courtesy of the YWCA of Black Hawk County

Through visiting and talking with peers, teens work through an identity-seeking process.

To be most effective in working with young teens, leaders should be cognizant of their own influences (both purposeful and unintentional) on the lives of these adolescents. Opportunities for success, and protection and security from negative social influences are strongly desired. Helping teens to explore many facets of their skills, abilities, and personality in a safe environment can make a tremendous difference in teen development. See Table 3C, page 92, for a summary of this developmental stage.

Table 3C *Young Adolescence (ages 12 to 14 years)*

Piaget's Theory of Cognitive Development: Beginning of Formal Operations
Erikson's Theory of Human Development: Identity vs. Role Confusion Crisis
Kohlberg's Moral Development Theory: Stage 3 and Stage 4

Characteristics	Description
Physical	A balance of energy output occurs. Abilities related to coordination and fine motor skills are well-developed. Most girls have reached puberty and experience the development of secondary sexual characteristics. Most boys are just beginning to experience sexual maturation. Large focus on body image for both girls and boys.
Cognitive	Logic and reasoning abilities are developed and continue to be practiced. Organizational skills and rules management are honed. Can understand abstractions and various viewpoints. Begin to learn how to test hypotheses; are developing a sense of self.
Socioemotional	Peers are a very important source of support. Teens are seeking independence from adults and family. Sociosexual relationships develop. Moodiness is not uncommon; self-esteem for girls begins to plummet. Boys strive to be "cool;" girls often follow media stereotypes for body image/success. Exploration in many areas is common.
Moral	Values clarification continues; teens are able to understand actions and consequences. Decisions are based on rewards and social acceptance/approval. Approval, loyalty, respect and trust are important aspects of self.

Leadership Implications
- Provide opportunities for own, and peer group leadership development.
- Try laissez-faire, democratic, or consultive leadership styles.
- Model positive social relationships and human relations skills.
- Lead and facilitate a variety of sophisticated activities.
- Allow and accept mood swings; understand lashing out at leader is not personal.
- Encourage nonstereotypical leisure pursuits; act as a guide, mentor, counselor.

Adolescence (15 to 17 years)

Physical Development

Well into being teenagers, fifteen-year-olds to seventeen-year-olds tend to be very concerned about their physical development and body image. Most males reach puberty during this period; most girls have already reached puberty. As physical growth outpaces their ability to adapt, boys' coordination takes a dip (they may appear gangly—all arms and legs). By this age most girls have accepted their postpubescent bodies. Skills acquisition becomes important and is made possible by physical capabilities—this is the age at which many physical skills are refined.

Mental/Cognitive Development

Many teens hold an idealistic view of the world and believe that situations can change if people just try hard enough. At this age the ability to handle abstractions, test hypotheses, and engage in problem solving come together. Cognitive abilities have reached a point of development where further growth results in increasing sophistication rather than the development of new skills. Teens have a wide variety of interests and a strong need to experiment and stretch themselves.

Socioemotional Development

Moving toward young adulthood, older teens strive to achieve self-identity, freedom from adults, and responsibility for themselves. Group affiliation remains important and mixed sex activities are sought. This stage of development can be difficult for teens as the pull for independence and desire for familial security coexist. Moodiness might reflect the struggle in maintaining changing relationships. Many teens in this age group often seem like two different people—one mature young adult, and one immature youngster.

Moral Development

While many teens remain in the belief that morality is based on peer approval (Stage 3), a large number of teens are moving into the stage of moral reasoning where what is appropriate is defined by legitimate authority (Stage 4). Rules, laws, and leader guidelines become the source of what is right and what is wrong. A sense of responsibility develops as many youth at this age begin working and thinking about higher education or self-sufficiency away from the security of family.

Implications for Leaders

Working with teens can be a challenge for recreation and leisure services leaders. The fragility and strength dichotomy often manifested by teens can be just as confusing for adult leaders as for the teens themselves. Certainly, leaders have much more freedom to communicate using reason and logic when working with teens as their abilities in those areas are fairly well-developed. Leaders who understand the struggle between needing the social approval of one's peer group and the desire to be one's own self will be more effective than those who do not understand these inherent difficulties.

The struggle with body image is evident for both girls and boys. Boys often become increasingly physical as they use their bodies in sports, athletics, and shows of physical prowess. Many girls discover that their bodies are capable of being strong and fluent as well. As this is a time of varied interests and strong skills, leaders who provide opportunities for trying new things will tend to be effective. In addition, it is important to allow this age group the freedom to experiment and practice making decisions for themselves, resolving conflicts, and working through relationships with a minimum of leader involvement. At the same time, genuine leader concern and respect for these young people is important.

Young Adulthood (18 to 25 years)

Physical Development

Young adults are at their physical peak; most physical abilities are well-developed and while nuances may be refined, increased physical prowess is unlikely. The activity level of young adults is relatively high, but it can be slowed somewhat by life changes (e.g., beginning a career, relocation, establishing a family). Structured competition and recreational play are desired by most people in this age group. Often a concern for fitness drives physical activity, and activity is typically secondary to job or career. Interests in physical activity often include both individual and group activities.

Mental/Cognitive Development

Building on the cognitive skills of the late teen years, young adults are creative and capable of handling abstractions quite well. Cognitive skills are sharp and are often considered at a peak during these years.

Table 3D Adolescence (ages 15 to 17 years)

Piaget's Theory of Cognitive Development: Formal Operations Stage
Erikson's Theory of Human Development: Identity vs. Role Confusion Crisis
Kohlberg's Moral Development Theory: Stage 3 and Stage 4

Characteristics	Description
Physical	Almost all girls and boys have experienced puberty and there is a focus on body image for both girls and boys.
	Skills are well-developed and specific skill (e.g., music, athletics) acquisition is important.
Cognitive	Most teens hold an idealistic view of the world.
	Logic and reasoning abilities are developed.
	Teens understand abstractions, problem solving, and hypothesis testing.
	Sophistication in cognitive abilities increases.
Socioemotional	Peers remain an important source of support.
	Mixed-sex activities are desired and sociosexual relationships develop.
	Moodiness is not uncommon; self-esteem for girls continues to drop.
	The struggle for own identity continues.
	Interests vary.
Moral	Values clarification continues; decisions are based on social acceptance/approval.
	Some are beginning to believe that morality is based on legitimate authority.

Leadership Implications

- Model positive values and social skills; offer structured opportunities for sociosexual relationship development.
- Provide skill instruction and activity strategies for honing of skills and cognitive development.
- Continue variety of leisure and leadership opportunities; provide opportunities for success and allow for failure.

Problem solving and hypothesis testing are further refined as young adults build on previous knowledge and experience. Intellectual development tends to increase in sophistication.

Socioemotional Development

It is during the young adult years that most people in our culture search for a life partner and a sense of stability; a family orientation is initiated. Enjoyment is often experienced in mixed sex activities and one's circle of friends expands through work contacts and neighborhood connections. This stage of socioemotional development is often characterized as the intimacy versus isolation crisis, as presented by Erikson. People take risks at this life stage to develop intimate and social connections with others.

Moral Development

In young adulthood people gain a perspective on life that, while it certainly addresses personal needs, also shows an awareness of the influences of society. According to Kohlberg, any young adults are in Stage 4, which addresses the acknowledgment of the rights of the legal system. Other young adults are in Stage 5, which is indicative of an assumption of a social contract where people strive to do the greatest good for greatest number. A sense of social consciousness develops for many.

Implications for Leaders

Leaders who work with young adults can expect a great deal of sensibility and stability in participant choices and actions. A sense of competition may drive some behaviors, and a knowledge of rules combined with life experiences can make it relatively easy for a leader to present activity instructions and directions.

Participants may seem to follow stereotypical activity patterns, although there certainly are individuals who step outside of these expectations. This age group, particularly true of males, tends to engage in the highest frequency of risk-related recreation and leisure opportunities of any age group. An attitude of life and vibrancy is expressed. Obviously, leader-participant communication is easier than at previous stages of development. This is due in part to the development stage, and in part due to the fact that most leisure leaders and participants in this age group are peers. A wide variety of activities and social groupings would help to meet the leisure needs of this age group. Treating individuals with dignity and respect and allowing them to be involved in leadership and decision-making processes tend to be effective leadership techniques.

Table 3E *Young Adulthood (ages 18 to 25 years)*

Piaget's Theory of Cognitive Development: Formal Operations Stage
Erikson's Theory of Human Development: Intimacy vs. Isolation Crisis
Kohlberg's Moral Development Theory: Stage 4 and Stage 5

Characteristics	Description
Physical	Physical peak; most physical abilities are well-developed. High activity level; structured activities and competitive recreation experiences are desired.
Cognitive	The cognitive abilities developed as teens continue to be honed; creativity is thought to be at a peak.
Socioemotional	The search for a life partner and a sense of familial stability occurs. People enjoy mixed-sex activities; circle of friends expands through work and neighborhood relationships.
Moral	An awareness of the greater society is seen. Some believe that morality is based on legitimate authority while others perceive the notion of an assumed social contract.

Leadership Implications
• Provide opportunities for physical and cognitive prowess to be expressed; provide a variety of structured and unstructured activities.
• Creative outlets are desirable; allow flexibility in choices of self-directed activities.
• Appeal to social contract in explaining rules and moral issues.
• Allow group development to occur naturally.

Middle Adulthood (26 to 40 years)

Physical Development

At middle adulthood, many people are still at their physical peak. Some slowing down is evident as family and career take priority, and finesse generally becomes more important than strength. Physical activities often take on a family orientation. Personal activity involvement tends to be focused on a few activities in which an individual works to hone her or his skills.

Mental/Cognitive Development

Cognitive skills and abilities of human beings are at a peak in middle adulthood. One's creativity, use of logic and reasoning, and understanding abstractions reach a high point and many people enjoy stretching their cognitive skills through mental challenges. An awareness of the influences of greater society and global issues on self and family occurs.

Socioemotional Development

Persons in middle adulthood generally are settled in their decisions relative to children and family. Often, the family orientation is one that goes in both directions; that is, there is a concern for both one's children and aging parents. For those without children, in the early years of middle adulthood there is often a "couple" orientation, and a focus toward developing one's work and career. Work-related stresses may begin to interfere with one's personal and leisure life.

Adults of all ages sometimes need permission to play.

Photo courtesy of Hartman Nature Reserve

Moral Development

Generally, by middle adulthood people have realized that for individuals in society to coexist, moral and ethical decisions must be based on an unspoken social contract (Stage 5). People must "buy into" certain social norms for society to flow smoothly. A simplified example of this is the convention of walking on the right side of the road or sidewalk. If the unwritten rule of staying to the right did not exist, navigating a busy sidewalk would be very challenging. At this stage some people are wrestling with developing and refining their own sense of ethics and principles (Stage 6). Personal integrity becomes an important factor in the establishment and maintenance of one's values and morals.

Implications for Leaders

Leaders who work with both young and middle adults can expect a good deal of sensibility and stability in participant choices and actions. People strive to do what is best and look to leaders to facilitate a leisure experience free from constraints typical of the workplace. Logic, reasoning, and sound explanations help adults to make behavior choices appropriate to the situation.

With their physical, social, and cognitive capabilities, adults are often able to lead themselves. Leadership then becomes a matter of providing resources and the space for adults to allow them to determine and engage in their own leisure experiences. It is common, when leading adults, for the direct leader to become more of an experience facilitator or program supervisor. As the supervisor, the leader might help resolve rule issues, respond to maintenance concerns, and generally oversee the area in which people are engaged in leisure. See Table 3F, page 100, for a summary of information.

Older Adulthood (41 to 60 years)

Physical Development

As individuals pass middle adulthood, changes in physical abilities become evident. For most people, there is a general slowing down with some changes in eyesight, strength, and flexibility. Metabolism begins to slow and weight gain is common; for women, menopause occurs. Physical activity tends to decline as personal work and family situations change.

Table 3F Middle Adulthood (ages 26 to 40 years)

Piaget's Theory of Cognitive Development: Formal Operations Stage
Erikson's Theory of Human Development: Intimacy vs. Isolation Crisis
Kohlberg's Moral Development Theory: Stage 4, Stage 5, and Stage 6

Characteristics	Description
Physical	Some adults are still at their physical peak; some slowing is evidenced as family and work interfere with activity level. Finesse becomes more important than strength. People work to further refine a few physical skills.
Cognitive	The cognitive abilities including creativity, logic, reasoning, problem solving, and hypotheses testing are well-developed.
Socioemotional	Settled in decisions relative to family structure; often a "couple" orientation. A focus on social position and status become important; this relates to the orientation toward family—both one's own children and aging parents. Work stresses are evident.
Moral	Some believe that morality is based on legitimate authority; others perceive the notion of an assumed social contract; and others are wrestling with their own sense of principles.

Leadership Implications
- Recognize the pull of family and work obligations on personal leisure efforts; be flexible in activity prerequisites, scheduling, and leadership techniques.
- Be prepared for great diversity in desire for structured and self-directed recreational and competitive activities.
- Laissez-faire, participative and coaching are effective leadership styles.
- Open communication with participants is important to effective leadership.

Mental/Cognitive Development

As with middle adulthood, people in this age group experience strong cognitive skills and abilities. Much of one's focus is on career; creativity and the use of mental capabilities are focused in that direction.

An understanding of global and social issues is increasingly important to individuals and families. It is during these years that people begin to experience a sense of their own mortality.

Socioemotional Development

A focus on social position and security in retirement becomes an issue with people in this age group. Family, grandchildren, aging parents and extended family also become increasingly important. Social relationships tend to be stable and long-lasting. Concern about the future and work-related stresses may influence one's emotional and mental stability. This is the life stage when it is common for adults to experience midlife crises—often a radical change in behaviors and attitudes occurs. Midlife crises are experienced by both women and men, and by people from all walks of life.

Moral Development

Similar to those in middle adulthood, people in older adulthood are operating on the assumption that a social contract (Stage 5) is necessary for society to function efficiently. Many individuals at this stage of life have developed and are striving to meet their own sense of principles and high ethical standards (Stage 6). Generally, personal integrity is an important personal quality for individuals in this life stage.

Implications for Leaders

Sensibility and stability in participant choices and actions are still primary themes in adult life. Life experiences may take on increased importance as people learn from past events and integrate that knowledge into their lives. Understanding that some physical changes occur as people age is helpful for leisure services leaders because there may be a slowing down in activity level and physical skills may not be as sharp as they once were.

Adults expect to be able to make their own choices surrounding their leisure experiences and are skilled at doing so. Many adults will balk at rules which seem to have no real purpose. Leader-participant communication and issues related to problem solving tend to be resolved through logic, reasoning, and consideration of each situation. Participative and facilitative styles of leadership tend to be very effective with adults of all ages. See Table 3G, page 102, for a summary of information.

Table 3G *Older Adulthood (ages 41 to 60 years)*

Piaget's Theory of Cognitive Development: Formal Operations Stage
Erikson's Theory of Human Development: Generativity vs. Stagnation Crisis
Kohlberg's Moral Development Theory: Stage 5 and Stage 6

Characteristics	Description
Physical	Changes in physical abilities occur; eyesight changes, strength and flexibility lessen. Metabolism slows and weight gain is common. Fitness and social contacts are typical motivations for activity.
Cognitive	Abilities including creativity, logic, reasoning, problem solving, and hypothesis testing are well-developed. Much focus is on one's career; an understanding of global and social issues is apparent.
Socioemotional	A sense of one's own mortality is experienced by many. A focus on social position and security in old age becomes important. Family is often a center of activity; work-related stresses are evident. Stable, long-lasting social contacts exist.
Moral	Most agree that an unwritten social contract exists and determines one's sense of morality. Some are refining their own ethical principles and standards for decision making.

Leadership Implications
- Be aware of the tremendous variety in skills, desires and interests in leisure.
- Nuances of strategy and sophistication in activities is appropriate.
- Leisure may be viewed as a step to social status and position; be aware of participant motivations and desired outcomes of leisure experiences.

Seniors (61+ years)

Physical Development

As medical and lifestyle changes are introduced and accepted people tend to live longer and healthier. Due to longer life spans, there is tremendous variation in physical abilities and limitations of adults aged 61 and older. While everyone experiences changes in balance, eyesight, hearing, strength, and flexibility, how each person is affected by and deals with these changes is based on one's own physical makeup, mental attitude, environment, and opportunities. Some people seem as young and vibrant as those many years their junior, while others are quite frail.

The great disparities between well, active seniors and frail elderly require that recreation and leisure services leaders be careful to avoid categorizing all older adults as having limited physical or cognitive abilities. Women tend to outlive men in all racial and ethnic groups; therefore, in this age group there are higher numbers of women than men participants.

Mental/Cognitive Development

As with the changes and differences in physical condition, there is a similar variation in cognitive and mental processes. Eventually mental processes slow, but as a whole, older adults remain sharp and in control of their mental capacities until well into old age. Some seniors are impacted by diseases such as senility and Alzheimer's disease which affect their mental capabilities, but these people are exceptions, and not the norm. Work-related stresses are reduced as retirement and life changes are likely to occur. However, as retirement arrives stresses related to a change in life (from worker to retiree) can occur.

Socioemotional Development

As people age, social connections become increasingly important. Oddly, this occurs at the same time that people begin to deal with social isolation (as life partners and friends die) and death. Conflict in response to the desire for and lessening of social contacts may occur. Much reflection over one's life is common as people realize their own mortality. Because of this a renewed interest in religion may occur.

Furthermore, retirement may result in great joy and an apparent rejuvenation, or it may cause new stresses as financial stability and quality of life may become important issues.

Moral Development

By this stage in life, as one's own mortality becomes evident, many people are living their lives with a focus on the greater society. After wrestling for many years with their own understanding of morality, many individuals by now have developed and live by a set of ethical principles and standards which follow a consistent system of values and principles (Stage 6).

Implications for Leaders

As with all age groups, leaders are cautioned to not put all older people in one category. The variation in physical abilities, cognitive capacity, and socioemotional states are tremendous. The accumulation of life experiences to share and to integrate into one's leisure life is vast. Leaders can learn much from those years of experience. In leading, remaining aware of pacing and other physical issues is important, as is providing real choices. Facilitation and participative leadership tend to be effective methods of leadership with adults; they tend to be very self-directed in their leisure choices.

Table 3H *Seniors (ages 61+ years)*

Piaget's Theory of Cognitive Development: Formal Operations Stage
Erikson's Theory of Human Development: Integrity vs. Despair Crisis
Kohlberg's Moral Development Theory: Stage 5 and Stage 6

Characteristics	Description
Physical	There is tremendous variation in physical capabilities; some seniors are in excellent health, others experience health problems.
	Most people experience some lessening in eyesight, hearing, balance, strength and flexibility.
Cognitive	Some slowing and lessening in cognitive abilities occurs.
	Stresses related to retirement and life changes may occur.
Socioemotional	Social connections and relationships with family and friends become increasingly important.
	Disease and death are faced often as friends and cohorts pass on.
	Social isolation can occur.
Moral	One's own sense of integrity and ethical principles is usually well-established by this point.
	The focus is on the needs of other's in society.

Leadership Implications
- Recognize a wide variety in physical and mental health and well-being in people in this age range.
- Focus on social interactions; treat all participants with the utmost of respect and dignity.
- Accept the knowledge, judgment and experience gained over a lifetime—utilize those strengths in participants.
- Introduce new activities, encourage personal leadership and choice in leisure.

Summary

This chapter has provided a basis for understanding people—the one common element in all leisure services settings. Being exposed to different theories or models of human development allows leaders to make effective decisions in their interactions with people of all ages. Being familiar with and understanding well-known models of development such as presented by Piaget, Erikson, Kohlberg, and Gilligan provide a firm rooting in learning about human behaviors.

Piaget suggested that individuals move through four stages of development: sensorimotor intelligence, preoperational, concrete operations, and formal operations whereby one's ability to process information cognitively becomes increasingly sophisticated. Erikson believed that people face various crises across the life span which trigger various types of growth. Those crises are: trust vs. mistrust; autonomy vs. shame; initiative vs. guilt; industry vs. inferiority; identity vs. role confusion; intimacy vs. isolation; generativity vs. stagnation; and integrity vs. despair. In investigating moral development, Kohlberg reported that people make moral decisions differently based on cognitive and emotional maturation. Gilligan examined gender differences in moral development in presenting us with the concept of an ethic of care.

It is important to remember that while people all pass through the various life stages and develop (cognitively, physically, emotionally, socially, and psychologically) not everyone does so at the same chronological age. In their development people are affected by social mores and stereotypes, genetic disposition, opportunities, their own abilities and limitations, and leader expectations. By understanding the basic elements of human development—physical, mental/cognitive, socioemotional, and moral—leaders can make appropriate choices in communication, activity leadership, conflict resolution, behavior management, and other aspects of direct leadership. Leaders are encouraged to continue to study issues of human development and to apply that knowledge to leadership situations.

The Front Line

Knowing and applying information about human development when leading leisure services activities can make a big difference in perceived competence of the leader. To this end leaders would be wise to:

- remember that knowledge about human development should be applied to communication with participants, in behavior management situations, leadership style choice, risk management situations, and all other aspects of leadership in leisure services;

- remember that very young children do not understand figurative language;

- avoid treating young children as miniature adults;

- recognize that much "sassing back" from teenage youth is not personally directed;

- realize that to learn and improve their own leadership skills, youth need various opportunities to practice various forms of leadership;

- avoid referring to older adults as "cute" (and other paternalistic adjectives);

- avoid discounting the life experiences of older adults;

- be careful to not assume that all adults are skilled in communication or conflict resolution; and

- bear in mind that all persons, no matter the age, have potential to develop leadership skills.

References

Bee, H. (1992). *The developing child* (6th ed.). New York, NY: HarperCollins Publishers.

Beilin, H. (1992). Piagetian Theory. In R. Vasta (Ed.), *Six theories of child development: Revised formulations and current issues* (pp. 85-132). London, UK: Jessica Kingsley.

Bocknek, G. (1980). *The young adult.* Belmont, CA: Brooks/Cole Publishing Company.

Edginton, C., Jordan, D., DeGraaf, D., and Edginton, S. (1995). *Leisure and life satisfaction: Foundational perspectives.* Dubuque, IA: Brown & Benchmark.

Gilligan, C. (1982). *In a different voice.* Cambridge, MA: Harvard University Press.

Goode Vick, C. G. (1989). *You can be a leader.* Champaign, IL: Sagamore Publishing.

Howe, F. (1993). The child in elementary school. *Child Study Journal, 23*(3), 229-338.

Howe, N. and Strauss, B. (1993). *13th Gen: Abort, retry, ignore, fail?* New York, NY: Vintage Books.

Hughes, F. and Noppe, L. (1985). *Human development across the lifespan.* St. Paul, MN: West Publishing Company.

King, E., Chipman, M., and Cruz-Janzen, M. (1994). *Educating young children in a diverse society.* Needham Heights, MA: Allyn & Bacon.

Sadker, M. and Sadker, D. (1994). *Failing at fairness: How our schools cheat girls.* New York, NY: Touchstone.

Sarafino, E. and Armstrong, J. (1986). *Child and adolescent development.* St. Paul, MN: West Publishing Company.

Schickedanz, J., Hansen, K., and Forsyth, P. (1990). *Understanding children.* Mountain View, CA: Mayfield Publishing Company.

Schuman, D. and Olufs, D. (1995). *Diversity on campus.* Needham Heights, MA: Allyn & Bacon.

Section II

Working with People:
Essential Skills of Leadership

Having recently completed the broad foundational material presented in the first section, you will find this section of the text, Working with People: Essential Skills of Leadership, more specific. Background information, reasoning, and specific techniques are offered within this section to aid in the usefulness of the material. To be both an effective follower and an effective leader, skills in working with others are absolutely essential. This section of the text is comprised of information and knowledge about people skills which are needed and utilized by leaders and followers alike.

The purpose in presenting this material is to provide information that can be used in the actual practice of leisure services leadership. It is well and good to write and read about group dynamics, for instance, but without actual practice and experience with groups, a leader's judgment may be lacking and she or he may be unsure which direction to turn. Therefore, upon studying the material in this section, students are strongly encouraged to "try out" and practice these essential leadership skills with a variety of groups.

Leadership is about relationships, and relationships are commonly formed in groups; thus, an examination of group dynamics, communication, managing difficulties, and managing and motivating participant behaviors is necessary. These are the issues presented in this section. To build on the material in the first section of this text, for each of these topics basic definitional information as well as guiding principles and specific techniques for working with a diversity of people is presented.

Throughout each chapter an attempt has been made to discuss the influences of demographics—such as sex, age, and ethnicity—on the various interpersonal skills and in the use of specific techniques. In this way, leaders are reminded that to work with people effectively requires an understanding of all people, especially those unique from themselves. In addition, a more thorough treatment of these issues is presented in Section III.

Research has shown that individuals who are perceived as effective in human relations skills are often also perceived as effective leaders. Therefore, an individual committed to learning and improving personal leadership skills will wish to focus in on these areas. This section of the text provides a starting point for learning these types of skills. By combining this knowledge with observations and personal experience, effective leadership is enhanced.

Chapter Four
Learning Opportunities

Through studying this chapter students will have the opportunity to:

- define group dynamics;
- understand the components that comprise groups;
- explore group development across and within stages;
- evaluate effective and ineffective groups; and
- understand how power and team building are integral to group dynamics.

Photo courtesy of the University of Northern Iowa Public Relations Department

CHAPTER

4

Group Dynamics:
The Essence of Leadership

Leaders are not leaders in a vacuum—they lead people, who are usually in a group. Therefore, group dynamics is the essence of leadership because without a group of followers, there would be no leader. As noted in earlier chapters leadership entails interpersonal influence in relation to group tasks and socioemotional concerns (Schmuck & Schmuck, 1992). These, plus the social, intellectual, and moral forces that produce activity and change in a group constitute group dynamics. Having a clear understanding of how groups work—group dynamics—will greatly enhance a leader's ability to be effective.

People within functional groups are interdependent with one another; that is, each group member is linked to all other group members. What one does impacts the others. For example, if one person does not do her or his part of a common project, the project will not be completed and all group members will be negatively affected. This interdependence among group members is viewed as having five primary ingredients:

- an affective or emotional component where group members experience feelings of disappointment, excitement, frustration, or contentment;

- personal and group motives—individual people have distinct reasons or motives for joining a group; likewise, a group has its own set of motives or reasons for being;

- individual roles—each member of a group fills a role, yet those roles can change within the group as needs, tasks, and people change;

- status which is gained through task performance (based on performance, individuals are perceived as having different status levels than others in the group and people outside the group); and

- specificity of group focus; in other words, the clarity of group goals and attention to those goals (Schmuck & Schmuck, 1992).

These five elements are necessary components of an effective group. If one element is weak or nonexistent, group effectiveness will be negatively affected. Recognizing and remembering that all groups have these elements will help a leader to more effectively meet group and individual needs.

Another group phenomenon to bear in mind is that social identity is bound up in group memberships; people are defined by groups to which they belong and take on certain roles such as sibling, scout, teacher, church member, or parent. Therefore the skills needed to work with groups vary; however, certain group skills are fundamental—decision making, trust building, communication, and conflict management—no matter the type of group with which one works.

Most scholars view a group as a system which is organized as a set of interrelated and interacting parts that attempt to maintain a balance

Figure 4.1   *Five elements found within a group.*

(Cathcart & Samovar, 1992; Schmuck & Schmuck, 1992). In other words, groups do not operate in isolation—external and internal forces act on groups continually. *Internal forces* include such things as individual group members and all their baggage (e.g., personalities, motives, emotions, self-esteem), levels and types of participation, overt and covert agendas, group norms, and perceived group status. *External forces* include time, spatial arrangements, lighting, acoustics, external stimuli and the physical environment (Johnson & Johnson, 1991; Schmuck & Schmuck, 1992). As each of these forces change, so too, do the dynamics within a group.

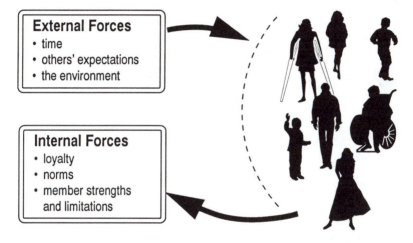

Figure 4.2 *Both forces from within and outside of a group impact on group dynamics.*

The nature of a group dictates much of the internal and external structures—underlying assumptions about how it operates. Within all groups expectations of individuals are developed and expressed; in turn, group members respond to these expectations. This was presented in the C-I-E model of leadership. There are two general group structures—collectivist and individualist. *Collectivist* cultures (and groups) work toward total sharing of in-group norms and goals while *individualistic* cultures (and groups) have as a primary focus the goals of individuals. No group exudes pure collectivism or individualism (Hinde & Groebel, 1991), yet groups do seem to be predominantly one or the other.

In collectivist groups the views, needs, and goals of the in-group are much more important than personal or individual needs, views or goals. Behavior is responsive to group needs and things such as loyalty, trust, and cooperation with in-group members is considered paramount. Achievement is perceived as group rather than individual accomplishment. This may be characterized by the statement, "It's amazing how much gets done when no one cares about who gets the credit." In-group members are perceived as homogenous and the underlying assumption is that in-group members have similar needs. Examples of cultures with this underlying framework include Native-American, Asian, and African cultures. In groups that follow this philosophy a leader would be wise to remember to celebrate and salute the group efforts rather than single out individuals for special attention.

Individualistic cultures, on the other hand, emphasize the individual within the group over the group effort. Personal rights, the pursuit of pleasure and achievement are perceived in personal terms—individual achievements are more important than group achievements. Attachment to other group members is minimal because the emphasis is on freedom and equality on an individual-by-individual basis. Examples of cultures with this attitude as an underlying feature are the European and [predominant] American cultures. Leaders who work with this type of group may need to spend a good deal of time helping individuals learn how to work within a group, and may wish to remember what is valued by the participant—individual mastery and achievement.

Collectivist Cultures

- share "in-house" norms and goals
- primary importance is group needs
- achievement is shared by all
- strong attachment to group

Individualist Cultures

- goals of individuals are important
- primary importance is individual needs
- achievement is seen as individual accomplishment
- emphasis on personal freedoms

Figure 4.3   *Many view culture as having two primary contrasting structures—collectivism and individualism.*

Definitions

As with all phenomena one is trying to understand, it is important to have agreement about meanings of terms; thus, in this section a review of definitions is presented. Several types of definitions exist for *group*:

- a number of individuals who interact with one another;
- a social unit consisting of two or more people who see themselves as members of a group;
- a collection of individuals who are interdependent;
- a number of people who are trying to satisfy personal needs through joint association;
- a number of people who are joined together to achieve a common goal;
- a collection of people whose interactions are structured by a set of roles and norms;
- a collection of people who influence one another; and
- a combination of the abovementioned definitions (Johnson & Johnson, 1991).

Most agree that for a group to be so identified, the members must define themselves as such and so too must outsiders (Brown, 1988). A group or team is more than the sum of its parts—it is a social system with its own structure and culture; members may come or go, but the base culture generally remains the same (Dimock, 1987). Groups do evolve and change over time with large changes in membership.

Group dynamics is the scientific study of behaviors in groups to increase understanding of the nature of groups, group development, and interrelationships between groups and others (Johnson & Johnson, 1991). It is the study of human interactions in specific group settings and is used to describe what is happening in groups and explain why (people in) groups behave the way they do. According to Sessoms (1991),

> To recreators group dynamics involves being aware of the many forces that affect the way individuals act in group settings, and, once aware of them, using those dynamics in a manner that enhances the quality of the group experience and moves the group toward achieving its goals. (p. 3)

Leisure services leaders must be well-aware of group dynamics and what it means in terms of their own leadership, and the growth and development of the group within which they work. If a leader does not know why a group is behaving the way it is, she or he may respond inappropriately to that group.

Groups: The Good and the Bad

Research has not been conclusive about whether or not groups are a good thing—some research indicates that groups are extremely beneficial while others report the opposing position. In a summary of research about groups Johnson and Johnson (1991) reported that groups are good because under most conditions, the productivity of groups is higher than the productivity of individuals alone. This phenomenon of the sum being greater than its parts is known as *synergy*. Synergy allows groups to make more effective decisions and solve problems more effectively than individuals acting alone. In addition, research reports that it is through group membership that the values of altruism, kindness, consideration for others, and responsibility are socialized in people. (It would be difficult to argue against these traits!)

Through group membership a person's quality of life is enhanced through the emotional bonds of friendship, camaraderie, love, excitement, and joy. In addition, achievement and task accomplishment are greater for group members than for individuals acting on their own. Furthermore, research has shown that a person's identity, self-esteem, and social competencies are shaped by group members and through group membership. Humans are social by nature and without cooperation, social organization, and groups of all kinds, this would be compromised. Belonging to groups then, is a good thing. Groups benefit both individuals and society as a whole.

On the other hand, there is some research that would indicate that groups are not all good. Again, Johnson and Johnson (1991) summarized the results of this research. They reported that people in groups tend to take greater risks than when alone and groups tend to take more extreme positions than individuals do alone—this can be both positive and negative. Also, in groups there sometimes is diffusion of responsibility so that members take less responsibility for attending to group tasks and group members; the perception exists that "someone else will do it."

Research also shows that when in large groups people have a tendency to feel anonymous; therefore, they may engage in ultra-extreme and socially unacceptable behaviors which they would not do when alone. This acting out within a feeling of anonymity is sometimes known as "mob mentality." Another drawback to groups is that perceiving others as members of a group makes it easier to depersonalize them and treat them poorly (e.g., discrimination and the effects of stereotypes). Furthermore, groups often force conformity and this is not always done in a positive fashion. Examples of this would be hazing and gang initiation.

While there are both positive and negative aspects to groups and their existence, groups nonetheless exist and will continue to do so—as social animals, humans *need* groups. In recreation and leisure services settings, leaders have the opportunity to help form and develop groups that exhibit positive values and are beneficial to both the group and individual group members. To be most effective in these efforts leaders need to understand why people join groups, what elements constitute a group, and what differentiates effective from ineffective groups.

Why Do People Join Groups?

People join groups for all different types of reasons and in order to best understand how groups function and why they act the way they do,

Photo courtesy of the Family YMCA of Black Hawk County

Some people join groups to work on personal fitness in a social environment.

leaders would be wise to find out from group members why they joined. Generally, people join groups in efforts to form relationships and to meet needs of affiliation; it feels good to belong to something identifiable and to be able to say, "I am a XXX member." An affinity for a particular group may be based on an attraction to other members (e.g., young people may join a group because group members are perceived as "cool"; adults may join because members are interesting and stimulating). Other reasons for being attracted to a particular group is due to the nature of the group goals or tasks (e.g., individuals want to help meet the group's goals), perceptions of prestige associated with the group (e.g., members may be perceived as having higher status than nonmembers), and it has also been shown that physical proximity to facilities influences group affiliation (e.g., the closer one lives to a group, the more apt she or he is to join) (Dimock, 1987).

Some of the other reasons people join groups are many. Some of these reasons are:

- social reasons (to meet new people);
- to learn a new skill, or to increase personal knowledge;
- self-enhancement or advancement (e.g., resumé builder);
- to share a common activity with a significant other (e.g., achieve intimacy);
- coercion (e.g., parents "force" children to join after-school groups);
- to make a statement (e.g., rebel against the "establishment"); and
- for self-identity.

Elements of Groups or Group Structure

Groups are such because they have certain characteristics that define the community of people. All groups share basic components although the direction or quality of these components differ across groups. As mentioned earlier, a group is a social system which consists of several elements or components; these components exist to provide structure and form to the group. Group elements typically include agreed upon rules (norms), cohesion, various tasks and functions, differing roles of group members, and common goals, among others.

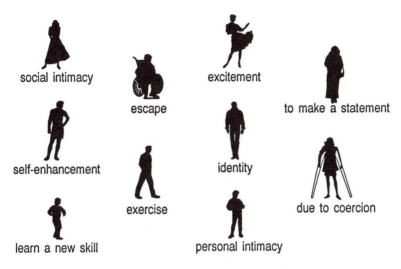

social intimacy

escape

excitement

to make a statement

self-enhancement

identity

exercise

due to coercion

learn a new skill

personal intimacy

Figure 4.4 *There are almost as many reasons for joining groups*
as there are different types of people.

Membership

Individuals who are members of a group define the attributes that make each group unique. As each person is added to a group the nature of the group flexes to accommodate the change. Leaders should remember that while a group has its own personality, each individual within the group remains somewhat individuated. Each member brings to the group her or his own history which includes personal "baggage," expertise, knowledge, biases, attitudes, feelings, and ways of interacting with others.

Cohesion

Cohesion is viewed as the glue that holds a group together. In physics, cohesion is characterized as an intermolecular attraction by which the elements of a body are held together; this is similarly true in group dynamics. Without an attraction of some sort to hold individuals in a group, there is no cohesion. Generally this attraction occurs due to socioemotional aspects (i.e., people in the group like one another), shared interests, common goals, and the meeting of individual needs. The more cohesive a group, the more the group acts with its own distinct identity.

Participation

Observable participation is an indication of involvement in a group—
verbal participation, physical participation, and emotional support.
Every group has differences in levels of participation among members,
and group members influence who participates, how much, and when.
Leaders may wish to monitor levels of participation within a group to
ensure inclusion of all members in activities and tasks of the group.

Influence and Style of Influence

Influence exists and fluctuates within groups. Different people have
differing levels and styles of influence over others in the group. In
addition, the group is influenced by outsiders and at the same time,
influences outsiders. Influence may be positive or negative in approach.
Some people try to influence by bullying others into agreement, others
use subtle manipulation, while others use logical arguments and positive motivation to influence others in pursuit of a goal. Furthermore,
influence has a resulting impact on a group—either enlistment (successful positive influence) or alienation (a result of negative influence).

Norms

Norms are the unwritten rules of a group. They are standards to which
group members tacitly agree to support and adhere, and which guide and
control member behavior. Norms usually express the beliefs and values
of the majority of group members as to what behaviors should and
should not take place (or are acceptable) within the group. Norms may
be made explicit or implicit; some help a group function, others hinder
group functioning. For instance, it may be the norm when one group
member meets another to engage in a physical greeting of some sort
(e.g., some male group members bump chests when greeting one
another; female members of a group may hug).

Atmosphere

Atmosphere is a term used to describe the climate or general impression
of being in a group. All groups have climates which can be described—
some are quite positive while others are negative. For instance, one may
instantly sense a high level of enthusiasm, excitement, and a positive
can-do attitude in one long-term care facility while another has an

atmosphere of despair, sadness, and underlying anger. A leader has a tremendous influence and impact on the climate or atmosphere of a group; her or his values, levels of acceptance and own moods will "rub off" on the group.

Leadership

Styles of leadership and leadership as it emerges from within a group are fundamental elements of a group. Leadership is an integral part of a group and meets one of the role requirements needed to accomplish tasks and meet group and individual needs. As mentioned in previous chapters, leadership styles vary as do the ways individuals within a group become recognized and accepted as leaders.

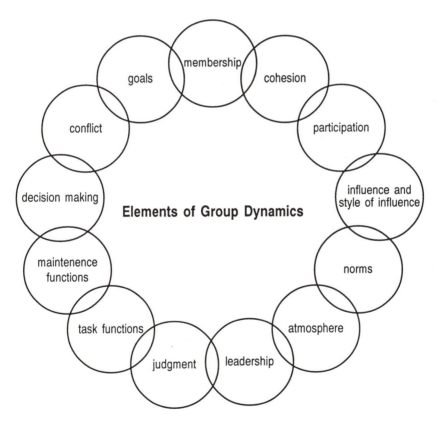

Figure 4.5   *All groups consist of similar elements, and all elements impact on group success.*

Task Functions

Task functions are those functions that directly relate to getting the tasks of the group accomplished, or getting the job done. Task functions tend to be outcome oriented and include such things as taking initiative to stay on task, working with resources, and keeping people focused on the goal at hand. An individual who reminds others to stay on track and follow the agenda (e.g., in a meeting) is engaging in a task function.

Maintenance Functions

In conjunction with task functions, maintenance functions are necessary for effective group functioning. Maintenance functions are those tasks associated with caring for individual group members and being concerned for the morale of the group. These functions help maintain harmonious working relationships with group members and enable group members to contribute maximally to the effective functioning of the group. For instance, the group member who checks in with others when they arrive and asks about their week is engaging in a maintenance function.

Decision Making

All groups are involved in decision making to some degree. How decision making occurs, who facilitates it, and what type of approach is used are critical to group processes. Johnson and Johnson (1991) indicate that an effective decision is one where:

- the resources of the group are fully utilized;
- time is well-used;
- the decision is of high quality;
- the decision is implemented in full by all group members; and
- the problem-solving ability of the group is enhanced.

Group decision making can be enhanced by:

- positive interdependence (where everyone is needed for success);
- individual accountability to other group members;
- members encourage and support each others' efforts;

- socially skilled members;
- debriefing and processing to get at group issues;
- accepting controversy; and
- the motivation to make high-quality decisions is evident.

On the other hand, effective decision making can be hindered by:

- poor group skills;
- a lack of group maturity (e.g., the group is young, or has not been together very long);
- making a quick decision based on the dominant and quickest response of the group;
- social loafing (i.e., slacking off);
- conflicting individual goals;
- a failure to communicate and use information;
- egocentrism of members;
- lack of heterogeneity;
- inappropriate group size;
- power differences and distrust; and
- a lack of time to thoroughly engage in the decision-making process.

There are several methods of decision making which have advantages and disadvantages depending upon the situation. Table 4A (page 126) presents several methods of decision making and the advantages and disadvantages of each.

Judgment

Judgment is essentially "knowing what you know and knowing what you don't know" (Petzoldt, 1984). It is a requisite skill of leadership, and when a group understands and utilizes good judgment, group decisions, actions, norms and general functioning reach a highly effective level. Judgment involves *knowledge* (i.e., of oneself, others, the environment, similar situations from past experiences); *skills and abilities* needed in the particular situation; *self-confidence* (i.e., one believes that whatever decision is made is based on sound reasoning and knowledge); *selflessness* (i.e., the decision made is made with the group

Table 4A Advantages and Disadvantages of Decision-Making Styles

Decision-Making Style	Advantages	Disadvantages
Authority without discussion leader makes decision with no input from the group	• useful for simple, routine decisions • good when short on time, or immature group • good in emergency or short time frame	• may cause resentment among group members • no commitment to implementing decision • group members not used as resources
Expert member group member with expertise makes decision for group	• good if one member is by far an expert • can begin trust building based on experience levels	• may cause resentment among group members • no commitment to implementing decision • group members not used as resources
Average of members' opinions add opinions and divide by group members	• good when time is short, but want some member input • good for simple routine decisions	• not enough sharing among members to get good commitment • conflict and controversy may hinder future decisions
Authority with discussion leader asks for input then makes decision on own	• uses some group resources • group members feel included • uses expertise of leader	• no group commitment to decision • members may feel put aside • does not resolve group conflicts
Majority vote the largest number of group members' opinions counts as the entire group's decision	• good when time is short and need group input • some commitment by the group is evident • quick and straightforward	• usually leaves disgruntled minority which may impact future decisions • full commitment is absent • full participation is absent
Minority control often a subcommittee or small executive group makes the decision	• can be used when everyone is not available • delegates responsibilities to a committee • good when only a few members have knowledge	• does not utilize all group members • no commitment by group • decision may alienate some or hinder future decisions
Consensus entire group talks through the process until a decision is made that all members can accept	• often creative and innovative • elicits commitment from all • uses resources of all members • useful when entire group involvement is desired	• takes a great deal of time and energy • requires skilled leader to facilitate • not good if short on time or in emergency

needs and welfare foremost in one's mind); *commitment* (i.e., one is committed to the role of leader and is willing to face the consequences for one's decisions); *expediency* (i.e., decisions are made quickly, but without waste); and *experience* (e.g., past experiences assist in the use of judgment) (Cockrell, 1991).

Conflict

A fully functioning group must experience conflict. Conflict, when handled appropriately, is a very healthy component of all groups. In fact, a group without conflict is seen as stagnant where few or no new ideas are formed and forward movement is absent. Disagreements and disharmony are important in helping people to think in new directions and consider situations from various viewpoints.

Goals

Groups exist for a reason and that reason is often presented in terms of group goals. Goals serve groups in that they provide a standard of excellence, serve as a source of stimulation for arousing involvement, act as a guide for member actions and integrating the behaviors, serve as criteria for justifying group actions, and are a basis for clarifying relations with outside groups (Zander, 1994). To reach group goals efficiently, all members must be committed to achieving them.

One reason groups form is to help people achieve goals they would otherwise be unable to achieve by themselves. Goals represent an ideal—a state of affairs which people value and wish to achieve. They give a group focus and direction; goals help to shape and motivate member behaviors. Member commitment to group goals is dependent upon several factors:

- how desirable the goals seem;
- how likely it is the group can achieve the goals;
- how challenging the goals are (moderate levels of challenge are desirable);
- expected satisfaction when goals are achieved;
- the extent to which members participated in setting the goals (the higher the member participation, the higher the commitment); and
- the level of group cohesiveness.

It is important to remember that while groups have goals, so too, do individual group members. Shared or common goals are critical to effective and successful groups. Group members should feel comfortable that the group goals are in concert with personal goals and that working toward one goal will support achievement of the other. The fact that group goals and individual goals are related to one another is known as *goal interdependence.* There are three basic goal relationships between member and group goals—cooperative, competitive, and independent (Jordan & Mertesdorf, 1994).

Goals may be *cooperative* in nature and positively aligned where reaching one goal is in support of reaching the other goal. For example, consider an individual who joins a wallyball team to learn to play wallyball to a high-skill level (i.e., personal goal); this goal would be positively related to the wallyball team goal to win games (i.e., group goal). These goals are said to be cooperatively related. This is the ideal goal relationship for effective and well-functioning groups.

The second type of goal relationship is *competitive.* Here inversely related goals exist where achieving one goal is done so at the expense of achieving the other goal. For instance, if an individual joins a group to increase her or his own status in the community yet the goal of the larger group is to share all credit for group tasks, then the actions of the individual will be in conflict with the group (and vice versa). In this case, the individual might act in such a way as to take the spotlight and claim credit for achievements which rightly belonged to the group. This would be in direct contradiction to the group's desires. On the other hand, every time the one individual did achieve something for the group and the group claimed credit, this might irritate the individual. A competitive goal relationship is the most damaging and contributes negatively to group success.

The third possible goal configuration is one of *independence.* This is where the goals of the individual have no relationship to the goals of the group. When one acts to achieve one's own goals, the group is not impacted, and vice versa. As an example of this type of goal relationship one might think of an individual who has joined a walking group for the social interaction, yet the group's primary goal is weight reduction for members. In this case the two differing goals do not interfere with one another, nor do they necessarily support one another. An independent goal relationship then, has little impact on group or individual success.

As can be seen, groups consist of many components that define and determine group success. All of the above elements may be found in

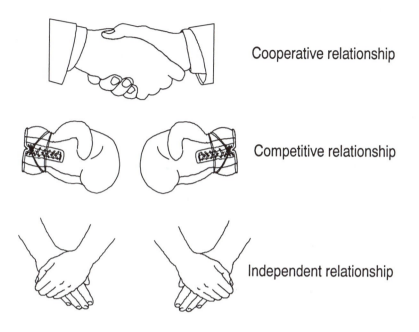

Cooperative relationship

Competitive relationship

Independent relationship

Figure 4.6   *There are three primary goal relationship possibilities between leaders and followers.*

groups; groups find their own identity by emphasizing some aspects and not others, and by uniquely defining each component. Leaders may have a great impact on the effectiveness of groups by being attentive to these components and by helping to define them in a positive fashion. Successful and effective groups are those in which these elements are acknowledged and consciously developed. While it is true that every group has these same elements, another fact of group dynamics is that each group is comprised of individuals. As such, it can be beneficial to understand a bit about individual behavior-style preferences to begin to comprehend why people behave the way they do.

Behavior Styles

Diversity (or heterogeneity) is a necessary element of successful groups. If everyone in a group was similar in style, ideas and energy, accomplishing group tasks would be extremely difficult and accompanied by much conflict. Therefore, leaders should look for diversity in people, in their preferences, ideas, ways of approaching problems, and the like.

Examining personal behavior style preferences is one way to look at group diversity. Everyone has a preference for work and behavior styles; some people are very fast in the way they approach problems and work, while others are more successful with a slower approach. Some individuals prefer to focus on the job at hand, while others are more concerned with the happiness and satisfaction of the people in the group.

There are many models that explain personal behavior style differences by examining four dimensions: fast pace, slow pace, task orientation, and people orientation. Utilizing a model popular in business and educational settings, leaders can see that based on these dimensions people may be characterized by four basic styles: director, socializer, relater, and thinker (Alessandra & O'Connor, 1994). In group dynamics people exhibit their personal styles through interactions with other group members, interactions with group leaders, and in how they approach the group tasks. All four styles need to be represented in groups as their strengths and weaknesses complement one another.

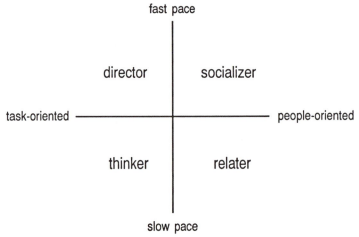

Figure 4.7   *Four primary behavior styles fit within two axes.*

Director

Individuals who favor the director style have a fast-paced approach to life and are task oriented; that is, they prefer to focus on the task to be accomplished rather than people in the group, and they tend to work quickly. People who favor this behavior style:

- think logically;
- want facts and highlights;
- like personal choices;
- enjoy risks;
- accept challenges;
- prefer control and leadership roles;
- enjoy competition;
- enjoy conflict and confrontation;
- are change oriented;
- are results oriented;
- are independent;
- are decisive; and
- prefer to make a bad decision rather than no decision at all (Phillips, 1989).

As a group member, the preferred mode for a director is one that is fast-paced and alone (or in charge). This individual prefers options and alternatives in group activities and the freedom to choose from among them. As members of a group, directors tend to be impatient with groupmates, particularly if they are making mistakes. In group meetings high director individuals tend to be intolerant of wasted time and lack of structure. Due to their need for control and independence, directors might emerge as group leaders or be high participators.

Socializer

Like a director, an individual who favors socializer types of characteristics operates at a fast pace. With an orientation that emphasizes relationships, however, socializers prefer to be with people rather than accomplishing tasks. They enjoy variety and stimulation, tend to think (and react) emotionally, and enjoy having others notice them. In addition, socializers:

- tend to be persuasive with others;
- seek recognition;
- prefer places to express their creativity;
- may not follow through with tasks;

- can be impulsive;
- are inattentive to detail;
- are irritated by routine;
- like innovation and change complexity;
- are enthusiastic; and
- may become irritated by a lot of rules and procedures which can be seen as interfering with creativity and expression (Alessandra & O'Connor, 1994).

Individuals who are primarily socializers like to be in groups; they need people. They enjoy being the center of attention and showing off to others. Because of their fast pace and orientation to others, socializers might need help with getting organized relative to group tasks. People who exhibit socializer traits often enjoy socializing during meetings more than getting a particular task done. Socializers might be late to meetings either because they got caught up with people elsewhere, or so they can make an entrance and be noticed. In groups socializers generally feel comfortable being the spokesperson for groups as they love the spotlight.

Relater

Relater participants prefer a much slower pace to things than people who are directors or socializers. Like socializer types, individuals who may be characterized as relaters are relationship oriented although their goal is group harmony and cohesion, not self-recognition. Relaters tend to think logically in a step-by-step progression, care about stability, and tend to dislike conflict. Relaters also:

- enjoy routines and avoid risks;
- need a lot of rules and procedures;
- prefer the status quo and security;
- need reassurance in facing challenges;
- enjoy being a member of a group;
- want documentation and facts;
- strive to maintain peace in groups;
- seek consensus from others;

- are concerned with inclusion of all; and
- want to be appreciated by others (Alessandra & O'Connor, 1994).

As group members, relaters tend to be easy going, low-key and strive to please everyone. They are very people oriented and friendship oriented, as well as loyal to the group. Relaters often make excellent managers because they focus on group members and morale. During meetings, relaters feel most comfortable when there is routine and structure in how the group functions. If there is going to be a change, relaters need to know why, and how it affects them; they prefer this notification in advance.

Thinker

Individuals who may be characterized as thinkers prefer a slow pace (similar to relaters). In addition, like those who are directors, thinkers prefer tasks over people. They tend to think logically and methodically and seek data to back up group processes and approaches. Because they prefer to have the information at hand before making decisions, thinkers tend to be cautious in their approach to group work. Furthermore, thinkers:

- are low risk takers;
- are perfectionists;
- are cautious;
- are task oriented;
- are detail oriented;
- need order and organization;
- are slow and very deliberate;
- need a lot of rules and procedures;
- avoid conflict;
- need to be right; and
- believe that no decision is better than a wrong decision (Phillips, 1989).

Participants who have the traits of thinkers prefer to have order and organization in group meetings and prefer to work carefully and alone.

As members of a group, thinkers would keep close track of group tasks such as minutes, following an agenda, and obeying the meeting rules. Quality of group work is a prominent concern of people who are viewed as thinkers.

Labeling Without Labels

The purpose of identifying these four behavioral styles is not so individuals can be labeled and placed into "boxes." Administrators, programmers, and leaders must be careful to avoid "writing off" individuals by thinking or saying, "He's always late; what else would you expect from a socializer?" "Don't make her the group leader, she's a thinker and will never make up her mind about a strategy;" "Give him that job, he's a relater and won't make a fuss about it;" or "She's so pushy, she must be a director." Use and abuse of labels may influence leader and group member expectations of individuals which can constrain individual potential as members of a group (York & Jordan, 1993).

Identifying the four predominant behavioral styles helps leaders to better understand the observable differences in people's behavior so that leaders and group members can be more tolerant and effective in dealing with others. By understanding the action choices of others and self, leaders can avoid making hasty judgments about behaviors, and control their own responses to participants based on observable behaviors.

Understanding people is the heart of recreation and leisure services. With increased knowledge of human behavior, recreation and leisure services professionals can provide guidance and leadership

Figure 4.8   Improving our understanding of others should help to avoid labeling people and casting them aside.

direction which meets the needs of a variety of people. Gaining insight into participant needs, desires, and style preferences provides leisure services leaders with information to mold programs and leadership techniques to meet the diverse needs of program constituents. Through sharing information about the dimensions of behavior with participants and recognizing those differences, leisure service professionals can enhance between-participant interactions of group members as well as leader-participant relations.

Group Development

Groups form and develop as does a living being. They go through life stages, mature, make mistakes, and learn continuously. Groups continually fluctuate, gaining and losing ground on various occasions. A group is more than a number of people simply sharing time and space; members interact and move through several stages together as they grow and mature into a distinct entity.

Leaders need to go beyond knowing about group development to *understanding* it. Without truly understanding how groups develop and function a leader is unable to act in the most effective fashion possible. Deciding on the level of leader involvement, the amount of structure to provide, and appropriate leadership styles all depend upon where a group is in its development.

Group development has commonly been viewed as a linear and sequential process. Researchers are now, however, beginning to view group development as nonlinear and cyclical. Experience indicates that while groups might move through several stages on their way to high performance, there is much cycling through several steps along the way. It certainly is not a neat, easily identifiable process. During each phase or stage of development group members are impacted by internal and external forces (mentioned earlier) which impact progress. A group may move "forward" in its development to the next stage and while in that stage group members may experience growing pains similar to earlier stages. As groups develop the movement appears to be directional (in an effective group), but the process is convoluted and intertwined with many subprocesses occurring at each stage.

Within the linear processes, group development has been presented in two different perspectives. First, as they form a group individuals express needs of inclusion. Once they feel a sense of

Photo courtesy of the Western Home

All groups work through similar phases as they develop into an effectively working group.

belonging and acceptance, the group moves into a control stage. During this phase of development group members struggle with the leader for control of the group. Finally, after resolving control issues, the group moves into an affection stage where they grow to truly like one another and become tied affectively (emotionally) as well as in task. According to this perspective, as groups break up individuals experience the same stages in reverse order: affection, control and inclusion.

The second common way of examining group development is through an approach that delineates what occurs as groups move through several stages. It examines group affect as well as leader roles. Leaders should remember that groups cycle back and forth through the stages as various situations arise. The acronym *GROUPD* is a mnemonic which explains the various stages through which a group moves: getting to know one another; relationship building; opposition and conflict; unity; productivity; and dissolution.

Getting to Know One Another

During this orientation phase of group development members seek clarification and direction from the leader(s). Individual roles within the group and member status are typically assigned based on the roles one fulfills outside of this group. Issues within the group tend to be discussed on a surface level and are often quite ambiguous. Mutual respect (on a surface level) is typically evident. This is a time of identity formation—determining who members are, and what is unique about this group.

As they feel their way into a new group, members may experience feelings of concern over their acceptance and sense of belonging in the group. There is both dependency on the leader and the established structure as well as anxiety about both of those things. Group members are often concerned about the leader's competence as well as their own relationship to the leader; at the same time, members are dependent upon the leader(s) for guidance and direction.

Leaders also experience identifiable feelings and situations. Often, at this stage of group development a leader is focused on providing structure and task clarification to members. In an effort to aid in the transition for each individual group member, leaders may wish to focus on involvement and participation levels of all. This is a time of information sharing to be sure that group members feel comfortable with the direction and goals of the group. At this stage, many leaders serve as facilitators to ensure that the group gets off to a successful start. Establishing the tone—acceptance, tolerance, safety—are primary considerations of a leader in this stage.

Relationship Building

Moving out of the orientation stage group members begin to form relationships *with* one another as well as *in relation to* one another (i.e., perceived status and within-group rankings). During this phase there is early agreement on the group norms and atmosphere or climate of the group. People are searching for an understanding of how they fit into the group, which niches they fill. Some give-and-take is evident among group members as the niche-finding occurs. Individual members make judgments of others relative to personalities, behavior styles, work ethics, and other group concerns.

Group members and leaders are building and defining relationships, as well. At this stage leaders and participants have defined their relationships with one another. Some leaders have very close relationships with individual participants and the group, while other leaders feel more comfortable with a sense of formal distance between themselves and the group members. Leader respect and credibility are usually fairly well-established at this stage, although leaders are continually tested.

Opposition and Conflict

Every group (if it is together long enough) goes through an opposition and conflict stage. It is a normal stage of group development and may be likened to a teenager breaking away from parents. Individuals within the group attempt to gain control of the group (take control away from the leader) and assert themselves as independent and viable in their own right. This is a time when leaders are tested and challenged either overtly or covertly. For example, a group in this stage might have strong disagreements and experience anger, frustration, and irritation with other group members or the leader. These feelings should be addressed with the entire group at this point with an aim toward working through the issues. If a leader realizes that this is a normal phase of group development, she or he is much more likely to accept the situation as growing pains rather than as a personal affront.

Because various intergroup power issues are the primary focus during this state, task avoidance is often the result. Members are determining the amount of autonomy they will have and the level of influence over themselves and others in the group. Individuals are trying to ascertain who is where in the "pecking order" of the group, and as a result, not much work toward goal achievement or task accomplishment is undertaken.

For leaders, particularly those who are caught unaware, this stage of group development can be one of the most difficult. Establishing a tone accepting of divergent viewpoints is important to ensure that all group members feel equally a part of the group activities. Due to the struggles experienced during this phase it is also important for the leader to encourage members to state their feelings; this assumes of course, that the leader has already established the group as a safe place to express and accept feelings as valid.

Unity and Oneness

This is a period of reconciliation, integration and cohesion. Group members have experienced and survived feelings of discord, and are now more clear and focused on the tasks at hand; goals have recently been restated and clarified. Often, leaders reemerge, more widely accepted than in earlier stages. Having been through difficult times, this stage is one where intimate discussions are likely to occur and the cohesion process begins. Risk taking and trust building are found within the group.

Figure 4.9   *Group development may be viewed as a stretched out Slinky. It is directional, but may double back on itself as various forces act upon the group.*

In this stage of development, the desire to be a group member is noticeable; if things are going well people are proud of their group affiliation. Members are learning to disagree without being disagreeable and group members are free to laugh and enjoy one another's company in the process of working toward group tasks. Group loyalty and an implicit agreement to abide by group norms is evident; there is a real sense of "we-ness." Norms are solidified, roles are accepted, and a unique group culture is recognizable to outsiders.

At this stage leaders might wish to disengage themselves from the internal workings of the group and allow the group to achieve its potential. Positive and negative feedback are often solicited from group members and the leader responds in kind. Group members are ready to take on additional tasks and delegation becomes an important leader skill at this time.

Productivity

In the productivity stage, the group works toward shared goals with enthusiasm and a solid understanding of one another's strengths and limitations. The group is an effectively functioning group, and is able to accept and use differences among members. Members take initiative and those initiatives are accepted by other group members.

Similar to the opposition and conflict stages, member challenges recur during this phase of group development. Unlike during the earlier stage, however, at this stage of development groups use the challenges to increase creativity and effective problem solving. Functional and personal relationships are strong, and the group is able to do what needs to be done. As they seek feedback from the leader and other members, the group becomes self-regulating and self-determining.

The leader may wish to assist (as needed) to restate or restructure goals to aid the group in meeting its needs. With a fully functioning group, the leader may play the role of the devil's advocate and question traditional or habitual ways of doing things. Facilitating the development of ongoing assessment methods for the group is also a task of the leader in this stage of group development. The leader's role has evolved from one of setting the tone and providing direction to helping to develop members to their fullest potential through evaluation of task and maintenance functions.

Dissolving or Disbanding

All groups cease to exist at some time. Some groups reframe and reinvent themselves, while others simply dissolve or disband as members' needs are met. This may occur gradually or abruptly. In this stage some groups experience an overoptimism about the power of the group (we can do *any*thing!!) followed by a denial of the impending dissolution.

Group leaders need to understand what occurs at this stage because it is not uncommon for a well-functioning group to seem to fall apart—members fight, withdraw, or appear to self-destruct. These behaviors are normal and not necessarily the fault of poor leadership or selfish group members. The pull of emotions is often difficult for members to address and they may react by withdrawing or striking out.

All groups grow, develop, and mature through several phases and, as mentioned earlier, these phases are intertwined and impacted by forces acting on the group. The intensity and impact of the growth process experienced by group members is influenced by leader preparation, group tasks, group skills, and the effect of internal and external forces. A basic knowledge and understanding of groups and how they develop can be beneficial to leaders as they attempt to positively influence the growth of groups. Solid leadership skills and a willingness to help groups work through the various stages can increase the effectiveness of groups in both task and maintenance functions.

Strong and Effective Groups

Leaders desire strong and effective groups. Strong groups are more stable, have greater control over member behaviors, do a better job of servicing member needs, and generate high levels of participation and loyalty than do weak groups (Foschi & Lawler, 1994). In strong groups, members are cognizant of various interrelationships which impact group effectiveness. Petzoldt (1984) first identified these relationships as they relate to behaviors on extended outdoor expeditions. The relationships are a consideration of all groups—the various configurations include the following.

Individual to Individual

Individuals are asked to be aware of personal habits and idiosyncrasies which might negatively impact other group members. For example, if one person has a habit of talking to a neighbor while others are talking (resulting in disruptive behaviors) she or he should become aware of this and try to stop. In this instance, the message is, "Each person has a responsibility to monitor her or his own behaviors and how those behaviors impact other individuals."

Individual to Group

In this relationship format, individuals are asked to acknowledge that while they are each an individual (and as such have rights), they also have a responsibility to the larger group. Individual behaviors should be examined relative to group needs. For instance, if a group member was late to meetings this would have an adverse affect on the larger group and such behavior should be stopped out of consideration for the group. The message is, "The group is important; helping the group to achieve group goals is the focus of my membership."

Group to Individual

Individuals need to be aware of how they impact the group; likewise, group members must also be aware of how they interact with individuals and be considerate of individual needs. Every person in the group should "count" and her or his ideas solicited and taken into consideration. In this relationship orientation the message is, "The group is made up of individuals who have varying abilities and limitations which must be valued and respected."

Group to Group

Each group has its own personality and way of looking at the world which may impact other existing groups. For smooth relationships and to be sure that all groups achieve their stated goals, groups are asked to examine their group behaviors and how that impacts other groups. An example of this would be groups who take large and noisy boom boxes into natural settings; the music may be exciting and stimulating to the one group, but obnoxious and ruinous of another group's outdoor experience. The message of this element is, "Groups have a responsibility to monitor their behaviors to avoid infringing on the rights of other groups."

Group to Administration

Groups work within organizational structures—both societal and agency related. As such, groups must respect and adhere to the values, mission, and focus of the agency (and society) to which they belong. Respecting and following a dress code and other agency and societal norms are examples of group to administration consideration. The message is, "A group is a reflection of the agency it represents."

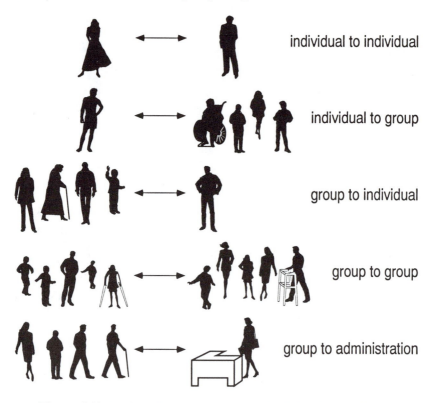

Figure 4.10 Within all groups a variety of relationship combinations are possible.

In addition to understanding and being cognizant of these relationships in effective groups, members interact freely, depend upon one another, want to remain as members, and as a group have social power (Zander, 1994). The strength and solidarity of a group is determined by personal need satisfaction of members. If a group meets the personal needs of its members, satisfaction is high and the group is strong. It has been found that the size of group impacts strength and effectiveness; five to 13 people are considered to be more cohesive and effective than larger (or smaller) groups. A participative leadership style increases satisfaction as do common goals, and things that make people feel special for belonging (Dimock, 1987). Other characteristics of effective and ineffective groups are found in Table 4B (page 144).

Effective group efforts require work; groups do not occur without some struggle with tasks and the socioemotional aspects of group members. The group skills and characteristics listed in Table 4B do not necessarily come naturally to people. Group members must learn the necessary skills, attitudes, and belief structures to work through the rough spots and persevere. Individual group members must be convinced that this group is for them, will meet their needs, and that cohesion will occur with the efforts of all. Effective groups are those in which members have a commitment to experiencing and utilizing the effects of synergy.

Barriers to Effective Groups

As mentioned above, effective groups do not just happen, the group leader and group members must have some level of commitment to making things work to reach their potential. As one might imagine, barriers to developing effective groups are many. Some of these barriers exist without conscious effort on the part of the individuals engaging in the behaviors. Nonetheless, the barriers affect not only individuals, but the functioning of the group, as well.

Petzoldt (1984) has indicated that an ineffective group is due to a breakdown in human relations caused by selfishness (in outdoor leadership, this is known as poor expedition behavior). In this sense, selfishness is characterized as being overly focused on one's self so that what is best for the group is set aside in efforts to do what is best for the self. Certainly, good leadership requires a letting go of this type of self-absorption; a leader who is not involved with and cognizant of the group will not be effective in helping group members achieve their goals. As can be seen in Table 4B, other reasons for group ineffectiveness exist. Poor group skills, a lack of commitment to group efforts and a lack of a common goal all can negatively impact group functioning.

Table 4B *Characteristics of Effective and Ineffective Groups*

Effective Groups	Ineffective Groups
• Are between five and 13 people in size	• Form cliques (subgroups)
• Share common goals which are clarified and changed as the need arises	• Have no focus or goals; goals may be imposed upon group members
• Meet the needs of group members (e.g., inclusion, control, affection)	• Ignore the contributions of select individuals
• Communicate openly and in all directions	• Communication is one way; if at all.
• Feelings and affect are accepted and addressed as needed.	• The affective component is downplayed, suppressed, or ignored.
• Decision making is mutual, group members are involved as much as the situation will allow.	• Decision making is by authority with little or no discussion.
• Controversy and conflict are viewed as signs of a healthy group and are dealt with from a positive learning approach.	• Controversy and conflict are viewed as negative and are ignored, suppressed, or denied.
• Cohesion is a primary focus and a real "we" approach to group tasks is taken.	• Cohesion is ignored, group members are controlled by authority; a "me" stance is adopted.
• Feedback and evaluation are ongoing and viewed as exciting learning opportunities.	• Feedback and evaluation are done sporadically, if at all; group members fear evaluation and feedback.
• Alternative ways of looking at things are encouraged and nurtured.	• Creative thoughts and approaches are squelched; the leader has rigid control.
• Leadership rotates based on the situation and group need.	• Leadership is hoarded and used as power and self-enhancement/aggrandizement.
• Participation is shared across all members of the group; involvement is high.	• Participation is by a select few; some monopolize, others withdraw.

One of the strong points of group dynamics, which when overused becomes a weakness, is peer (or group) pressure and the influence to conform. Used in a positive sense, group pressure assures that group members adhere to norms, agree to the group goals, and have a level of commitment to the group. When overused or overemphasized, however, group pressure can squelch individual ideas and creativity, force individuals to comply with situations with which they do not agree, and subsume individual identity within the group.

Groups that have large and obvious status differences between group members may experience difficulties in becoming fully functioning. A problem of having too much homogeneity (sameness) within the group can be detrimental, as well. Furthermore, an unacceptable physical environment (e.g., too hot, too cold, dilapidated, too stark) will likely have a negative effect on group functioning. If people are uncomfortable they are unlikely to be concentrating on the task or people at hand.

As one might imagine, poor leadership also presents problems for effective group functioning. Being overly dictatorial with a mature, highly experienced group may result in a stifling of group abilities, boredom, or irritation. On the other hand, being too removed from the group when it is in need of guidance can also result in a group not working up to its potential.

Group Roles

Yet another element of group dynamics that may serve as a barrier to a group is that of group roles. Group roles are fluid; that is, people change the role they fulfill from time-to-time (one day someone may be clowning around and entertaining the group when on another day that same individual is seeking information and opinions from group members). While it might be true that one group member might be more apt to fill a certain role, on any given day each group member has the capability of falling into one or more of either positive or negative roles. The behaviors, attitudes, thoughts, and moods of each group member constitute the characteristics or position one will play within the group at a given time. If negative group roles are allowed to dominate the group process, the group will be ineffective in its efforts.

Positive Group Roles

Positive roles are parts people play which help a group achieve its goals while, at the same time, maintain high group morale. By fulfilling these roles individuals contribute to the effective functioning of the group. Some of these positive group roles are:

> **Clarifier:** An individual who seeks clarification and assists others in seeing things more clearly.

> **Compromiser:** Seeking the middle road, a compromiser helps members see ways of agreeing through disagreements.

> **Consensus Seeker:** The person who is concerned that all members are equally involved in the group and decision-making processes.

> **Encourager:** Often viewed as the cheerleader, the encourager supports and encourages group members to do their best.

> **Gatekeeper:** A gatekeeper is an individual who checks in with group members as tasks move ahead to be sure that tasks are being completed and that everyone is being included.

> **Harmonizer:** Concerned for the welfare and morale of group members, the harmonizer tends to help people smooth over conflicts and see what similarities are shared.

> **Initiator:** One who initiates or serves to get things started—both in task and people functions.

> **Opinion/Information Giver:** This person shares her or his own opinions and knowledge in group sessions when appropriate.

Opinion/Information Seeker: A balance to the opinion/information giver, the seeker strives to include group members through asking them to express their thoughts and opinions. Facts and knowledge associated with the group tasks are solicited from group members.

Problem Solver: This individual names and addresses problems and issues as they arise, and helps group members to solve problems.

Summarizer: A person who provides a summary of what has occurred helps to keep things in perspective.

Timekeeper: Needed by all groups, a person who fulfills the timekeeper role keeps tasks on time and the group moving toward group goals in a timely fashion.

Negative Group Roles

Because groups consist of many members all of whom are unique and experience a variety of influences, some members fulfill negative roles. Negative roles are those that impede or hinder group functioning; these roles may interfere with group tasks and/or group morale. Any positive role taken to the extreme could have a negative impact on the effectiveness of a group. In addition, other negative roles include those listed below:

Blocker: An individual who stops forward movement with a "yeah, but" or "we've always done it this way." Arguing, resisting, and disagreeing beyond reason are other behaviors of a person in this role.

Clown/Entertainer: This person feels compelled to interrupt group functioning with inappropriately placed humor and antics. This serves as a disruption and moves the group off task; ineffective functioning results.

Digressor: Similar to the entertainer, a digressor takes group members off task and into unrelated tangents. The behaviors may be friendly and open, but disturb group goal achievement.

Disassociator: One who fulfills this negative group role disengages from working toward group goals. She or he tends to daydream, talk to others, or leave the room for no apparent reason.

Instigator: An individual who initiates irritations in others and gets them excited or upset about topics irrelevant to the tasks at hand is known as an instigator.

Scapegoat: Scapegoat is another negative group role whereby an individual gets blamed for everything that does not go well within the group.

Leaders who understand what and who constitutes an effective group will likely be successful in their leadership efforts. In addition to understanding group development and the components of a group, it is helpful to understand the phenomenon of power and how it is used by and affects individuals and groups.

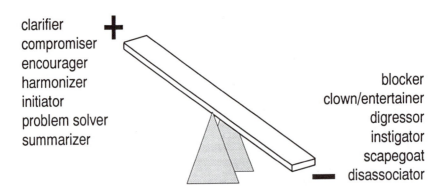

clarifier
compromiser
encourager
harmonizer
initiator
problem solver
summarizer

blocker
clown/entertainer
digressor
instigator
scapegoat
disassociator

Figure 4.11 People fill both positive and negative roles within groups.

Power

Power is a phenomenon related to leadership and group dynamics. It is generally perceived as the influence an individual (or group) wields over another. In addition, power generally has been viewed as a finite construct where in order for one person to have power, another has less or none. In other situations power is viewed as infinite where the more one gives away the more one has. In either case, there are ten types of power. Individuals, groups and leaders all use one or more of these types of power in different situations.

Coercive

In a vein similar to Reward (page 150), followers believe this individual has the capability of punishing them; the powerful person has the ability to withhold resources. In this case a leader who has the ability to suspend participants from a sports league would be viewed as having coercive power.

Connections/Networking

In this day and age when networking is considered vital to one's professional development, an individual who has varied and strong connections with others in the field is often perceived as having this type of power. Networking is characterized by the adage, "It's not what you know, but who you know."

Empowerment

Empowerment is *power to do*; power which is shared with others. In this view power is not viewed as finite, but rather as expansive. Giving power to others enables them (and you) to accomplish more and experience a sense of self-esteem. People are empowered when they are taught the skills and given the resources to meet group goals.

Expert Power

Others accord a person with power because they believe this individual has special knowledge or expertise about the best way to do something. This type of power is usually attributed to an individual in a specific task situation. For example, an individual who has the knowledge to understand the meaning of gang symbols will likely be given power when in gang-tagged (with graffiti and symbols) territory.

Helplessness

Helplessness power is used by all people at one time or another. People claim to be infirm or helpless and in that way induce others to do something for them. Examples of this include seeking help with a crafts project claiming a lack of skill to complete it, and requesting help with heavy equipment by acting helpless when trying to move it.

Informational

This person has access to information which can impact another. A good example of this type of power is a secretary—she or he takes phone messages (and can "lose" them), files paperwork (which can be "misplaced"), and knows when meetings are being held (but can "forget" to tell you).

Legitimate

In this situation the one with legitimate power is seen as having the right to do something (usually by way of position) and others have the obligation to follow. For instance, students generally allow teachers legitimate power and participants generally attribute this type of power to leisure services leaders.

Referent (Charisma)

The person with referent power is admired and looked up to; she or he may have personal charisma and charm which draws others to her or him. Examples of this type of power have been attributed to people such as John F. Kennedy, Mahatma Gandhi, and Eleanor Roosevelt.

Reward

Followers believe this individual has the capability of rewarding them; the powerful person has control of resources which are perceived as rewards. For instance, if a recreation leader has the ability to give free pool passes to well-behaved participants, she or he would be perceived as having reward power.

Social Status

Often, those with higher levels of social status as indicated by their position in the community, occupation, and/or history of altruism are perceived to have more power than those with little social status. Social status may also be attributed to team captains, gang leaders, and the president of an organization (e.g., class president, president of the state recreation association).

As one might suspect, power can be used in both positive and negative ways. Power often implies an imbalance in perceptions of capabilities and as such can leave those who are perceived to lack power feeling less than adequate. Leaders, however, can use power positively to enable others and help them reach their full potential. Wisely used, power is a valid aspect of leadership and group dynamics—an effective leader will consistently consider the impacts of various types of power on group members.

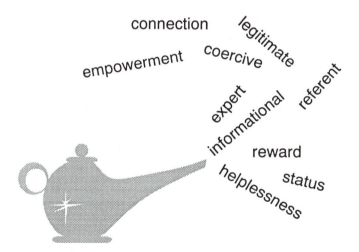

Figure 4.12 Researchers have identified ten possible types of power relationships between group members.

Team Building

In conjunction with knowledge of groups, power, and leadership, comes the concept of team building. People often use the word *team* when describing a group; yet, there are differences in what constitutes a group and a team. The word *team* often brings to mind athletic teams where a strong climate of mutual trust, cohesion, and purpose exist. The inference is that the group

> has a particular process of working together, one in which members identify and fully use one another's resources and facilitate their mutual interdependence toward more effective problem solving and task accomplishment. (Reddy & Jamison, 1988, p. 77)

In addition, teams are collaborative, have a strong discernible identity, a sense of solidarity, and an attitude of interdependence. Teams are often viewed as groups which exude a sense of family.

To develop an effectively functioning team, group leaders and group members must be committed to the process and willing to accept responsibility to make things happen. It must be understood that team building is a process, not a one-shot approach to group development. In developing a team group members should strive to meet the following team essentials.

Take Care of Yourself

For example, flight attendants on airplanes direct capable individuals (in the event of an emergency) to put on their own oxygen masks before attempting to assist others so that the helpers do not lose consciousness before helping either the individual needing assistance or themselves. This is true in groups, as well. If individual group members do not first take care of themselves, they will be unable to adequately tend to group mates.

Take Care of Each Other

If everyone takes care of everyone else, each person will receive the benefit of the others' concern. This is the positive aspect of "what goes around comes around," and tends to enhance and encourage cohesion and team building.

Take Care of Facilities, Equipment, and Supplies

A group without the tools and resources necessary to accomplish its tasks will be ineffective. Teams maintain resources knowing that those tools are important for long-term success.

Have Balance in Your Life

Another component of taking care of oneself is balance; it enhances individual well-being. Healthy people tend to be happy, physically well, and capable of taking on a variety of tasks.

Give the Other Person the Benefit of the Doubt

Avoid harsh or quick judgments of others and situations. Being too quick to judge is one of the most insidious barriers to effective teams. Remember to allow people to be human—including yourself—everyone makes mistakes.

Photo courtesy of the Conestoga Council of Girl Scouts

Team building requires trust and a group effort working toward a common goal.

Bring Your Best to Each Situation

If each person consistently presents herself or himself to do the best possible in every situation, the synergy and energy will expand and great things will happen. This also involves using all of one's talents and energies.

Put the Other Person First

By putting the other person first, no one will be left out and everyone will be treated on equal footing. This "other-esteem" will enhance self-esteem for all. It might be wise to follow the Platinum Rule: "Do unto others as they would want to be done unto." (Note how this differs from the Golden Rule: "Do unto others as you would have them do unto you.")

Think "We" and Support Other Group Members

If people are supportive (even in their disagreements), trust will build and people will be willing to take risks. Trust and risk taking behaviors are two components necessary for team building. These both take time to develop, yet are easily destroyed. Being alert to this will aid positive group growth.

Meld Your Goals with the Group Goals

With shared goals, each group member has a better opportunity of knowing why she or he is doing what she or he does, and will better understand the consequences of their actions. If your (individual) goals are distinctly incompatible with group goals, perhaps it is time to find another group.

Appreciate the Strengths, Diversity, and Limitations Each Person Brings to the Team

Without the ability to use and work with the differences, limitations and strengths brought by others, a number of conflicts would be likely. Groups and teams are enriched by diversity. Leaders who are skilled and knowledgeable about issues of diversity are likely to be highly successful.

Effective teams do not simply "happen." They take attention, nurturing, and ongoing evaluation throughout the life of the team. Team building is a continuous process—it takes time and commitment by all those involved. Basics for developing and maintaining a strong team include mutual understanding; goal agreement; trust; risk-taking behaviors; physical, emotional, and psychological safety within the group; an understanding of and willingness to embrace diversity; and effective decision-making processes. By taking care of self, others, and equipment and by addressing all team essentials, exciting and effective teams can be developed.

Summary

Leisure services leaders work with groups in a variety of settings and in a variety of situations. Therefore, understanding groups and group dynamics becomes a critical skill for leisure services leaders. Groups are complex structures that consist of many elements and have internal and external forces acting on them. Affect, group focus, status, personal and group motives, and individual roles all contribute to make a group what it is. Some groups are collectivist in nature; that is, the primary focus of the group is on its collective self; while other groups have an individualist perspective whereby individual freedoms are perceived as more important than the collective group.

People join groups for a variety of reasons. By understanding the reasons people have for joining, leisure services leaders can be well-prepared for group and individual behaviors. People join others to engage in social behaviors, learn new skills, for self-enhancement, to achieve intimacy, because they were coerced into doing so, for self-identity, and to make a statement. Leaders can utilize the above knowledge in increasing comprehension about group structure. Group structure consists of membership, cohesion, participation, influence and style of influence, norms, atmosphere, leadership, task and maintenance functions, decision making, judgment, conflict, and goals.

Within groups, of course, are individuals, and individuals have preferred behavioral styles. Some tend to be fast paced while others are slow paced; on another dimension some people are task oriented, yet others are more people oriented. As groups of individuals, all groups pass through many stages of development which are intertwined with and loop back on one another throughout the development process. Group members first get to know one another, then build relationships; next opposition and conflict occur, after which unity is restored. Once reformed, group productivity tends to be high. Understanding how groups develop helps a leader to more effectively lead, facilitate, and encourage group growth.

There are identifiable differences in effective and ineffective groups just as there are identifiable group roles members play (which change regularly). These were discussed in terms of better developing teams and understanding power relationships between group members. Power can be utilized to enhance or inhibit group functioning. Learning about the various forms of power allows a leader flexibility in addressing and working with groups of all kinds.

The Front Line

When working with groups leaders will often be in positions to help group members learn about the process of being a group and developing into a team. By asking group members a variety of questions about the dynamics observed within the group, leaders can facilitate learning so that group members experientially discover what is needed for effective functioning. Leaders might consider asking the following types of questions:

Participation: Did all group members participate equally? Who participated the most? the least? How were silent group members treated? How was participation defined? Who contributes the most to the task? to the affect of the group?

Influence: Who were the most influential members of the group? What made them influential? Who was more influential—those most verbal or intermittently verbal? What outsiders influence the group? How can you tell? Does any one group member seem to manipulate others? how?

Norms: What are the group norms? How were norms defined by the group? Who seemed to define the norms? Does everyone adhere to the norms? What happened when individuals did not follow the norms? Which norms are implicit? explicit?

Atmosphere: How would you describe the atmosphere of the group? What makes you define it that way? Who influences the climate of the group? How do they do that?

Leadership: Who is the leader of the group? What makes her or him the leader? What leadership style is primarily used? Does anyone not follow this leader? What impact does that have on the group?

Task Functions: What are the tasks of the group? Who serves to develop group goals and objectives? Who keeps the group on task and on time? Who initiates the group work? How do others react to these individuals?

Maintenance Functions: Who appears to take care of the group members? Is there one person who ensures member involvement? Does the leader exhibit more task or maintenance functions? Who is concerned for the well-being of the group members?

Decision Making: What style of decision making is used most often? Are all group members included in all decisions? Are all ideas heard and acknowledged? How do those who are excluded react? Is the decision-making process effective? How can you tell? What impedes effective decision making?

Communication: Describe the communication process. Was it effective? ineffective? Why? What hindered/ helped effective communication? What would you suggest as guidelines to enhance communication?

References

Alessandra, T. and O'Connor, M. (1994). *People smarts.* San Diego, CA: Pfeiffer & Company.

Brown, R. (1988). *Group processes: Dynamics within and between groups.* Cambridge, MA: Basil Blackwell, Inc.

Cathcart, R. and Samovar, L. (1992). *Small group communication* (6th ed.). Dubuque, IA: Wm. C. Brown Publishing.

Cockrell, D. (Ed.). (1991). *The wilderness educator.* Merrillville, IN: ICS Books.

Dimock, H. (1987). *Groups: Leadership and group development.* San Diego, CA: University Associates, Inc.

Foschi, M. and Lawler, E. (Eds.). (1994). *Group processes: Sociological analyses.* Chicago, IL: Nelson-Hall Publishers.

Hinde, R. and Groebel, J. (Eds.). (1991). *Cooperation and prosocial behaviour.* New York, NY: Cambridge University Press.

Johnson, D. and Johnson, F. (1991). *Joining together: Group theory and group skills* (4th ed.). Englewood Cliffs, NJ: Prentice Hall.

Jordan, D. and Mertesdorf, J. (1994). The effects of goal interdependence between leisure service supervisors and employees. *Journal of Applied Recreation Research, 19*(2), pp. 101-116.

Miles, J. (1991). In D. Cockrell, *The wilderness educator.* Merrillville, IN: ICS Books.

Petzoldt, P. (1984). *The new wilderness handbook.* New York, NY: W. W. Norton & Co., Inc.

Phillips, B. (1989). *Dancing with porcupines.* Ventura, CA: Regal Books.

Reddy, W. B. and Jamison, W. K. (Eds.). (1988). *Team building: Blueprints for productivity and satisfaction.* Alexandria, VA: NTL Institute for Applied Behavioral Science and University Associates, Inc.

Schmuck, R. and Schmuck, P. (1992). *Group processes in the classroom* (6th ed.). Dubuque, IA: Wm. C. Brown Publishing.

Sessoms, H. D. (1991). In H. D. Sessoms and J. Stevenson, *Leadership and group dynamics.* Boston, MA: Allyn & Bacon.

Sessoms, H. D. and Stevenson, J. (1981). *Leadership and group dynamics.* Boston, MA: Allyn & Bacon.

York, S. and Jordan, D. (1993, October). Programming with style. *Leisure Today,* 38-40.

Zander, A. (1994). *Making groups effective* (2nd ed.). San Francisco, CA: Jossey-Bass Inc., Publishers.

Chapter Five
Learning Opportunities

Through studying this chapter students will have the opportunity to:

- examine the communication process;
- evaluate effective and ineffective communication;
- identify requisite skills of active listening;
- understand how elements of culture interact with the communication process; and
- delineate how one can improve communication effectiveness.

Photo courtesy of the University of Northern Iowa Public Relations Department

CHAPTER 5

Communication Skills
for Leaders

In anger a small child may stomp her or his foot and exclaim, "I'm not talking to you!" This sends a powerful message. In fact, we send messages—communicate—through everything we do. We can never *not* communicate. We communicate through the way we walk, the clothing we wear, the sound of our voice, the use of silences, and the words we use. People are constantly "reading," deciphering and listening to what we have to say. A leader, then, would be wise to pay attention to what she or he is saying—through words, body movements, silences, and external coding (i.e., the way one dresses).

Leisure services leaders communicate with supervisors, peers, participants and the general public at various times throughout their careers. To maximize communication effectiveness, the communication, while different for each audience, should nonetheless be articulate and accurate. Effective communication consists of much more than simply talking. It also involves listening, speaking, delivering, selling, giving, and receiving information (Genua, 1992). Communication is used to manage conflict, create and maintain relationships, persuade others, understand groups and group dynamics, and transmit cultural norms. It is both an art and a science and is a critical skill for leaders.

Shared meanings are the very crux of effective communication. When I say, "It's raining cats and dogs," we must have a shared agreement that this means it is raining quite heavily or some people will be looking for animals to drop from the sky. Without shared meanings (which are based on shared experiences), communication is full of confusion and misinterpretations. Shared meanings develop over time when people learn to agree on the meaning of certain sounds. By changing one's voice tone, volume, or pitch, these meanings can change. For instance, a change in voice tone can change a simple statement from a request to a command—we key in on power differences and the nuances of verbal language.

Effective leadership requires a knowledge of basic communication skills and practice with communication in a variety of settings. This chapter presents information related to the communication process in general, and verbal communication, in particular. The following chapter addresses nonverbal forms of communication—body language, writing skills, and symbolic language.

Models and Definitions

Communication is a process or system of exchange and interaction which is directed at conveying meaning and achieving understanding (Brody, 1991; Burgoon, Dawson & Hunsaker, 1994; Heath & Bryant, 1992). It occurs within, between, and outside of groups and is a regular component of human relationships. Ideas, opinions, facts, and feelings are shared in this process. Communication may be verbal, nonverbal, written, sensory (e.g., touch, smell), and demonstrative. Because communication is a crucial leadership skill, leisure services leaders are encouraged to develop skills in all of the areas.

Figure 5.1   Communication may occur through several means and mediums.

Models are ways to represent various constructs or ideas. In this instance, a model of the communication process of sending and receiving messages is presented. (See Figure 5.2, page 166.) Most models include similar elements: a sender of the message; a message or intended communication; a channel through which the message is sent; noise which interferes with the process; a receiver of the message; and feedback from the receiver to the sender. Each of these components has a task or function directly related to making the intended message understood as sent. Whether a person is a sender or receiver is primarily a function of time and circumstance rather than any firmly defined role. This means that in the same interaction one person may be both the sender and receiver depending upon the flow of the conversation.

Sender

The *sender* is the one who initiates an interaction and has a message she or he wishes to send to a receiver. Before the message can be sent the sender must first have an intention or desire to communicate. Next, the sender goes through various cognitive processes to encode, or put into words, what it is she or he wants to say. Both the intended message and the motivation for sending the message are important in the encoding process. Sender intentions and motivations can influence the tone and manner in which a message is sent (and subsequently received).

Message

Many feel that the *message* is the most important element of communication; it is after all, the object of the interaction between people engaged in the process. Messages may take many forms—verbal and overt (i.e., person says exactly what is on her or his mind), verbal and hidden (e.g., double entendres), nonverbal (e.g., through body language), written (e.g., memoranda, letters), and symbolic (e.g., hair styles, logos, clothing choices). Problems arise when there is confusion about the message as it gets sent to the receiver. Confusion and misinterpretations are quite common because communication and language are culturally based. This means that words and symbols have different meanings to different people; common meanings are generally a result of shared culture.

Channel

The *channel* is the medium through which a message is sent. The channel might be a paper memorandum, face-to-face communication, a video recording, an audiotape, telephone, or computer system. Each type of channel has advantages and drawbacks to effective communication. Some of the channels are meant to be primarily one-way, while others encourage two-way communication. Some, such as the use of paper memoranda, are two-way channels, but have periods of delay where the receiver must first have the memo in hand before the communication cycle may be completed (i.e., the message interpreted, then a response drafted and sent through similar channels).

Receiver

To continue the process, once a message is crafted and encoded by a sender and a channel for communication is selected, a recipient of the message must exist. This *receiver* perceives the incoming message and then must attend to the message, and decode or interpret what is being communicated. Whether the message is being sent verbally or nonverbally, in order for the interpretation to be similar to what was intended, the sender and receiver must share meanings.

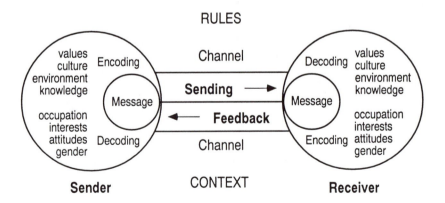

Figure 5.2   *A basic communication model (York, Jordan, & Safford, 1995).*

Feedback

Feedback is an element of communication which rounds out or lends a wholeness to the communication process. Feedback is a reaction given by the receiver (initially) which tells the sender that the message was understood, or was unclear and clarification is needed. As with all methods of communication, feedback may be verbal, nonverbal, or a combination of both. Feedback is very important to the communication process and to be most effective should be given freely, expeditiously, and succinctly.

Feedback is utilized as part of the complete communication cycle and is often given when observing behaviors or actions of another (e.g., behavior management). In any case, to be most effective feedback should be *very specific*. It should be focused on the particular behavior or words in question. For example, consider the following exchange:

Sender: "It's time to go, I'd like everyone to help pick up."
Receiver provides feedback seeking clarification: "What would you like us to pick up, and what should we do with it after picking it up?"

In many ways feedback provides clues about the accuracy of the sent message, motivation of the receiver, clarification of the message, and interest level of the receiver. Nonverbal cues such as a hand to the back of the ear ("I can't hear you") are often effective means of providing feedback to speakers. A communicator constantly scans the audience and looks for cues from listeners. Picking up on and responding to feedback are important skills of communication and help the effectiveness of the communication process.

Noise

Anything that is not directly a part of the communication cycle and interferes with the successful sending and receiving of a message is called *noise*. Noise may be internal to the communicating parties (e.g., personal biases, practicing one's response, thinking about something else), or external to the communicators (e.g., sounds from passing vehicles, music, other people talking). If not addressed, noise can render communication efforts ineffective.

To be complete, communication should cycle through all elements of the process. If any one element is lacking, incomplete or misinterpreted, communication efforts will be negatively impacted. In striving for effective communication, leaders should seek to enhance their skills in all aspects of the communication process. In addition to this, it may be helpful to understand the various functions of or reasons for communication.

Photo courtesy of the Western Home

Effective communication requires both a receiver and a sender who alternate roles.

Functions of Communication

Like group dynamics, communication is a dynamic process—it is always changing, being revised, and involving different people. It consists of both a task (content) and an affective (emotional) component (i.e., job to be accomplished and feelings related to group processes) (Burgoon, Dawson, & Hunsaker, 1994). Within the task and process components, communication has several different functions, and an effective leader understands which function of communication is being addressed when.

While all communication has multiple levels of meanings and serves several purposes simultaneously, function provides some cues as to the intent of the sender and ongoing motivations of those involved in the communication process. It helps focus and clarify the message.

Communication may be used as persuasion, to share information, to express oneself, to command others, and to resolve conflicts.

Persuasion/Influence

Communication may be used to persuade or influence others in their thoughts or actions. For example, a recreation aide might wish to persuade or influence elderly residents in a care facility to participate in recreational activities; a Morale, Welfare and Recreation (MWR) Youth Services Director might wish to persuade parents to enroll their child in upcoming special events; or a park ranger might wish to persuade canoeists to pack out all their trash.

In this function one individual communicates with the intent of convincing or persuading another to take a certain course of action. There are ethical issues involved in persuading others to certain courses of action and leisure services leaders would be well-served to adhere to a strong ethical position when engaging in this type of communication.

Information Sharing

Recreation and leisure services leaders do a lot of sharing information with people—at some time or another we share facts and information with colleagues, supervisors, town council members, participants, and nonparticipating constituents. Oftentimes this communication is one-way whereby a leisure services leader simply informs others about schedules, policies, upcoming events, or how to play a particular game. Other times, information sharing is two-way as in activity instruction or "town hall" meetings.

Social/Expressive

Social/expressive communication is at the heart of interpersonal communication. People communicate with others to engage in social interaction (connect with others) and to express themselves creatively and emotionally. Social/expressive communication efforts are a large part of human communication patterns, yet this is an area in which many have limited skills. For example, in the predominant U.S. culture it is common to suppress and ignore feelings and operate on a cognitive or mental plane. Nonetheless, expressing oneself socially and creatively is important to people and is a legitimate function of communication.

Some people pride themselves on their ability to express themselves creatively, and to make connections with others.

Command/Instruct

Another common purpose of communication is to command, direct, or instruct others. Most often utilizing a one-way approach, leaders engaged in this function direct or instruct participants or subordinates to do something—stop an activity, pick up equipment, attend a meeting, or follow rules. Oftentimes this communication is used to maintain safe environments for all.

Conflict Resolution

Conflict resolution is a very important reason for and function of communication. Resolving problems in a positive and creative fashion is critical to task accomplishment, effective group growth, and personal development. To be effective, conflict resolution must be desired by those involved and be a conscious goal of communication. Conflict management skills are required for effective leadership; a later chapter of this book is devoted to the subject.

No matter the function or reason for communicating, communication effectiveness varies in each interaction. As people, messages, channels, and noise change, the effectiveness of communication may be affected. Identifiable factors exist which influence each communication process. These are addressed in the next section.

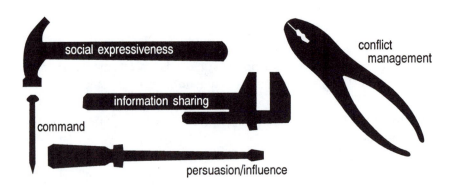

Figure 5.3   *There are five primary functions or tools of communication.*

Effective Communication

Many factors influence the communication process; they may be elements internal to those communicating or external to the communication process. Internal factors that influence the communication process include the need for shared meanings between the sender and receiver, sender and receiver biases and prejudices which might impact the communication process, individual readiness, and the individual communication skills of those involved. External factors that might influence the effectiveness of communication include the physical environment, timing issues, and noise. The physical environment (e.g., room temperature, arrangement of furniture) can have an impact on participant readiness to receive communication messages.

Other factors that influence communication effectiveness are the varying emphases placed on either task accomplishment or morale within the group. If a group is very focused on task completion, for instance, communication related to emotions, affect, and group feelings would not only be unwelcome, but perhaps, distracting. In addition to group focus there are personal factors such as credibility and trustworthiness that impact the communication process.

Credibility and trustworthiness of both senders and receivers are necessary for effective communication to occur (Bolton, 1979; Hayes, 1994; Verderber & Verderber, 1992). Credibility is addressed through issues such as task competence as well as communication, character (i.e., issues of personal integrity), composure under stress, sociability and likableness, and extroversion (Burgoon, Dawson, & Hunsaker, 1994). The use of appropriate grammar, considering the emotional impact of what is said, knowledge about the possible ambiguity of word and phrase choice, and understanding the needs of the sender and receiver also contribute to one's perceived competence (Verderber & Verderber, 1992). Many of these issues fall under the guise of professionalism.

Effective communication involves an understanding of professionalism and a sound knowledge of and an ability to use basic communication skills in writing, oral communication, and nonverbal communication. A sense of professionalism is communicated in the way one dresses, wears one's hair, and carries one's self. For example, participant confidence tends to be greater in leaders who are dressed in uniforms (sometimes as simple as a polo shirt and matching shorts), or neatly pressed clothes (such as a nice shirt, tucked into neat slacks) than in a leader who wears cutoff jeans and a T-shirt that reads, "Who me?"

In addition to exuding professionalism, leisure services leaders convey messages through basic communication skills which must be developed and continually improved upon throughout one's lifetime. Leisure services professionals tend to stress oral presentation skills (e.g., leading songs or games, giving instructions, speaking on the telephone) and place less emphasis on other forms of communication. In addition to being accomplished speakers and presenters, however, leisure services leaders must also be skilled in written communication. Reports, inventories, memos, promotional materials, policy manuals, and schedule books are just a few of the areas in which a solid command of the written language is necessary.

Increasing Communication Effectiveness

Effective communication occurs when the intended message is the one that is received and the exchange of information is accomplished efficiently. As can be seen from the model of communication presented earlier, there are many places where effectiveness might be strengthened or compromised. To increase the quality of the communication process leaders will want to subscribe to the following techniques.

Speak and Write at the Audience Level

Children require different communication patterns than do adults, and teens require an approach different from children. Leaders should be well-aware of when the communication is going to take place with people who are culturally different from themselves; attempts should be made to reach the audience at its level of readiness, and not where the leader *thinks* the group should be (or below its level). If one is communicating with adults who know English as a second language, the choice of words and word arrangements should be taken into account.

Communicate to Share Ideas

Many young leaders get caught up in communicating to "puff" themselves up and to make an impression on those with whom they are communicating. This type of impression management interferes with effective communication because it is egocentric rather than being other-oriented; the message is not content-focused, but rather self-centered. Being conscious of the function and reason for communication will aid in maintaining clarity of purpose.

Consider Both Fact and Feeling Aspects of Communication

Too often words are chosen or information is delivered in a way that is offensive, shocking, or hurtful to those receiving the messages. All communication has an emotional component to it and matching one's words and message to the audience lends itself to effective communication. Leaders should also bear in mind that potential audiences often extend beyond those who are immediately present. What is communicated in one situation "gets around" in short order.

Recognize...

If ever there was one thing to remember, it is that there can be a large difference between intent and interpretation. Simply because a sender meant to send a particular message does not mean that was the message received. What becomes important at that time, then, is the message as interpreted and perceived by the receiver. This is particularly true when working with young children (ages three to seven years) who are still in the stage of literal understanding. Using a figure of speech would be ineffective in communicating an intended message because youngsters interpret messages figuratively.

Good communicators are able to choose what to say from a variety of options—they understand the other person's point of view, monitor their own behaviors to better understand how others perceive them, and choose the most appropriate way to converse (e.g., informal, formal, use of humor). Furthermore, leaders understand the cultural context in which communication occurs. In addition to these traits of good communicators, Johnson and Johnson (1991) presented the six Cs of effective communication. In considering the suggestions listed below, leaders should note that as with all communication efforts, these style issues are culturally based. The following Cs identify effective communication:

- clear (language and messages should be unambiguous);
- concise (being succinct and concise minimizes misinterpretation);
- correct (effective communication is correct communication);
- complete (the communication cycle should be complete for a message to be fully understood);
- courteous (being courteous and considerate of receivers and their needs enhances communication); and

- convincing (to be effective, communication should be convincing in its logic and reasoning).

In any culture effective communicators are very aware that words have tremendous power. People take to heart very much the words and tone that leaders use. The use of "I," for instance, sets the stage to share personal opinions and feelings; "you" is a phrase that can project blame or pride, "but" is a negating word that sinks the heart of listeners as in, "you did well, but..." (but negates everything that came before it); "yes," a very positive can-do word; "no," a word that should be used sparingly; "should" and "ought to" are two words that infer a heavy responsibility, i.e., "what happens if one should, but does not do...?" Leaders have tremendous power and influence over their constituents through various ways of communicating.

No matter how much one knows about and practices effective communication, misinterpretations and miscommunications are bound to occur. This is because so much of the communication cycle is out of the control of any one person. As with understanding that effective communication aids in successful communication, so too does knowledge of miscommunication aid in avoiding common pitfalls—preparing for miscommunication can minimize its negative effects.

Miscommunication

To minimize miscommunication people must first come to understand five basic principles of communication relationships: (1) we can never know the state of mind of others, (2) we depend on ambiguous symbols to explain other's attitudes, (3) we use our own (defective) coding system to decipher signals, (4) we may be biased in interpreting other's behaviors, and (5) we are not as accurate as we think we are in interpreting others' messages (Gudykunst, 1991). Keeping in mind these principles, it is easy to see how miscommunication might occur. In fact, we might wonder how we *ever* manage to communicate well!

Miscommunication is a breakdown in the communication process; it can occur in several ways:

- the sender improperly encodes the message;
- the message may be ambiguous;
- the channel may not be the best choice for the message;
- the noise may be too intrusive;

- the receiver may misinterpret the message; and
- the feedback might be inadequate.

The result of miscommunication, of course, is that the intended message is not the message received. This results in actions on the part of the receiver that do not coincide with the intent of the sender. Frustration, anger, inefficiency, and lack of task completion are a few of the results of such communication miscues.

To get better at communication one must practice. This is true of oral, written, or nonverbal language. In addition, being open to learning and feedback is critical for improvement to occur. Along with repeating an important message three times, using demonstration and practice by receivers are desirable to overcome potential barriers to communication.

Barriers to Communication

Communication is incredibly complex and while we engage in it constantly, most people do not communicate well (Bolton, 1979). The good news is that communication skills are learned; poor communication habits can be minimized and good communication skills can be enhanced. In spite of this, barriers to communication exist in many places. In fact, people often interject barriers into the communication process without realizing it.

Whether one is a sender or receiver, "people issues" may arise which act as barriers to communication. The sender might put up barriers through engaging in one or more of the following behaviors:

- prejudging the receiver;
- avoiding the real and immediate concerns of the receiver;
- having disorganized thoughts;
- having strong emotions;
- trying to share too much information at one time;
- using inappropriate language or nonverbal signs; and/or
- mismatching communication style with receiver.

Receivers also put up barriers to effective communication. Receiver barriers include:

- prejudgment of the sender;

- poor listening skills;
- defensiveness;
- strong emotions;
- incorrect assumptions;
- different connotations for words and intonations; and/or
- mismatched communication styles with sender.

Group problems also contribute to communication problems. Barriers to communication that arise out of group problems include:

- a lack of cohesiveness;
- a lack of openness to opposing views;
- a lack of willingness to talk;
- unacknowledged culture differences;
- biases inherent within the group; and
- ineffective leadership.

Verbal Language

Communication may occur through verbal and nonverbal and paraverbal language. In addition, written communication and the use of symbols may also be used to convey meaning to others. Verbal language is so commonplace and such an integral part of our lives that we rarely give it serious thought. As leisure services leaders, however, we must always bear in mind that other people will form opinions of us based on our verbal presentation: the use of the language, "proper" or standard English, our ability to articulate, and clarity of message. This is true whether engaged in one-on-one communication in person or on the phone, giving a presentation, or being overheard in a casual conversation by passersby. Therefore, it is wise to learn and practice good verbal communication skills as much as possible.

It is important to remember that language is imprecise. Words have both a denotation, which is a dictionary definition, and a connotation, which is the personal meaning of a word. To improve use of language, communicators should strive to expand their vocabulary (often accomplished through increased reading), use simple language, choose action words, choose to illustrate abstract ideas so people get a picture of what is meant, and use compare and contrast techniques to aid in comprehension (Gibson & Hanna, 1992).

Verbal communication involves many specific skills. Internalizing these skills into one's communication patterns and seeking feedback about use of these skills will improve one's ability to communicate with a variety of people. Effective communicators:

- know how to say the right thing at the right time;
- know the necessity of sometimes remaining silent;
- work on skills to improve their verbal facility (increased vocabulary, reading, exposure to cultures other than one's own);
- know how to keep certain information protected (all information need not be public information);
- know what information is and is not appropriate for each unique situation;
- understand that personality influences behaviors;
- understand gossip and how it affects relationships;
- know how to access information; and
- know the importance of nonverbal messages and how to improve them (Genua, 1992).

In addition to these skills, effective communicators are also aware of how tone of voice, intonations, pitch, use of silence/pauses, speed, and volume affect verbal communication. For instance, lowering the pitch of one's voice and "clipping" one's words may convey an attitude of authority; and asking a question such as, "Would you please help get set up?" conveys a different message than a flat command, "Please help with the setup."

Effective communicators are very cognizant of the impact of their language on others. Leaders must always bear in mind that using sexist, racist or other demeaning language will affect how and what is being conveyed. Language that is other than inclusive will send messages about the sender, the agency she or he represents, and how receivers are perceived. Care should be taken to respect and be concerned for all individuals, no matter how they differ from others.

Listening

In order for verbal language to have any influence someone must be listening. As most people have learned over time, to truly listen requires work—it does not simply happen. It is interesting to note that listening takes up more waking hours than any other activity, yet 75% of oral communication is ignored (not listened to) (Worchel & Simpson, 1993). This is an amazing statistic! Listening *does* take effort, and it is a reciprocal and active process. This means that someone has to be listening in order for communication to have an effect. Listening is a skill that everyone can learn and one which leisure services leaders should work to develop. To fully utilize the communication process no aspect of it can be passive—every step requires active, conscious effort on the part of those involved. There are several types of active listening (Cathcart & Samovar, 1992; Gibson & Hanna, 1992):

> **Empathic listening:** This is a form of active listening which involves relationships and sharing feelings. Empathic listening is an intimate process and involves an understanding of and the ability to reflect the feelings, needs, and intentions of others back to them. For instance, when listening to an irate customer an empathic listener might say (in a calm, well-modulated voice), "I see you feel strongly about this."
>
> **Comprehensive listening:** Listening to understand the material presented; listening for facts, ideas and themes the speaker is trying to share is the goal of comprehensive

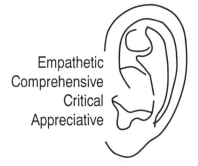

Empathetic
Comprehensive
Critical
Appreciative

Figure 5.4   Listening is a process and may involve slightly different skills depending upon the needs of the situation.

listening. This is the common form of listening students use when learning in classes. It involves a "holistic" type of listening.

Critical listening: This involves listening to evaluate ideas as they are expressed. Generally, it is used when trying to make judgments about persuasive messages of others. For example, when engaged in the fact finding period in the problem-solving process, leaders will use critical listening skills to ascertain pieces of truth from those involved in the conflict.

Appreciative listening: Listeners who engage in listening for pleasure are appreciative listeners. Appreciative listening stimulates the mind and senses through listening to others. This is often the type of listening used by leaders when listening to elderly participants reflecting on their lives.

In order to understand intended messages of any kind one needs to *want* to listen. This desire and commitment to listen enables the receiver to pay attention to the context of what is being said and identify and interpret the feelings of the speaker. Receivers can improve listening skills by practicing the three primary skill clusters of listening: *attending, following,* and *reflecting.*

Attending Skills

Attending is the process of deciding which sounds are to be focused upon. It describes how listeners pay attention to what is being said and how the message is being conveyed. In order to best attend to a speaker, listeners often model an attending posture. An attending position is one where the listener faces the speaker squarely, has an open posture (no arms and legs crossed), leans toward the speaker, maintains eye contact, and appears relaxed. At times, the listener's body may mirror the posture of the speaker. In essence, attending is the nonverbal indication that a listener is paying attention and is well-focused on the speaker.

Following Skills

Once a listener indicates an attentiveness toward the speaker, following skills become important. Exhibiting nonverbal door-openers (e.g.,

Photo courtesy of the Black Hawk County Community Playhouse

Effective communication requires effective listening which involves attending to the message.

eyebrows raised, an inviting look on face), making interpretive statements (for clarification and acknowledgment), and using attentive silences and verbal prompts to continue talking are all examples of these skills. Being attentive and following what is being said indicate active listening. The third cluster of active listening skills consists of reflecting skills.

Reflecting Skills

Used to ensure understanding, reflecting skills include paraphrasing, reflecting meanings and feelings back at the speaker, and summarizing what has been said (Worchel & Simpson, 1993). Reflecting skills provide an opportunity for the speaker to restate issues if needed, and to see that the listener truly comprehends the message as it is being sent. Listeners should be careful to avoid inappropriate responses. Inappropriate responses include those which are irrelevant (ignores the speaker and message), tangential (an irrelevant response more tactfully done—some acknowledgment of the speaker, then the subject changed), incongruent (the response is in opposition to statement), and interruptions (breaking in before another finishes) (Verderber & Verderber, 1992).

As with verbal language, effective listening requires much practice. It can be difficult to learn at first because many of us have picked up poor listening habits. Problems with listening may originate with the receiver, the sender, or be found in any part of the communication cycle.

Factors Influencing the Ability to Listen Effectively

Listener problems include not listening (or poor listening skills), a lack of motivation to listen, and an inability to make sense of the message. Speaker difficulties include speaking too quickly or too slowly, being unclear, and choosing an inappropriate time or place for communication. In addition, the message may be poorly structured or have too much or too little detail, and be based on incorrect assumptions. Furthermore, if the environment is too noisy or uncomfortable, listening will be negatively affected.

Listening, speaking and sending messages occur among and between all types of people. Due to the diverse nature of society, effective leaders understand that communicating with others may not be as clear-cut or simple as we would like. We have a tendency to assume others are like ourselves in values, thoughts, and attitudes. These assumptions are not always accurate, however, and can lead to ineffective communication. Effective communicators strive to identify their own assumptions about others, and to learn more about the values, beliefs, and attitudes of those different from themselves.

Intercultural Communication

Intercultural communication occurs any time the communication process is initiated by one individual who holds one set of cultural beliefs and is received by individuals who hold a different set of cultural beliefs. For purposes of this text *culture* is defined as an identifiable group of people who share customs, language, patterns of speech, meanings, religion, relationships, and values. In this sense intercultural communication occurs between teenagers and older adults, women and men, and people of various racial and ethnic backgrounds.

Language can be used to impress, influence, and exert power over people. Power in speaking comes from the receiver's perceptions and stereotypes about the status, prestige and competence of the person communicating. Speaker status is affected by listeners' perceptions of that speech; for example, the rate or speed, intonations, word choices, or accent. For instance, low-power speakers tend to use tag questions, qualifiers, and a questioning tone of voice when speaking. Tag questions such as "...don't you think?" or "...if you agree?" are tacked on the end of a sentence. Rate of speech is related to perceived speaker competence (up to a point) where those who speak more quickly are perceived as more competent than slow talkers. In addition to speech rate, voice intonations and intensity also relate to speaker power; those in high power are perceived as being intense communicators—they make assertions, are firm, and have a conviction to their communication (Ng & Bradac, 1993).

All of us should be concerned with making generalizations about people because all too easily, these global statements soon come to be known as truth. Generalizations *can* be very helpful in that they help us order and make sense of the world; however, inappropriate use of generalizations can result in unfair and inaccurate stereotypes. To be the best communicator possible, leisure services leaders should understand how various groups *tend* to communicate while avoiding the trap of believing that all members of a group *should* communicate that way. Our perceptions about language and communication are different from others' because learning contexts are different; the cultures in which people are raised vary tremendously (Cathcart & Samovar, 1992).

As we examine intercultural communication it becomes evident that the greater the cultural and linguistic knowledge, and the more one's beliefs overlap with others, the more effective the communication will be (Gudykunst, 1991). This means that the more we have in common with others, the more effective the communication between us.

Ethnic Variations in Verbal Communication

Ethnocentrism is the belief that one's own culture is correct and others' are incorrect and improper. Unfortunately, this is a position to which many people adhere. Ethnocentrism results in stereotypes, overgeneralizations, and inaccurate judgments about various groups. It also can interfere with effective communication. When we realize that the top ten languages spoken as a first language worldwide are: Chinese, English, Spanish, Hindi, Arabic, Bengali, Russian, Portuguese, Japanese, and German (Gibson & Hanna, 1992) and that each has many dialects within it, difficulties in communication are inevitable.

Cross culturally there can be confusion in communication goals or in interpreting the main point of a conversation. For instance, in Asian

Photo courtesy of the University of Northern Iowa Public Relations Department

Intercultural communication involves sending and receiving in at least two sets of cultural belief systems.

cultures one typically begins a conversation with background material (e.g., general information about a topic) and then moves on to the main point. In western talk (i.e., the dominant U.S. style) the point is made first and the explanation follows. Expectations and perceptions might lead one to believe that Westerners are frank and rude and that Asians are difficult to understand and "read" (Scollon & Scollon, 1995).

It is helpful to remember that language is ambiguous by nature, and that people draw inferences about meaning based on their world-view. Those inferences are drawn from the language, tone, nonverbal language, and other communication cues used. Therefore, depending upon the culture in which one was raised, one might arrive at the conclusion that a speaker is highly intelligent, manipulative, confident, or concerned only about the task at hand.

Furthermore, how one uses language expresses degrees of familiarity ("Yo!"), politeness ("Yes, sir"), and shared knowledge/world-view ("phat"—a term used by teens to mean "cool"). Intonation in how one uses words changes the meanings associated with those words, as does timing. For example, the way one asks the question, "Did you do that?" changes based on whether or not the one asking is pleased, angry, perturbed, or mildly amused that you "did that." Thus, cultural differences arise out of not knowing or understanding other's communication styles—meanings of words, intonation, nonverbal language, and so on.

Other ways that language across ethnic groups affects communication is in the use of what is sometimes called *family* or *street* language. In the study of African-American dialects (termed Ebonics), for instance, it has been learned that certain aspects of the language differ from standard English. Consider the following:

- In Black English the word "be" is used in place of am, is, or are;

- In addition, the "sk" sound is often reversed as in "I aksed you a question;"

- The use of double negatives is common; "Nobody knows nothing;"

- The "l" sound is dropped in words like "help," and the "r" sound is dropped in words like "door;" and

- Another key difference is that in Black English the last consonant cluster is often dropped (Stanton, 1995).

These differences become understandable when one knows that African-American English has its roots in the days of enslavement when Africans were forcibly taken from their tribes and prohibited from speaking any language. Some standard English sounds (i.e., "th") were not a part of the tribal language, and as those who were enslaved began to communicate, they had to develop their own usable language. Sounds and intonations became distinct from the now "standard" (i.e., white, middle class) English. For recreation and leisure services leaders understanding Black English (and other ethnic forms of standard English) is important to more effectively communicate with staff, participants, and the general public.

Racism in Verbal Communication

In addition to recognizing various dialects, another issue related to ethnicity and communication is covert and subtle racism in all forms of communication. Language perceived as racist or sexist may alienate or irritate listeners so that they are no longer able to discern the intended content of the message. An underlying message being sent by a speaker using racist language is one of exclusion and disregard for listeners.

Therefore, leaders will want to be cognizant of such exclusionary language. While racism can be observed throughout the communication process it is most obvious in one's choice of words. Being aware of the meanings of words across cultures is necessary to eliminate this problem. For example, identifying all people of Hispanic heritage as Mexicans (or Hispanics) does not acknowledge that some have origins in Latin countries, others in the South Pacific, and still others in Spain. This misidentification is exclusionary in that it negates distinct cultural groups.

In other racist communication one might hear blatantly racist words when individuals are involved in arguments or fights (calling each other names based on ethnic group affiliation). In addition, it is important to recognize and put a stop to more subtle uses of racist language as in the phrase, "yellow coward." This phrase has its roots in World War II references to the Japanese and continues to be a negative use of language.

Other subtle forms of racism in communication occur when a person is defined by her or his ethnic heritage when it has no relevance. This is common in news reports where individuals are identified as Black or Asian in crime stories, but white perpetrators are not identified as being Caucasian. In leisure leadership this could be a problem when describing individual behaviors to others: "The Black boy shoved Tommy;" "Wow! Look at the fine crafts project that Kim did! She's Hmong, you know." Leisure services leaders each would be wise to examine their own cultural biases and prejudices, and to listen to themselves and others when speaking to avoid "innocent" (but hurtful) remarks.

Gender Variations in Verbal Communication

As a term, sex is used when referring to biological distinctions and gender is used when referring to a sense of culturally defined femaleness and maleness (i.e., femininity and masculinity). In examining the use of language between the sexes, we will use gender as the defining element; there is little evidence of biological differences in women's and men's language.

Communication is a process that involves bargaining and negotiation. We have already discussed how communication occurs in context, involves codes, and is an interchange or transaction between those involved in the process. In examining transactions between women and men many believe that the communication differences between women and men are due to varying socialization patterns and/or power differences between the sexes.

Tannen (1990) has conducted extensive studies of female and male communication patterns and reports that females tend to use language to build and maintain relationships while males tend to use language to establish and maintain personal power. This means that women use language to focus on the connections between people. They tend to smooth hurt feelings, be concerned about group morale, and address issues of people liking one another. Men, on the other hand, use language to establish positions of power, status, and prestige among others involved in the communication process. Tannen has identified nine dimensions of communication on which women and men differ:

> **Intimacy-Independence:** Women desire intimacy in communication while men strive for independence.

> **Connection-Status:** In their efforts towards intimacy women are involved in connecting with others while men are engaged in communication to enhance their status.

> **Inclusion-Exclusion:** The different orientations report that women have a tendency to be inclusive and men exclusive in group task accomplishment.

> **Relationship-Information:** Again, in concert with a focus on intimacy and connection, women are relationship oriented while men are information oriented.

> **Rapport-Report:** Women are concerned with developing rapport with others while men have a tendency to focus on outcomes.

> **Community-Contest:** A sense of community and cooperation are evidenced in women's communication while competition and contest are more evident in men's language.

Problems-Solutions: Women often present situations as problems to be worked through together while men are drawn toward devising quick solutions to those problems.

Novice-Expert: Women often perceive and present themselves as novices while men perceive and present themselves as experts.

Listening-Lecturing: When communicating, women are more apt to listen and men are more apt to lecture.

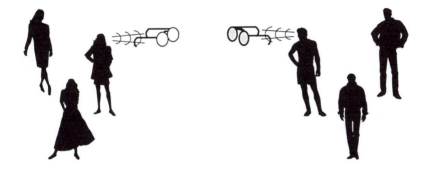

Figure 5.5   *In most cultures females and males perceive communication differently. Many believe this is due to the effects of socialization.*

Some would argue that these distinctions are also common in relationships between low and high power people (e.g., frontline worker-supervisor relationship; child-parent relationship). Speech patterns of people in low-power situations (e.g., women, children) include a greater use of the following types of statements than for high-power (e.g., men, supervisors) individuals:

- the use of *word qualifiers* such as "kind of," "I guess," and "maybe";
- *tag questions* placed at the end of assertions as in, "... don't you agree?";
- *compound requests* such as adding "... if you would like" to one's thought;

- *polite forms of language* such as saying, "thank you for your time";
- *disclaimers,* usually stated at the beginning of a statement such as, "this might not be right, but...";
- *intensifiers* such as, "very," "really," and "surely";
- *verbal fillers* which are often linked to a tentative speech pattern: "well," "okay," and "ummm"; and
- requests that might serve to *discount own ideas* as in, "I'd like to hear from others on this" (Pearson, West & Turner, 1995; Scollon & Scollon, 1995; Tannen, 1990).

Sexism in Communication

Sexist language is used by females and males alike, often without an understanding of the impact of such language. Generally there are three types of sexism in language; ignoring one gender (using a supposedly generic "he"), defining a gender in relation to something else (e.g., women *and* children), and in deprecation of a gender.

Research has shown that there is no such thing as a generic "he" and that using the male pronoun when addressing or dealing with mixed groups is exclusive and sets a tone of "males only" (Pearson, West & Turner, 1995). This is also true if leaders consistently use male-based examples as in, "the Director, he ..." and, "the Firefighter and his dog..." This technique of ignoring females is a sexist use of language.

The other two ways in which sexism is identified in language is by defining a gender in relation to something else, and in deprecation of a gender (when adjectives discredit one gender as in, "that's a *girl's* toy!"). To avoid the first pitfall leaders should be careful to use *parallel terms*; that is, terms which are like one another in connotation. Examples of this include women and men (not girls and men), girls and boys, and ladies and gentlemen (not ladies and men). Generally, in the predominant U.S. culture females and males are labeled as girls and boys as children; as they mature they are identified as either young women and young men or women and men in their midteen years. Just as identifying adult males as boys is inaccurate (and often a put-down), so too is referring to a woman of 25 or even 68 as a girl; this is considered a sexist use of language.

Communication is used for a variety of functions and one of those purposes is to wield power over others. Language in the form of sexist or racist remarks, no matter how "innocent," denigrates members of the targeted group. Leaders can combat racism and sexism in language by doing the following:

- examine personal verbal, written and symbolic language for inclusiveness (i.e., of both sexes, people with disabilities, people of color, and people of various ages);

- be aware of works, images, and situations that suggest that everyone of one race, sex, or ethnic group is the same (leaders will want to pay particular attention to promotional materials);

- avoid qualifiers that reinforce stereotypes (e.g., "She's smart—for a woman.");

- identify by sex, race, or ethnicity *only* when relevant;

- be aware of language that has sexist, racial or ethnic overtones or connotations to some people;

- avoid patronizing others (e.g., "cute" elderly);

- substitute substantive information for sexist or racist clichés; and

- review all media, and office and promotional materials to be sure representation of people is broad.

Summary

Communication skills are fundamental to effective leadership. Communication is a process which includes a sender, message, channel, receiver, feedback, and noise. For effective communication to occur, there must be agreement between the sender and receiver in terms of the underlying meanings of the message. Sender and receiver roles change as positions in the communication process change.

There are five basic functions to communication and leaders utilize communication for these reasons at various times: persuasion, information sharing, social/expressive, to command, and in conflict resolution. Effective communication must be developed and continually practiced to improve. It entails understanding the receiver, communicating to share ideas, attending to the message one sends, and actively listening. Miscommunication may occur at any stage of the communication process.

Miscommunication may occur due to barriers put up by the sender, receiver, or the environment. Barriers to communication may arise due to many factors: a breakdown in the communication process, poor listening skills, lack of motivation, and inept skills. To be an effective communicator one must overcome these issues. One of the most important aspects of effective communication is listening. There are several types of listening: empathetic listening, comprehensive listening, critical listening, and appreciative listening. Each of them requires the listener to attend to the sender, use following skills, and reflect the communication back to the sender.

In addition to these elements, effective communicators understand issues related to intercultural communication which occurs any time the process begins in one set of cultural expectations and must be interpreted in another. Ethnicity and gender (as well as other elements of diversity) influence the communication process. Word usage, voice quality, and other variations in language may exist between individuals who exist in different cultural worlds. Effective leaders take into consideration their own skills, levels of awareness, and the audience when engaging in the communication process.

The Front Line

Listening is a critical skill for leaders who have been identified as leaders through all avenues—legitimate, elected, appointed, emergent. Research has recently been completed which identified listening as a key component of perceived effective leadership. Bechler and Johnson (1995) studied undergraduate college students in small group communication courses at two universities. Subjects were randomly assigned to task-oriented groups, which met a minimum of six times; the mean group size was 5.5 members. Each group was split in half (for purposes of responding to research questionnaires) and half completed a leadership assessment questionnaire—asking which group members were most like and unlike a leader. The other half of the group completed a listening assessment questionnaire defining the most and least skilled listeners in the group.

Findings indicated that those individuals ranked as most like a leader were also ranked as good listeners. Individuals perceived to be leading the groups (the emergent leaders) were perceived as listening to group members throughout the process. Poor listeners were not perceived as having good listening skills, nor were they viewed as group leaders.

Implications for Leaders

In leisure services leadership, small groups are formed and reformed continuously. Small task-oriented (i.e., focused on doing a job) groups occur at all levels of leisure services. Coaches form small groups when planning league schedules; therapeutic recreation specialists form small task-oriented groups when devising patient plans; instructional staff gather together in efforts to provide both educational and fun programs; and boards of directors form subcommittees to focus on particular tasks. In each of these examples, leaders emerge from within the various groups to facilitate group efforts toward accomplishing a task.

The findings of the Bechler and Johnson study indicate that emergent leaders, effectively chosen from within a work group by peers, are also perceived as good listeners. It would make sense, then, for an individual wishing to develop and hone her or his leadership skills to practice active listening skills. For emergent leaders to be perceived as effective in a leadership role, they must also be perceived as good listeners. Being attentive, asking clarifying questions, including all group members in work efforts and discussions, and being sensitive to individual needs all fall within effective listening skills. According to this research, practicing and seeking feedback on one's listening skills is one key to effective leadership.

References

Bechler, C. and Johnson, S. (1995). Leadership and listening. *Small Group Research, 26*(1), 77-85.

Bolton, R. (1979). *People skills.* Englewood Cliffs, NJ: Prentice Hall.

Brody, E. W. (1991). *Managing communication processes: From planning to crisis response.* New York, NY: Praeger.

Burgoon, M., Dawson, E., and Hunsaker, F. (1994). *Human communication* (3rd ed.). Newbury Park, CA: Sage Publications, Inc.

Cathcart, R. and Samovar, L. (1992). *Small group communication* (6th ed.). Dubuque, IA: Wm. C. Brown Publishing.

Genua, R. (1992). *Managing your mouth.* New York, NY: AMACOM.

Gibson, J. and Hanna, M. (1992). *Introduction to human communication.* Dubuque, IA: Wm. C. Brown Publishing.

Gudykunst, W. (1991). *Bridging differences: Effective intergroup communication.* Newbury Park, CA: Sage Publications, Inc.

Hayes, J. (1994). *Interpersonal skills.* London, UK: Routledge.

Heath, R., and Bryant, J. (1992). *Human communication theory and research.* Hillsdale, NJ: Lawrence Erlbaum Associates.

Johnson, D. and Johnson, F. (1991). *Joining together: Group theory and group skills* (4th ed.). Englewood Cliffs, NJ: Prentice Hall.

Ng, S. and Bradac, J. (1993). *Power in language: Verbal communication and social influence.* Newbury Park, CA: Sage Publications, Inc.

Pearson, J., West, R., and Turner, L. (1995). *Gender and communication* (3rd ed.). Dubuque, IA: Brown & Benchmark.

Scollon, R. and Scollon, S. W. (1995). *Intercultural communication.* Cambridge, MA: Blackwell Publishers.

Stanton, J. (1995, October 29). Crossing the language gap. *Waterloo Courier,* Metro Section. Waterloo, IA.

Tannen, D. (1990). *You just don't understand: Women and men in conversation.* New York, NY: William Morrow & Co.

Verderber, R. and Verderber, K. (1992). *Inter-Act: Using interpersonal communication skills* (6th ed.). Belmont, CA: Wadsworth Publishing Company.

Worchel, S. and Simpson, J. (Eds.). (1993). *Conflict between people and groups.* Chicago, IL: Nelson-Hall Publishers.

York, S., Jordan, D., and Safford, S. (1995). *Personal leadership series facilitators guide.* Unpublished manuscript.

Chapter Six
Learning Opportunities

Through studying this chapter students will have the opportunity to:

- articulate the types and functions of nonverbal language;

- explain and demonstrate nonverbal skills in body language;

- describe the role of leadership in elements of nonverbal language such as chronemics and physical appearance;

- identify the cultural, gender and power issues inherent in nonverbal communication; and,

- understand the use and importance of quality writing skills in effective leadership.

Photo courtesy of the YWCA of Black Hawk County

CHAPTER

6

Nonverbal Communication:
An Important Skill

As mentioned in the previous chapter, listening and communicating involves paying close attention to the person sending the message. This close attention allows a listener to not only *hear* what is being said, but also to *see* what is being said. After all, the communication process is not complete without considering both the verbal and nonverbal aspects of interactions. It has been estimated that between 60% and 75% of what is said is transmitted nonverbally (Burgoon, Dawson & Hunsaker, 1994). This is an amazing figure when one thinks about how much we talk!

While nonverbal language and ascribed meanings vary by culture and subculture (for instance, tapping one's temple with the forefinger means "You're crazy!" in Europe; except in Holland where it means, "How clever!"), it tends to be the more trusted aspect of communication. People (especially children) are more apt to believe the message communicated nonverbally than the verbal message if there are any perceived contradictions. In addition, interpreting nonverbal language provides insight into others' states of mind, intent, and personal meanings inherent in the communication. While commonly the more trusted form of communication, nonverbal language is also perceived as an ambiguous element of language. This may arise from the fact that interpretations of nonverbal communication differ based on gender, ethnicity, power relationships, and other aspects of culture.

To effectively use one's knowledge of nonverbal communication, leisure services leaders need to be good observers and decoders of others' nonverbal messages. In addition, leaders need to be effective senders of such messages (be aware of their own nonverbal messages).

Being able to correctly observe and interpret another's nonverbal language will help in understanding the entire message being sent. In addition, a leader can strengthen or differently emphasize what is being said by being cognizant of her or his own use of nonverbal language.

In this chapter, nonverbal language will be discussed including the use of one's body in communication; symbolic communication (through symbols such as logos); and written language, an underemphasized and much needed skill of all leisure services leaders. Nonverbal communication serves several functions within communication interactions.

Functions of Nonverbal Communication

Functions of nonverbal communication are varied, and in some way, enhance the spoken word. In general, nonverbal communication may serve to assist in impression management, to indicate membership, regulate communication, provide feedback, to repeat or emphasize a verbal message, as a substitute for words, and to express a variety of social relationships (Daly & Wiemann, 1994; Gibson & Hanna, 1992; Hayes, 1994; Kalbfleisch & Cody, 1995; Patterson, 1983; Verderber & Verderber, 1992).

repeat or emphasize verbal communication

impression management

substitute for words

sign of membership

regulate communication

express social relationships

Figure 6.1   *Nonverbal language serves many functions in communication.*

Impression Management

Impression management includes those behaviors where one engages in efforts to control or influence the manner in which others perceive oneself. This includes both efforts to increase one's credibility (e.g., status and prestige) as well as efforts to maintain a level of deception (e.g., telling a white lie). To some extent most people are continually engaged in efforts related to managing how others perceive them. For instance, every time a leisure services leader steps in front of a group of participants to lead an activity the preparation she or he undergoes, the choice of clothing she or he wears, and the techniques and leadership styles utilized all contribute to managing her or his self-impression in front of others.

Sign of Membership

An individual may indicate membership within a certain group or club by engaging in certain nonverbal behaviors and displaying certain symbols. Young people in gangs do this (e.g., crossing one's arms in a particular manner and wearing gang-associated colors indicates membership in a particular gang) as do professionals in particular organizations (e.g., shaking hands in a certain fashion or secret handshakes, wearing agency-associated clothing such as uniforms or suits). Nonverbal communication can send messages of belonging, inclusion, and group pride and cohesion.

Regulate Communication

One of the more subtle yet powerful functions of nonverbal communication is to regulate the flow of conversation. It is through this mechanism that people understand when to remain silent while others finish their thought and when to take their turn in the conversation. Without this function people would interrupt others frequently, and would not know when to stop or start speaking. This is most evident when engaging in casual conversation with others. One might hold up a finger to prevent another from speaking, or use one's eyes to hold one's turn in the conversation.

Providing Feedback

For leaders, nonverbal messages from participants are crucial to effective leadership. The feedback one receives through participant facial expressions, level of fidgeting, and other nonverbal mediums helps a leader know when to change approaches, speed up, slow down, or continue to follow the path one has chosen. Similarly, feedback informs speakers involved in casual conversations about listener comprehension and readiness for additional information.

Repeat or Emphasize Verbal Message

All of us have had experience with repeating or emphasizing spoken words with nonverbal language. For instance, a pounding fist emphasizes the verbal message as does pointing, gesturing with one's arms, smiling, and an "open" stance. Many leaders are skilled with a certain "look" (i.e., facial expression) that communicates, "I mean business," which induces rapid compliance in listeners.

Substitute for Words

Often nonverbal language is used as a substitute for spoken words—these are called emblems. Emblems include the thumbs up sign for "I agree," or "good job," (in the U.S.) the "okay" sign made with the thumb and index finger, and nodding one's head to indicate "yes."

To Express Social Relationships

Various meanings and expressions of relationships are accomplished through nonverbal language. They include communicating *power and dominance, compliance* with another's wishes, *sharing emotions*, and *social intimacy*.

Power and Dominance

Leaders (and others) use nonverbal language to influence other people using power differences. Examples of this include standing (with crossed arms) over someone who is sitting; pointing at someone in close proximity; and patting a person on the head—all of these are expressions of power. Power and dominance issues are evident in nonverbal interactions between females and males, people of varying ethnic backgrounds, and in parent-child relationships (Kalbfleisch & Cody,

1995). Leaders may use their power through nonverbal language to induce compliance from participants.

Compliance

Compliance is generally thought of as yielding to another's request or demand. Like verbal language, nonverbal interactions are reciprocal; therefore, for efficient smooth communication if one acts in a dominant manner the other party usually will be compliant. Nonverbal compliance may be indicated by smiling, bowing one's head, lowering one's eyes, or making a sweeping gesture with one hand as if indicating, "as you wish."

Affect Management

Affect management refers to the management or regulation of the emotional component of communication. Leaders often are called to manage affect when tempers rise and conflict occurs. Nonverbal language can help to mediate intense surges of emotion. Smiling, sitting with an "open" posture, and lightly touching another on the forearm are all nonverbal behaviors that may help to diffuse strong emotions. Nonverbal communication may also be used to "hype up" participants and encourage excitement. Wide-open eyes, a big smile or grin, and large gestures such as waving the arms about can incite a group to "get rowdy."

Photo courtesy of the YWCA of Black Hawk County

Nonverbal communication is sometimes used to provide feedback to a speaker.

Social Intimacy

Another subfunction of expressing social relationships is maintaining or regulating the amount and tenor of intimacy or familiarity experienced by two parties. Shaking hands sends a different message than giving a hug, and warm, friendly eye contact results in perceptibly different responses than an aggressive stare. Nonverbal language says much about the relationship between those communicating.

Body Language

The need for leisure services leaders to accurately decode as well as appropriately encode and send nonverbal messages was mentioned earlier. As one begins efforts to increase skills in this area, developing keen observation skills becomes important. It is interesting to note that research has shown that females tend to be better at decoding than males (Burgoon, Dawson, & Hunsaker, 1994; Kalbfleisch & Cody, 1995; Pearson, West & Turner, 1995). This has been generally attributed to the notion that in the predominant U.S. culture (like many others), women have less social power than men and, therefore, pay closer attention to all communication clues.

The lower level of social power and status reportedly leads young girls to pay close attention to others (as they grow up). Boys, on the other hand, do not need to pay as close attention to others because males already have access to resources by virtue of being male. This results in girls and women being socialized to cue in to other's nonverbal messages with more intensity than boys and men.

Recent research indicates that it is the position of low power, rather than gender, that results in increased accurate decoding of others' nonverbal messages (Carbaugh, 1990; Daly & Wiemann, 1994; Kalbfleisch & Cody, 1995; Pearson, West & Turner, 1995). This would lead one to surmise that people of color and people of low socioeconomic status also have a tendency to be relatively accurate decoders (i.e., interpreters) of others' nonverbal cues.

Many who study communication in general, and nonverbal communication specifically, report that nonverbal communication consists of several elements of body language as well as paraverbal communication. The most common elements of nonverbal communication which are investigated include use of space (proximity), touch, eye contact, facial expressions, gestures, posture, physical appearance, and use of time. *Paraverbal language* refers to those sounds made by people which are not distinguishable as words, yet have definite meaning (e.g., um, uh, uh huh, tsk, pshaw).

Proximity

Proximity refers to the use of space, both used or filled with one's body as well as with furniture or possessions. In other words, it is the study of how much space a person takes up with her or his body when sitting, walking, or standing. In addition, proximity addresses how an individual uses and fills up space with possessions such as books, papers, coats, and brief cases.

In the communication process, dominant people are known to control more space than less dominant people. This means that dominant individuals take up more space by (for example) sitting with their arms spread out. Furthermore, they might lay their belongings on the backs of empty chairs to claim additional space, and they tend to use large amounts of office space by spreading out the placement of furnishings. In addition, high dominant people tend to establish themselves physically above others—their chair might be raised higher than others, they might stand while others are sitting, or in some other fashion literally raise themselves above others. Leaders who wish to send a message of power and dominance, then, will want to position themselves higher than participants, and take up space with their bodies.

Higher dominant individuals are accorded greater personal space than submissive people; that is, others allow dominant people to move into their space relatively freely while the opposite is not necessarily true. This might be seen in agencies where the executive director might simply walk into an employee's office without knocking, yet the employee would never think of entering the director's office without first knocking and being invited in.

The elements of gender, ethnicity, and power interact with all aspects of communication. Relative to use of space, women use less personal space than do men; they take smaller steps, sit "smaller" in chairs, and either take up less space in offices or create multiple intimate spaces in large offices (Kalbfleisch & Cody, 1995). Power differences can also be seen in examining the use of space by members of various ethnic groups. For example, Asians tend to consume less space when standing, walking or sitting than do Europeans; and Caucasian Americans tend to take up more space when doing these things than do other U.S. ethnic groups.

Consider the use of personal space in talking to others. In the dominant U.S. culture talking, or social, distance is 18 to 36 inches. Therefore, when talking with others in a social setting we expect them to remain at least 18 inches away from us. If (nonfamily/nonintimate) people get closer than this we feel uncomfortable and tend to back away in efforts to maintain the 18 to 36 inch social distance. In other cultures, however, such as in some Middle Eastern cultures, social speaking distance is much closer and individuals may be offended if the one to whom they are speaking is at "arms length." As with all elements of communication, in examining spatial differences, understanding cultural norms becomes important in interpreting whether an individual is "in your face" or simply acting within her or his cultural expectations.

To be effective, leisure services leaders need to consider and be aware of the conscious use of space in leading activities and participants. It is important to match one's use of space to the needs of the situation. For instance, when leading large groups a leader will want to be visible; this may mean standing on top of something to be higher than participants, moving to one side of the room, or a combination of manipulating lateral and vertical space. When desiring to calm individuals down or in dealing with people who are shorter than the leader (e.g., a person in a wheelchair, a short adult, a child) a leader should remember the impact of "towering" over the participant and consider sitting or bending down to the level of the individual with whom she or he is speaking. This is particularly important in conflict management and problem-solving situations.

Figure 6.2   *Leadership involves a conscious use of both personal and environmental space.*

Touch

When researching touch in nonverbal communication, investigators measure the intensity (e.g., light, resting touch or heavy, pressing touch), direction (who touches whom), duration (how long the touch lasts), frequency (how often touches occur), and the instrument of touch (e.g., hand or object). Touch commonly occurs in the course of regular conversations to signal an upcoming change in turn taking. For instance, if another individual is speaking and I have something I would like to say, I might lightly place my hand on the forearm of the speaker indicating that I have something I would like to interject. Touch is also used when comforting others, managing behaviors, or demonstrating activity rules.

Cultural, gender, and power differences exist related to touch; higher dominant individuals tend to touch others' possessions more often than do low-power people. This is also true for touching people. Females are touched more than males and males are more apt to touch females than other males (Kalbfleisch & Cody, 1995). In some cultures touch, such as hand holding between people of the same sex, is acceptable and indicates a bond of friendship. In other cultures, this type of touch is considered taboo.

Touch can be a very powerful tool and can be used to soothe hurt feelings, to exert power, or to gain attention. Of all the nonverbal tools at a leader's disposal, touch is one which requires judicious use. A touch on the arm, pat on the back, or congratulatory hug can easily be misinterpreted and/or misused. For people who are survivors of sexual abuse, even an "innocent" touch on the shoulder may be interpreted or experienced as a sexual advance or personal invasion.

It is best, therefore, prior to touching anyone to ask the individual for her or his permission to be touched. For instance, if a youngster has been hurt by another child's remarks, and comes to the leader with tears in her or his eyes, before reaching out to hug that child, the leader should ask if the child wants a hug. Or, if in explaining an activity the leader needs to reposition someone she or he should ask, "Is it okay if I touch your arm?" prior to doing so. Furthermore, it is best to touch participants only in the view or presence of others. This way, if a question about the appropriateness of a touch arose at a later time, witnesses would be available to speak to what occurred.

It is the responsibility of the leader to understand the assumed power that goes with her or his position. Any touch from a leader, then, has the potential of being received in a way different than intended. Leaders who are aware of when and how they use touch tend to be safe and appropriate in their contacts.

Eye Contact

In the dominant U.S. culture people believe that eye contact is important in open and honest communication. It has been said that the "eyes are the window into the soul" and many believe that the eyes allow another to see earnestness and sincerity. In typical conversations people engage in more eye contact when listening than when speaking. Eye contact in listening is interpreted as an indicator of active listening and listening for understanding. It shows that the listener is fully engaged; it is difficult to daydream while looking an individual straight in the eyes. For leaders it is very important to engage in eye contact when speaking as well as when listening. Effective leaders will scan the room as they talk (i.e., making eye contact with participants) to invite feedback and keep participants engaged in the event or activity. Eye contact from the leader helps participants in feeling welcomed and valued.

There are cultural, gender, and power differences in how much and when eye contact is used and, as with other elements of nonverbal communication, an effective leader will have some level of understanding of these differences. For instance, in some Asian cultures individuals do not make eye contact when talking to elders and authority figures. In this instance direct eye contact is considered aggressive and disrespectful. In the dominant U.S. culture women and low-power individuals spend more time gazing at others (engaging in eye contact) than do men and high-power people. This has been attributed to the need of low-power individuals to attend to the moods and desires of high-power people in attempts to ensure others' needs are met. Understanding these types of differences will help in minimizing misinterpretation and miscommunication when interacting with others.

Facial Expressions

When decoding nonverbal communication patterns people look at the whole picture—quick observations are made of how an individual is standing, her or his posture, any gestures used, and the degree and intensity of eye contact. As this quick scan is conducted people key in on facial expressions in an attempt to correctly understand the message being sent. Facial expressions include smiles, forehead and face "scrunches" (often associated with not understanding something or disgust), frowns, and other facial expressions one can make with eyes, mouth, nose, eyebrows, and forehead.

Much understanding of messages (particularly as they are reflected back to us in terms of feedback) comes through correctly interpreting another's facial expressions. As leaders teach or instruct in activity leadership they look at participants to assess the messages being sent through facial expressions—boredom, fatigue, engagement, impatience, and so on. Once these nonverbal messages are received and interpreted the leader can make adjustments in her or his style of leadership, the pacing, or whatever best fits the situation. Another example of the usefulness and effect of facial expressions may be found in "the look."

Photo courtesy of the Black Hawk County Community Playhouse

Facial expressions can communicate clear and unambiguous messages.

Some leaders are very effective with "the look," which seems to have the power to silence loud participants and stop undesirable behavior. In addition to perfecting "the look," a second powerful tool of leisure services leaders is the smile. Appropriately used smiles (as with all nonverbal language) can aid in de-escalation of conflict, set the stage for a friendly and comfortable atmosphere, and make people feel welcomed. At the same time, leaders should be aware that smiles can be used inappropriately. For instance, if a leader smiles when being firm in an attempt to stop certain behaviors, conflicting messages might be sent. Conflicting messages are confusing and easily misinterpreted (or ignored). Smiling when angry or when needing to be authoritarian can be an area of concern for female leaders. Women (and lower power individuals) are prone to smile more than males, and often when trying to be firm and express anger. This often results in an increase or no change in undesirable behaviors.

Gestures

The sweeping motions of one's hands made when describing the "fish that got away" is an example of a gesture. Generally, the more power one has, the more sweeping the gestures one uses. This is related to proximity and the use of space discussed earlier. People who take up a small amount of space will tend to keep their hands, arms, and possessions close to their bodies. In using large spaces, more expansive gestures tend to be used.

Gestures may be used to get a group's attention, emphasize a point, or to provide clarity. For example, if a leader wants the group's attention she or he might clap her or his hands; to emphasize a particular point a leader might pound her or his fist; and if a leader asked participants to go into the next room and someone asked "Where?" the leader could point in the appropriate direction.

As one might imagine, gestures are culturally based; that is, those within a culture understand how to use and decode gestures accurately. Because gestures are culturally based there is much room for misinterpretation in crosscultural interactions. As an example, gangs have very elaborate nonverbal communication patterns; gestures are particularly important as symbols of being in or out of a gang. These gestures have meaning relative to membership, "brotherhood," safety, and upcoming activities. There have been many instances of individuals inadvertently using a "gang-only" gesture and being severely beaten for their "transgression."

Posture

The manner in which one walks, sits and stands constitutes posture. Most people believe that they can tell (from looking at and decoding body posture) if a person is happy, depressed, anxious, confident, or experiencing a host of other moods. The tallness with which one stands, the bounce in a step, and overall tenseness of one's body serve as various nonverbal cues. Leaders will want to be aware of the messages they send with their bodies because most participants receive their cues and motivation for behaviors from watching leaders and other participants. A leader who exudes confidence, energy and an upbeat attitude usually will engender similar attitudes and feelings in others.

Physical Appearance

While not a direct result of communicating through body movements, one's physical appearance certainly sends messages. The type of clothing one wears, choice of hairstyle and color, use of makeup, and the manner in which one wears them in ensemble, all communicate something about the individual. While certain hair styles might be in fashion (e.g., purple spikes) and send messages of individuality or rebellion against "the establishment," those same hair styles may not communicate confidence and competence in a leader. A professional, clean, and neat appearance is needed for effective leadership.

As with other elements of nonverbal communication it is important to recognize cultural differences—clothing or hairstyles that might be considered antiestablishment when worn by one person could be an expression of cultural pride in another. Clothing, hair style, tattoos, and body jewelry all may signify confidence, individuality, or group membership. Members of athletic swim teams, for instance, have been known to shave their heads prior to an important swim meet in a show of team spirit, cohesion, and to get "psyched up." Observers know at a glance that those with shaved heads are on the team and share a common goal.

As leaders develop their own understanding of what it means to be a professional and to engender an atmosphere of respect, credibility, and competence, it becomes clear where the lines should be drawn. For example, leaders who wear neatly pressed uniforms (shorts and T-shirts), wear their hair in "mainstream" fashions, and use makeup sparingly are typically perceived as more competent, credible, and worthy of respect than leaders who look unkempt or excessively fashionable.

Chronemics

Another related element to nonverbal communication that affects all leisure services leaders is called chronemics, or the use of time. In the predominant U.S. culture, time is perceived as being linear (it has a beginning and an end; once it is past it is gone forever) and is valued (people perceive their time as important to them). As such, being on time for meetings, events, and other gatherings is considered both polite and important. A leader who is consistently punctual is usually perceived as being respectful of others and as having credibility and competence.

As with other elements of nonverbal communication, the way one uses time can express power relationships as well as serve other functions. Making an individual wait until 2:20 when she or he had an appointment at 2:00 may be an indication of a power ploy—the individual who controls the resources (in this case, time) is more powerful than the other. If being late for an appointment is inevitable, alerting the one being inconvenienced by having to wait is the courteous and respectful thing to do.

In addition to time being used as a power issue, time must also be considered within the context of culture. In some Latin cultures, for example, time is perceived as cyclical (it follows natural rhythms) and "being on time" may mean "within an hour or two." Understanding differences allows a leader to prepare for and make a more accurate interpretation of what has occurred and react accordingly.

Because there are both cultural and individual differences in perception of time, one cannot assume that all staff or participants share values related to punctuality. Therefore, planning and conducting activities that allow for adding participants as they arrive will be important when leading activities with mixed groups. In this manner, people who arrive early and late can be accommodated and not left to feel disrespected or belittled.

Nonverbal language is that which is communicated without the spoken word. It tends to be the most trusted form of communication,

Figure 6.3   *Some cultures are strongly influenced by mechanized time while others rely on natural rhythms and cyclical time.*

although at the same time it may be perceived as ambiguous and difficult to understand exact meanings. The communication process is an interaction between people; therefore, power, gender, and cultural issues are intertwined with all aspects of it and will influence the accurate interpretation of nonverbal language.

Paraverbal Language

Nonverbal language consists of many elements—those that do not involve sounds such as body movements and physical appearance, and those that include sounds, but are not distinguishable as spoken words. These sounds or noises individuals make are known as *paraverbal language*. Paraverbal language includes noises and elements of speech which are used to enhance the spoken word. Pitch, rate, volume, inflection, accents, silences and pauses, and miscellaneous sounds are all considered aspects of paraverbal language.

Pitch

Pitch may be described as a musical note that the voice most closely resembles. Women generally have higher pitched voices than men; and boys' voice pitch lowers when they reach puberty. For most people, lower pitched voices (and noises) are easier to distinguish from other sounds and understand, and are more comfortable on the ear than are higher pitched voices or noises.

It is helpful if leaders recognize that in the U.S. culture we have come to associate authority with lower pitched voices. This is evidenced in television commercial voice-overs (e.g., the off-screen voice assuring the consumer that the item is a good buy), radio disc jockeys, and even in the voices people use when trying to stop misbehaviors (e.g., lifeguards tend to lower their voices when they shout, "Walk, don't run!" at the pool). On the other hand, higher pitched and softer voices are desirable when trying to soothe participants. Elevator voice recordings, recorded voices welcoming travelers to rest stops, and computer-generated voices at places like Disney World tend to be "female" voices. Leaders, then, will want to be aware of the pitch of their own voice and modulate it as needed to meet the needs of the situation.

Rate

Speech rate varies across individuals, groups by geographic region, and by culture. Some people speak quite rapidly (often a stereotype of those reared in the northeastern United States) while others speak much more slowly (considered typical of those who live in the southern U.S.). We have come to liken speech rate to speaker competence and intelligence often assuming (to a point) that the quicker one speaks, the more competent and intelligent that individual is. In reality, of course, speech rate has little to do with competence or intelligence. Understanding the perception of speech rate may help a leader in selecting an appropriate rate of speech when speaking to different groups.

Volume

The loudness of how one speaks and the way a person projects her or his voice are related to volume. Some people are loud talkers while others speak so softly that it is difficult to hear them. To be effective in accomplishing tasks, leaders need to practice using a well-modulated voice that becomes louder or softer as the situation calls for it. Projecting one's voice requires maintaining a conversational tone and inflection, yet increasing in volume. This increase in volume is not the same as shouting or yelling. Shouting or yelling often has a negative, punishing tone to it, while increased volume simply allows people who are at a distance from the leader to hear what she or he is saying.

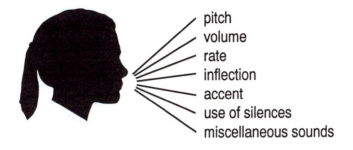

pitch
volume
rate
inflection
accent
use of silences
miscellaneous sounds

Figure 6.4   *Used appropriately, paralanguage enhances both verbal and nonverbal language.*

Inflection

No matter the language one speaks, it is usually evident to others who also speak the same language whether the person speaking is asking a question or making an assertion. The manner in which one's voice goes up or down in pitch at the end of a sentence usually indicates the type of statement being made. In the dominant U.S. culture a question "goes up" at the end while a statement or assertion tends to drop at the end. People who speak with an "up" inflection at the end of statements are often perceived as less capable and less sure of themselves than those whose speech drops at the end of a sentence. Inflection is somewhat regionalized; for example, people living in the south tend to use sentences that end going "up."

Accents

Some people believe that everyone has an accent or characteristic way of pronouncing certain words. Others believe that only those other than themselves have accents. What is likely is that to someone somewhere, every person pronounces certain words in particular ways which tend to be distinct to a particular region of the country. As with speech rate, many have come to associate particular accents with competence and intelligence of the speaker. Stereotypes (or incorrect assumptions) abound and leaders would be wise to be aware that a flat, Midwestern-type accent is often perceived with a good deal of authority and believability, while those with southern "drawls" often find their intelligence questioned.

Silences and Pauses

Silences and pauses are used in communication so frequently that many of us do not notice when they are used. Those who use silences and pauses effectively can hold the attention of a group and draw them into the communication process. One effective use of silence is after asking a question. Educational research has shown that most teachers ask a question, pause momentarily, then move on if the individual does not have an immediate answer. Typically, however, it takes several seconds for people to gather their thoughts and respond in an appropriate fashion. Waiting for five to ten seconds to elapse before rephrasing a question or going on to someone else (Sadker & Sadker, 1994) would be useful for leaders who wish to engage others in meaningful dialogue.

Miscellaneous Sounds

In "normal speech" people commonly use sounds such as "ummm," "ahh," and "hmm" to serve as space savers and turn holders. In conversation, when an individual pauses in midsentence to complete a thought she or he will often use a sound to prevent another individual from entering the conversation. Should another individual wish to enter the conversation, but realize the time is not yet right, she or he may insert one of these sounds to indicate that she or he desires a turn speaking next. In this way, paraverbal language helps to regulate communication.

In addition to the typical sounds used to hold one's speaking turn, we also make other sounds; "tsk," "pshaw," and "huh?" are three of those paraverbal sounds that serve an important function in communication. Depending upon their use (e.g., timing, when in conversation) these sounds may serve to indicate a particular thought or emotion (e.g., disbelief, discounting, confusion). There are many other sounds which are used to emphasize a point, serve in the place of words, convey an emotion, or save a turn. A leader who understands the use of these sounds will be a more effective communicator than one who does not understand the use of paraverbal language.

In addition to body language, physical appearance, and paraverbal language, communication also occurs through use of symbols. In leisure services settings symbols are used in everyday situations: on letterhead, staff uniforms, promotional materials, and agency vehicles, to identify a few.

Symbolic Language

Symbolic language is the use of symbols to convey a message. This may be seen in the use and proliferation of logos (on T-shirts, posters, promotional materials, agency vehicles) and signs which have a clear meaning. For instance, if a group were to see a set of golden arches up the road most would realize that a McDonald's restaurant was ahead. Similarly, the symbol of a red circle with a diagonal slash mark through it has an international meaning of "No whatever-is-in-the-circle."

Symbols as language can be very powerful and are often used as indications of membership in an organization. Athletic teams wear logos and symbols on their clothing which helps team members to identify one another. This is also true of corporations, gangs, and neighborhood associations. Symbolic language has great significance for a sense of belonging and inclusion.

Recently there has been much attention focused on the use of symbols that perpetuate derogatory or stereotypical portrayals of ethnic groups. This is most commonly seen related to schools, colleges, and professional sports teams with team logos and mascots. An example of this is the controversy over the name, logo, and fan chants of the Atlanta Braves. The "tomahawk chop" is a nonverbal gesture made by fans that to some Native Americans is denigrating and perpetuates stereotypes. The messages sent by the visual depictions of an organization are strong and memorable. Leisure services agencies and leaders of those agencies

no entry   wheelchair-accessible restrooms   campground   no pets (except those assisting the blind)

parking   recycle   food   fragile

Figure 6.5   *Symbolic language can communicate a simple message in an efficient manner.*

may wish to consider all possible implications of using certain symbolic language to represent the agency prior to selecting a symbol.

Written Language

Communication skills for leaders include the ability to speak, listen, use paraverbal language effectively, understand symbolic communication and the ability to write in a professional manner. Often, at the direct leadership level verbal and nonverbal language skills are emphasized and little or no mention is made of writing skills. This may be due to the fact that most direct leaders are frequently in front of participants using verbal and nonverbal communication skills. The writing required of leaders often is infrequent and less valued than physical leadership. With the advent of computer technology, however, business and professional writing skills have become even more essential than before the advent of these various forms of communication.

Many leisure services leaders hold the erroneous assumption that writing skills do not matter and that the departmental secretary will serve as the editor and proofreader of all paperwork. This is far from the truth. Many agencies do not have access to this type of editorial assistance and clerical personnel are not always skilled in these areas. Furthermore, the general public will be exposed to a leader writing promotional copy, business letters, signs in the facility, and client reports, and will form opinions about her or his capabilities based on this contact. Learning how to write professionally, therefore, is essential to effective and competent leadership.

Leisure services leaders at all levels write their own reports, memos, and business letters and must have good writing skills to do this efficiently and effectively. Specifically, writing will occur in reports (e.g., accident/incident reports, inventories, client progress reports, contracts, and the like), letters (e.g., to potential employers, registrants, sponsors, parents, and equipment manufacturers), and in promotional materials (e.g., signage, schedule books, flyers, special event information, and public service announcements). While each of these requires slightly different types of writing, each demands basic skills in grammar, composition, spelling, and layout.

Writing may occur on hard copy (e.g., paper, letterhead) or on computer (e.g., Internet, World Wide Web) and in either case, good writing requires practice and feedback. It is very easy to let incomplete or sloppy work be sent out on electronic mail, for example. Leaders who are committed to a sense of professionalism tend to basic rules of writing in composition and spelling. Effective and high quality written material should be:

- readable by the intended audience (for instance, language and style are different if the material is intended for children or adults);

- precise and to the point (begins at the beginning, says what needs to be said, and ends);

- accurate in detail (vague or inaccurate information may lead to miscommunication);

- complete thoughts (ambiguous thoughts or half-finished ideas leave the reader wondering what the message was to be);

- worded in the active voice ("Tomika led the activity" rather than, "The activity was led by Tomika"); and

- well-focused relative to the purpose of the communication (e.g., being persuasive, sharing information, expressing social relationships).

Figure 6.6   *Leisure services leaders must be skilled in several forms of written communication.*

As with verbal language in written communication, using appropriate grammar, proper spelling, complete sentences, and nonsexist and inclusive language are important to communicating the intended message. Once written materials are complete they are usually available for a variety of constituents to review. Leaders would be wise to remember that many individuals (e.g., participants, the general public, employers) will develop their first impression of the leader through samples of the leader's writing. Competence, intelligence, and sensitivity are a few of the positive characteristics people ascribe to authors of materials. Taking the time to write and design written materials professionally and continually seeking improvement in that area are signs of mature leaders.

Summary

Nonverbal communication is a complex aspect of the communication process. It serves to aid in impression management, as a sign of membership in a group, and to help regulate the communication interaction. This is accomplished through providing feedback, emphasizing a verbal message, holding a turn, and serving as a substitution for words. In addition, nonverbal communication expresses a variety of social relationships such as power and dominance, compliance, affect management, and social intimacy. It tends to be the more trusted form of communication.

Elements of body language such as proximity, the use of touch, eye contact, facial expressions, and gestures constitute some of what is considered nonverbal language. Other elements include physical appearance, the use of time, and paraverbal communication. Effective leaders are aware of their own and other's uses of these aspects of the communication process. In addition, it is crucial to recognize and acknowledge cultural differences in nonverbal language so as to avoid embarrassing situations.

Symbolic language utilizes signs and symbols to portray messages. Examples of this are found in leisure services agency logos and on street signs. In addition to wise use of symbolic language, good professional writing skills are required of direct leaders in many situations—leisure services leaders are often involved in report writing, developing signs and schedules, writing letters, and memoranda. Therefore, developing solid writing skills is an important skill for leisure services leaders at every level. The communication process operates in several media including verbal, nonverbal, and paraverbal skills, as well as symbolic and written language.

The Front Line

A recent article published in the *Chronicle of Higher Education* (McDonald, 1995) reported that leaders can transmit fear (a highly undesirable trait in a leader) by looking down, hesitating, making rapid, jerky motions, or by seeming to freeze when in difficult situations. McDonald indicated that the:

> traits people expect in body language of leaders include a certain amount of smoothness in movement, an absence of threatening behavior to subordinates, and the capacity to adapt to different social situations. (p. A6)

A warm smile at the appropriate time can make people feel safe and respond positively to the leader.

To better understand her or his own use of nonverbal and paraverbal language, a leisure services leader may wish to be videotaped in a variety of leadership positions. Studying videotape of oneself engaging in leadership activities is often very effective in helping to improve communication skills. Through observing videotapes of leadership activities leaders learn such things as: overuse of paraverbal language (e.g., "you know," "uhhh"), stiffness or constraint in movements or overly aggressive gestures, lack of eye contact with participants, lack of smiling or overuse of smiling, and contradictions between nonverbal language and the verbal message. All of this feedback can help a leader improve her or his direct leadership skills.

References

Burgoon, M., Dawson, E., and Hunsaker, F. (1994). *Human communication* (3rd ed.). Newbury Park, CA: Sage Publications, Inc.

Carbaugh, D. (Ed.). (1990). *Cultural communication and intercultural contact.* Hillsdale, NJ: Lawrence Erlbaum Associates.

Daly, J. and Wiemann, J. (Eds.). (1994). *Strategic interpersonal communication.* Hillsdale, NJ: Lawrence Erlbaum Associates.

Gibson, J. and Hanna, M. (1992). *Introduction to human communication.* Dubuque, IA: Wm. C. Brown Publishing.

Hayes, J. (1994). *Interpersonal skills.* London, UK: Routledge.

Kalbfleisch, P. and Cody, M. (Eds.). (1995). *Gender, power, and communication in human relationships.* Hillsdale, NJ: Lawrence Erlbaum Associates.

McDonald, K. (1995, January). Nonverbal language and leaders, *The Chronicle of Higher Education, XLII*(17), pp. A6-A7.

Patterson, M. (1983). *Nonverbal behavior: A functional perspective.* Secaucus, NJ: Springer-Verlag New York, Inc.

Pearson, J., West, R., and Turner, L. (1995). *Gender and communication* (3rd ed.). Dubuque, IA: Brown & Benchmark.

Sadker, M. and Sadker, D. (1994). *Failing at fairness: How our schools cheat girls.* New York, NY: Touchstone.

Verderber, R. and Verderber, K. (1992). *Inter-Act: Using interpersonal communication skills* (6th ed.). Belmont, CA: Wadsworth Publishing, Co.

Chapter Seven
Learning Opportunities

Through studying this chapter students will have the opportunity to:

- be exposed to the benefits and advantages of conflicts and problems;
- understand how difficulties escalate across a spectrum of struggle intensity;
- discover various approaches to handling difficulties;
- integrate knowledge of the sources of conflict with conflict management strategies; and
- explore the methods of leader involvement in mediating difficulties.

Photo courtesy of Black Hawk County Community Playhouse

CHAPTER

7

Managing Difficulties

Leaders of parks, recreation, and leisure services face a variety of problems, conflicts, and difficulties in their positions. Examples of common difficulties include equipment that breaks down, a participant has a question about payment of an invoice, a group of participants are dissatisfied with quality of services, and there may be disagreements between participants in structured programs. Common difficulties, then, range from simple problems related to equipment to complex conflict resolution issues involving multiple parties. Difficulties and struggles are a normal and natural aspect of working with people in various environments and are found in every leisure services setting. Therefore, developing an understanding of difficulties and how to manage them is a vital skill for leisure services leaders.

A problem tends to be relatively objective and involves a situation or objects, while a conflict usually involves difficulties between people. A problem often is a question to be considered, solved, or answered and it may be a situation, matter, or person that presents a perceived perplexity or difficulty. Problems might involve such dilemmas as a glitch in a computer program, attending to ineffective promotional strategies, or addressing changing staffing needs. Conflicts frequently arise out of problems and are feared and avoided by many leaders. Conflict (and other difficulties) is a natural process, however, which is inherent in all important relationships (Hocker & Wilmot, 1991). As such, a conflict is an expressed struggle between two or more interdependent people who perceive differences in goal activity. This means that people are linked together and something arises that interferes with the relationship and what they desire to accomplish. As one might imagine, by its very nature communication is integral to conflict. In fact, communication *creates* conflict, *reflects* conflict, and is a *vehicle* for the productive management of conflict (Hocker & Wilmot, 1991). Conflict, like communication, is a mutual activity; essentially, it takes two (or more) people for conflict to exist.

Conflict is beneficial in many ways. According to Worchel and Simpson (1993), conflict:

- forces people to examine their self-concepts;
- forces individuals to seek evidence to support their positions;
- results in self-examination;
- provides a sense of identity; and
- stimulates creativity.

Others have indicated that conflict also aids in problem awareness, improved solutions, and serves as a catalyst for change. Conflict is necessary to healthy group development as it is vital to growing and maturing relationships. Without conflict, relationships stagnate and wither away (Tjosvold, 1993). As discussed in Chapter Four, each process or stage of group development requires some degree of conflict to occur for the group to move into the next phase of maturity.

While conflict and problems are beneficial in many ways, relationships continually embroiled in conflict are not healthy. This, of course, is also true for instances where conflicts are lacking or consistently avoided. As stated by Worchel and Simpson "... it is not the conflict that is the problem, but rather the management and response to conflict that determines the health of the unit" (1993, p. 79). Leisure services leaders can exert a positive influence on the outcome of problems and conflicts faced in leisure settings.

Leaders, after all, often have the authority to "make things happen" and manage the difficulty to the satisfaction of all. In addition, the role of managing difficulties is appropriate for leaders because they are in positions of responsibility to meet others' needs, are accountable to supervisors and the public, and are often in a facilitating role. Furthermore, leisure services leaders are responsible for quality service, and the appropriate management of difficulties typically results in improved services. In addition to these pragmatic issues, many leisure services leaders also engage in problem management due to personal ethics or obligations related to the issues in question.

What is Conflict Resolution and Difficulty Management?

Conflict resolution refers to the process of resolving disagreements with the use of specific conflict resolution skills. These basic skills (expressing emotions clearly, defining the problem specifically, reflective listening, and creative brainstorming) are set into a step-by-step framework for addressing the problem (Koch & Jordan, 1993). Depending upon the situation, the skills of the disputants and the seriousness of the problem, the involved individuals may work to solve their own problem (i.e., negotiation), or they may ask someone else to serve as a conflict manager (i.e., mediation). Whatever technique is used, the goal of conflict resolution is to create a win-win solution (Hocker & Wilmot, 1991).

There are many ways to look at the development of conflict and other problems. Whatever model one utilizes to better understand how issues develop into conflicts, it should be noted that most researchers agree that the process is generally linear, yet also loops back on itself. If managed at any one stage, one "spins off" of the conflict development and management loop; if things are not resolved one continues on to the next stages.

The Struggle Spectrum

Keltner (1994) presents a "Struggle Spectrum" which illustrates the staged development of various types of difficulties faced by people in conflict. The difficulties range from mild differences to a violent interaction (e.g., fight). As one can see from Table 7A (pages 226-227), maintaining and diffusing conflicts at the disagreement level is important. Once a struggle moves to the dispute stage goals are no longer intertwined and escalation is likely. Leisure services leaders should be prepared for all degrees of struggle as each type of difficulty is faced to some degree in the leisure services field.

Consider the following example of struggle development. Two girls are playing board games; one moves her piece down the board and the second child thinks the first went out of turn. Child 2 tells Child 1 to go back, because she went out of turn (mild difference). Child 1 does not believe she was out of order and says she will keep her piece where

Table 7A   **The Struggle Spectrum.** If not managed early in the
process, conflict escalates from left to right on the chart.

CONDITIONS	STAGE 1 Mild Difference	STAGE 2 Disagreement	STAGE 3 Dispute
Processes Leading to Resolution	discussion	discussion negotiation	argument bargaining
Problem-Solving Behavior	joint problem solving	contentions over choices	rational proof & game playing by rules
Relationship between Parties	partners, friends & acquaintances	rivals	opponents
Goals	includes other	includes other	excludes other
Orientation to Each Other	cooperative & amicable	disputative conciliatory	win-lose 1 hostile
Communication	open-friendly	open, but strained	limited tense
Decision Making	mutual decisions	joint decisions and agreements	joint decision in mediation; third party decisions in arbitration
Intervention Process	none needed	mediation by neutral party	mediation or arbitration by neutral party
Possible Outcomes	integrated agreement; mutual satisfaction	accommodated agreement with both satisfied	compromise agreement or one wins, but one or both dissatisfied
Intractability Potential	very low	low	medium

NOTES:
A. Mediation is relatively useless in Stages 1, 4, 5, and 6, but may be used in Stage 4 under special arrangement.
B. Win-Lose escalates from Level 1 to Level 3. The longer it exists, the more intense it becomes.
C. Neutral third parties have no stake in the outcome of the struggle. They include mediators, arbitrators, judges and juries.
D. Parties lose their joint decision-making power when mediation is no longer applicable.

Table 7A The Struggle Spectrum (continued)

STAGE 4 Campaign	STAGE 5 Litigation	STAGE 6 Fight or War
persuasion pressure	advocacy debate	violent conflict
emotional and logical strategies	selective proofs before judges or juries	psychological or physical violence
competitors	antagonists	enemies
excludes other	excludes other	eliminates other
win-lose 2 estranged	win-lose 3 alienated	irreconcilable
restricted & planned	blocked & controlled	closed except for violent acts
vote by constituents or third-party decisions	third-party courtroom; decisions by judge or jury	each side seeks control by forcing the other
arbitration by neutral party or election-vote	arbitration or judge or jury	force of police or other military or power intervention
a win or draw. winner pleased with loser accepting but dissatisfied	one wins and winner celebrates. loser frustrated, etc.	one prevails. other or both destroyed or harmed. high fear in both
high	high	very high

NOTES (continued):
E. When issues are not resolved at one stage, the tendency is to move to the right on the continuum.
F. De-escalation from right to left is possible under special circumstances.
G. Disputes may become intractable (stalemated) at any stage in the process and may thus require special efforts to "unfreeze" them.

Keltner, J. S. (1992). The Struggle Spectrum. Reprinted with permission of Hampton Press, Cresskill, NJ.

it is; Child 2 is not successful in getting Child 1 to remove her piece and begins to get angry (disagreement)—the conflict escalates.

At this point Child 2 yells for the activity leader to come over and state the rules—"if you go out of turn you have to move your piece back;" Child 1 still disagrees that she is out of order (argument) and refuses to move her piece (both children are now visibly upset and yelling at one another). Child 2 resorts to whining and making nonverbal threats (e.g., closed fist, angry facial expression) to try and persuade Child 1 to move her piece off the board (campaign). Child 2 is unsuccessful and shouts for the activity leader again to make Child 1 stop cheating, take her piece off the board, and rule that Child 2 won. Child 2 wants the staff member to make the decision related to who is correct (litigation). This effort also fails and Child 2 resorts to dumping the game board upside down and striking Child 1 (violence and fight).

This movement from mild difference to violent interaction can occur very rapidly—in a matter of five to ten minutes. If the youngsters (or the leader) had basic conflict management skills, it is possible that they could have resolved the issue of turn taking early and continued to play in harmony. Without these skills, the situation escalated out of control.

Escalation

Throughout the above scenario, the situation escalated—that is, it got worse. The conflict was not successfully managed during any of the many levels of conflict and it moved quickly through the process until it reached a point of violence. In any conflict, regardless of cause, there are certain behaviors that are almost guaranteed to escalate the problem and other behaviors that will generally have the opposite effect. Whether or not the steps of a conflict resolution process are being followed, individuals can choose to make matters worse or move toward diffusing the conflict by exhibiting certain behaviors. Conflicts are likely to get worse when:

- people raise their voices;
- people make themselves physically larger (e.g., by standing up);
- personal space is invaded (e.g., "getting in someone's face");

- other people get involved in the problem and take sides;
- past conflicts are brought up (e.g., especially if the phrases "you always" and/or "you never" are used);
- one or both disputants feel threatened in some fashion; and
- there is an increase in acting out anger, fear, or frustration (Koch & Jordan, 1993).

De-escalation

Escalation serves to increase the difficulties and emotions involved in a conflict; de-escalation helps to mitigate emotions and reduce difficulties. De-escalation strategies, even if used by only one of the disputants, tend to make a conflict far more manageable than if not used. In the same way that escalating behaviors are chosen, individuals can also de-escalate conflicts by choosing to:

- speak in a calm and evenly modulated voice;
- sit down and maintain an open posture;
- allow for a comfortable distance between disputants;
- talk directly to the person with whom the conflict exists;
- focus on the problem at hand and stay away from personality issues; and
- identify and express emotions appropriately (Koch & Jordan, 1993).

Reasons and Sources of Conflict

Conflicts and problems arise for a variety of reasons. Understanding these reasons will help leisure services leaders in their attempts to manage difficulties in which they are involved, and when facilitating others to manage their own differences. Researchers studying the issue see conflicts arising out of three basic sources: *distribution of resources, individual psychological needs,* and *conflicts over values* (Cox, 1993; Crawley, 1994; Hocker & Wilmot, 1991; Koch & Jordan, 1993). These sources of conflict exist for people of all ages and lifestyles.

Resources

Conflicts over resources generally are manifested in power struggles where one person perceives an inequity in the distribution of resources. Young children might engage in conflicts over control of toys or equipment, teens might experience difficulties over control of certain parts of town (e.g., "turf" issues), and adults might engage in struggles over money and time. Resources include both tangible resources such as trophies, use of adaptive equipment, and court time; and intangible resources such as self-esteem, authority, and prestige or status. Leaders can minimize resource conflicts by ensuring that tangible (i.e., equipment) and intangible resources (i.e., leader attention) are equitably distributed.

Individual Psychological Needs

In addition to competing for resources, another reason people engage in conflicts is due to individual social and psychological needs. Competing or incompatible goals, power discrepancies, personality clashes, conflicting motivators, and unmet needs such as the need for security and the need for belonging all fit within this category. If the disputing individuals are experiencing different needs and do not recognize their own needs, conflict is likely to arise. For instance, if one participant in a group has a need to express her or his creativity while another group member operates out of a need for physical rehabilitation, conflict might arise over how to achieve both goals. Leisure services leaders would be well-served to consider individual needs when leading various programs.

Values

The third general category of sources of conflict or difficulties includes value differences. Value differences typically arise out of cultural differences, religious beliefs, or personal belief systems. Values that vary from one individual to another include those related to the rights of others, work, leisure, honesty, loyalty, the law, and the environment. Conflicts over values are the most difficult to resolve because they are deeply entwined in one's identity and are developed over years of exposure and reinforcement.

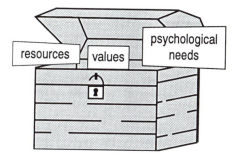

Figure 7.1   *Three basic sources of conflict impact each one of us on different levels.*

Factors that Lead to Difficulties

Many factors contribute to the likelihood of difficulties occurring. For instance, the more opportunities one has for interactions with others, the more likely conflict of some type is to arise. The visibility of differences between those interacting also impacts the likelihood of conflict; that is, the more visible and obvious the differences, the more likely the conflict. In addition to the tangible factors leading to conflict, perceived incompatibility (i.e., people believe they will not get along with or like one another) also influences the nature and strength of difficulties (Sims & Dennehy, 1993; Väyrynen, 1991).

Approaches to Conflict

Whether addressing issues related to conflict management or problem solving, similar approaches to managing difficulties may be taken. Not all approaches are equally beneficial in all situations and there are times when some approaches are actually detrimental to relationships and the successful management of the conflict. Nonetheless, the approaches are valid for leisure services leaders in different situations. The five most common approaches to managing conflicts include *avoidance, accommodation, competition, compromise,* and *collaboration* (Bannon & Busser, 1992; Brightman, 1988; Burgoon, Dawson & Hunsaker, 1994; Hocker & Wilmot, 1991; McLean & Weitzel, 1991).

Avoidance

Many individuals are well-skilled at conflict avoidance. When a difficulty arises individuals who are skilled in avoidance techniques might engage in denial ("What problem? There is no problem!"), shift topics ("Problem? Say, did you hear about the new facility being built down the road?"), make noncommittal comments ("Problem? It certainly does need to be addressed."), make irreverent remarks ("Problem? Ah, they'll get over it!") or ignore the issue completely.

An avoidance approach is an unassertive method to dealing with very real issues. It often indicates a lack of respect for oneself and fear of dealing with the issue or person involved. Often, this approach is used when the leader is hesitant to hurt someone's feelings, when the leader is fearful that others will cease liking her or him, and when one does not want to take the time to address the concern. Avoidance usually results in a lose-lose situation—no one comes out ahead and the difficulty remains.

Accommodation

Accommodation is another nonassertive approach. In this instance, however, rather than avoiding the issue, the facilitator attempts to cooperate with (do a favor for or yield to) others. Accommodation involves doing as the other needs or requests; it is essentially obliging the other party. For instance, a leader might handle a conflict over a shared facility by giving in to the most vocal and persistent participant rather than actually addressing the issue at hand. Accommodation is often viewed as a win-lose relationship and may reflect a lack of confidence in self.

Competition

Competitive reactions to difficulties may be seen in verbal aggression and confrontation between two (or more) individuals; this is often characterized as a one-up relationship. In a competitive approach to conflict, each party seeks to overpower and dominate the other. Often, personal criticism and attacks are utilized as are hostile jokes or questions, and a denial of responsibility for the situation. Competitive reactions to conflict may be observed in arguments by young children over who gets to play with which toy—there is a great amount of grabbing, shoving and screaming by both parties involved. Teens and adults also engage in competitive approaches to conflicts. A competitive approach to problem solving is perceived as a win-lose relationship, and while it serves the needs of one, it is unhealthy for all disputants.

Compromise

In compromise each side gives in or concedes some aspects of its position to the other. It is reflective of a give-and-take philosophy where the goal is to obtain an equal exchange in the resolution or management of the conflict. Often when they compromise, participants feel as though neither party has achieved a satisfactory conclusion to the issue. An example might be a disagreement over which activity to play for the last twenty minutes of a session. The parties might agree to play two games for ten minutes each, which is not enough time for either participant to truly enjoy her or his favorite activity. This approach may be viewed as a lose-lose or weak win-win conflict management approach.

Collaboration

Collaboration is the most preferred difficulty management technique. It involves each individual attempting to work toward meeting the goals of the other and doing so together. It is distinguished from compromise in that in compromise each party gives up something to move ahead. In collaboration each party looks to work together and combine resources in moving ahead. In collaboration both parties work jointly and accept responsibility for the final decision. It is a win-win position for all involved. An example of collaborative problem solving might be in meeting two different needs—one group member has a need for status, another a need to complete the task. They might work together to accomplish the task and then address the status issue through publicly naming those directly responsible for the task completion.

Selecting the Best Approach

Brightman (1988) suggests that a two dimensional model be utilized to examine the options in managing difficulties. In it, one examines the level of assertiveness and the degree of cooperation between the involved parties (see Figure 7.2, page 234). This is similar in concept to the Managerial Grid presented in Chapter Two which identified a wide range of leadership behaviors based on two dimensions.

According to Brightman (1988) interpersonal conflict may be handled by examining two dimensions—level of assertiveness and

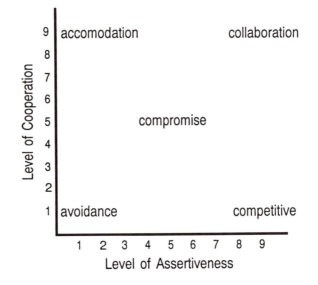

Figure 7.2   The five common approaches to managing conflicts may be placed on an assertiveness-cooperation grid.

level of cooperation.   A position low in cooperation and low in assertiveness would be characteristic of the *avoidance* approach. An individual at these coordinates does not take a strong position with regard to the conflict; constructive problem solving is usually not possible utilizing this technique. One who is high in assertion and low in cooperation usually is exhibiting a *competitive* approach to conflict management. Little discussion is evident, conflicts are not addressed, and others are often bullied into agreement.

A leader demonstrating a high cooperation and low assertion combination is likely manifesting conflict management as *accommodation*. For this individual, group harmony is the ultimate goal, yet problem solutions are often ineffective. A mark in the center of the grid showing a medium amount of both cooperation and assertion typically results in *compromise*. Involved parties seek middle ground, and each gives up some of what they want. In a high cooperation and high assertion position one is in the *collaboration* mode. Here, individuals confront disagreements openly, people listen to one another, disagreements are not perceived as personal, and effective management of the difficulty results.

Effective Conflict Management for Leisure Services Leaders

To be effective in managing various types of difficulties, leaders need to understand that when in conflict people will see things very differently from one another; perceptions of the problem situation differ and by varying degrees. Perceptions are based on personal filters (i.e., how one sees the world), first impressions of those involved, and past experiences. Leaders who are aware of their own feelings relative to the situation (e.g., the other person, the environment, personal fatigue, timing), who focus on the entire situation, who seek to change positions and understand varying viewpoints, and are aware of their own biases and prejudices related to the persons involved tend to be more effective than others in managing difficulties (Crawley, 1994).

A leader who is a *constructive conflict manager* has many traits: an ability to understand and deal with difficult emotions; empathy and the ability to earn trust; openness and sensitivity to others; emotional balance (i.e., understands own feelings and their impact on the situation); self-awareness and integrity; the ability to take a nonjudgmental stance; the capacity to learn from experiences; a willingness to be assertive; the ability to think creatively and deal with complex factual material; and an ethic of thoroughness and professionalism. Effective and well-respected leaders also exhibit these traits.

Guidelines for Constructive Management of Difficulties

Learning to manage conflicts and solve problems is an ongoing process of new and improved skill development, and it is often helpful to follow a set of general guidelines when learning new skills. It is also important to remember that dealing with conflict management and problem solving can be a very emotional and complex situation—for both the conflict manager and those directly involved in the issue. Managing difficulties well requires creative thinking, self-awareness, a knowledge of management techniques, and strong communication skills. The following guidelines may help leaders in successful conflict management:

- address the emotional issues first by acknowledging and validating each person's feelings ("You seem very angry right now");

- as a facilitator, be clear about what you see, how you judge, and how you react to people and situations (I have a tendency to judge quickly so I should take a moment to gather my thoughts before making up my mind);

- practice "no fault" thinking (This situation is not the fault of any one person; it exists and must be addressed);

- as a facilitator, understand and take charge of your own feelings and behaviors (I am fatigued and might not see things as clearly as I should);

- step back and take a balanced view of the situation;

- observe and analyze the conflict from three perspectives: mine, yours/theirs, and the "fly on the wall";

- respond positively to what is done and what is said ("I appreciate your willingness to work through this");

- remember that managing conflict is a process (what occurs during the management process is just as important as the end result);

- keep process activities and statements in the first person; use "I" statements (An "I message" is a four part statement: "I feel (name the emotion), when (this occurs), because (identify the effect on self), and I would like (this to happen)."); and

- beware of and avoid power plays and power issues between disputants.

Constructive management of problems and conflicts involves being self-aware as well as being willing to consider all sides of an issue. Remember that within each person's perception a bit of the truth is found. It is also helpful to remember that perceptions are very real to each individual. Discounting individual comments and insights as "wrong" or "stupid" may lead to a future unwillingness to address conflict in a proactive and straightforward fashion.

Models of Conflict Management

Having discussed the inevitability and nature of conflict, the five basic approaches one can take to managing conflict, and general guidelines for addressing conflict, we will now turn our attention to the actual management of those conflicts and problems. A standard approach to addressing various difficulties moves from first identifying the issue through several interim stages to implementing and evaluating the proposed management solutions (Brody, 1991; Cockrell, 1991; Hitt, 1993; Savage, 1991; Schwarz, 1994).

Seven-Phase Model of Managing Difficulties

A seven-phase model to successful management of various types of difficulties has been developed by combining many of the models offered by several authors (Bannon & Busser, 1992; Bethel, 1990; Brody, 1991; Crawley, 1994; Savage, 1991; Schwarz, 1994; Worchel & Simpson, 1993).

Phase 1—Define the Objectives for the Solution

First, it is important that the objectives for the solution be in congruence with agency objectives. This means that a leader must have a solid understanding of the agency mission and philosophy so that as solutions are discussed the leader is assured the solutions fall within the scope of agency values and practice. Both short-term and long-term issues should be identified and articulated. How does managing this issue in this manner relate to the existing values structure of the agency? How does addressing this issue in this manner relate to the long-term goals of the agency?

Once goals, objectives, and values are clearly stated it will be important to agree to the *process* of conflict management. Agreeing to and openly articulating where, when and how the process will occur is necessary to serve as a basis for the work ahead. These logistical concerns are important so that all involved parties agree to and operate within the same ground rules.

Phase 2—Identify the Problem

At this stage it is important to spend some time and collect facts surrounding the conflict. The goal of this phase is to diagnose the problem; therefore, identifying and determining the underlying causes of the problem is very important. Many problems are not as straightforward as they might appear on the surface. For instance, if two individuals are arguing over a minor rule infraction the real issue might be that one participant feels ignored and disrespected by the other. In this example and in many "real life" situations, psychological needs often manifest themselves in seemingly unrelated manners.

Seeking information from as many individuals as possible (while at the same time keeping an open mind) helps to present a clear and relatively complete picture of the actual situation. It also will be helpful to list the driving forces that seem to perpetuate the problem. When does the difficulty arise? What seems to escalate the problem? When does the problem dissipate? This information helps later in data analysis and interpretation.

Phase 3—Data Analysis and Interpretation

After identifying and stating the problem those involved in facilitating and managing conflicts will be interested in analyzing and interpreting the data (i.e., facts). To do this it is helpful to determine the factors that seem to influence and change the conflict. A conflict manager will want to make observations of both positive and negative factors involved in the changes surrounding the conflict. Using past experiences and good judgment in examining the entire situation will be needed at this stage. Once all the information has been gathered, what does it all mean? Understanding the context in which an issue arose and the people involved are important elements of this stage.

Phase 4—Facilitate Creative Solutions

Facilitating creative solutions often is the most enjoyable aspect of managing conflicts and problems. It is the time when new, fresh, and creative ideas are sought and welcomed. In fact, at this stage, the negative emotions often associated with the issues at hand are set aside to allow for freedom of expression and a sense of play in the brainstorming process. Brainstorming is the most commonly used technique to facilitate the development of creative solutions; and many people are familiar with the concept. A common error in brainstorming, however, is to undervalue the process and get off track and into justifying and qualifying suggestions. To be effective, brainstorming principles should be strictly followed.

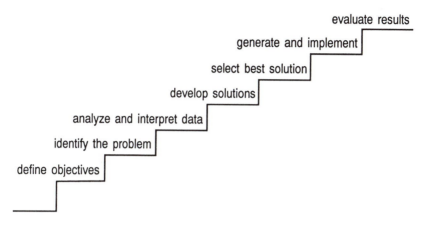

Figure 7.3   *The Seven-Phase Model for managing problems*

Principles of brainstorming:

- Arrange the group so that each member can see one another; a circle arrangement is often the best option. Being able to make eye contact with others in the group lends itself to supporting an open atmosphere. An open and "safe" atmosphere is vital to effective brainstorming.

- Be aware of the impact of the physical environment on the brainstorming process. Room temperature, lighting, and the comfort level afforded by the chairs in which people are sitting impact the flow of creative thought. Comfort is important.

- A large quantity of ideas (rather than quality) is desired at this point. Aiming for quantity tends to encourage new thoughts and keeps the pace moving quickly. An overconcern for quality at this stage can inhibit freewheeling thought and stifle ideas.

- Freewheeling and zany ideas are welcomed; in fact, the crazier and more creative the ideas the better. It is often out of one of the most "unreal" ideas that elegant solutions are found.

- Group members should avoid critical judgments and qualifiers attached to ideas. Encourage individuals to present their ideas and then move on to the next brainstorming idea.

Lengthy justifications and explanations tend to inhibit the creative process. Likewise, if group members feel that as soon as they say something another person is going to judge it "stupid" or "weird," people will stop participating.

• Participants should strive to combine and piggyback on ideas. Once ideas are out on the floor they belong to the group and adding to them, looking at them backwards, combining two or more, and modifying them in some other fashion all lead to creating additional creative ideas. Everything goes!

• Everyone should be strongly encouraged and helped to fully participate. There are many occasions when the best ideas for a solution come from the most unexpected (and often quietest) source. The facilitator might consider a system of some sort whereby a large group is divided into smaller groups and then are brought back together; or a situation where everyone shares one idea before any one person may share additional ideas. Encouraging and facilitating participant involvement and managing idea flow are both important in effective brainstorming.

• Use analogies, metaphors, or "animal viewpoints" to encourage different ways of looking at the situation. An *analogy* is where the situation is likened to something else as in, "A problem is like meatloaf because it is constituted of many different ingredients which can be examined to see the individual components." A *metaphor* is a figure of speech in which a word or phrase that ordinarily designates one thing is used to designate another, thus making an implicit comparison, as in "a sea of troubles." Finally, *animal viewpoints* ask individuals to examine the situation from the perspective of a worm, fish, bird, or turtle. All of these techniques allow for unique and creative perspectives to be brought to bear.

• As they are generated, write ideas on an overhead or flip chart for viewing. This enables group members to piggyback on ideas and helps to retain information.

Photo courtesy of the University of Northern Iowa Public Relations Department

Managing difficulties requires thoughtfulness in working through a process.

Phase 5—Select from Among Alternatives

Once brainstorming is complete the next step is to select one or more choices from the brainstormed list. This can be a difficult process. At this stage, it is important to engage the critical thinking abilities of the participants to best delineate and then evaluate the advantages and disadvantages of each possible solution. It is important to examine the pros and cons of *each* possible solution, no matter how zany the idea. Stopping short often results in premature selection of a solution which may not be the *best* option. When evaluating the possibilities the facilitator will want to assist participants in considering the consequences and viability of each option. In addition, it is important to rearticulate the decision-making method and degree of group involvement in the decision-making process. Listing the pros and cons on newsprint in view of everyone often helps with critical thinking processes.

Phase 6—Generate Strategies and Implement Decisions

Once a solution has been selected, participants will need to brainstorm strategies and actions to implement the decision, and then, implement the decision. The conflict management process will be wasted if a selected solution is not tried and given a chance to work. Again, the brainstorming process is effective at this stage of the process. Strategies to initiate implementation of a conflict management decision are very important to resolving the issue in a satisfactory manner.

Phase 7—Evaluate the Process and Outcome

After the solution has been implemented, leaders and participants will want to evaluate both the problem management process and the outcome. Were the objectives met? Is the issue managed to the satisfaction of all participants at this point? Is the momentum back on the "right" track? At this stage, checking in with task, human relations, and conceptual issues will allow those involved to determine the level of success.

Following these techniques to manage difficulties may appear to be a relatively mechanical process, but it involves many different leader skills. Effective communication and group dynamics skills are integral to successful problem management. In addition, personal leadership style and competencies such as assertiveness are also beneficial to the difficulty management process.

Assertiveness in Managing Difficulties

Assertiveness involves a range of behaviors which arise out of particular attitudes related to perception of self and the handling of various situations. Being assertive means standing up for one's own rights while being sensitive to the rights of others, and then accepting responsibility for the consequences of one's actions. While most view assertion as a three stage continuum of behaviors (i.e., passive, assertive, and aggressive), Crawley (1994) has suggested a four stage continuum (i.e., *aggressive, passive, manipulative,* and *assertive*).

Aggressiveness

Aggressiveness is based on a lack of respect for others; it involves directly standing up for personal rights in such a way as to violate the

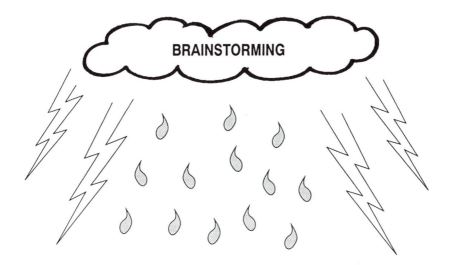

Figure 7.4   *Brainstorming is like a thunderstorm where ideas flow like raindrops and creativity flashes like lightning.*

rights of others (Silberman & Wheelan, 1980). The usual goal of aggression is dominating and winning, usually through humiliating, degrading, or overpowering others so that they become unable to stand up for themselves. Aggressive people often get what they want and may perceive themselves as powerful.   Others, however, will frequently resent an aggressive person and respond in equally negative fashions (Crawley, 1994). Leaders who are aggressive will rarely retain personal credibility or respect from the group.

Passive Behaviors

Passive behavior involves violating one's own rights by failing to express one's own feelings and thoughts honestly (or doing so in such a way that others disregard those feelings) (Silberman & Wheelan, 1980). Being passive shows a lack of respect for one's self; the goal often is to appease others and avoid conflicts. Some people who are by nature, passive, feel that being passive leads to a quiet life and one free of unpleasant conflicts and problems.   On the other hand, many individuals do not respect people who do not stand up for themselves, and they often take advantage of passive people (Crawley, 1994).

Passive behaviors in leaders is usually ineffective, particularly when attempting to facilitate problem management.

Manipulative Behaviors

Being manipulative is based on a lack of respect for self and others. It involves expressing one's needs in an "underhanded" fashion in an attempt to craft and "coerce" particular responses from others—usually to one's personal benefit. Manipulative people may succeed in persuading others to behave in certain ways and may even be successful at dodging unpleasant situations. However, being manipulative often results in resentment by others and a loss of respect. Most people do not like being manipulated (Crawley, 1994). Manipulative leisure services leaders quickly lose the respect of participants and are often stymied by group members in their leadership efforts.

Assertiveness

Assertiveness indicates a respect for self and others. It involves standing up for one's own rights in direct, honest, and appropriate ways which do not violate other's rights (Silberman & Wheelan, 1980). Being assertive often results in others understanding one's needs and respecting an individual for who she or he is. Assertiveness may also lead to confrontation with people who disagree with the individual, however, and with requests being denied. Effective assertiveness makes use of the four part "I" statements discussed on page 236.

Selecting appropriate assertive behaviors can result in positive approaches to various types of difficulties. Leisure services leaders can help participants develop assertive behaviors and make use of them in the conflict management process. The use of assertive behaviors often aids in the handling of the emotional aspects which are an integral aspect

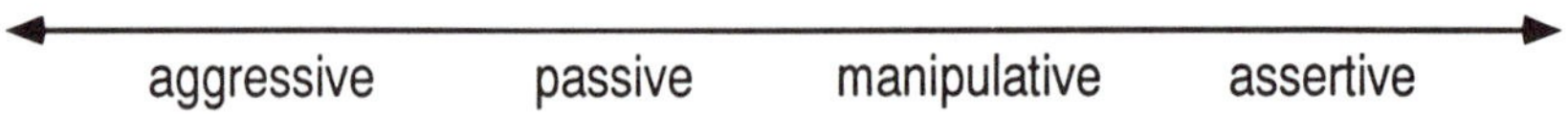

```
←————————————————————————————————————————→
    aggressive      passive     manipulative    assertive
```

Figure 7.5   *Levels of assertiveness vary as on a continuum.*
While individuals tend to have a baseline level of
assertiveness, we all fluctuate depending on the
circumstances.

of all conflicts and problems. An assertive leader is more effective in all aspects of working with groups than leaders who utilize other types of behaviors.

Emotions and Managing Difficulties

The emotional element of conflict and other difficulties is often neglected in the conflict management process. This may be due, in part, because in the predominant U.S. culture, people are taught that emotions are to be held in check and not revealed—in many instances an emotional person is considered a weak person. Nonetheless, emotions persist in conflict situations, and if not acknowledged and addressed, can be detrimental to successful problem management.

One of the more prevalent emotions in conflict and dealing with problems is anger. Anger has been given a "bad rap" in that many believe that anger is never appropriately expressed—being angry may even be perceived as irrational. As many therapists will attest, however, well-handled anger can be beneficial in many settings. Appropriately used, anger promotes confronting problems and elaborating on positions held by those involved (Tjosvold, 1993). It also fuels ongoing improvement in the area of concern as parties work toward managing the issues that triggered the initial bouts of anger.

Anger may be viewed as similar to physical pain in that it sends a signal that helps individuals determine the source of irritation—the underlying causes of the problem. Furthermore, anger focuses and motivates people, and moves people to action (Tjosvold, 1993). It is difficult to do nothing when an individual expresses anger about a situation.

In cooperative relationships (where the goal is to work and succeed *together*) anger can serve to reaffirm interdependence, strengthen the need for collaboration, energize the parties involved, and increase both self-awareness and awareness of others. Expressing anger allows for a ventilation of emotions which can be relaxing and serves as a physical release. As with all emotions, there are appropriate and inappropriate ways to express anger. Leisure services leaders who understand how to use anger as well as how to help others manage it, will be increasingly effective in helping to manage conflicts.

To express anger constructively leaders should:

- establish a cooperative context (show a commitment to the relationship and avoid provoking anger simply because of the ability or position to do so);

- state and explain their position (describe feelings, be specific, take responsibility for own anger, be consistent in verbal and nonverbal messages, use assertion);

- avoid "out of control" expressions of anger (e.g., shouting, throwing items, projecting blame);

- question and understand differing views (e.g., check assumptions, be sensitive to other viewpoints, check the reactions of those listening);

- integrate and create options (use constructive conflict management, ask for help in developing solutions);

- agree and "shake hands" (once the issue has been successfully managed, put the anger away, avoid hanging on to it, make the expression of anger cathartic); and

- reflect and learn (e.g., celebrate joint success, reflect on the experience—what was learned that can be used in the future?).

Using anger within the context of assertive behaviors can enhance successful conflict management. People have a right to know how each disputant feels (as well as what she or he thinks) about a particular situation. In helping others to manage their anger and other feelings in a constructive fashion, leaders may engage in behaviors known as mediation.

Mediation and Leadership Responsibilities

Conflict management typically begins when at least one disputant recognizes the need to find a solution to the problem and initiates the process. Although it is almost always best for two individuals to resolve their own conflicts, there are many occasions when the use of a mediator is the best choice for finding the elegant solution. An *elegant solution* is one where all parties are satisfied, the atmosphere remains positive, and relationships are strengthened.

The role of the mediator is to facilitate the parties involved in the dispute to reach an agreement themselves (Keltner, 1994). In this manner, mediation involves a third party to help individuals move through the conflict management process (Crawley, 1994). According to Crawley it might be wise to consider mediation when:

- relationships are important and people care about one another;

- those involved want to retain control of the outcome (they want to avoid having an outsider dictate the way to manage the problem);

- both sides have a good case and it is difficult to discern which is "better;"

- speed and timing are important (the issue must be addressed *now*);

- confidentiality is important;

- both sides see a need to let off steam (a third party can help to keep things from getting overly personal); and

- neither side wants things to go further up the [grievance] line.

Furthermore, a mediator can be helpful when one disputant feels that the other person involved in the dispute is in a more powerful position than she or he. Although this power discrepancy (which may be related to size, age, sex, personality, seniority, or other reasons) may be more perceived than real, it is a limiting factor in face-to-face negotiation where those involved in the conflict manage the situation themselves.

Mediation is also useful when the parties do not communicate openly with one another; the parties do not have the skills, desire or trust to manage the difficulties effectively; or the parties cannot find an acceptable solution themselves. The presence of a mediator may also be helpful when the conflict is a long standing one, when past efforts to negotiate have failed, or when one of the involved parties seems reluctant to engage in negotiation.

The mediation process is simply a matter of providing guidance in the conflict management process described earlier in this chapter. In some cases, the mediator might be the only person in the situation who is familiar with this process. In that case the conflict manager begins the process by explaining how it works and expressing appreciation to all parties for being willing to work out the problem. Establishing ground rules (a matter of good manners) for the mediation meeting is also important. Participants need to agree not to interrupt each other, to be honest, and to try to find a solution together. Throughout the process the conflict manager also asks clarifying questions to make sure that points are clearly understood and makes certain that each disputant gets approximately equal time.

The mere presence of a third party who is independent of the disputants may help with the resolution of a dispute (Keltner, 1994). Mediator presence often helps in objectifying the situation. A leader who is serving as a mediator should strive to maintain an emphasis on establishing meaningful communication between the disputants, who eventually will identify their own mutually acceptable (i.e., elegant) solution.

The Mediation Process

The mediator helps the participants through the following process (adapted from Koch & Jordan, 1993):

Step 1—Set the Tone

State your positive intentions. For example: "I think we have a problem and I'd really like to work together with you to solve it for both of us," or "Thank you for taking the time to meet with me today. I look forward to solving this problem together."

Step 2—Define and Discuss the Problem

Using "I messages" and active listening, define and discuss exactly what the problem is. It is important at this step for each disputant to have an opportunity to state her or his views and to restate what the other person has said, in order to be sure that the interests of both parties are clear. Each person should be given equal and uninterrupted time to state her or his view of the problem or issue.

Step 3—Summarize Progress

Once it appears that the problem has been described from both points of view, each person should spend a few minutes summarizing the situation from her or his viewpoint. The mediator serves to assist in clarification, if needed.

Step 4—Explore Alternative Solutions

This is the time to ask and answer the question, "What can I do to solve this problem?" Avoid criticizing ideas and list as many alternatives as possible. In fact, using and following the principles of brainstorming might be helpful during this stage. Explore possible solutions for each part of the problem and discuss what the future consequences for each idea might be. Keep in mind that effective solutions must be agreeable to both parties (specifically regarding what will happen, who will do it, and when) and balanced—that is, each person should contribute to the solution.

Step 5—Set a Time for Follow-up

Before ending the mediation session, agree on a time to check back with those involved to make sure the solution is working. This encourages all parties to be accountable and helps to address any unexpected problems which may arise.

Following and practicing mediation steps and the conflict management process can be helpful to mitigate all types of difficulties a leader might face in leisure services settings. The steps to mediation provide a logical framework from which to address a variety of issues. It would be wise

LEADER

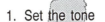

1. Set the tone
2. Define and discuss the problem
3. Summarize progress
4. Explore alternatives
5. Follow up

Figure 7.6 *The mediation process involves a third party— usually the leader or trained peer conflict manager.*

to remember that while the steps to mediation and conflict management are clear and straightforward, in "real" situations the process might not be as clear cut. People react to various situations in unique and unpredictable ways and these behaviors can cause glitches in the difficulty management process. Leader practice is critical to successful use of these techniques.

Summary

While not often perceived as such, conflicts and problems can be very positive—they may serve to jump start a group, encourage creative thinking, and help individuals clarify their positions. Difficulties range on a spectrum from mild differences to violence (fight); movement from one extreme position on the continuum to the other extreme can occur quite rapidly—this is known as escalation. Escalation can occur when people raise their voices, make themselves larger, involve outsiders, bring up past issues, and/or feel threatened in some manner. Leisure services leaders can be instrumental in helping to de-escalate conflict.

Reasons for conflict arise out of differences in perceptions of the distribution of resources, different psychological needs, and opposing or conflicting values. Values conflicts tend to be the most difficult to address because they affect individuals at their core. With knowledge about how conflicts can escalate and why people face conflict, leaders can choose an approach to facilitating the successful management of that conflict. There are five common approaches to conflict: avoidance, accommodation, competition, compromise, and collaboration. These approaches vary in terms of level of assertion and level of cooperation required of the disputants. Collaboration is often the most highly sought after approach as it leads to successful management of conflicts.

A seven-phase model of conflict management was presented where one moves from defining the objectives for the solution to evaluating a decision after it has been implemented. The process involves all disputants, and if followed, can provide a structure for addressing each party's needs. In addressing conflict and disagreement from any perspective, assertiveness is a desirable characteristic. Assertiveness falls along a four-point continuum along with aggressiveness, passive behaviors, and manipulative behaviors.

To facilitate the management of difficulties leisure services leaders may be called upon to serve as mediators for participants. In this situation it is important to address emotional issues of the situation, practice "no fault" thinking, take a balanced view of the situation, use positive "I" statements, and address the situation from three perspectives: yours, mine, and the fly on the wall. Mediation is a process whereby the leader merely facilitates the conflict management process with those involved; when followed and practiced it can be highly effective.

The Front Line

A very simple process for leader facilitated mediation has been presented by Koch and Jordan (1993). It is a quick and positive process for resolving conflicts. The first step is to have two (or more) disputants who are interested in resolving an issue. Next, the disputants must agree to certain conditions:

(1) disputants must agree to work to solve the problem;

(2) disputants must agree to speak honestly; and

(3) disputants must agree not to interrupt, use name calling, or physical violence.

The role of the mediator is to facilitate the process, not to resolve the issue for the disputants. In this respect, the mediator provides the structure and the opportunity for the disputants to work through the issues. The following steps, facilitated by the mediator, can help to reach an agreeable solution:

(1) have the disputants move with the mediator to a private place and sit down;

(2) remind the disputants of the conditions as stated above;

(3) ask Person 1 to tell what happened and how she or he feels;

(4) ask Person 2 to tell what happened and how she or he feels;

(5) ask Person 1 what she or he can do to help solve this problem;

(6) ask Person 2 what she or he can do to help solve this problem;

(7) get agreement from each disputant regarding what each is willing to do;

(8) ask if the disagreement is resolved;

(9) ask each person what she or he could do differently if a similar disagreement should arise again; and

(10) congratulate the disputants for managing the problem!

References

Bannon, J. and Busser, J. (1992). *Problem solving in recreation and parks* (3rd ed.). Champaign, IL: Sagamore Publishing.

Bethel, S. (1990). *Making a difference: Twelve qualities that make you a leader.* New York, NY: Berkley Publishing Group.

Brightman, H. (1988). *Group problem solving: An improved managerial approach.* Atlanta, GA: Georgia State University Business Press.

Brody, E. W. (1991). *Managing communication processes: From planning to crisis response.* New York, NY: Praeger.

Burgoon, M., Dawson, E., and Hunsaker, F. (1994). *Human communication* (3rd ed.). Newbury Park, CA: Sage Publications, Inc.

Cockrell, D. (Ed.). (1991). *The wilderness educator.* Merrillville, IN: ICS Books.

Cox, T. (1993). *Cultural diversity in organizations.* San Francisco, CA: Berrett-Koehler Publishers Inc.

Crawley, J. (1994). *Constructive conflict management.* San Diego, CA: Pfeiffer & Co.

Hitt, W. (1993). *The model leader.* Columbus, OH: Batelle Press.

Hocker, J. and Wilmot, W. (1991). *Interpersonal conflict* (3rd ed.). Dubuque, IA: Wm. C. Brown Publishing.

Keltner, J. (1994). *The management of struggle: Elements of dispute resolution through negotiation, mediation and arbitration.* Cresskill, NJ: Hampton Press.

Koch, S. and Jordan, D. (July/August, 1993). We can work it out: Resolving staff conflicts. *Camping Magazine, 21-25*

McLean, J. and Weitzel, W. (1991). *Leadership—Magic, myth or method?* New York, NY: AMACOM.

Savage, T. (1991). *Discipline for self control.* Englewood Cliffs, NJ: Prentice-Hall.

Schwarz, R. (1994). *The skilled facilitator: Practical wisdom for developing effective groups.* San Francisco, CA: Jossey-Bass, Inc., Publishers.

Silberman, M. and Wheelan, S. (1980). *How to discipline without feeling guilty.* Champaign, IL: Research Press.

Sims, R. and Dennehy, R. (Eds.). (1993). *Diversity and differences in organizations.* Westport, CT: Quorum Books.

Tjosvold, D. (1993). *Learning to manage conflict: Getting people to work together productively.* New York, NY: Lexington Books.

Väyrynen, R. (Ed.). (1991). *New directions in conflict theory.* Newbury Park, CA: Sage Publications, Inc.

Worchel, S. and Simpson, J. (Eds.). (1993). *Conflict between people and groups.* Chicago, IL: Nelson-Hall Publishers.

Chapter Eight
Learning Opportunities

Through studying this chapter students will have the opportunity to:

- explore various approaches to behavior management;
- examine a variety of behavior management techniques for inclusion into one's own repertoire;
- consider methods of selecting behavior management techniques;
- explain how motivation is related to behavior management; and
- put into practice motivation techniques as preventative behavior management.

Photo courtesy of the YWCA of Black Hawk County

CHAPTER

Managing and Motivating Participant Behaviors

People expect to be free *from* the pressures of work and free *to* do as they please when engaged in leisure. In fact, *freedom from* and *freedom to* are integral components of several leisure theories. This expectation of freedoms from and to is part of what leads to the need for managing and motivating participant behaviors.

Everyone is different in this respect; they have different expectations, preferences and behavior styles when involved in leisure services. Because of these differences people sometimes behave in ways that are not always considered acceptable to others. In other words, people do not always do and behave as leaders ask or as they would like—this is true for adults as well as young people.

Throughout society there have been tremendous changes in people, social mores, and social values over the past several years. These social changes have resulted in a need for new assumptions about behavior management. Consider the information found in Table 8A (page 258) as a way to understand the changes in the need for behavior management.

In addition to the changes identified in Table 8A, there is general agreement that a shared sense of morality has lessened and that people in today's society are more apt to engage in confrontational, rude, and violent behaviors than in the past. As in all social venues, these changes in social mores could lead to violence and aggression in leisure service settings. It is more likely, however, that a recreation leader will face more basic behavioral disruptions in the course of leadership.

This chapter will define terms, explore approaches to behavior management and present various behavior management systems. As a

Table 8A A Comparison of Behavior Management Issues

In the Past	Today
• Youth were considered innocent.	• Youth are street-wise.
• Physical punishment was condoned.	• Corporal punishment is banned.
• Public agencies were immune from most lawsuits.	• Lawsuits are likely no matter the type of agency.
• Leadership was autocratic.	• Leadership is participatory.
• Problem youth were separated from the mainstream.	• Problem and troubled youth are integrated in schools and neighborhoods.
• Acts of violence were relatively uncommon.	• Acts of violence are commonplace; violence has moved from fists to guns.
• Severe behavior problems were limited to inner cities and slums.	• Severe behavior problems are found everywhere.

Adapted from Ramsey, R. (1994). *Administrator's complete school discipline guide.* Englewood Cliffs, NJ: Prentice Hall.

part of behavior management, motivation theories will be addressed as well as specific techniques for motivating participants.

Definitions

The term, *behavior management* has been used interchangeably with other words such as discipline and behavior modification, yet each term has different meanings. They all do relate to the desire to maintain individual behaviors in a desirable and socially acceptable fashion.

Behavior Management

Behavior management is the preferred term for altering or maintaining positive relationships and actions in recreation and leisure services leadership because it tends to be the more accurate in terms of identifying what the leader is attempting to accomplish. Leaders are interested not necessarily in controlling other's behaviors (although that, too, is sometimes necessary), rather leaders are concerned with managing or guiding the actions of others to conform to an established set of expectations. Behaviors are actions or reactions of people in response to external or internal stimuli. Therefore, it makes sense that to manage or guide those behaviors, the internal and/or external stimuli should be addressed.

Discipline

Discipline is one element of behavior management. It refers to one person initially controlling behaviors of another through training. The ultimate goal is *self*-discipline where an individual controls her or his own behaviors to meet both internal and external expectations. As a verb, to discipline usually implies control obtained by enforcing compliance or order on someone. It often involves the use of punishment to gain submission to rules and authority. There are both advantages and disadvantages to using external discipline—an effective leader strives to help participants achieve discipline over themselves.

Behavior Modification

Behavior modification is a term commonly used in the therapeutic element of the leisure services field. It has its foundation in operant conditioning and utilizes a great deal of reinforcement toward the "ultimate goal of eliciting behavior that is controlled, constructive, predictive, and orderly" (Seaman & DePauw, 1989, p. 277). Individuals' behaviors are conditioned through the use of positive and negative reinforcements so that desirable behaviors are increased and undesirable behaviors are decreased (i.e., made extinct).

Although it is often assumed that behavior management is a tool which is used with children only, both adults and children receive benefits from structured environments and a sense of discipline or order. In addition, the environment, facilities, program, and other participants also benefit from guiding participant behaviors in certain fashions. It is interesting to note that adults often engage in the same undesirable behaviors as children (e.g., whining, fighting, shouting, being disrespectful to the leader, refusing to participate, not listening to instructions), yet when adults engage in these behaviors they are not labeled as misbehaving. Thus, misbehavior is simply a label placed on certain types of actions exhibited by young people.

Generally, actions defined as misbehaviors are goal-directed; the person misbehaving is usually trying to meet certain personal needs. The manner or approach used to meet those needs might be perceived as immature or considered antisocial; this is what usually leads to the negative label of misbehavior. Misbehavior is a judgment or perception of an adult that a young person's behavior is bad. In other words, it is a value judgment made by an adult (Gordon, 1989).

Oftentimes, recreation leaders define any disruption to an activity or leadership opportunity as misbehavior. As Seeman (1994) pointed out, however, all disruptions are not behavior problems. Some disruptions are to be expected in the course of leadership no matter the age of the participants. Disruptions may be no more than evidence of exuberance, excitement, or high-intensity interest. In addition, people with developmental, emotional, behavioral, or learning disabilities may be perceived as misbehaving because they do not act in a manner consistent with their chronological age or as society deems appropriate. As leaders gain experience, it becomes easier to distinguish behavior management issues from simple participant excitement.

Power and Behavior Management

When dealing with undesirable behaviors inexperienced leaders may resort to "pulling rank" over participants. They may try to bully or intimidate participants into appropriate behaviors. These types of behaviors are examples of one type of leader power over participants. Leader power comes from the position one holds and might include the power to eject someone from a facility, deny access to equipment, or to otherwise interfere with one's leisure experience. It is important to remember that, even if leader power is not used in a negative way with participants, the perception of leader power exists. Inappropriate and negative use of one's power may lead to participant resentment or rebound, where a power struggle between participants and leaders occurs.

To facilitate positive leisure experiences for others, leaders would be wise to be aware of their position of power and use it in a fashion to help participants achieve their leisure goals. In relation to discipline, power can be viewed as being on a continuum with the leader retaining all the power (i.e., external discipline) on one extreme and the participants having full control over power to discipline themselves (i.e., internal power) on the other end. Self-discipline is the most effective for managing behaviors and involves less leader intervention (see Figure 8.1).

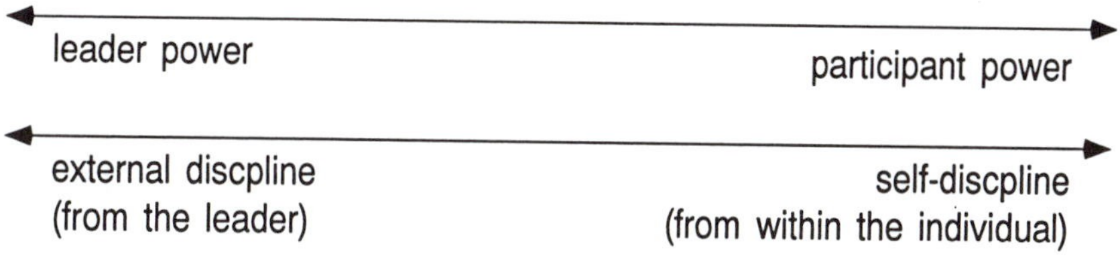

leader power   participant power

external discpline   self-discpline
(from the leader)   (from within the individual)

Figure 8.1   *Leader power and behavior management are related through discipline.*

Approaches to Behavior Management

There are many approaches to behavior management which have been developed over the years. Many of the models were established through the study of sociology and psychology and have roots in behaviorism, humanism, and other aspects of social psychology (Goldstein, 1995). This section will provide snapshot information about several of the more commonly used behavior management models in leisure services.

Preventative Management

An effective leader experiences fewer disruptions from participants than does an ineffective leader due to the skilled use of leadership techniques. One of those techniques is *preventative management*. The goal of preventative management is to minimize or prevent behavior difficulties from occurring. Therefore, this technique includes using effective leadership techniques (beginning with preparation) to keep participants engaged in fun and exciting experiences.

In addition to exhibiting strong leadership abilities, preventative management utilizes frequent monitoring of participants so that potential problems can be "caught" before they occur. Furthermore, frequent monitoring allows a leader to "catch" participants acting in desired manners— "catch them doing something right!" The use of clear rules and appropriate praise are also elements of a preventative management approach. As an example, a leader using a preventative management approach would ensure that there is enough equipment for full participation and that the activity space is well-marked. This would minimize participants vying for use of equipment and would help participants to know activity boundaries.

Moral Education

The use of *moral education* as a model to change behaviors is one favored by many. It has drawbacks relative to participant understanding, however. In their attempts to alter behaviors leaders ascribing to this theory commonly use discussions of real-life dilemmas and role playing as techniques to help participants understand why their behaviors are undesirable, and why they should change those behaviors. For instance, a leader using this approach with a child who has just bitten another child might sit the biter down and have a heart-to-heart discussion about the negative aspects of biting or hurting someone; the leader might ask, "how would you feel if someone bit you?" Moral education also may include participant involvement in agency leadership and policy development when rules, policies and procedures are developed.

Affective and Communication Models

Approaches to behavior management that target one's emotions and feelings about various behavioral issues are categorized as *affective and communication models*. Within this category leaders work with participants on values clarification and interpersonal skills training. Feelings and emotions are addressed as the leader attempts to determine causes for undesirable behaviors. In addition, active listening on the part of the leader is stressed in these models because open communication is a prerequisite for trust, expression of emotions, and dealing with problems openly. For example, if a leader were to follow this approach when dealing with an argumentative adult, she or he might ask the individual to come into the office and talk things through. Through active listening, the leader would try to determine what participant feelings (e.g., frustration, anger) were causing the conflicts and work with the individual to minimize such issues from recurring.

Behavior Modification

As mentioned earlier, *behavior modification* has its base in operant conditioning which was popularized through B. F. Skinner's early experiments. Using this approach effective leaders would begin with direct instruction (relative to the desired behaviors) with involved participants. Once initial instruction has occurred, behavior modification relies heavily on the effective use of reinforcement techniques to alter behaviors. In addition, "time-out" is commonly used often as a

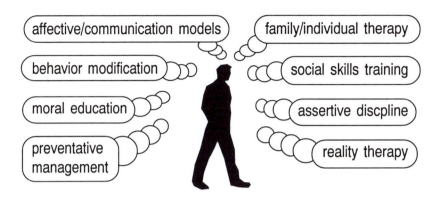

Figure 8.2   *Approaches to behavior management are varied.*
Generally leaders follow one or two predominant
approaches.

negative reinforcement tool. People who use behavior modification are well-rehearsed in techniques such as shaping, chaining, fading, and extinction.

Assertive Discipline

Assertive discipline requires that leaders be assertive in addressing undesirable behaviors. That is, leaders need "to be firm, stand up for personal rights and express thoughts, feelings, and beliefs in *direct, honest* and *appropriate* ways which do not violate another person's rights" (Silberman & Wheelan, 1980, p. 8). The associated discipline is a systematic use of behavior modification techniques designed to achieve desired results. Open and honest communication, often framed in a series of "I" statements is the hallmark of this model. For instance, a leader facing an abusive parent at a youth sports event might approach the parent and say, "When that language is used with the coaches, a bad example is set for the youth. In addition, it is disruptive to the game. I need you to stop the verbal abuse so that the game may continue uninterrupted. If you do not stop, you will be removed from the field."

Reality Therapy

The premise of *reality therapy* is that in order for people to change their behaviors, they must first be confronted with what they are actually doing (people are often unaware of their behaviors). Therefore, in this approach, confrontational questioning is utilized in one-on-one and group settings. An example of confrontational questioning would be to ask a person who is whining (e.g., about wanting her or his turn) what she or he is doing. A typical response would be, "I want my turn...." The leader again would ask, "What are you doing just now?" This would continue until the participant recognized and acknowledged that she or he was whining. The leader then might choose to use logical consequences—any time a person whined, she or he would not get what she or he requested.

Social Skills Training

One of the most prevalent myths surrounding people who enter into leisure service settings as participants is that they have received quality and appropriate social skills training at home and school (Bolton, 1979). Leaders tend to expect participants to be nice, ask for things politely, and know how to interact appropriately with others. This, however, is an incorrect assumption. Many participants (of all ages) do not have the appropriate and necessary social skills to function well in diverse social situations. Therefore, leaders who believe in this model of behavior management would commonly utilize direct instruction, modeling and practicing skills, and coaching behaviors. As an example, a leader might help a person who gets into numerous fights to learn basic conflict management skills. Opportunities to practice and use the skills would also be made available until the person became proficient at conflict management.

Therapy (Behavior and Family)

Oftentimes when participant actions are extreme, a variety of cognitive-behavioral or operant techniques are utilized in a therapeutic setting. Because these forms of intervention are considered therapy, only certified, licensed, or trained therapists should use them. Leisure services professionals who are not therapeutic recreation specialists, might be involved in therapy interventions through making referrals for those participants in need.

As with learning about various models and theories of leadership, learning about models and approaches to behavior management is useful for recreation and leisure services leaders. The models provide a basic foundation for the approach a leader takes when utilizing various behavior management techniques. Often, leaders use a mix or combination of two or more of the previously mentioned approaches to behavior management. Many of the specific behavior management techniques provided in this chapter are used with various approaches. We will now move into investigating purposes of behavior management and why behavior management is necessary.

Purposes of Behavior Management

As a leader considers the use of an approach to behavior management and the implementation of specific techniques it is important that she or he understands the purpose behind managing behaviors. Is it to maintain control? Is it for participant safety? Is it to enhance leader/participant power differences? It is common for agencies to establish basic reasons and expectations for behavior management; individual leaders then implement those policies based on the requirements of the immediate situation.

Typically, behavior management is desirable for safety reasons. Through effective use of behavior management techniques, safety of self, other participants, the facility and equipment is ensured. Furthermore, the use of behavior management techniques allows for the smooth conduct of recreation and leisure activities; if people's actions are managed well, a leader is free to give instructions and work with participants as needed.

At the direct leadership level, through the use of various techniques leaders may desire to *control* others' behaviors for many reasons. While controlling others' behaviors can be difficult (since each individual is truly the only one who can make choices relative to her or his own behaviors), a certain level of control may be achieved, particularly with children. This is often accomplished through such means as controlling access to equipment and limiting the times of day a facility is open. When "in control" a leader usually is directive and authoritarian in her or his leadership style; it is clear who is "in charge."

At other times a direct leader may wish to use behavior management to *instruct* or *educate* others. Participants learn what is appropriate and is not appropriate through leader explanations about the decisions made, and through leaders being clear and unambiguous about what is and is not acceptable. Once participant behaviors are managed effectively, it is possible to teach tasks needed to accomplish an activity or how to deal with people (i.e., social skills, interpersonal or human relations skills). To achieve long-term educational goals a leader would typically engage in ongoing coaching and guiding behaviors.

Whether the purpose is to maintain safety, control, or education/instruction, behavior management is necessary. Leader intervention and implementation of behavior management techniques is needed because of the shift in values and social expectations of people. The chosen techniques may be very subtle and unnoticeable to participants, or they may be very obvious.

Why Behavior Management is Needed

Leisure services settings are microcosms of society and as such are not immune from the larger problems that occur in home, school, and work. As experience tells us, any time people are involved there is potential for inappropriate or undesirable behaviors. Therefore, behavior management in some form is desirable to help maintain safe and enjoyable leisure environments. Problem behaviors range in severity from minor disruptions (e.g., a participant talking out of turn) to very serious situations (e.g., a gang fight with weapons). Some of the more common problem behaviors that face direct leaders in leisure service settings include:

- stealing,
- talking back,
- fighting,
- refusing to participate,
- destruction of equipment,
- disrespect for leaders,
- disruptive activity behaviors,
- racial intolerance,
- value differences,
- inflexibility/poor adaptability,
- lying,
- demeaning others,
- arguing/verbal abuse,
- overly demanding of leader's attention,

- whining, and
- sexual harassment.

All of these identified problems may be exhibited by adults, youth, girls, boys, people of various socioeconomic groups, and people who represent all cultural backgrounds. It is quite common for these behavior problems to have their roots in deeper issues. Many times the behaviors being exhibited are hiding problems such as low self-esteem, victimization or abuse in the home, and health and medical issues. It is always wise to try to determine the underlying causes of behavior problems while also dealing with the surface issues.

For example, if a male teenage participant is sexually harassing a female participant (e.g., making sexual comments, spreading rumors, making sexual gestures), the leader certainly must act on those behaviors. In addition, to lessen the chance of the behaviors recurring, it is important to determine what is causing the male to harass the female participant. The sexual harassment may be a result of low self-esteem of the male teen, the teen questioning or testing his masculinity, conforming to peer pressure, acting in a way that he has seen modeled by adult males, or a simple lack of empathy.

In this instance short-term behavior management is necessary to protect the rights of the female teen. Activity-based interventions might be utilized to address the longer term issues. For instance, activities designed for the male teen would allow for success, model appropriate behaviors, provide alternatives to peer conformity, and/or explain the impact of such harassment on the victims. While this example described a need to protect a person, in other situations it might be necessary to protect equipment, facilities, or the social order.

Factors Affecting Behavior Management

It is not possible to make global statements about how to handle specific instances of misbehavior. Certainly, general rules-of-thumb can be established which serve as guides for handling certain types of situations. However, people are much too diverse and every situation too distinct to make hard-and-fast rules about how to handle undesirable behaviors. This is not to say that rules cannot be made and followed consistently and equitably—this, in fact, is very desirable. Rather, it is important that leaders consider all aspects of a situation before making a judgment relative to the undesirable behavior and subsequent intervention.

Among the human elements to consider when making behavior management decisions are the developmental ability involved, age, gender, and cultural background of the participants. Environmentally, a leader should consider such things as temperature, lighting, activity pacing, and spatial arrangements. These issues should not be used to excuse undesirable behaviors, but rather should be used to develop a deeper understanding as to the causes of inappropriate actions. Understanding underlying causes helps a leader in advising or teaching participants how to handle themselves more appropriately.

Developmental Ability

All human beings move through various life stages which were discussed in depth in Chapter Three of this text. To be most effective when utilizing behavior management techniques leaders should bear in mind that as people pass through the various developmental stages they grow cognitively, affectively, physically, and socially. At various times of life some people will not have the sophistication to fully understand the repercussions of certain behaviors. At other times they may not be physically capable to do as asked. Those with emotional, behavioral or developmental disabilities are often incapable of making appropriate judgments relative to their own behaviors. Understanding human development, then, is important in selecting appropriate leader actions.

developmental ability
age
gender
culture
maturity
leader experience

Figure 8.3   *Many factors influence the choice of behavior management approaches and techniques.*

Age

Combined with a knowledge of developmental stages, understanding age differences is helpful when deciding which behavior management approach would be most effective in what situation. Young children may be unable to articulate their needs and therefore may act out to gain what they desire. Particularly when in the heat of the moment, leaders should remember that children are not miniature adults; therefore, the expectations of and consequences for undesirable behaviors must be different for youngsters than for adults.

Gender

A relatively subtle influence on behavior management is gender. Leaders may not recognize its influence in their perceptions and use of various behavior management techniques, but it exists nonetheless. In many instances it is considered acceptable for males to engage in certain behaviors (a "boys will be boys" attitude) whereas it is unacceptable for females to engage in similar behaviors (it is "not ladylike"). In addition, leaders often apply or enforce rules differently for females and males. Leaders will want to be aware of different standards based on the participant's gender and make adjustments to avoid falling into stereotypical behaviors and expectations.

Cultural Background

As society becomes increasingly diverse, every recreation leader will be required to have a basic understanding of cultures other than her or his own. In general terms, one should recognize that people from various cultures do not handle all situations alike. For instance, in the predominant U.S. culture people are expected to make eye contact with others—particularly when being addressed by a leader due to a behavior problem. However, for some people of Asian heritage, making eye contact is considered rude and aggressive—particularly when being addressed by a leader due to a behavior problem. In addition to differences in eye contact, cultural differences may be found in the use of vocalizations (e.g., loudness, pacing, intonation) and in the use of physical contact between peers and others (e.g., shoulder punches, chest bumps). These differences do not necessarily equate to inappropriate or undesirable behaviors.

In addition to misinterpretations based on culture, gender, age, or development stage, other factors influence individuals engaging in undesirable behaviors. Often the factors that affect behavior management contribute to underlying reasons why people act out. Understanding these reasons can help the leader in difficult situations.

Why People Act Out

Why do people act in ways that are inappropriate? Why do both adults and young people engage in undesirable negative behaviors? People act out for a variety of reasons; among other things they might be tired, in a bad mood, or simply uninterested in the activity. It is important to ascertain underlying reasons for negative behaviors because, as mentioned earlier, an effective leader will wish to address the cause of misbehavior through behavior management techniques (in addition to the individual acts). Ramsey (1994) reported global issues such as growing diversity and racial tension, the impact of drugs, a shift of values, the advent of gang cultures, and the normalization and glamorization of violence through the media as underlying reasons for people of all ages acting out.

As one might imagine, there are as many individual reasons for undesirable behaviors as there are people. Through research conducted in schools in the early 1990s the underlying reasons for young people acting out listed in Table 8B were identified by youth and their teachers (Ramsey, 1994; Seeman, 1994). Some reasons are related to effective leadership and can be addressed through improving leadership skills, and other reasons relate to individual participant issues.

It is interesting to note that of the reasons listed, more than half of the reasons relate to effective leadership and can be mitigated through a change or improvement in leadership skills, and another 20% relate to actions of both the leader and the participant and can be partially addressed through effective use of leadership skills. Effective leadership, therefore, can have a tremendous impact on participant success and enjoyment.

It is not uncommon for professionals entering the leisure services field to mistake undesirable behaviors as personal attacks on themselves. As can be seen from the data presented here, however, participants have many reasons for acting out, few of which have anything to

Table 8B *Reasons Youth Act Out*

• Leader's fear of litigation	• Conflicts with agency personnel
• How the activity was set up	• Personality conflicts
• Because the leader seemed to pick on someone	• Underskilled for activity; to avoid failure
• Because the leader would put people down; leader did not care about youth	• Problems at home
• Overlabeling of youth	• To test personal power
• Leader was not interactive enough	• Curiosity/testing the adults
• Because the leader was not genuine	• Low self-esteem
• Leader did not explain well enough	• Lack of appropriate social skills
• Not enough equipment	• Depression
• No participant input into programs	• Immaturity
• Did not understand, so did not pay attention	• Medical problems (e.g., vision, hearing, ADD)
• Unmet needs	• To get leader attention
• Because of physical discomfort	• Fear (e.g., of abandonment, intimacy)
	• Boredom
	• Feelings of not belonging

Resources: Ramsey, 1994; Seeman, 1994.

do with the leader personally. Most participants do not purposefully target their inappropriate actions *at* leaders.

Principles of Behavior Management

Behavior management techniques are a necessity of all recreation and leisure services leaders. To be prepared for a variety of situations each leisure services leader should develop a repertoire of behavior management techniques to be used with adults and young people. To be most effective this repertoire should be a match for the leader's style as well as fit within the policies and aims of the agency. The agency in which one works sets the tone for how behavior management is approached by staff members. Expectations, which may or may not be articulated, are established related to personal behaviors exhibited by both staff and participants (e.g., verbal abuse, fighting, disrespect, stealing). Oftentimes, policies are developed to provide guidelines for staff indicating how and when staff should step in to resolve escalating conflicts, call for assistance, and handle other behavioral concerns.

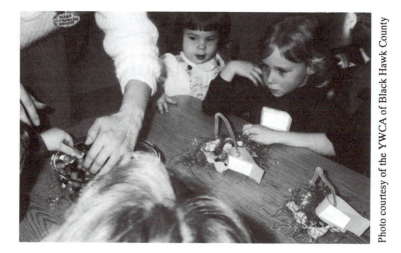

Photo courtesy of the YWCA of Black Hawk County

Children often react with hurt feelings to certain behavior management techniques.

As the approaches discussed earlier indicated, there are many behavior management techniques available and all have different success rates depending upon the situation. It is best if a leader develops a range of techniques which suit her or his preferred style of leadership. In this way, when a particular technique is not effective with a participant, the leader can try another approach. It is not uncommon for a leader to utilize several techniques before finding one that is effective for a particular individual. Behavior management techniques vary from unobtrusive (i.e., it is difficult to observe the leader taking action) to very obtrusive (i.e., it is obvious that the leader is trying to gain control), and there are many variations. If a leader considers the factors involved, attempts to determine the underlying cause(s), and follows the basic principles found in the following section, effective management of behaviors will likely occur.

Principles serve as guideposts or general suggestions to help leaders in the decision-making process. There are several steps that leaders can take to ensure some success in managing the behaviors of leisure services participants.

Make It an Agency Process

Behavior management should be systemic; that is, every agency should have a philosophy or approach to behavior management in which it trains staff. This philosophy usually involves a proactive component as well as an intervention plan. Guidelines related to intervention and enforcement typically are developed at the agency level and shared with staff in staff training or through the staff manual. Resources to help resolve causes of misbehaviors and ways to help people meet their needs are commonly included in the behavior management system.

Be Proactive

Leaders who consistently model and send positive messages tend to have few behavior problems. Ramsey (1994) has suggested that the following messages permeate an agency to establish an atmosphere of mutual respect:

- all people have value as human beings and deserve respect as worthwhile persons;
- there is more than one way to be human, to learn, and to contribute;
- despite differences, people are more alike than different; and,
- there is strength in diversity.

Establishing an atmosphere of respect and identifying expectations related to responsibility for one's actions are proactive behavior management techniques. One of the simplest and effective proactive steps leaders can do is to learn participant names, pronounce them correctly, and use them often.

Be Prepared

Disruptions of some magnitude occur in every leadership opportunity. To be ready for such events, an effective leader maintains a "bag of tricks" (i.e., repertoire of techniques) with which she or he feels comfortable. Arranging space and equipment in such a way as to avoid tempting misuse or misbehaviors, and playing "What if?" so that all contingencies have been considered are aspects of being prepared. A well-known adage highlights the importance of planning: "Proper prior planning precludes poor performance."

Determine Who Has the Problem

There are times when the problem caused by the undesirable behavior is experienced only by the leader; other times it is experienced solely by the participant; and yet other times, the problem is shared by the leader and the participant (Gordon, 1989). It is the participant's problem if the behavior is causing problems for that participant (e.g., refusing to participate only impacts that individual); it is the leader's problem if the behavior is causing problems for the leader (e.g., talking back to a leader in front of others); the problem is shared if it results in difficulties for both the leader and participant (e.g., breaking equipment—the participant has no equipment to use and the leader must scramble for replacement gear). Determining who has the problem helps to clarify potential leader actions.

Feedback

In the course of engaging in behavior management techniques some type of feedback must be given to the participants involved. Feedback is the initial communication that is passed from leader to participant and is related to a particular incident. It is an element of communication that ensures a cycle where all participants are actively involved in the communication (i.e., the communication is two-way). To be effective in helping to change behaviors, feedback should be:

- given immediately after the behavior (desired or not desired) occurs;
- very specific;
- focused on behaviors rather than the person; and
- understandable to the recipient (this varies based on developmental abilities).

Immediacy

Handling a situation as quickly as possible after it occurs tends to result in effective behavior management. Providing immediate feedback to those involved catches them "in the moment" and makes it easier to deal with the undesirable actions.

Avoid Neglecting the Entire Group

If the group is left unattended while the leader is dealing with one individual, the message will be that to get the leader's attention one should engage in undesirable behaviors. In addition, ignoring a group while handling one person might lead to safety concerns; also, it is unfair to group members. As a rule of thumb, the disruption caused by the leader when addressing misbehavior should not be larger than the disruption caused by the misbehaving person (Jones & Jones, 1995).

Focus on the Behavior, Not the Person

It is very important that a participant knows that it is her or his actions and behaviors with which the leader is concerned, and not her or him as a person. Messages perceived as personal attacks on participants will result in defensiveness and a lack of cooperation. For example, "Chris, pushing people is unacceptable behavior" targets the behavior while, "Chris, you are bad!" is aimed at the person.

Protect and Maintain the Dignity of the Participant

When utilizing behavior management techniques with a specific individual, a leader should strive to avoid addressing her or him in the presence of others (although this is not always possible). Humiliation is a strong emotion and will cause not only the individual in question to react negatively, but also the entire group may rebel. Whenever possible, those who are engaging in undesirable behaviors should be taken aside and the issue dealt with out of the eyes and ears of others.

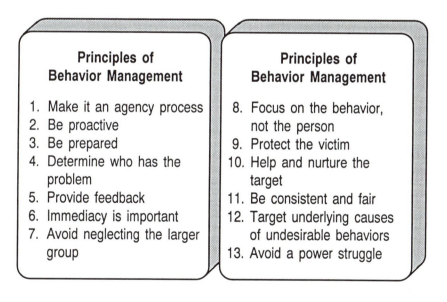

Principles of Behavior Management

1. Make it an agency process
2. Be proactive
3. Be prepared
4. Determine who has the problem
5. Provide feedback
6. Immediacy is important
7. Avoid neglecting the larger group

Principles of Behavior Management

8. Focus on the behavior, not the person
9. Protect the victim
10. Help and nurture the target
11. Be consistent and fair
12. Target underlying causes of undesirable behaviors
13. Avoid a power struggle

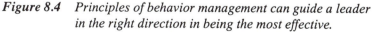

Figure 8.4   *Principles of behavior management can guide a leader in the right direction in being the most effective.*

Help and Nurture the Target of Misbehaviors

If the target of inappropriate behaviors is another participant (e.g., through harassment, name calling, fighting) attend to and nurture the victim. Particularly in instances of personal attacks, leaders have a tendency to admonish or punish the one misbehaving and ignore the target of those actions. It is desirable to attend to the needs of the emotionally or psychologically injured person, just as one would with a physically injured person, and empathize and nurture her or him. This accomplishes several things—it lets the target of the negative behaviors know that the leader does not condone the actions of the attacker, it gives the victim positive leader attention, it helps to soothe hurts, and it models preferred behaviors.

Be Consistent and Fair

While children may be the most vocal about their displeasure if they perceive that something is unfair or not being consistently applied, adults will also resent inconsistencies and unfairness. Being consistent and fair while keeping in mind that all situations and people are unique can be a challenge for a leisure services leader, however, it is best to have this as a goal. Consistency provides a sense of security as participants can count on a leader to act or react certain ways in particular situations.

Target Underlying Causes of Undesired Behaviors

Acting-out behaviors might be thought of as medical signs that a person exhibits when she or he is ill. The signs certainly need to be treated, and it is also important to get to the cause of the illness. This is true of behavior problems as well. If only the behaviors are addressed and the underlying causes are left untouched, undesirable behaviors will continue and may escalate.

Avoid a Power Struggle

Engaging in argumentative behaviors with participants—no matter their age—is counterproductive. Leaders would be wise to hold their emotions in check so as to avoid an "I'm right"—"No, I'm right" conflict. One way to deal with a participant who seems to desire a power struggle is to provide options so that it is the participant's choice as to what occurs. For instance, asking a participant to hold a ball still or put it away provides her or him with a choice. Simply telling the person to put the ball away will likely be perceived as a command and could result in a power struggle.

These basic principles work within the various approaches to behavior management discussed earlier and help lay the groundwork for a successful leadership experience. Leaders will want to implement these principles using a style that is comfortable to them—not all leaders are equally skilled in the use of all techniques. Specific management techniques build on the principles of behavior management and are described in the next section.

Behavior Management Techniques

Having prepared well for the leadership opportunity and taken a proactive position with regard to behavior management with a group, it is now time to consider individual behavior management techniques. As mentioned earlier, techniques for managing behaviors range from simple and unobtrusive to complex and obtrusive. It is usually wise to try unobtrusive measures first to manage behaviors; only if those attempts prove unsuccessful should a leader then move into the more obvious and obtrusive techniques. In this section behavior management techniques are presented in order from unobtrusive to obtrusive.

Unobtrusive or Preventative Techniques

Some preventative and unobtrusive techniques have already been addressed in this chapter. Depending upon the approach to behavior management one is utilizing, the type or style of behavior management will differ. The purpose of preventive techniques is to minimize the likelihood of behavior problems from occurring. These techniques include:

- defining limits;
- planning for contingencies in advance (i.e., playing "what if?");
- providing ongoing clarification as needed;
- establishing routines;
- being sure that participants are challenged at an appropriate level;
- being inclusive of all participants;
- avoiding some activities; and

- meeting basic needs (e.g., physical, safety, belonging, achievement, self-actualization).

One of the goals of behavior management is to induce compliance or to influence participants to behave in a particular fashion. Eventually, the goal is to influence participants to want to behave as expected on their own. Goldstein (1995) reported that certain unobtrusive variables affect compliance among participants. While the sophistication level might differ, these techniques produce similar positive reactions in people of all ages, backgrounds, and abilities.

Use a Question Format

While leaders do not wish to appear to beg for compliance or behavior norming, phrasing a directive in the form of a question softens it and may make it more palatable than if it were a straightforward directive. A question format is less authoritarian than a directive, and is usually more easily accepted by participants.

Use Distance and Proximity Control

Quite often, simply moving closer to an acting out participant is enough to cause her or him to cease the undesirable behaviors.

Eye Contact

Using eye contact and perfecting "the look" lets participants know that the leader is aware of their actions, and a firm look sends a message to stop.

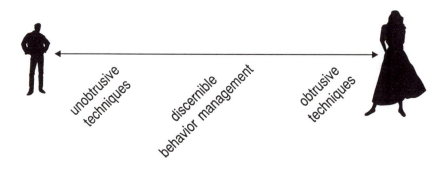

Figure 8.5   *Behavior management techniques move from very subtle to overt interventions—the leader, participant, and situation dictate the degree of obtrusiveness.*

Make Two Requests—No More

As long as the leader knows that a participant understands the request, two requests to stop a behavior are sufficient; ask twice and then intervene with the preferred leader follow-up behaviors (e.g., logical consequences, punishment).

Allow Time for Compliance

After the request has been made, allow a minimum of five to ten seconds (with no other leader-participant conversation) for the person to change her or his behavior. There are times when five to ten minutes should be allowed—it depends on the situation.

Make More Start Than Stop Requests

Avoid a tone of negativity by asking participants to begin a specific action rather than stop one. For instance, if a youth was running around a pool, rather than asking that youngster to stop running (which leaves all sorts of wonderful options open such as cartwheeling, skipping, or rolling), the leader might ask the person to start walking heel-to-toe around the pool.

Be Sure the Requests Are Specific and Descriptive

Comprehension is very important in influencing desired behaviors. A request from a leader should be specific, as literal as possible, and descriptive so that the need for clarification is minimized.

Use Genuine Reinforcement of Positive Behaviors

When compliance is achieved, praise those actions using "I" statements. Participants can tell when a leader is making positive comments for the sole purpose of influencing them to behave a certain way; therefore, leader authenticity is desired.

Redirect the Activity

Often participants act out due to difficulties with the activity—they are bored, do not understand how to play, or the activity is not meeting their present needs (if a child needs to expend energy, a quiet board game will not keep her or him engaged). Changing the activity in midstream to accommodate needs is an effective way to redirect behaviors. Leaders should take cues from the participants as to what type of activity (or rest) to begin next.

Use Regulated Permission

Regulated permission is a technique that accommodates a participants' immediate needs. For example, if the leader is having difficulty keeping participants on task because they seem to have a need to run around and make noise, a leader using regulated permission would encourage three to five minutes of running around and making noise. After the designated time period has passed, participants would be guided into the next task.

Tolerate Some Misbehavior

People are people and will act in ways not always acceptable to the leader. This is to be expected; therefore, if the undesirable behaviors are not causing difficulties for others or presenting a safety concern, it may be appropriate to ignore the behaviors. When people are in groups they expect others will fidget, whisper, and move about. Leaders would be wise to remember the cliché: choose your battles.

Praise vs. Positive "I" Statements

Praise is a form of feedback and as such should be specific and related to behaviors rather than a person. Because praise is a feeling, value, or thought of the leader, it is best to couch it in "I" statements rather than "you" statements (Gordon, 1989). In this way the issue remains with the person who owns it. For instance, "I appreciate you helping to put away equipment; it makes my job easier" is better than "you did a good job with the equipment today." The "you" message may imply that something is amiss on days the person did not help and can lead to guilt, hurt feelings, and a feeling of being criticized; it also may communicate a lack of respect for others. An "I" message alerts participants that the leader is human and has needs, too (Gordon, 1989). Guidelines for effective praise have been developed and may be found in Table 8C.

Discernible Techniques

Discernible techniques are those that fall between being unobtrusive and outright obvious interventions. They are often integrated into basic leadership skills and techniques for teaching an activity or task, and therefore, tend to be more pointed than unobtrusive techniques. Discernible behavior management techniques are more noticeable than unobtrusive techniques, but not as obvious as obtrusive methods.

Table 8C Giving Appropriate Praise

Giving praise is very similar to giving general feedback; there are several principles to bear in mind to ensure that praise is both appropriate and effective in reaching desired goals. Usually praise contains both affect (feelings) and content (the message) and is targeted at a specific individual or group.

- Be specific and target the behaviors, rather than the person; avoid global statements. Rather than commenting, "Wow! You did great today!" tell the individual what exactly she or he did great.

- Use "I" statements when identifying affect (i.e., "I appreciate the way you picked up the equipment today!")

- When you indicate that something is "good," be sure to indicate what was good about it. For instance, in the example above, did the leader appreciate the way the group picked up equipment today because the group did it without being asked? or because it was done quickly, quietly, or neatly? or because the leader wasn't feeling well and the group helped her or him out? or because it showed responsibility or commitment? or....

- Know when to use praise in public and when it is best done privately. For example, to praise one person loudly in front of others who have been acting out may cause an increase in undesirable behaviors by the others. If an individual might be embarrassed by public recognition, it may be best to give praise privately.

- Be sure that verbal praise is "in sync" with nonverbal language. People are more apt to believe the nonverbal message over the verbal one if there are inconsistencies.

- Follow verbal praise with consistent treatment of the individual.

- Be genuine and truthful in your praise of another; avoid exaggerations. Most people are perceptive and can recognize exaggerated praise; it is often interpreted as "buttering up" the target of the praise and can backfire.

- Understand cultural nuances surrounding praise. In many cultures, giving praise to one person is undesirable and is thought to draw undue attention to that individual. In this instance, praising the group may be best.

- Try to catch people doing something right and use praise often. This helps to articulate expectations and desirable behaviors.

- Avoid using phrases like "perfect!" Perfection is rare and this type of praise may give a false sense of ability. After all, one cannot improve on perfection. Instead, use phrases that accurately describe the situation.

- Give praise when it is due and try to use it often—remember the above principles, however.

Positive Discipline

Discipline refers to a set of techniques used in behavior management to maintain orderly social behaviors so that meaningful learning can occur (Munn, Johnstone & Chalmers, 1992a; Munn, Johnstone & Chalmers, 1992b; Nelson, 1987; Savage, 1991; Silberman & Wheelan, 1980; Windell, 1991). It often includes direct instruction, the use of punishment, and an overall tone of leader control to induce compliance in others. Positive discipline helps to move the sense of control from the leader (external to the individual) to the individual (internal to the individual). See Table 8D for characteristics of positive discipline.

Modeling

By demonstrating desired behaviors and then allowing for individuals to practice these behaviors participants learn to understand leader expectations. When using modeling, for example, a leader might have participants learn and practice how to quiet down when the leader needs their attention.

Rules

The use of rules is necessary for the managed presentation of recreation and leisure services activities. Yet, rules do not have to be overly constraining and "ruin people's fun." Rather, rules are designed, implemented, and enforced to manage what otherwise could be chaos. In most leisure services settings there are many different interests and desires being expressed by participants simultaneously. Without rules of some sort, very few people would have their needs met. The following principles apply to the successful use of rules:

Rules should have reasons. Arbitrary rules serve no purpose other than to enhance leader power. When participants realize this, the leader loses much respect and authority. Have reasons for rules and share those reasons with participants. Most rules are designed to keep participants, leaders, equipment, and facilities safe from harm.

Design rules in conjunction with participants. As much as possible, develop rules with participants. When rules are developed cojointly by participants and leaders, participants are much more likely to understand and follow the rules.

State rules in positive terms. Avoid a long list of "No" statements as rules. "No gum. No candy. No drinks. No running. No shouting, etc." leaves one wondering just what she or he *is* allowed to do. In addition, it establishes a negative tone and often results in the leader

Table 8D Positive Discipline

• Successful experiences are provided and highlighted.
• Honest answers are given by the leader.
• Responsibility for things that really matter is put in the hands of the participants.
• Self-discipline is the ultimate goal and efforts lead participants toward achieving this.
• Leaders hold realistic expectations of participants based on their knowledge of human development.
• Personalization and individual attention are given to each participant.
• Second chances are given; people are allowed to make mistakes.
• Is systematic.
• Utilizes active listening.
• The leader gives recognition for effort as well as achievement.
• Encouragement is used.
• Equal access is ensured for all participants.
• Flexibility is needed to accommodate each situation.
• Structured choices are provided to participants.
• Self-evaluation related to one's behaviors is conducted on a continuous basis.
• Authentic feedback is provided as opportunities arise.
• Acceptance of failed efforts as a part of learning is emphasized.
• The leader emphasizes genuine respect for differences.

looking for people to break rules. As much as possible, state all rules in a positive fashion. For example, "Please protect the grass by walking only on the sidewalk," "Please keep voices at a conversational level."

Keep rules clear and succinct. The more descriptive, and short and sweet a rule is, the easier it is to understand. Keep individual rules unambiguous and concise, and ensure that rules are packaged the same way.

Rules should be equitable. Rules should be designed to affect all participants in a similar fashion and be enforced equitably. For instance, the rule of "No hats inside" could be discriminatory to Jewish men who wear yarmulkes for religious reasons. When developing rules leaders and participants need to consider all the elements of a situation and make a judgment related to how a particular behavior will be handled based on those factors.

Rules should define responsible behaviors. If participants do not know what behaviors are expected, they will be unable fully to comply with the rules.

Clarify, practice, and monitor rules continuously. Leaders can help participants meet rule expectations by continuously clarifying them. In addition, participants will need time to practice following and meeting the rules. Both participants and leaders can monitor progress related to rules.

Rules should be appropriate for participants. Be sure that rules are appropriately matched to participant developmental stage. Expecting too much from participants can be likened to setting them up for failure.

Rules must be enforceable. Unenforceable rules are simply threats. To be effective, design rules that can be followed and enforced.

Follow through with enforcement. If rules are not enforced or enforced only sporadically, they will tend to be ineffective.

Give a warning. People of all ages tend to respond better to directions if given a heads-up that something is about to (or should) change. For instance, when it is necessary to put equipment away or swim time is about over, alerting participants ahead of time is a courteous way to help them make the psychological switch from involvement to ceasing activity. Expecting anyone to put a ball away *now* or get out of the pool *now* without advance notice is almost guaranteeing a lack of compliance.

Have only a few rules. If participants feel overwhelmed by the sheer number of rules they may feel overly constrained and that they are not trusted. Have as few rules as possible and follow through on them.

Bearing in mind these principles when developing rules will help make the policies that exist useful and doable. Rules provide structure and help teach about expectations of leaders. Use rules, but use them carefully.

Positive Reinforcement

Positive reinforcements are used to increase the frequency of desired behaviors (Sherrill, 1993). *Primary reinforcers* include edible and sensory reinforcers (e.g., candy, a pat on the back). *Secondary reinforcers* include tangible materials (nonconsumable items such as trophies, certificates, and stickers), privilege reinforcers (e.g., being first, being allowed to play longer), activity reinforcers (e.g., playing special activities, choosing the activity), generalized reinforcers (e.g., tokens, points that are traded in), and social reinforcers (e.g., a verbal "nice job" or a nonverbal smile) (Wolfgang & Wolfgang, 1995).

Rewards are an integral aspect of positive reinforcement, yet there are many disadvantages in using rewards to increase (or decrease) particular behaviors. Many believe that rewards are used too frequently and as such, tend to lose their value to participants. In fact, if used inappropriately rewards may be perceived as bribes. In addition, participants can often acquire rewards on their own—rewards are not contingent upon the leader. Furthermore, it is not uncommon for misbehaviors inadvertently to be rewarded and desired behaviors to go unrewarded. Eventually the absence of a reward feels like punishment (Gordon, 1989). A leader will want to consider all the options before deciding to use rewards as an integral part of behavior management.

Punishment

According to Sherrill (1993), punishment is anything that decreases a particular behavior. Typically, punishment has a negative connotation and involves taking away privileges or reinforcements; to be punished is not a desirable thing. Jones and Jones (1995) oppose the use of punishment because it does not teach about the more desirable behaviors, it simply punishes the individual. In addition, punishment has been shown to inhibit learning and allows the one being punished to project blame on the punishers.

Windell (1991) indicated that use of punishment can lead to the four Rs: *resentment, revenge, rebellion,* and *retreat* (sneakiness) on the part of participants. Further supporting the position of not using punishment in behavior management, Gordon (1989) reported that youth often cope with punishment by: resisting, defying, being negative, rebelling, sassing, retaliating, striking back, hitting, being combative, breaking rules or laws, lying, deceiving, getting angry, blaming others, bullying others, withdrawing, trying to be in a position of "one-up" on everyone, giving up, feeling defeated, becoming fearful and shy, getting ill, becoming overly submissive, and using drugs. Obviously, none of these coping mechanisms can be considered positive responses. If the goal of behavior management is to change behaviors and influence participants to behave in certain ways, punishment as a tool is to be avoided.

Social Contract

The use of a contract in behavior management is frequently successful for participants of all ages. A contract should be a shared effort because effective contracts outline what is expected of both the participant and the leader. In a behavior contract it is common for a leader to be identified as being responsible for helping the participant achieve her or his behavioral goals by "being there" when needed, giving a nonverbal signal which might serve as a reminder to the participant of the contract, or engaging in some other tangible action to aid in behavior control. The purpose of a contract is to help someone change behaviors and not to give the leader an easy out if the person is unsuccessful.

A behavior contract is a formal (preferably written) agreement between the leader and participant for the participant to behave in a certain fashion. Desired behaviors are identified as are the consequences for failing to meet contract stipulations. It is most effective when negotiation of all behavior contracts is systematic (no matter with whom they are used). As an example, Goldstein (1995) suggested a process of developing a behavior contract with a child.

First, the leader would explain what a contract is and provide examples of types of contracts. To insure understanding the leader then would ask the individual to describe another example of a behavior contract. Next, the leader would explain the need for a contract and identify the specific behaviors which are to be addressed in the contract. Both leader and participant negotiate the elements of the contract—a timeline is established, criteria for achievement are delineated, the leader's role is made explicit, evaluation procedures are identified, and a date for renegotiation is selected. The contract is then written out; if the participant is old enough the leader might consider having her or him write it out. Once written, both the leader and the participant sign the contract, and each of them keep a copy (Goldstein, 1995).

To be most effective, contracts should be drawn up privately and in a positive fashion; reasons are given for the need for the contract as well as each of the contract elements. Often, it is helpful to have a bonus clause to reinforce persistent efforts or outstanding behaviors by the participant. Contracts are not always successful—they fail for a variety of reasons. If penalties are too punitive or the person does not understand the agreement, a contract will not work; if the leader fails to consistently respond to the contract, its effectiveness will be lessened. In addition, if the leader is not available to dispense reinforcers when needed or to enforce the contract, it will lose its effectiveness.

Obtrusive Techniques

Most obvious to participants and onlookers, obtrusive behavior management techniques often get the attention of the entire group. With these techniques there is little question that the leader has noticed and is acting on inappropriate or undesirable behaviors.

Time-Out

Time-out is a technique used with both adults and youth; with adults, time-out is usually referred to as penalty time (as in soccer or hockey). As a behavior management technique with youth, however, time-out tends to be overused. Many parents, teachers, and leisure services leaders have fallen into using time-outs for every minor infraction, and it has lost much of its effectiveness to alter behaviors. Often, time-out is used because it is convenient for the leader—the participant is out of the way and not causing problems (at the moment). Because of its minimal effectiveness in changing behaviors, however, time-out should be a last effort technique.

To maximize the effectiveness of time-out, the leader should explain the entire process before using it (i.e., why the person is being put in time-out, where the time-out area is located, and how long the participant will remain in time-out). The time-out setting should be well-lit, ventilated, and clean; a storage closet is usually **not** a desirable location. To avoid having participants vying for time-out select a place where people do **not** want to go and is visually isolated from the activity. For safety reasons, the leader should be able to see the area at all times.

One of the reasons that time-outs are not effective is because many leaders expect participants to "sit and think about what they did" and are thus assigned an excessive amount of time (15 minutes or more in time-out). Even the best intentioned child (and adult) cannot think about her or his inappropriate behaviors for 15 minutes. A more appropriate reason to use time-out is to remove an individual from an environment where she or he is overstimulated. Time-out becomes a tool to help people "gather themselves" together and calm down.

Used as a last resort, time-out is a serious behavior management technique and to maintain this tone, the amount of time spent in time-out should be dictated by the leader and not the participant. A good rule of thumb is to require a participant to remain in time-out for *no longer* than her or his age. Therefore, a five-year-old usually should spend no more than five minutes in time-out. Certainly, leader judgment should be used and this time adjusted as the situation warrants; seven to eight minutes is usually a maximum length of time for any individual in time-out. Requiring the youth to be quiet for 30 seconds before rejoining an activity when released from time-out helps to maintain a controlled activity level (Wolfgang & Wolfgang, 1995).

Consequences

In behavior management terms consequences are defined as reactions to activity or behavior choices. There are three basic types of consequences:

(1) *arbitrary consequences* whereby reactions have nothing to do with the undesirable behavior. As an example, if a participant does not put the equipment away when asked, she or he must do ten push-ups;

(2) *logical consequences* whereby reactions are connected to the action through reason or logic. For example, if an individual does not put equipment away when asked she or he must put away not only the equipment she or he was using, but must also pick up all the other equipment as well; and

(3) *natural consequences* are results that occur as a natural outcome of the action. As an example, if participants did not put away equipment when asked, putting away equipment would take longer, and participants would be late for and perhaps unable to engage in the next activity.

There are proponents both for and against the use of the three types of consequences in behavior management. Most agree that arbitrary consequences have the least value in terms of long-term effectiveness of managing participant behaviors. Logical and natural consequences have some impact on successful behavior management.

Guiding Principles for Applying Consequences

As with rules, there are principles for applying effective consequences. Generally, the use of consequences should be in line with the behavior management philosophy of the agency. If education is the primary objective of behavior management, certain types of consequences would be more effective than if the primary goal were simple crowd control. Consider the following when implementing consequences:

Catch participants doing something right. If the underlying premise of behavior monitoring is to catch participants doing something right, there will be fewer behavior problems with which to be concerned than if the leader was always looking for participants to do something wrong (e.g., break a rule). Reinforce the appropriate and desirable behaviors so that these will occur with increased frequency.

To be most effective, consequences should be appropriate to the rule infraction. "Make the punishment fit the crime" is an adage that has application here. Demanding that participants wash a car, sit in time-out for 30 minutes, or run laps for using profanity is usually not very effective in reducing the use of profanity. Consider how and when the profanity was used, how it affected other participants, how it impacted the success of the program, and how it affected the leader before identifying and selecting potential consequences.

Consequences should be clear and understood. Well-informed participants can make better choices relative to their behaviors than those who are not informed. When enforcing rules be sure to explain the consequences of breaking those rules and be sure that participants understand them by asking clarifying questions.

Balanced and "doable" consequences are usually accepted. Building on the notion of being sure that the consequence matches the infraction, consequences tend to be accepted when it is evident that they are balanced and "doable." Doable consequences are those that are enforceable. For instance, it would not be unusual to hear an untrained and emotionally-responding leader say to a child, "If you don't stop swearing I'm going to tape your mouth shut!" Suffice it to say that taping shut the mouth of another is very unwise; that type of response is merely a threat which tells more about the emotional reaction of the leader than the actual consequences to come. Participants know that a leader is not going to tape shut their mouths; this type of threat is ineffectual and may result in overall reduced leader effectiveness.

Leave emotions out of it. As mentioned briefly in the point above, emotional leaders tend not to think clearly and often act in ways that are not only unprofessional, but could be damaging as well. One of the more difficult lessons to learn about other people's behavior is that it very rarely is directed personally at the leader. Acting out usually occurs because a need is not being met, problems at home or school are interfering with an individual, or the participant is uncomfortable. Therefore, effective use of consequences (as well as reinforcements and punishment) should be free of leader emotions. If the leader is emotionally calm, the participant often is calm and, therefore, the consequences are more palatable.

Do not withhold physical necessities. There are still leaders (e.g., uninformed youth coaches) who punish or instill arbitrary consequences of withholding physical needs such as water, food, and shelter if a youngster acts in an undesirable fashion. This is a very dangerous practice. If when standing in line for water, for instance, participants begin to push one another, a logical (although inappropriate) consequence might be to remove the pusher from the line and not let her or him have water. Withholding water from an individual has the potential to cause life-threatening illnesses and should be avoided. This is particularly true in a warm, humid environment where participants have been active.

Ask for participant involvement. Oftentimes, asking the participant what consequences should follow a rule infraction is very effective because it puts the responsibility upon the participant rather than the leader. The leader's role, then, is to modify the suggestion to be sure it meets the other principles of using consequences.

Physical Intervention

There is much discussion about the use of physical intervention in behavior management. When discussing physical intervention, thoughts often turn to corporal punishment such as spanking or slapping. The use of corporal punishment in any form is an unwise behavior management technique. Concerns over child abuse and lawsuits have effectively resulted in a ban on the use of such contact no matter the situation. Physical intervention in other forms, however, is sometimes necessary. If a participant is likely to hurt herself or himself, others, or property, action to stop the individual must be taken.

Physical intervention ranges from a hand lightly resting on the shoulder to actual "bear" hugs where an individual is completely physically restrained. To minimize the likelihood of misinterpretation and misuse, and to protect the leader(s), it is best if these types of intervention be used only in the presence of another adult. In addition, if the situation will allow for it, the participant should be verbally alerted that the leader(s) is about to touch, bear hug, or reach out for the participant.

Any physical interventions used should be employed in the best interest of the participant, not for the convenience of the leader. Therefore, the care and well-being of the participant should be foremost in the leader's mind. As with the use of all behavior management techniques, physical intervention should be emotion-free. If a leader is caught up in the moment, the possibility of a struggle and inappropriate (e.g., violent) use of intervention arises. It is best to avoid using physical intervention when possible. Typically, these types of techniques are used infrequently and as last resorts.

Ineffective Behavior Management Techniques

When leaders get tired or things are not going well there is a tendency to fall back into old behaviors and techniques—most of which are ineffective in changing behaviors and, at the least, are unprofessional. Ramsey (1994) reported a variety of techniques which do not work and should be avoided. They include yelling (participants may face similar verbal abuse at home); physical punishment (lawsuits are likely any time a leader physically punishes a participant); corporal punishment (outlawed in most states and unwise because it can backfire); and, calling parents (many parents are uninvolved or are unable to be involved to the extent needed). See Figure 8.5 on page 293 for other techniques to avoid.

If the principles of behavior management are recalled and a repertoire of techniques are utilized, it is very likely that behaviors will conform as desired without having to resort to techniques which do not work.

Selecting Techniques

People are unique; this is what makes the field of leisure services exciting, challenging, and rewarding. Knowing that all people are different and that at some time all people will act in undesirable manners, how does a leader know which technique to use when? There are several factors that help determine the most effective technique. French, Henderson, and Horvat (1992) indicated that leader style preference is a large determining factor as is the personality and style of the participant. French, Henderson, and Horvat also recommended that techniques be changed over time as they tend to lose their effectiveness if used over and over again with the same participants.

Leader knowledge, experience, and comfort level with the various techniques are probably the most influential factors in selecting behavior management techniques. In addition to these factors the needs of the individual participant should be primary in determining which technique to use when. Until one gains experience in behavior management and working with groups, it would be best to have a repertoire of techniques and work through them from unobtrusive to obtrusive until the behavior is changed in the desired fashion.

To help in minimizing the need for extensive use of behavior management techniques, it is suggested that the leader encourage and teach participants how to ask for what they need (e.g., attention, rest, more involvement) rather than act out to gain it. In addition, participants tend to engage in fewer misbehaviors when the leader meets them as they enter the facility, uses their names, and listens well (Ramsey, 1994). Leaders who recognize their own biases and prejudices and do not take things personally also tend to be more successful than those who do otherwise.

When instituting behavior management, leaders sometimes make mistakes. Mistakes in behavior management techniques are called *miscalls* (Seaman & DePauw, 1989). Miscalls include such leader errors as overreacting to a withdrawn person and feeling compelled to include her or him immediately (often accompanied by a leader command for the participant to have fun); the need to have all the attention on oneself (e.g., any fidgeting or whispering is taken personally); and, displaced anger (e.g., taking it out on participants). Furthermore, sometimes leaders become tired of being understanding (being understanding requires a commitment and energy) and leaders may see participants mirror a piece of themselves which they do not like. Other leader miscalls include the need to maintain absolute control; mistaking excitement and enthusiasm for disruptions; blaming participants when they are not at fault; and, the leader being incongruent and inconsistent. Being aware of these potential miscues can help a leisure services leader avoid common behavior management errors.

Motivation

Behavior management and motivation go hand-in-hand. If a leader has the skills to help motivate participant involvement in activities, there will be fewer behavior problems than if participants are not motivated

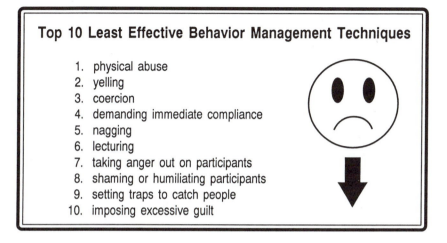

Figure 8.5   *Leaders should avoid the techniques on this list—
these are the ten* least *effective behavior management techniques used by leaders.* Adapted from
Windell (1991).

to participate or behave appropriately. Thus, understanding motivation
theories and models provides leaders with background information to
better prepare for direct leadership. It is a very complex phenomenon
and due to space limitations only an overview of motivation will be
discussed here.

First, it is necessary to understand that all people are motivated.
They may not be motivated to do as the leaders desire, nor to behave as
deemed appropriate; yet people are, nonetheless, motivated. Motivation generally refers to the forces outside of a person which cause
behaviors (i.e., extrinsic motivation) and those from inside a person
which focus behaviors toward goal achievement (i.e., intrinsic motivation) (Seaman & DePauw, 1989; Sherrill, 1993). Leaders are encouraged to learn more about motivation and motivation theories so that they
might be fully effective when working with groups.

Theories of motivation commonly focus on unmet needs and most
needs, are thought to be learned (Russell, 1986). Generally the motivation process involves an internal drive or need that causes certain actions
or behaviors to occur which are directed toward achieving a goal (to
meet the need).

Maslow's Hierarchy of Needs

One of the more well-known theories or models of motivation is Maslow's Hierarchy of Needs (Bass, 1990; Bijou, 1992; Chemers & Ayman, 1993; Edginton & Ford, 1985; Hunt, 1991; Kraus, 1985; Niepoth, 1983; Russell, 1986). According to this model, people will act to meet lower order needs before striving for higher order needs. Maslow believed that people are initially motivated by biological or physiological needs such as the need for food, water, sleep, and sex. Therefore, if a participant is hungry or thirsty she or he will be motivated to eat and drink before doing much else. If food and water are not available or if the need goes unrecognized, misbehaviors might result. For instance, people who are hungry may be tired and "cranky" until they have had food.

Once physiological needs have been met, Maslow believes participants are motivated by a need for security. Security includes not only physical safety and security, but also psychological and emotional safety. Therefore, if an individual feels threatened, she or he will act in ways to regain a sense of security. This might include staying close to the leader, fighting back, or withdrawing from the situation.

Humans are social beings and as such have a need for love, belonging and social contacts. This is the next level of needs according to Maslow. Wanting to be a part of the group, to fit in, and to be accepted are strong drives once security and physiological needs have been met. Adolescents and teens often act in ways to gain acceptance by a peer group.

The last two levels of needs in Maslow's hierarchy are the needs for esteem and self-actualization. Esteem needs include the needs for achievement and recognition by others. Participants strive to master skills and to gain recognition (e.g., attention from the leader, a pat on the back, a trophy) for those skills. If leaders and others do not give such recognition, participants may act out to gain the leader's attention. People with low self-esteem may be moody, aggressive or withdrawn.

Self-actualization needs may be defined as the needs described by the now popular phrase, "be all that you can be." Self-actualized people are motivated and satisfied from within themselves, dare to take risks, and are not afraid of failure. According to Maslow all humans strive to reach this potential (Bass, 1990; Bijou, 1992; Chemers & Ayman, 1993; Edginton & Ford, 1985; Hunt, 1991; Kraus, 1985; Niepoth, 1983; Russell, 1986).

As leaders consider the various elements of motivation and the reasons behind people acting the way they do, it is wise to bear in mind that people float up and down this hierarchy, and may be striving to meet several needs at the same time. Therefore, if a participant is acting out it may be helpful to discern which needs are driving the behaviors. By addressing the underlying needs, the undesirable behaviors will cease. For instance, a participant may not have slept well the previous night, feel as though others are picking on her or him, and may feel ostracized from the group. According to Maslow's hierarchy, this individual will strive to "fix" these imbalances through various actions. Undesirable techniques might include fighting and engaging in name calling.

Figure 8.7   *Maslow's Hierarchy of Needs offers a clear look at the primary motivators of participants.*

Flow

Another way to look at participant needs is to examine the concept of *flow* (Csikszentmihalyi, 1990). Flow is a zone of enjoyment and pleasure which exists between boredom and anxiety. When engaging in leisure activities people strive for enjoyment and a (psychological) place where they feel competent. If an activity is difficult or challenging and a participant is a novice, she or he will probably feel anxious. This anxiety may lead to acting out behaviors as the participant tries to avoid failure. If, on the other hand, a participant is highly skilled at an activity and the activity is too easy or lacking in challenge, she or he may experience boredom. As with anxiety, a participant feeling bored might act out in an effort to be more challenged. Therefore, leaders should strive to determine if the activity is overly challenging or too simple for participant skill levels. By adapting activities and the way one leads, flow can be facilitated for many. A leader, then, strives to match participant skill and challenge levels in an effort to help them experience flow.

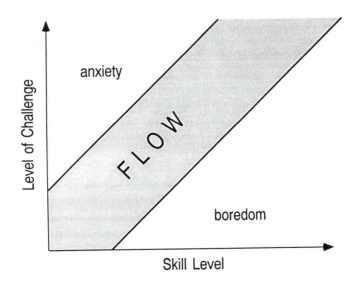

Figure 8.8   *The concept of flow involves matching skill levels with the level of challenge.*

Facilitating Motivation

If the supposition that all people are motivated is true, then one might well be wondering about the role of a leader in motivating participants. Leaders can establish an environment which will provide an atmosphere that directs the way in which a person is motivated. An environment can be established that will enhance and guide participant motivation to match the leader's expectations for behaviors. Leaders can augment participant motivation by manipulating three environments: *physical*, *psychological*, and *socioemotional*.

Physical Environment

The physical environment can be manipulated through use of room colors, posters, lighting, noise, temperature, and external stimuli. For instance, it is known that the color red increases heart rate and respirations—it serves to excite people. Most blue tones, on the other hand, act as a calming influence. Bright lights affect participants differently than does subdued lighting. Room temperature can affect the level of alertness (e.g., warm temperatures often cause people to get sleepy, cooler temperatures make people more alert). Different music affects people differently, establishing various moods.

Psychological Environment

Leaders can manipulate the psychological environment by establishing an atmosphere that encourages achievement, mastery of skills, esteem, and knowledge. Motivating participants may occur through ensuring an appropriate level of challenge and difficulty in activities so that success is achieved. By maintaining and communicating expectations of success a leader also can manipulate the psychological environment. Allowing opportunities for participants to make choices and providing immediate feedback also influence the psychological environment.

Socioemotional Environment

The socioemotional environment includes the elements that affect one's sense of belonging and affect (feelings). Leaders can manipulate this environment by helping participants see links between their efforts and outcomes. Providing a supportive environment that meets one's need to belong and feel like a member of the group is an important element of the socioemotional environment. Modeling interest, enthusiasm and intensity in the activity, and outlining meaningful objectives in which participants are interested are two other techniques that might increase the effectiveness of this environment.

People become involved in activities if they think they can be successful. Therefore, if activities are designed for participant success based on developmental stage, motivating need, and other participant factors, it is likely that they will be motivated to fully and actively participate rather than act out in undesirable manners. In addition, participants will be motivated to the degree that they value the rewards of participation. The more an individual values a particular activity, the more she or he will behave in appropriate ways. Furthermore, Jones and Jones (1995) have found that the quality of relationships involved in an activity is a motivating factor. Leaders who strive for high-quality relationships for participants will be more successful than those who do not.

Summary

In this chapter you have had an opportunity to discuss and explore several approaches to behavior management; preventative management, moral education, affective and communication models, behavior modification, assertive discipline, reality therapy, and behavior and family therapy. Each of these approaches provides a philosophical orientation to how a leader handles the management of other's behaviors. A leader may follow one approach or a combination of several in behavior management efforts.

Just as there are many ways in which people differ from one another, so there are many contributing factors to how and why people act out. Age, developmental ability, cultural understanding, and gender all play a role in how people act in leisure settings. Through understanding the underlying principles of behavior management leaders can accommodate and acknowledge differences in people, while still attending to the undesirable behaviors. A variety of specific behavior management techniques were presented, from unobtrusive to discernible to obtrusive in nature.

Because motivation and behavior management are closely related, the concept of flow and Maslow's Hierarchy of Needs were presented. Comprehending what motivates people and how to facilitate that motivation are great aids in managing participant behaviors. It is anticipated that as with all leadership skills, each leader will integrate various techniques and methodologies into her or his particular leadership style as appropriate. Managing behaviors is necessary to facilitate high quality recreation experiences for participants. In that sense, rules and guidelines serve not to constrain individual leisure and ruin people's fun, but rather to manage diverse situations in the best interest of all.

The Front Line

Remembering the following *principles of motivation* may help when desiring to facilitate intrinsic motivation and positive behavior management in participants (i.e., self-instilled):

- All people are motivated.
- People are motivated for their reasons, not yours.
- There is no single best or all-purpose motivational pattern (in other words, everyone is different).
- A motivational strength overused, or used when inappropriate, can become a weakness (e.g., a person who is motivated by perfection might end up never completing her or his tasks because the jobs are never perfect enough).
- People use different behaviors to get their needs met.
- People are naturally motivated to get their needs met.
- People choose whether to live by needs alone (e.g., some people think that if their needs are met, that is, physiological, safety, belonging, achievement, and self-actualization, that is all that counts).
- People *cannot* live by needs alone (e.g., values help to temper the need motivations to fit within social dictates).
- Productive motivation begins with awareness (i.e., once an individual is aware of her or his primary motivators, she or he can be very productive in how that motivation is used).
- People have natural ways of behaving which can be predicted.
- When you understand someone you can better predict her or his behavior.
- Motivation is where our behavior begins *and* returns (i.e., motivation is an ongoing cycle that influences every aspect of our lives) (Merwin & O'Connor, 1988).

References

Bass, B. (1990). *Bass and Stogdill's handbook of leadership* (3rd ed.). New York, NY: The Free Press.

Bijou, S. (1992). Behavior analysis. In R. Vasta (Ed.), *Six theories of child development: Revised formulations and current issues* (pp. 61-83). London, UK: Jessica Kingsley Publishers, Ltd.

Bolton, R. (1979). *People skills.* Englewood Cliffs, NJ: Prentice Hall.

Chemers, M. and Ayman, R. (Eds.). (1993). *Leadership theory and research.* San Diego, CA: Academic Press, Inc.

Cherry, C. (1983). *Please don't sit on the kids.* Belmont, CA: Fearon Pitman Publishing.

Csikszentmihalyi, M. (1990). *Flow: The psychology of optimal experience.* New York, NY: Harper & Row.

Edginton, C. and Ford, P. (1985). *Leadership in recreation and leisure services organizations.* New York, NY: John Wiley & Sons.

French, R., Henderson, H., and Horvat, M. (1992). *Creative approaches to managing student behavior.* Park City, UT: Family Development Resources, Inc.

Goldstein, S. (1995). *Understanding and managing children's classroom behavior.* New York, NY: John Wiley & Sons.

Gordon, T. (1989). *Teaching children self-discipline.* New York, NY: Times Books.

Grossnickle, D. and Sesko, F. (1994). *Promoting effective discipline in school and classroom.* Reston, VA: National Association of Secondary School Principals.

Hunt, J. (1991). *Leadership: A new synthesis.* Newbury Park, CA: Sage Publications, Inc.

Jones, V. and Jones, L. (1995). *Comprehensive classroom management.* Boston, MA: Allyn & Bacon.

Kraus, R. (1985). *Recreation leadership today.* Glenview, IL: Scott Foresman & Company.

Merwin, S. and O'Connor, M. (1988). *The mysteries of motivation.* Minneapolis, MN: Carlson Learning Co.

Munn, P., Johnstone, M., and Chalmers, V. (1992a). *Effective discipline in primary schools and classrooms.* London, UK: Paul Chapman Publishing.

Munn, P., Johnstone, M., and Chalmers, V. (1992b). *Effective discipline in secondary schools and classrooms.* London, UK: Paul Chapman Publishers.

Nelson, E. (1987). *Positive discipline.* New York, NY: Ballentine Books.

Niepoth, E. W. (1983). *Leisure leadership.* Englewood Cliffs, NJ: Prentice Hall.

Ramsey, R. (1994). *Administrator's complete school discipline guide.* Englewood Cliffs, NJ: Prentice Hall.

Russell, R. V. (1986). *Leadership in recreation.* St. Louis, MO: Times Mirror/Mosby.

Savage, T. (1991). *Discipline for self control.* Englewood Cliffs, NJ: Prentice Hall.

Seaman, J. and DePauw, K. (1989). *The new adapted physical education: A developmental approach* (2nd ed.). Mountain View, CA: Mayfield Publishing Co.

Seeman, H. (1994). *Preventing classroom discipline problems* (2nd ed.). Lancaster, PA: Technomic Publishing Co., Inc.

Sherrill, C. (1993). *Adapted physical activity, recreation, and sport* (4th ed.). Dubuque, IA: Brown & Benchmark.

Silberman, M. and Wheelan, S. (1980). *How to discipline without feeling guilty.* Champaign, IL: Research Press Company.

Windell, J. (1991). *Discipline: A sourcebook of 50 failsafe techniques for parents.* New York, NY: Macmillan Publishing Company.

Wolfgang, C. and Wolfgang, M. (1995). *The three faces of discipline for early childhood.* Boston, MA: Allyn & Bacon.

Section III

Synergy in Leadership:
Pulling It All Together

Synergy is a term used to describe the notion that the sum of the parts is larger, bigger, and more powerful than the whole. It also implies an important linking together of the various pieces. The final section of this text presents material that is overtly necessary for effective leisure services leadership. Issues of diversity, values, ethics, risk management, direct leadership techniques, and social and professional concerns are vital to all discussions surrounding leadership. Successful and effective leaders have a solid understanding of how these elements impact leadership situations.

The purpose of this third section of the text, therefore, is to provide thought-provoking material to serve as a kind of fabric for leisure services leadership. The issues found in upcoming chapters are woven throughout all leadership decisions and are necessary to help leaders successfully meet the diverse needs of leisure participants.

It is not possible for this text (or any other) to be all things to all people; everyone learns in her or his own way. Some quickly grasp abstract concepts and build practical knowledge on that base, while others learn through experience and backtrack to related conceptual issues. In this text, an attempt has been made to provide a mix of information—conceptual, theoretical, practical, and thought-provoking—that might serve to meet the needs of a diverse readership. Readers are encouraged to review sections that may have been a bit muddied in earlier study, and to place the information in context with current learning and goals. Leadership development is like learning in that they both occur through book knowledge as well as through experiential efforts—and material must be continually reviewed to fully make sense.

As one reads the chapters in this section, then, and begins to pull together the material from throughout the text, the synergy that develops from these efforts will aid in the holistic development of leadership skills. An effective leader is one who is competent in technical skills, human relation skills, and conceptual skills and understands how the three skill areas are inextricably linked.

Chapter Nine
Learning Opportunities

Through studying this chapter students will have the opportunity to:

- understand the importance of diversity for effective leadership;
- examine the construct of culture and how it impacts leisure services leadership;
- increase their knowledge of the dimensions of diversity;
- recognize the impacts of unearned privilege on access to resources; and
- examine several techniques for leaders to effectively meet the needs of a variety of constituents.

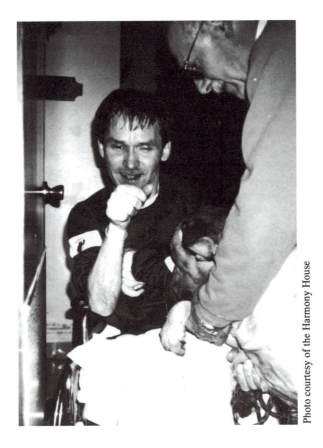

Photo courtesy of the Harmony House

CHAPTER

9

Diversity and Leisure Services Leadership

Leisure services settings are places where people go to engage in enjoyable activities, to be with others with whom they feel safe and whose company is stimulating, and to perhaps learn new skills or knowledge. Leisure services leaders work in these settings and strive to facilitate the various types of leisure experiences participants seek. Leaders have a responsibility to ensure (as much as possible) that every leisure participant has the opportunity to reach the potential in leisure she or he desires. For this to occur, the environment must be conducive to a feeling of belonging, personal growth, and offer a variety of experiences. In many cases, such an atmosphere is lacking. Consider the following scenarios:

- Women from a local college basketball team are at the recreation facility over winter break shooting hoops during an open gymnasium period. A group of young men come in and run them off saying, "Let us men show you girls how the game is really played—basketball is a man's game."

- A Black family enters the library and a friendly librarian steps up and offers to show them where the books are shelved that would be of interest to them—she takes the family to the section that deals with African-American history.

- A group of boys ages 11 to 13 are engaged in a rough and tumble game on the football field. When the recreation supervisor asks them what they are playing they shout, "Smear the queer!"

- A 65-year-old man mails in his registration for a low-impact aerobics class and is called by the center staff who want to be sure the man knows he is "signing up for a ladies activity."

- A person who uses a wheelchair wants to play racquetball and is told she cannot because "black rubber soles are not allowed on the court" and the tires on her chair are black rubber.

In each of the above situations potential participants were faced with prejudice and discrimination which negatively impacted their leisure experiences. Whether based on age, gender, race, disability or perceived sexual orientation, prejudice and discrimination have the potential to inhibit and constrain the leisure of those being labeled. As facilitators of leisure experiences, recreation and leisure services leaders are in a position to protect, facilitate, and enhance the leisure experiences of others.

Because leaders work with people of all backgrounds, understanding the issues surrounding diversity is required to be an effective leisure services leader. Having some knowledge of the different ways in which people learn, communicate with one another, and participate in leisure can help a leader be responsive to the needs of all participants. An attempt has been made throughout each chapter of this text to address issues of diversity as they apply to the material being discussed. To

Figure 9.1   People differ from one another on many dimensions.

augment that material, this chapter is devoted to providing additional information about various elements of diversity and multiculturalism to assist leaders in better understanding the issues involved.

Understanding the Basics

As with all constructs it is important to gain an understanding of how terms are used. This chapter utilizes terms that are used in everyday language, but for which people often hold different meanings. *Diversity* is what this chapter is all about. It is a concept referring to a celebration of differences among people that seeks to encourage the appreciation of those differences (and similarities) in the pursuit of equality and fairness (Hernandez, 1989). *Dimensions of diversity* refers to the various dimensions, traits, or characteristics on which we differ. There are core and secondary characteristics upon which others make assumptions about us. They include such things as sex, age, class, and level of education, among others (Loden, 1995; Loden & Rosener, 1991).

The assumptions others make about us based on the dimensions of diversity are known as *stereotypes*. Stereotypes are part of a perceptual and cognitive process whereby specific traits are ascribed to people based on their apparent membership in a group—they are by no means always accurate, and may be either positive or negative (Cox, 1993; Gudykunst, 1991). For instance, a negative stereotype might be one where all members of a cultural group are believed to be substance abusers. A positive stereotype might be when an individual is perceived as highly intelligent simply because she or he belongs to a cultural group. According to King, Chipman, and Cruz-Janzen (1994), stereotypes are perpetuated by:

- denying they exist (e.g., "This is 1996; people don't believe in stereotypes any more.");

- ignoring them or accepting them when they occur (e.g., in response to a sexist remark—"Uh huh, that's true.");

- denying that they affect our lives (e.g., "Stereotypes don't affect me—I'm accepted for who I am.");

- denying that they affect other's lives (e.g., "They need to stop playing 'victims'—people don't get fired from jobs because of stereotypes."); and

- supporting them through our own behaviors, for example: exclusion and tokenism, stereotyping, biased language, imbalance and inequality such as giving value to only one side of the story, unreality (e.g., misinformation), isolation, and segregation.

Closely related to stereotyping is *prejudice*. Prejudice is a preconceived belief or preference for one thing, place, or people over another; it is an irrational hatred or fear of a group of people and individual members of that group (Hirsch, Kett & Trefil, 1993). *Discrimination* describes the acts taken on the basis of prejudice; it is differential treatment of one group which can create a situation of disadvantage for another group.

Various cultural groups will be discussed throughout this chapter. *Culture* is often perceived as the sum total of the way people act and live their lives. It consists of shared assumptions, beliefs and values (usually unspoken); learned responses; and ways of being, knowing and doing. Culture is transmitted through language, material objects, rituals, institutions, and art from one generation to the next (Cox, 1993; Hirsch, Kett, & Trefil, 1993).

Culture is also viewed as a dynamic, creative and continuous process; it is an orientation to life that includes an intertwined system of values, attitudes, and beliefs that give meaning to individual and collective identity (Hernandez, 1989). Althen (1994) thinks of culture as an iceberg. The tip of the iceberg, which is one ninth of its total size, may be represented by the aspects of culture which are visible to others—words, behaviors, customs, and traditions. Just under the surface of the water are the beliefs held by the cultural group. They are surfaced in varying situations, but for the most part, remain hidden. Far under the water are the values, assumptions, and thought processes of the culture; these are very difficult to access and understand by people who do not belong to that cultural group, and sometimes, by cultural group members, themselves.

By understanding that people differ in beliefs, values, assumptions, customs, and ways of knowing we begin to comprehend the complexities of working with people in leisure services settings. While humans are similar to one another in many respects, there are also significant ways in which people differ from one another. Leaders who are able to work with both the similarities and differences in people are likely to experience success in their leadership efforts.

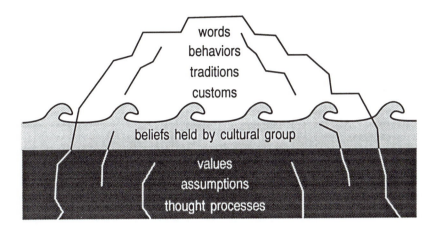

words
behaviors
traditions
customs

beliefs held by cultural group

values
assumptions
thought processes

Figure 9.2 *Culture may be perceived as an iceberg with various elements above and below the water line.*

Approaches to Dealing with Diversity

It is important to note that there currently are two prevailing schools of thought related to examining differences and issues of diversity. One group of people subscribes to the notion that to focus on differences will only serve to divide people further apart. According to individuals who subscribe to this philosophy, it is best to let historical issues lie and to move forward working toward common goals and shared needs. We should only focus on how people are alike and let go of the feelings of being different. Indeed, it seems logical to believe that if celebrating diversity is the ultimate and most highly valued end (of all human values), a sense of commonalty and unity would be extremely difficult to attain.

The other school of thought believes that to overcome prejudicial attitudes, whether they be based on race, sexual orientation, gender, or other characteristics, people must first be willing to examine their own attitudes and beliefs about differences. To truly get at the root of "isms" (e.g., racism, ableism, sexism), both personal as well as systemic prejudice and discrimination must first be uncovered. Once these issues are recognized, action may then be taken to deconstruct discrimination and work toward equality, common goals, and shared needs.

To focus on differences in efforts to better understand others seems to lend itself to breaking down discrimination and moving forward—

together. Gaining a better understanding of one's own perceptions of differences and similarities in people may help in developing a leadership style and approach which is relatively free of bias, and effective with most constituents most of the time.

Changes in Diversity Issues

In the past, culture was commonly perceived as referring to traits that were deemed characteristic of people who belonged to various racial groupings (e.g., Black culture, Native-American culture). In recent years we have seen an expansion of the definition of culture to include all of the core dimensions of diversity (e.g., gender, race, sexual orientation, physical/cognitive abilities and qualities, and age) (Althen, 1994; Loden, 1995; Loden & Rosener, 1991). This means that it is now believed that people with disabilities have an identifiable culture as do the elderly as do people who are gay, and so on.

As new knowledge is gained through research, a trend is emerging that suggests that the impacts of discrimination are a result of power differences between cultural groups; these differences arise out of historical and political factors associated with the particular culture (Althen, 1994). This means that between Black people and Caucasian people (i.e., people of European ancestry) for instance, prejudice and discrimination arise out of a power relationship more so than from a racial relationship. In the U.S., Caucasian people have more power (i.e., better and easier access to resources such as money, good jobs, and housing) than do Blacks. Discrimination, then, is systemic. It goes beyond personal attitudes and is perpetuated by the mores and norms of the dominant culture.

Recognizing that power differences exist hand-in-hand with discrimination often helps in understanding the need to disassemble such system-wide prejudicial attitudes. As a leader in the field of human services it is necessary to see that all people, no matter who they are, should have equal access to basic needs such as housing, food, transportation, and leisure experiences.

Another trend relative to the examination of issues surrounding diversity is the move from attempting to assimilate cultures into one "melting pot" to the notion of *pluralism*, which is learning how multiple groups can coexist as one while retaining their own cultural identities (Loden, 1995). More and more people are beginning to realize that there is strength in diversity and that all people do not need to be exactly alike. Learning how to live, work, and play together within differences is the goal for increased life satisfaction.

As can be seen, an understanding of diversity is vital for an effective leader. Knowing how to best serve people of different backgrounds and cultures is the first step to celebrating diversity in leisure services leadership. Consider the following information: by the year 2000 it is estimated that in the U.S. the Asian-American population will increase by 22%; the Hispanic-American (including Latino) population will see an increase of 21%; the African-American population will experience a 12% rise; and Caucasian Americans will increase their numbers by 2%. By 2015 Hispanic Americans will outnumber Black Americans (York, 1994). From these population increases it has been estimated that by 2015 Caucasian Americans will be a minority in terms of numbers of people (Hirsch, Kett, & Trefil, 1993; York, 1994). Leisure services leaders will be faced with addressing and meeting the needs of very diverse constituent groups.

Dimensions of Diversity

Loden and Rosener (1991) present a model of diversity which has been adapted for use in this text. There are many dimensions or elements of diversity, some of which are considered core dimensions and others secondary dimensions of diversity. When examining the dimensions of diversity it is important to remember that people are not different from one another on just one dimension. People are a composite of many elements of diversity and each diversity element can serve to help or hurt in terms of negative (or positive) social responses to that person.

While not necessarily accurate, many people perceive the dimensions of diversity as bipolar; that is, people tend to categorize individuals into belonging to "one or the other" categories. This polarization of the dimensions of diversity is seen in the overt valuing of one end of the continuum over the other. For instance, being Caucasian is more highly valued (and receives better and more perks) than being Black; male is more highly valued than female; and able-bodied is more highly valued than disabled.

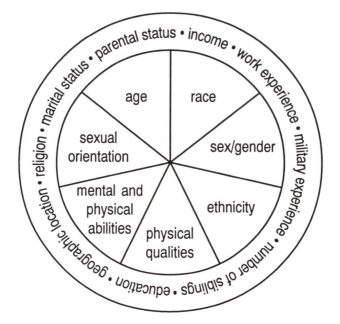

Figure 9.3   *Loden and Rosener (1991) presented core and secondary dimensions of diversity on which all people differ.*

Core Dimensions

Most of us expect other people to be just like us in ways such as likes, dislikes, values, assumptions, behaviors, and we base our expectations and judgments of their behaviors on these perceptions. For instance, if we have a habit of sending notes of appreciation to others when they have done something nice for us, we tend to expect others to do the same in return. If so, when we do not receive thank-you notes after doing another individual a favor, we may become irritated and hurt, and attribute the lack of a note to bad manners or a moral deficiency. Because people are distinct from one another and live with different elements of diversity than us, however, they have sets of experiences which lead to developing unique ways of looking at the world.

The core dimensions of diversity seem to have the largest impact on individual perceptions of the world. For the most part, these are part of the human composite we observe upon seeing and meeting people, and are extremely difficult, if at all possible, to change. As a way of maintaining order and processing information in a relatively efficient manner we have a tendency to put people into perceptual categories based on these core dimensions. It is the meanings and values that we ascribe to these various elements of personhood that result in prejudice and discrimination.

Sex/Gender

Sex is the biological difference in females and males present at birth; gender is the way we perceive femaleness (i.e., what it means to be a girl or woman) and maleness (i.e., what it means to be a boy or man) and is socialized in and taught to people throughout life. It is possible to be a female in sex, yet masculine in gender; it is also possible to be male in sex and feminine in gender.

The prevailing attitude in the U.S. is that male sex and masculine gender are favored—males who behave in a characteristically masculine fashion have greater power in terms of access to resources, than females and people who are feminine. This attitude is visible in leisure services settings in the basketball scenario presented at the beginning of this chapter. The men believed they had the right to take the court away from the women and did so without hesitation or second thoughts.

Age

People often overlook age when addressing issues of prejudice and discrimination, yet there are clear instances of age being used to label people and constrain them from reaching their full potential. Many people hold negative stereotypes of teenagers (e.g., they are self-serving and lazy) while others hold negative beliefs about older people (e.g., they have low mental capabilities and are physically frail). In leisure settings jumping to conclusions about an individual's abilities or interests based on age, or treating people in a certain manner because of their age, may limit full involvement in the leisure experience. A full discussion of human development is provided in Chapter Three.

Ethnicity/Race

It has been common to use the term *race* when referring to a group of people who share a genetic makeup which results in biological characteristics that can be used to distinguish one group from another (e.g., people of Asian heritage have eyefolds and small noses; people of European descent have round eyes and relatively pale skin color). The accuracy of the term, *race*, is being questioned as new research is being reported which indicates that all humans are biologically related to one another.

*Age is one dimension
of diversity that all
people will face.*

Photo courtesy of the Western Home

Ethnicity has referred to the commonalties passed down through history and tradition from one generation of people to the next. As a term, ethnicity is a more accurate description of the culture with which one identifies than is race. King, Chipman, & Cruz-Janzen (1994) have noted seven components that constitute ethnicity: a historical link, shared geographic beginnings, linguistic commonalties, shared religious beliefs, common social class status, mutual political interests, and a joint moral (values) base. Individuals who have most or all of these seven aspects of ethnicity in common would be considered to share an ethnic heritage and culture.

The assumption made by the friendly librarian in the scenario at the beginning of this chapter that a Black family would only be interested in books about African Americans is a subtle form of prejudice based on race/ethnicity. Before asking the family about their interests, the librarian made an unfounded judgment and limited the family's exploration of the library. This faulty assessment was likely based on both skin color and assumptions about the ethnicity of the family.

Sexual Orientation

Sexual orientation includes identifying as gay, lesbian, bisexual, and heterosexual. For many, this core dimension of diversity is the more easily hidden of all core elements of diversity (one cannot tell if someone is straight or gay simply by looking at her or him), yet it still engenders strong social reactions.

People of all sexual orientations engage in a variety of leisure activities and are involved in every type of leisure services organization. Leisure services leaders have long catered to the needs and desires of people who are heterosexual—family programming, husband-and-wife activities, dances—yet, the needs of gay, lesbian, and bisexual participants have essentially been ignored.

To be most effective, leaders would be wise to recognize the specific needs of *all* constituents. Particularly vulnerable to severe social sanctions are gay, lesbian, and bisexual adolescents and teens. These group members often experience tremendous stresses as they discover their sexuality in an atmosphere of hate and misunderstanding. The early chapter scenario of young boys playing a game called, "Smear the queer" is an example of homophobic attitudes found throughout society—even in children's games.

Photo courtesy of the YWCA of Black Hawk County

People differ in ethnic affiliation; some celebrate that affiliation through style of dress and special events.

Physical/Cognitive Abilities and Qualities

In this dimension of diversity cognitive and physical disabilities are addressed as are other physical qualities which might foster negative reactions—obesity, wearing thick glasses, having severe acne, or being "ugly" in cultural terms. Too often people with disabilities and other "less than perfect" physical qualities are ignored in as far as equal access to services and leisure services opportunities. Assumptions and pre-judgments about desires and capabilities are often made upon seeing a person who is obese, a person with Down syndrome, a person with a seeing-eye dog, or a person who has prominent birth marks. As depicted at the beginning of this chapter, disallowing a person who uses a wheelchair from full participation in leisure due to the fact that her or his wheelchair has rubber tires (which is not something to be altered) is an example of (seemingly well-justified) discrimination.

Photo courtesy of the Family YMCA of Black Hawk County

Among people with physical and mental disabilities, there is tremendous variation.

Secondary Dimensions

Secondary dimensions of diversity include elements of self which are not necessarily visible, and which may change over the course of one's life. Elements that fit into this classification of diversity include: marital status, class, parental status, socioeconomic status, educational level, type of occupation, military experience, types of leisure activities in which one engages, geographic area in which one grew up (and now lives), religion, and other components that comprise a person. As with the core dimensions, throughout various cultures there is one aspect of each of these secondary diversity dimensions that is more highly valued than the other and which receives unspoken privileges.

As we get to know more about a person than can be seen with our eyes (i.e., the secondary dimensions of diversity), we usually modify our first impressions. For instance, if we recently met an individual who is of Asian-American heritage (stereotype: highly intelligent), female (stereotype: not as intelligent as male), 16-years-old (stereotype: focused and college oriented), heterosexual (stereotype: "normal"), and able-bodied (stereotype: healthy), our first impression would likely be positive toward this individual; she does, after all, fit the American model of a soon-to-be successful employee and contributing member of society. However, as we get to know this teen better, we learn that she had a baby last year (teen parent status); many of us would modify our first impression to include stereotypes of irresponsibility and sexually promiscuity. Whether or not any of these assumptions were accurate could not be determined until we learned much more about this individual.

Diversity and Privilege

It has been mentioned that for each element of diversity there is a preferred state of being which is valued more highly than another. For example, in the dimension of physical/cognitive abilities and qualities the preferred state of being is able-bodied and attractive (according to one's culture). Being able-bodied and attractive is more highly valued than being disabled and unattractive—attractive able-bodied people are well-treated by society and receive many *unearned privileges* because of their physical appearance. Unearned privileges are special advantages, permissions, rights, or benefits granted to an individual purely on the basis of their physical appearance (or other dimensions of diversity) (McIntosh, 1989). Such an advantage, right, or benefit is often exercised to the exclusion or detriment of others resulting in discrimination.

People in each of the privileged classes or categories on the valued end of the diversity continuum are taught to not see the privileges bestowed upon them; most are very unaware of their own privileges based on the dimensions of diversity they represent (McIntosh, 1989). The awareness and knowledge of personal privilege is believed necessary to first become aware of, and then reduce prejudice and discrimination.

McIntosh (1989) enlightened readers by presenting a number of examples of unearned skin color–based privileges; they are in adapted form below. White privilege includes:

- being able to go shopping without being harassed or followed by security personnel;
- being certain people did not get out of the pool when I got in because of my skin color;
- being able to swear, dress grubby, and not answer letters without others attributing these behaviors to the bad morals, poverty, or illiteracy of my race; and
- getting a job without coworkers thinking I got it because of my race....

In addition, there are privileges of being male:

- assured of not waiting in long lines in public to use the bathroom;
- can be rude and short with people without being referred to as a bitch;
- can be physically athletic without someone questioning my sexuality; and
- have the ability to get my hair cut and clothes pressed for less money than a woman....

Privileges of being heterosexual include:

- the protection of marriage, should I want it;
- it is acceptable to engage in some public displays of affection with my significant other;
- receiving less costly family rates at parks, recreation and leisure services settings; and
- I am unlikely to be fired from my job because of my sexuality....

Privileges of being thirty-something include:

- the assumption of being able, college educated and having some level of knowledge;
- good insurance rates on my automobile;
- full access to all rides at an amusement or theme park; and
- can be assured that people will listen to my opinion....

Privileges of being attractive and able-bodied include:

- I can be assured of getting prompt and efficient service at a restaurant;
- the local recreation and leisure services facilities are fully accessible to me;
- when I have a flat tire alongside the road someone is likely to stop and help; and
- leisure services leaders will be pleasant with me and comfortable in my presence....

Privileges of being in the middle or upper class include:

- my chances of getting a bank loan for a vacation are fairly assured;
- I can find housing in an area where others will share similar values;
- my family will never go without heat or food for lack of paying a bill; and
- I can afford to use the local leisure services facilities as I wish....

Each of the dimensions of diversity has with it an amount of unearned privilege and power based solely on exhibiting that element of diversity. This in turn, is equal to unearned advantage for some and disadvantage for others. If people are to be treated fairly and without bias, an acknowledgment of these privileges must first occur. Effective leaders understand that those who are privileged by chance of birth are afforded privileges while others are essentially being penalized for their birth situation. It is through this systemic notion of the "haves" and "have-nots" that discrimination becomes institutionalized throughout society.

Knowing About Differences

An awareness of differences is the first step to working effectively with people who think and act differently from people with whom we are familiar. Consider the following story as presented by Edwards (1991) and cited in Sims and Dennehy (1993, p. 2):

> The second grade teacher posed a simple enough problem to the class: "There are four blackbirds sitting in a tree. You take a slingshot and shoot one of them. How many are left?" "Three" answered the seven-year-old European with certainty. "One subtracted from four leaves three." "Zero" answered the seven-year-old African with equal certainty. "If you shoot one bird, the others will fly away."

This story illustrates how two different people can understand the world differently from one another—and how both can be correct. Neither one is more right than the other and everyone is enriched by understanding both viewpoints. In most situations there is more than one right answer; recognizing this benefits leaders in their efforts to resolve conflicts, engage in problem solving, and make decisions relative to leadership efforts. Diversity in people and viewpoints offers strength in creativity, problem solving, and in seeing the big picture.

Another reason it is important to acknowledge differences is because it is known that people who "must function in situations where they feel alone and estranged will experience increased levels of stress

Figure 9.4   *People understand the world differently from one another and these differences tend to be complementary rather than divisive.*

and might not be able to show the competence they are capable of [sic]" (Chemers & Ayman, 1993, p. 194). The stresses arise from differences in values, norms, roles and attitudes, negative stereotypes, constantly interpreting what is occurring, and from being continually "on" (Seelye & Seelye-James, 1995). Leaders who recognize these types of stresses will likely be understanding of the possible frustrations participants might face. A connection with participants facing these stresses could be made which would help with achieving social integration and meeting each individual's leisure goals.

Age

At various ages across the life span people have different abilities and skills. As we age we gain maturity in physical size, physical abilities, social skills, and cognitive abilities. Our ability to reason, use language, and manipulate objects increases with age—to a point. When reaching old age, physical abilities fall off as do some cognitive functions. Readers are encouraged to review the chapter about human development for additional information about differences in abilities across the life span.

Leading People of Varying Ages

When talking with and leading the very young it is important to remember that they are literal in their understanding. The use of adages or clichés can be very confusing to youngsters during this period. Teens often wrestle with issues of self-identity and esteem, and a primary concern is gaining a sense of belonging. Mid-aged adults face concerns about family and stability and often seek leisure as a diversion or stress reliever. Older seniors should be treated with dignity and respect; activities should be adapted for changing physical and cognitive needs. Leaders who are age- and developmental-stage appropriate in activity choice and delivery, and in communication with participants will generally be more successful than those who try to lead the same way for every one.

Race/Ethnicity

Ethnicity has been discussed in some detail earlier in this chapter. Leaders would be wise to gain information about ethnic groups with which they might work because each culture is very complex in its attitudes, beliefs, values structures, and leisure preferences. It is also

Photo by Mowatt Photography; Courtesy of the Western Home

Leisure services leaders will lead groups of all ages and with varying physical capabilities.

important to recognize that within each culture individuals are unique; not all Hispanic women believe in the same issues, for instance. Gender, age, physical abilities and qualities, and sexual orientation all interact with one's ethnicity to result in differences within ethnic groups. Learning through observations, interactions, and personal research would be important to gain a solid understanding of various ethnic groups.

As the numbers of people from outside of the U.S. continue to increase due to both legal and illegal immigration, leisure services leaders will be faced with developing and providing services for people who speak English as a second language (ESL). As recent arrivals to the U.S., these individuals may experience feelings of alienation, distrust, and of not fitting in. Stresses associated with these feelings may inhibit full participation and enjoyment of leisure.

Leading People Who Are of Various Ethnic Backgrounds

Recognize that various ethnic groups are different in perception and use of time, conception of team versus individual, use of language and patterns of communication, leisure preferences, and values. Ethnic groups are *not* different in terms of intellectual, physical, or emotional abilities and needs. Learning about specific ethnic groups will reveal appropriate leader approaches. Certainly, going beyond celebrating ethnic festivals, hanging posters of famous people of color, and eating ethnic foods is required of leisure services leaders. Understanding a culture necessitates getting well beneath the "tip of the iceberg."

When working with people who speak ESL, leaders should bear in mind that speaking more loudly does not increase comprehension, although it can increase listener anxiety. Being patient, speaking slowly, using gestures, and leading through physical demonstration will help in leading people who have limited comprehension of English. Leaders will want to check for understanding by asking individuals to demonstrate desired behaviors and avoid questions that can be answered with a "yes" or "no." These techniques, of course, are effective leadership techniques no matter who the participants are.

Physical/Cognitive Abilities and Qualities

At various times in U.S. history people with disabilities have been viewed as subhuman (e.g., vegetables), menaces (e.g., scary) to society, objects of pity, holy innocents (e.g., special or exceptional), diseased organisms, objects of ridicule, and eternal children (Havens, 1992). These views are changing throughout most of the U.S., although vestiges of these attitudes remain. An estimated 40 million people in the U.S. are disabled; 44% of those individuals are physically disabled, 32% exhibit various health impairments, 13% have sensory impairments, 6% are reported to have mental disabilities, and 5% of disabled individuals have other disabilities (Havens, 1992).

The Americans with Disabilities Act (ADA)

The Americans with Disabilities Act of 1990 makes it illegal to discriminate against a person on the basis of her or his disability. Leisure services leaders are in direct contact with those who have disabilities and should be well-aware of the spirit of the ADA so as to facilitate a full range of leisure experiences for all people. The ADA states that leisure services providers **shall not**:

- deny a qualified person with a disability the opportunity to participate or benefit from services available to people without disabilities;
- offer less effective opportunities for the disabled;
- provide separate aids, benefits, or services for people with disabilities unless those aids are necessary to make services available;

- aid or perpetuate discrimination in any form; nor
- use facilities or sites that result in the exclusion of people with disabilities.

Furthermore, the ADA states that leisure services providers **shall**:

- make reasonable accommodations for people with disabilities to enable full enjoyment of services, programs, and facilities; and
- provide services, programs, and activities with the most interaction possible (Eichstaedt & Kalakian, 1993).

In terms of leadership, leisure services leaders are required by law to lead programs and services in such a way as to fully include people with disabilities in activities. Specific leader actions vary for different types of disabilities. In general, leaders are cautioned to be conscious of *learned helplessness* exhibited by some people who have disabilities, particularly in clinical settings.

Learned Helplessness

Learned helplessness refers to inappropriate participant dependency on the leader(s). A participant who is overly dependent upon the leader is limited in personal growth and may not reach her or his potential in terms of leisure experiences. To minimize learned helplessness, leaders should:

(1) be conscious of demands from participants who lack the confidence to do tasks themselves;

(2) show acceptance of participants who have specific needs, but do not give in to their demands if they are excessive or irrational; and

(3) help participants to see the patterns of their helpless attitudes.

Leaders can use activities and leadership interactions to build the participants' self-esteem and provide opportunities for participants to try, succeed, and fail in an accepting and safe environment (Austin, 1991).

Leading People with Physical Challenges

Physical challenges include disabilities such as cerebral palsy, muscular dystrophy, spinal cord injuries, amputations, arthritis, epilepsy, and multiple sclerosis. These physical disabilities are as varied as are those who are disabled. Some individuals with paraplegia seem very disabled while others appear to allow their physical limitation to interfere very little with their activities. Difficulties associated with these disabilities may be attributed to physical issues as well as the emotional and social struggles each person faces.

Leaders would be wise to assume, unless proven otherwise, that someone with unintelligible speech understands on a higher level than her or his communication indicates; physical disabilities do not necessarily impede cognitive functioning. If unsure of what is needed, leaders would be wise to ask the person with the disability what adaptations work best for her or him; generally people with disabilities know their own needs. As much as possible, allow the person with the disability to do what her or his peers do; preferences for leisure activities are influenced more by age and gender than by disability.

To be fully accepting and inclusive of people with physical disabilities, treat the individuals with disabilities as others are treated; avoid overprotecting individuals who have disabilities. Finally, to help other participants feel comfortable with those who have disabilities teach the nondisabled about issues related to the disability. This can be done casually in the conduct of the activity and does not necessitate structured educational sessions.

Leading People with Health and Sensory Challenges

Many health conditions are not visible and must be identified through noninvasive and nonthreatening means. Leaders should be aware that, at times, people with chronic diseases such as cancer, asthma, HIV, AIDS, and diabetes may be limited in their ability to participate in certain activities. As is true for all participants, leaders should know the location of completed medical and permission forms at all times. This way, if an emergency should arise, specific health information is available. *Sensory impairments* include visual impairments which range from total blindness to tunnel vision and varying degrees of light perception; and hearing impairments which include difficulty with hearing certain tones, being unable to distinguish sounds from background noises, and deafness.

*Some individuals have both
physical and cognitive
disabilities.*

Photo courtesy of the Harmony House

With participants with health impairments, leaders need to be aware of medical limitations, yet be careful of being overprotective. If there are questions related to participant safety, the advice of a physician or other experts should be sought. If an injury occurs, treating all participants by following universal precautions (precautions against the transmission of bodily fluids) is an absolute necessity. If everyone is treated in this fashion, there is no discrimination, and more importantly, the leader is protected from potentially serious health concerns.

For those who have sensory impairments, leaders should be articulate and speak clearly. People who are visually impaired (as well as those who do not have a clear view of the leader) will appreciate the limited use of directional terms. This means being careful in telling a participant to move "over there" (where is "there?") or "go to the corner" (which corner? where is it in relation to me?). Furthermore, leaders who wear brightly colored or decorative clothing may inadvertently cause visual difficulties for people who have partial sight and are distracted by such patterns.

If participants are hearing impaired or deaf and are lip reading, it is important for the leader to stay in front of them and avoid mumbling or exaggerating lip movements. Be careful of turning away from a person who is lip reading and avoid using gestures which block a clear view of one's face and lips. Written instructions may be helpful for people with hearing impairments and physical demonstrations may be helpful for those with visual impairments.

Leading People with Temporary Physical Disabilities

Leaders have a tendency to ignore the needs of those with temporary physical disabilities. This includes those individuals who have broken or sprained limbs, are recovering from health problems such as a heart attack or a severe illness, and those who are temporarily limited in sight (e.g., their glasses are broken or their vision is impaired by injury). In any case, those who have temporary disabilities are in need of leisure experiences just as are others. Being aware of medical concerns and limitations as well as following leadership techniques as mentioned throughout this text are warranted.

Leading People with Behavioral Disorders

Within the category of behavioral disorders there are three subgroups:

(1) persons with serious personality and adjustment disorders (these individuals may be psychotic and have schizophrenia, severe autism, or require hospitalization due to some other serious behavior disorder);

(2) persons who are "neurotic" may have problems with ego strength, self-concept and poor social adjustment; and

(3) other behavioral disorders which include people who have experienced emotional distress (e.g., trauma, abuse, divorce) (Winnick, 1995).

As with leading people with physical disabilities, it is important for the leader to become acquainted with the particular behavioral disorder to best meet the needs of each individual. Most people with behavioral disorders require some level of structure in leisure activities; "open gym" time may not provide enough structure to allow those who have behavioral disorders to succeed. In addition, leisure services leaders should clearly inform participants of expectations and available leader assistance.

As with behavior management techniques, modeling and reinforcing appropriate behaviors are important with people who have behavioral disorders. As activities and rules change, leaders should plan for a gradual transition to allow people time to adjust to the shifts in actions and mindsets. Leader fairness and consistency are vital to this population as is an understanding that participant expressed anger and aggression are not necessarily directed at anyone in particular. Particularly for people with behavioral and emotional disorders, leaders should use touch and physical intervention with discretion; it may be that the disorder is a result of inappropriate touching and abuse. Consistency and caring are important leader traits for success in working with people who have behavioral or emotional disorders.

Leading People with Mental Retardation

Mental retardation is generally classified into three categories: those who are classified as *educable* function on a second through fifth grade level. These individuals are able to adjust to fairly high levels of independence within a community. Those who are classified as *trainable* are those who typically work and live in a supervised group home. For people with this level of mental retardation the primary focus is on developing self-help skills. The third classification of mental retardation is *severe/profound*, which includes those who may not be able to take care of their own basic needs. A significant level of supervision is required throughout the lifetime of these individuals (Austin, 1991; Sherrill, 1993).

For people with mental retardation (and other developmental disabilities) leaders should strive to keep instructions concrete and straightforward; avoid abstractions and use of figurative speech. Using contact with actual equipment rather than illustrations or representations helps some people with cognitive and developmental disabilities understand activity instructions. Because cognitive processing takes time for these individuals, it is important to allow plenty of time for changeovers, transitions, and changes in routine.

Using the participant's name prior to giving instructions helps to get and maintain attention. Repetition helps to develop routines and is an effective way of helping people with cognitive disabilities to remember activity rules and directions. Leaders who include the ongoing practice of social skills and a broad range of fine and gross motor skill involvement in activities for individuals with mental retardation tend to be effective in their leadership efforts. Leaders will want to be cognizant of the impact of external stimulation on this population of individuals. People with cognitive and developmental disabilities may react strongly and aggressively if exposed to an overabundance of stimulation (e.g.,

Figure 9.5   *In many situations it is best to limit participant stimulation.*

flashing lights, loud and conflicting noises, bright colors, lots of activities) at one time. Helping people with cognitive and developmental disabilities to focus will often facilitate their success.

General Leadership Hints When Working with People with Disabilities

All leisure services leaders will, at some time in their career, work with people who have some type of disability. A minimum level of personal comfort and a knowledge base is required to work effectively with a wide variety of people. It might be helpful to become familiar with one's own biases, discomfort and fears of working with disabled people. Often, people who are able-bodied are fearful of hurting an individual who has a disability and this is a cause of some level of unease. If there are concerns about hurting an individual, ask that person if such actions would be harmful. Most people with disabilities are well aware of their own limitations.

Another fear of many leaders unfamiliar with leading people with disabilities is a fear of offending, often due to inappropriate use of language. A general rule of thumb when referring to someone with a disability is to put the *person* first. This, of course, assumes that mentioning the disability is pertinent to the conversation. When putting the person first, language changes from *the blind person* to *the person who is blind*; or from *the MR* to *the person with mental retardation*. Deaf people have expressed a preference for being referred to as deaf people. It is important to remember that those who use wheelchairs are not "wheelchair bound"—many people who use wheelchairs move freely from their wheelchair to other furniture quite readily. People who do not have disabilities are commonly referred to as nondisabled or able-bodied, not "normal." Again, if one is unsure of appropriate language—ask. A willingness to talk openly with a person who has a disability is necessary to overcome personal unease and biases.

Sexual Orientation

Gay, lesbian, and bisexual people differ from heterosexuals in terms of emotional and social-sexual attraction, but are similar in leisure preferences. There certainly are no differences based on sexual orientation in physical, cognitive, or emotional abilities. Specific needs of gay (this term usually refers to homosexual males, although homosexual females may use this term to self-identify, as well), lesbian and bisexual participants generally fall in the area of emotional support and social opportunities. There are many leisure services providers that specifically cater to the needs of gays, lesbians and bisexuals, particularly in tourism; and there are an increasing number of public agencies responding to the needs of gay youth.

Leading People Who Are Gay, Lesbian, or Bisexual

As with the other dimensions of diversity, an effective leader will take stock of her or his own biases related to people who are gay, lesbian, or bisexual. Because homosexuality tends to be hidden, there exists a common misperception that "there are no gay people in our community." By all figures used to estimate the number of people in the U.S. who are gay, it stands to reason that every parks, recreation and leisure services facility provides services to people who identify as gay, lesbian, or bisexual.

To be effective in addressing the needs of all constituents, leaders should be sensitive to the issues and assumptions that exist in the local community and then strive to develop and maintain a safe environment for all community members. One can do this by modeling acceptance of gay, lesbian, and bisexual people; being both proactive and reactive to disparaging remarks made by uninformed participants; by using inclusive language ("partner" or "significant other" rather than "spouse"); and by protecting and supporting an individual should she or he become the target of abuse.

Sex/Gender

At different stages of development females and males are both similar and different. When young, physical differences between the sexes are minimal. Then girls move ahead of boys for a couple of years after which boys move ahead of girls, at least in terms of physical size and strength. In late adulthood physical prowess is again somewhat equalized. Differences in intellectual capabilities are minimal across the life span. Social and emotional differences exist in as much as people have been socialized into gender roles. If one is feminine she or he might seem yielding, emotional, unassertive, "soft," and interested in social activities rather than physical games. If one is more masculine in demeanor one might be physical, assertive, boisterous, and "tough."

Leading People of All Genders

Having grown up in society all people who share a common culture also share the socialization messages of childhood. Some messages stick with us more strongly than others, but we have all been influenced by our upbringing in society. In the process of examining biases and discomfort relative to ethnicity, disabilities, and sexual orientation, leisure services leaders should also examine their own biases and assumptions relative to sex-appropriate thoughts, attitudes, and behaviors.

Many leaders treat females and males differently; some tend to take a "boys will be boys" approach to tolerating some behaviors and attitudes in one sex and not the other. Again, being conscious of language usage (discussed more fully in Chapter Five) may be the first step to equitable leadership for the sexes. Recognizing that all people, regardless of sex, have the right to equal leisure opportunities should help guide a leader in her or his choice of behaviors and words. Examples of sex bias are evident at every age: when treating a young child whose knee was scraped on the sidewalk, does the leader comfort the child, put a bandage on the injury and send the child off with a hug (which is a common leader treatment of a little girl), or does the leader tell the child to stop crying, grow up, and get back out there and play (which is a common response to a little boy)?

People differ on multiple dimensions of diversity, and on each of these dimensions there are socially preferred states of being. If one has the good fortune to be born with these valued traits, that individual is likely the beneficiary of many increased privileges. Recognizing and understanding how society develops and supports these unearned privileges helps in comprehending the discrimination and prejudice faced by others. Leading people with a knowledge of the core and secondary dimensions of diversity will assist a leisure services leader in leading with sensitivity and an orientation to equal access to leisure services; it will help a leader in becoming pluralistic.

Becoming a Pluralistic Leader

Loden and Rosener (1991) presented a number of tenets to which individuals may subscribe in efforts to become *pluralistic leaders.* Pluralistic leaders are those leaders who believe and are committed to leadership that reaches all constituents, regardless of the dimensions on which they differ from the mainstream. First, pluralistic leaders have and support a vision and values that support diversity across **all** dimensions. Pluralistic leaders, therefore, attempt to be pluralistic in their lives, and not just on the job. Supporting this is an ethical commitment to the fair treatment of all, and elimination of discrimination. To make this happen, pluralistic leaders must have a broad knowledge of the dimensions of diversity, and an openness to change based on new knowledge about personal limitations.

Pluralistic leaders understand the interdependence of all people—peers, employers, participants, and stock holders. To this end, leaders who are committed to diversity are well aware of promotional materials and agency presentation of people (such as, is there representation of people with disabilities, people of color, females, and people of various ages in written materials?). In addition, pluralistic leaders are willing to "call" people on their prejudice and attitudes in a way that educates rather than berates.

If leisure services leaders believe that all people deserve equal access to full leisure experiences, they will strive to make leadership and programming equitable in all settings. Underlying principles that may help with promoting equal access to leisure could include the beliefs that:

- diversity is important for social, political, economic, and moral reasons;
- the greater leisure services system has not served all equally well;
- all people are unique and different from other people;
- all people are whole people with many different qualities;
- all people have unknown potential for growth and development;
- multicultural presentations of leisure is appropriate for all;
- pluralistic leadership is effective leadership; and
- leadership is a crosscultural encounter (Loden, 1995; Protheroe & Barsdate, 1991).

Being a pluralistic leader implies two responsibilities—one to the notion of accepting all people for who they are and what they bring to the situation; and two to the ideals of effective leadership. If, in their leadership efforts leisure services leaders strive to meet the needs for dignity and respect of all humankind, there will be healthy conflict; and out of that, will arise effective and successful leadership. All people, no matter what their differences from one another, inhabit the same small world (made smaller by the incredible potential of computers); therefore, learning to live and lead one another with sensitivity can serve to improve the human condition.

Summary

This chapter has presented information to augment the material found throughout the text relative to leading diverse populations. Culture as the shared beliefs, attitudes, values, and traditions of an identifiable group of people was discussed in terms of culturally sensitive leadership. There are generally two approaches to dealing with diversity: to focus on diversity and celebrate it, and to simply work toward shared goals and ideals without addressing diversity outright. In either case, people differ and are similar in core and secondary dimensions of diversity. Core dimensions include race/ethnicity, age, sex/gender, sexual orientation, and physical and cognitive abilities and qualities; secondary dimensions include education, marital status, religion, work history, socioeconomic status, and others.

Within each dimension of diversity society attributes value and those who have characteristics of the more highly valued traits tend to receive very subtle privileges. It is through the system of privilege that people are treated differently based on core and secondary dimensions of diversity. Understanding this helps leisure services leaders to address diversity and be inclusive of everyone. Knowing about differences (and similarities) assists leaders in selecting activities, communicating with participants, managing behaviors, programming, and working with groups. Becoming a pluralistic leader is a goal of those who wish to strive for the ideals of transformational leadership.

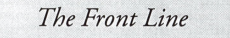

The Front Line

Consider this:

If the world were a village of 1,000 people, it would include: 584 Asians, 124 Africans, 95 Eastern and Western Europeans, 55 people from the States of the former Soviet Union, 52 North Americans, and 6 Australians and New Zealanders. They would probably have difficulty in communicating because: 165 of these people speak Mandarin, 86 people speak English, 83 people speak Hindi/Urdu, 64 people speak Spanish, 58 people speak Russian, 37 people speak Arabic, and the other 507 villagers speak more than 200 other languages (source unknown).

References

Althen, G. (Ed.). (1994). *Learning across cultures.* Washington, DC: NAFSA: Association of International Educators.

Austin, D. (1991). *Therapeutic recreation: Processes and techniques* (2nd ed.). Champaign, IL: Sagamore Publishing.

Chemers, M. and Ayman, R. (Eds.). (1993). *Leadership theory and research.* San Diego, CA: Academic Press.

Cox, T. (1993). *Cultural diversity in organizations.* San Francisco, CA: Berrett-Koehler.

Eichstaedt, C. and Kalakian, L. (1993). *Developmental/adapted physical education* (3rd ed.). New York, NY: Macmillan Publishing Co.

Gudykunst, W. (1991). *Bridging differences: Effective intergroup communication.* Newbury Park, CA: Sage Publications, Inc.

Havens, M. (1992). *Bridges to accessibility.* Dubuque, IA: Kendall/ Hunt Publishing Co.

Hernandez, H. (1989). *Multicultural education.* Columbus, OH: Merrill Publishing Co.

Hirsch, E., Kett, J., and Trefil, J. (Eds.). (1993). *The dictionary of cultural literacy.* Boston, MA: Houghton Mifflin Company.

King, E., Chipman, M., and Cruz-Janzen, M. (1994). *Educating young children in a diverse society.* Needham Heights, MA: Allyn & Bacon.

Loden, M. (1995). *Implementing diversity.* Chicago, IL: Irwin.

Loden, M. and Rosener, J. (1991). *Workforce America: Managing employee diversity as a vital resource.* Homewood, IL: Business One Irwin.

McIntosh, P. (1989, July/August). White privilege: Unpacking the invisible knapsack. *Peace and Freedom*, 10-12.

Protheroe, N. and Barsdate, K. (1991). *Culturally sensitive instruction and student learning.* Arlington, VA: Educational Research Services.

Seelye, H. and Seelye-James, A. (1995). *Culture clash: Managing in a multicultural world.* Chicago, IL: NTC Business Books.

Sherrill, C. (1993). *Adapted physical activity, recreation, and sport* (4th ed.). Dubuque, IA: Brown & Benchmark.

Sims, R. and Dennehy, R. (Eds.). (1993). *Diversity and differences in organizations.* Westport, CT: Quorum Books.

Winnick, J. (Ed.). (1995). *Adapted physical education and sport.* Champaign, IL: Human Kinetics Publishers, Inc.

York, D. (1994). *Cross-cultural training programs.* Westport, CT: Bergin & Garvey Publishers.

Chapter Ten
Learning Opportunities

Through studying this chapter students will have the opportunity to:

- understand the role of ethics and values in leisure leadership;

- explain the ethic of care in leisure leadership;

- explain the rights and justice position of ethics;

- discuss ethical issues as related to participants; and

- consider the place of values and ethics in one's own life.

Photo courtesy of the YWCA of Black Hawk County

CHAPTER

10

Values and Ethics in Leisure Leadership

Leadership is based on relationships. Relationships between leaders and followers, leaders and participants, and leaders with groups of participants are integral to all leisure services settings. Within these relationships the values and beliefs that individual leaders hold are made evident in their choice of actions and words. The more visible one is, the more visible one's beliefs, values, and ethics. Leisure services leaders tend to be very visible people. Through leading and being in front of groups of all types leaders expose themselves to the scrutiny and judgment of others.

In general, people look for high ethical standards in leaders; therefore, leaders need strong values and ethics to guide them in decisions and in all dealings with constituents. *Ethical beliefs are about how things ought to be; they describe the "right" way to do things.* Our own beliefs about how life should be and how it should be conducted reflect our beliefs about how life is and what is possible.

Ethics are taught and learned through a variety of avenues: modeling, discipline and training, social interaction, and through socialization into sex roles (McGrath, 1993). While these methods of transmission may be culturally based, it is important to note that right and wrong, and good and bad, go beyond culture. What is right and what is wrong is right and wrong for humanity, not just for select individuals who happen to fall into the "right" category. In fact, Hunt states, "…there are de facto universal moral standards" (1991, p. 17). These include such values as doing no harm, respecting living things, and respecting others' property, among others.

Oftentimes the terms ethics and morals are used synonymously. Ethics, however, are not the same as morals; they are an outgrowth of morality. *Ethics* represent actions based on a concept of right and wrong, and *morals* represent a personal philosophy of right and wrong. Ethics, then, are characterized by high standards of honest and honorable dealings based on morals (Bethel, 1990). The stronger the ethical behaviors—the higher the integrity, and the "better" the leader.

This chapter presents material about ethics, morals, values, and beliefs as they pertain to leisure services leadership. You will quickly discover that there are no easy answers—ethical dilemmas are very difficult to address and work through to the satisfaction of all those involved. After discussing background information in the early part of the chapter, several case studies are presented for you to read and work through. This will enable you to practice basic steps to ethical decision making, and become better acquainted with your own ethical positions related to particular ethical dilemmas.

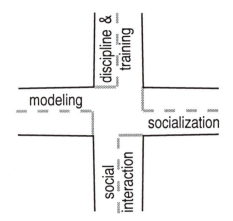

Figure 10.1 Ethics are learned primarily through four different avenues.

The Role of Values and Ethics in Leisure Leadership

Leadership, like teaching, is a moral activity (Goodlad, Soder & Sirotnik, 1990). It has been said that in leadership, the position gives one authority, but it is one's actions that generate respect (Kouzes & Posner, 1987). Leaders, due in part to the role they fill, lead by example; people are continuously watching and taking note of leader actions. It is important, then, that leader behaviors be consistent with the words she or he uses or respect and trust will be lost. By their words and actions leaders exemplify what is important—to them as well as to the agency they represent. In their positions, the expressed morality of leaders has an impact on the morality of followers. Leaders are, after all, role models. All participants, especially children, observe, discuss, and imitate leader behaviors. *Everything* a leader does while in contact with participants carries moral weight—responses to participant questions, giving instructions and directions, discussions, problem management, every comment and every action—illustrates the moral character of the leader.

Earlier in this text various models of leadership were discussed, one of which was transformational leadership. Transformational leaders are characterized by asking group members to:

> transcend their own self-interests for the good of the group, organization, or society; to consider their longer-term needs to develop themselves, rather than the needs of the moment; and to become more aware of what is really important. (Bass, 1990, p. 53)

In asking group members to take this position, leaders espouse their own beliefs about what is important. Considering long-term needs and the good of the group over one's self are important qualities of an ethical leader.

Without followers, of course, there are no leaders. Followers legitimize leadership by attributing leaders with credibility, trust, and loyalty; and by accepting the leader's ability to influence them. Leaders act in ways to make these things occur. In this way leadership and followership are interdependent, reciprocal and active systems. Followers ascribe leader legitimacy to the leader who demonstrates expertise in needed areas, entrepreneurship and initiative, and stewardship

Photo courtesy of the YWCA of Black Hawk County

Everything a leader does, says, and is carries moral weight.

(Chemers & Ayman, 1993). Thus, legitimacy comes from the beliefs of people that leaders are competent (experts), personally compelling and dynamic (entrepreneurial or charismatic) and trustworthy (stewards). These are positive qualities for which leaders can and should strive so as to lead people in an ethical fashion.

Ethics as Guides

Leaders use ethics to guide themselves and to set examples for others. Strong ethical values raise the level of conduct for both leaders and participants. Leaders generally perform three functions relative to values and ethics:

(1) they constantly define and communicate ethical behavior through their words and actions;

(2) they translate that definition so that everyone understands the ethical position taken—this builds trust; and

(3) leaders facilitate resolution of ethical conflicts that arise—this strengthens relationships and the agency or organization.

In this light, then, leaders have a responsibility to speak out *for* ethical behaviors and justice. In fact, leaders must *live* high ethics. Leaders show what they value by their actions, how they spend their time, the clothes they wear, the priorities on their agendas, by the questions they ask, people they see, places they go, and behaviors and results they recognize and reward (Kouzes & Posner, 1987). For instance, a leader who spends the majority of her or his time visiting with participants, smiling, and making everyone feel welcome likely values relationships. On the other hand, a leader who prefers to complete paperwork, leads activities, and tends to avoid close relationships with participants may more highly value tasks or solitude over relationships.

Leaders build trust and loyalty by behaving ethically and consistently from a solid values base (Bethel, 1990). Trust and loyalty are important for effective leadership at all levels; the impact of leadership is like a ripple effect of a stone in a pond. To determine sources of ethical influence a research study was conducted in which people were asked to rank the importance of various individuals in influencing their ethical conduct. The study respondents indicated that (from most to least important):

- the behaviors of their superiors had the strongest influence on their own behaviors;
- this was followed by the behaviors of peers in the agency in which they worked;
- the ethical practices of the profession to which they belonged;
- society's moral climate; and
- the existence of formal agency policies related to ethical standards (Hitt, 1990).

Furthermore, it was reported that people have a tendency to live up to or down to the leader's standards.

Foundational Values

Values are those traits, characteristics, and beliefs people esteem highly in themselves and others. When people value something, they judge it to have worth—value; it is what is important to the individual and for what she or he will stand. Values include determining the relative importance of intangible things such as religious beliefs, honesty, and trustworthiness. These intangibles are important in that they provide guidance to people's lives in terms of two particular areas: (1) *modes of conduct or behaviors* (how to behave), and (2) *desired end-states, or goals* (what people strive for) (Edginton, Jordan, DeGraaf & Edginton, 1995). Individuals who are unclear in the values they hold important may experience values confusion. These people often are inconsistent in behaviors, lack persistence, and may appear apathetic. Those who are clear and understand their own values tend to be very positive people, enthusiastic, and proud of who they are (Hunt, 1991; McGrath, 1993; Robbins, 1992). It is desirable that leaders be aware of and clear about their own values so that they can be most effective in their dealings with participants.

Research has been conducted that asked leaders and followers about the importance of values for leaders. From this research, Bass (1990) reported that important values for leaders include:

- a need for achievement;
- orientations toward both task and people;
- a willingness to take risks; and
- a willingness to trust others.

Effective leaders have been purported to require a good sense of self-understanding of their own values, beliefs, and morals, and solid self-efficacy. Self-efficacy refers to a belief that one is responsible for, and in charge of, her or his own fate. Leaders with these traits tend to cope well with stress, and are perceived as highly effective and well-liked.

It was mentioned earlier that leaders exemplify what is important, and it is through living their values that leaders influence followers. Like the ripple in a pond, leaders have a powerful impact on those they serve, whether the participants be children, adults, or people in between. The values leaders hold, of course, permeate everything they do and say. This can be beneficial in that values help guide the leader's:

- perception of situations and problems to be faced;
- approach to possible solutions to those dilemmas;
- view of others (e.g., her or his interpersonal relationships);
- perception of individual and group success as well as how to achieve success;
- determination of what is and is not ethical behavior; and
- the extent to which the leader accepts or refuses organizational pressures and goals (Hitt, 1990).

Perceptions of Ethics

Leaders rely on their values and sense of ethics to help them in all leadership actions and decisions. A leader who is well-aware of and consistent in her or his ethics, generally is a well-respected and effective leader. Values and morals evolve as one matures both as a person and as a leader. As discussed in Chapter Three, a common evolution through moral development is to move from seeking pleasure and/or avoiding pain, to abiding by rules and authority, to conforming to social norms and mores, to living through one's own conscience (i.e., being authentic and inner directed) (Bee, 1992; Hughes & Noppe, 1985). The most mature and effective leaders tend to be inner directed and self-monitored relative to moral positions—they rely on their own values to define what is right and what is wrong.

Consider the following scenario: a leader is responsible for closing and securing the recreation center each evening. On one evening there is a concert for which she or he has tickets, and the tickets were extremely difficult to get. The concert is sold-out. To remain open until closing time would make the leader late for the concert, and would pose difficulties in getting good seats; in fact, she or he might not even get into the show. Unable to get anyone to cover and close up for the evening, the leader had to work and is now considering closing up early. A leader who acts out of a moral base of seeking pleasure and/or avoiding pain would attempt to decide which pleasure or pain would be greater—closing early, getting to the concert, and likely losing her or his job; or staying until closing, retaining the job, but likely missing the concert.

A leader acting out of the second phase of moral development might wrestle with closing early based on the rules and policies of the agency. Agency policy indicates that the center should be closed early only in case of dire emergency; therefore, a leader at this stage might

follow the rules and remain open. At the next level of moral development a leader would determine the ethics of closing early based on the
moral tone of society. Generally, society dictates a sense of industrious-
ness and a work ethic; closing early for personal gain is not a socially
accepted practice and the center would remain open. A leader who is
ethically directed from within would likely choose to remain open out
of a recognition that to close early would negatively impact others—it
would be self-serving—and a sense of professionalism demands that
the center remain open until official closing time. This leader has a level
of self-sacrifice in her or his position of leadership.

In addition to these stages of moral development different people
measure what is ethical based on different sources: religious beliefs,
reason and logic, what is best for the greatest number of people, the end
results, and hedonism (i.e., self-pleasuring). People often place their
perceptions of right and wrong on a psychological continuum with
absolute "right" on one end, and complete hedonism on the other.
Hedonism is when one acts out of a desire for the highest level of
pleasure and/or self-gain. Ethicists, or those who study ethics, spend
their time studying and examining these various viewpoints in attempts
to better understand the human condition. One of the difficulties with
studying ethics in a society that believes in science to prove or disprove
facts is that *ethics is not an exact science*. It is fluid, amorphous, and
belies scientific proofs. Ethics are based on beliefs about what is good
and right, not facts or scientific proof.

Promoting Positive Social Values

To many, engaging in leisure is a freeing experience and in their leisure
some individuals expect to be free from all obligations and constraints.
To be totally free of constraints, however, would mean that individuals
would be acting outside of the "social contract." This social contract is
comprised of the laws, norms, and mores of society to which members
of society tacitly agree. By agreeing to live within these boundaries,
chaos is avoided and acceptable levels of community and humanity are
maintained. Therefore, leisure without *any* constraints is highly undesirable. It is during times of total disregard for social and ethical
boundaries that illegal and immoral activities take place.

As purveyors of leisure and the *good life*, leisure services leaders
have a responsibility to exude and promote positive social values. To

live and lead ethically demands such; it helps to maintain a humane society. Underlying values, morals, and ethics serve not only to guide leaders in their actions, but also to guide others and minimize social chaos. *Chaos* occurs when there is a lack of social order and values to bind people together. If there were no value for other people, their property, or even activity rules, leadership would be extremely difficult, participants would be unhappy, unfulfilled, and perhaps injured; and property might be damaged. An ethical leader has a responsibility to establish a standard of behaviors and words that will lead others to live their lives on a highly ethical plane. In this way, all of humanity (and the environment) is served.

In the United States the values of democracy, justice, human rights, equity, freedom, responsibility, reason, diversity of opinion, quality of life, and world peace are primary values, and all of them impact on leisure (Hitt, 1990). Each of these values constitutes the ethical structure of society, and provide guidelines for decision making and action related to moral issues. For example, in playing competitive games of skill leaders will often strive to organize teams so that they are equitable in terms of the skill levels of players. Furthermore, most leisure services professionals believe in individual freedoms to choose

Photo courtesy of the Conestoga Council of Girl Scouts

Values, like some activities, are taught through modeling what we see and believe.

from among alternative leisure pursuits, in the notion that each individual is responsible for her or his actions, and that leisure is an avenue to achieve a modicum of quality of life. These are positive social values which are within reach of all leisure services leaders in the conduct of business.

Ethical Decision Making

In addition to utilizing values and ethics as a way of maintaining the social contract, leisure services leaders use values when facing the many ethical dilemmas in their careers. When addressing ethical conflicts, problems, and issues leaders need to consider the factual, conceptual, *and* moral issues involved. Moral issues may be characterized by moral statements that include a prescription of conduct (an "ought" or "should" statement), leader impartiality (remaining objective), a sense of overriding importance, and independence from arbitrary authority or rules (Harris, 1987). When attempting to determine how to approach ethical issues, the leader is really asking, "What is good and what is right?"

In addressing ethical dilemmas, Hitt (1990) suggests considering four spheres of concern: *the end results, the agency or organization, society,* and *individual needs.* To help work through ethical issues, Phipps (1993) presents a two-step approach to ethical decision making. Generally speaking, the two steps that Phipps advocates are *identifying important considerations* and then *determining the emphasis among the three considerations.* Following is a brief discussion of these two steps as originally cited in Edginton, Jordan, DeGraaf, and Edginton (1995).

Step One

Identify the *important considerations of a decision*, focusing on obligations, ideals and effects:

> (1) Obligations—Are there any involved? What are they? Who has them?

An obligation is something that one is committed or bound to based on a formal contract, promise, or demands of a conscience. The leader making the decision must determine what promises or contracts she or he has made as well as take an inventory of her or his conscience. In the decision-making process one has to consider not only what obligations exist, but who (involved in the issue or problem) might have obligations.

Obligations might lie with supervisors, colleagues, and participants in addition to the leader making the decision.

(2) Ideals—To what ideal or ideals does the action relate?
In addition to understanding existing promises or weighings of a conscience in the decision-making process, leaders also need to consider what ideals exist. An ideal is a standard of beauty, perfection or excellence. It is important to note that this standard may be different for each individual, and is influenced by the social mores of the time. In considering the ethics of a problem, then, leaders must consider what ideals are important in a particular instance. Ideals exist related to every aspect of life; the environment, relationships, use of resources, tolerance, policies and procedures, and other aspects of every person and organization.

(3) Effects—Who is affected by the action, and how?
Leaders must consider all the 'players' in every decision to be made. Ethical decisions can have far reaching impacts, and to the best of one's abilities, both near and far effects should be determined. For instance, consider the agency that wrestled with the decision to allow a 13-year-old boy to pitch three baseball games in a row in an effort to win a league championship. The decision would impact the well-being of the boy, his future (if he injured his arm), his teammates, younger players who might observe and wish similar treatment, the league, other youth sports, parents, and so forth. All effects must be identified and made part of the decision-making process to fully comprehend the situation.

What obligations exist?

To what ideal(s) does the action relate?

Who is affected—how?

Figure 10.2 When addressing ethical decisions a leader must examine the obligations, ideals, and effects within the situation.

Step Two

Determine where the emphasis lies among the three considerations listed above. The judgment for which of the three considerations is most crucial for any given situation lies with the individual making the decision. Sometimes obligations are the most critical consideration and a leader makes the decision based on those obligations. At other times the ideal or the effects (short-term and long-term) outweigh the other two factors and essentially "make" the decision. Phipps (1993) suggests that leaders use the criteria as adapted below.

(1) When two or more obligations conflict, choose the more important one.

Which obligation is the most important is a consideration that must be decided by the leader engaged in the moral dilemma. In choosing the most important obligation one refers back to personal values structures and sources of morality. As an example, a child might report physical abuse to a counselor and ask the counselor not to tell anyone. In this scenario obligations exist to the child for both privacy and respect (as well as to her or his long-term well-being), and to the legal system which requires reporting of suspected child abuse. Although the obligations may seem in conflict in this scenario, the more important obligation is to the long-term well-being of the child, which, in effect, meets the other obligation to the legal system.

(2) When two or more ideals conflict, or when ideals conflict with obligations, choose the action that honors the higher ideal.

If a leader is faced with a moral dilemma which has two or more ideals where she or he might think, "if life were perfect such and so might be the situation," then she or he is faced with choosing one of the ideals over the other. According to Phipps (1993), that ideal also has precedence over obligations. Promises are outweighed by the perfect solution. For example, an ideal of fair play might be outweighed or put aside in the interest of the health and safety of players.

(3) When the effects are mixed, choose the action that produces the greatest good or the lesser harm.

When considering who is affected by an action, and how, this two-step decision-making process indicates that leaders must consider the impact of all of the effects. If an effect has short-term benefits, but long-term detrimental impacts leaders should choose the action that produces the greatest good or lesser harm. For example, if an activity leader reports that participants are stealing crafts and supplies, there are a number of effects that would need to be considered prior to action being taken. Depending upon the action taken, there will be both short-term and long-term effects in terms of repercussions to the agency, negative publicity, impact on the alleged thieves and their families, other programs that use supplies, and upon the individual bringing the accusation. In this scenario effects and obligations are the most salient aspects of the moral dilemma. Each leader will have to decide for herself or himself which of the effects, *in light of the obligations*, produce the greatest good or lesser harm.

As can be seen, ethical decision making is not an easy nor a clear-cut process. In fact, ethical dilemmas will present some of the most wrenching problems faced by leisure services leaders. Leaders who are clear in their own values and moral position, and who take a transformational approach to leadership, usually will be respected and appreciated for their consistent manner in handling difficult situations.

Ethic of Rights and Justice or Ethic of Care?

As mentioned earlier, ethics arise out of morals, and morality is viewed as one's sense of what is right and good, and what is wrong or bad. In the predominant U.S. culture, ethics are generally decided around what is fair and right for the individuals involved. This approach has been termed the *ethic of rights and justice*. Thus, to determine the ethics of a situation a leader would attempt to determine what is fair, right, and just for those involved in the dilemma. Often, rules are applied across the board because, "it wouldn't be fair to the others if you weren't held to the same standard." Rules exist to be applied in difficult situations, and to apply them in every situation is considered right and just. Leaders have policies, procedures, and rules to follow which they impart to others. An ethic of rights and justice is typified by a values base of rules and authority.

Another view of ethics which responds more on a relationship and individual basis is an *ethic of care*. Whereas the ethic of rights and justice defines what is right by equal application of rules in an attempt to remain impartial and fair, an ethic of care defines what is right by the needs of the individuals involved. Seeing and responding to the needs of others, and acting out of a sense of relationship and a need to maintain connections describes an ethic of care. Therefore, if one were to subscribe to an ethic of care one would respond to moral and ethical issues out of caring and concern for others, and not necessarily following exactly what is right and fair through the application of rules and policies.

An ethic of caring has two elements:

(1) *the disposition to care*—to fulfill the needs of others. This assumes a commitment to an ideal of caring where everyone in the world cares for other beings; and

(2) *an obligation to care for*—which is caring expressed in action (Manning, 1992). From this perspective day-to-day interactions with others creates a web of reciprocal caring. The caring might be manifested in caring for others physically, psychologically, emotionally, or spiritually.

The notion of *caring for* involves a measure of self-sacrifice on the part of the caregiver. Leaders, then, need an element of self-sacrifice to ascribe to an ethic of caring. By their very nature, human relationships

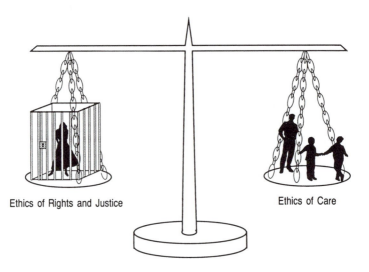

Figure 10.3 Differing views of ethical positions

require a level of caring—being receptive, accepting, and on-call for others—which requires commitment and practice (Manning, 1992). Therefore, leaders require commitment and practice in caring and being open in order to achieve the ideals of caring.

Personal Integrity

When asked, followers indicated that they admire leaders who exhibit the following characteristics: integrity (is truthful, trustworthy, has convictions), competence (is capable, effective, qualified), and leadership (is inspiring, decisive, and provides direction) (Kouzes & Posner, 1987). Participants measure leader integrity through the leader's actions and behaviors; they look to see if leader actions match leader words, if leaders are consistent, and if leaders can articulate their own values.

Integrity is the value placed on self—it requires a level of self-awareness and self-value. Respected people are those who know their own values, take a stand for what they believe in, and profess their own standards. These individuals are said to have personal integrity. To be ethical leaders, leaders must first know their own values and what is important to them. Once knowing and understanding these values, leaders with integrity live by these values—and do so consistently (Robbins, 1992). Leaders who have integrity make and keep commitments to themselves and others; they are trustworthy.

Winning trust is a long-term process which needs continual nurturing and development. Attributes that lead to trust include integrity, reliability, openness, and being consistent in these characteristics over time. In the trust building process participants will consider their history with the individual leader, and take into account the leader's reputation. Because of this, leaders need to avoid perceptions of impropriety. A good, solid values system, honesty, a straightforward demeanor, and standing up to one's promises are all needed to achieve personal integrity. When weighing and judging the integrity of an individual, we often ask about the strength of her or his convictions—does the person stand up for what she or he believes in? Does it feel safe to be with that person?

Hitt (1990) has presented the relationship of trust and leadership in this syllogism:

- trust is required for effective leadership;
- without personal integrity, there can be no mutual trust; and
- therefore, without personal integrity, there can be no effective leadership. (p. 206)

In addition to trust, other elements of integrity include competence, authenticity, openness, responsibility and a solid sense of self (or identity) (Hitt, 1990; Sonnenberg, 1994). *Identity* is knowing who one is and who one is not; identity provides a sense of wholeness and integration; is grounded in hierarchy of values; and allows one to sustain sameness and continuity of essential patterns in the face of changes. All leaders need a sense of *authenticity*: the capacity to be one's self and not the roles one fills. In addition, authenticity allows one to communicate expectations, give and receive honest feedback, and admit mistakes.

Integrity involves *responsibility*; realizing that each person lays the groundwork for what she or he will be; being aware that one has the freedom to choose; being faithful to one's convictions; putting all of one's self into little as well as big things; being accountable for decisions and their consequences; realizing that one can be accountable for inaction as well as action; and admitting mistakes and correcting them (Hitt, 1990; Robbins, 1992). The reason integrity is critical for a leader is because when a leader with integrity is presented with a problem, participants and followers can be assured that the same standards (i.e., values and principles) utilized to make simple decisions will be utilized in considering difficult situations. The leader is honorable in her or his actions and words.

Principled Leadership

Covey (1991) presented the notion of "principled leadership" as he examined the relationship of ethics and personal integrity to the role requirements of leaders. Covey perceives principles as natural laws of the universe that pertain to all human relationships. Principles apply at all times and in all places; they are manifested in values, ideas, norms, and teachings that empower people. Principles are objective and external to an individual.

In discussing principled leadership in businesses and organizations Covey (1991) suggested four levels of principled leadership: (1) *personal* (i.e., trustworthiness), (2) *interpersonal* (i.e., trust),

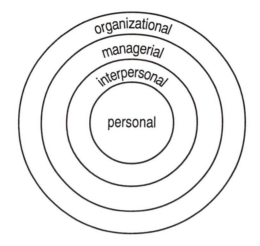

Figure 10.4 *Levels of principled leadership begin within each individual leader.*

(3) *managerial* (i.e., empowerment), and (4) *organizational* (i.e., alignment). First, leaders develop a personal trustworthiness—others can depend on them to do what is right and be consistent in behaviors and words. As leaders become comfortable with their own values and moral base, trust begins to develop between themselves and others. This trustworthiness is first developed within and then projected onto relationships with other people. Once self and interpersonal values are established, principled leaders then use their values base to empower others—in their own ethical positions as well as in day-to-day tasks. Becoming aligned with organizational values follows as leaders influence and are influenced by the agency with which they work.

According to Covey (1991), principle-centered leaders are characterized by the following traits:

- a desire for continual learning;
- a service orientation;
- radiating positive energy;
- a strong belief in the value of other people;
- leading balanced lives (e.g., family, work, leisure);
- view life as an adventure;
- are synergistic in their efforts to work with others; and
- exercise self-renewal.

Principled leadership sets up a leader for success—the respect and trust of participants, positive decision making, solid interpersonal relationships, and accomplished tasks. A principle-centered leader is often characterized as being highly professional in her or his handling of people and tasks.

Professionalism and Leadership

Professionalism describes a quality of practice, how members of the profession integrate obligations with knowledge and skill in ethical relationships with clients and customers. Professionalism affords a level of status to the professional and allows participants to measure leaders against established "professional standards" (Goodlad, Soder, & Sirotnik, 1990). Leaders would be wise to hold themselves to higher standards than anyone else might have of them. In this way, highly ethical practices are likely to become habitual.

The National Recreation and Park Association (NRPA), which is the primary professional organization to which leisure and recreation practitioners and academicians typically belong, developed and recently revised a code of ethics to help guide the profession. Initially the code of ethics was developed in response to a concern about the professionalization of leisure services practitioners; it was revised in recognition of the various ethical issues that face members of the profession almost daily.

The following NRPA Professional Code of Ethics is excerpted from an issue of *Parks and Recreation Magazine* (Clark, 1995):

> The National Recreation and Park Association has provided leadership to the nation in fostering the expansion of recreation and parks. NRPA has stressed the value of recreation, both active and passive, for individual growth and development. Its members are dedicated to the common cause of assuring that people of all ages and abilities have the opportunity to find the most satisfying use of their leisure time and enjoy an improved quality of life.
>
> The Association has consistently affirmed the importance of well-informed and professionally trained personnel to

continually improve the administration of recreation and park programs. Members of the NRPA are encouraged to support the efforts of the Association and profession by supporting state affiliate and national activities and participating in continuing education opportunities, certification, and accreditation.

Membership in NRPA carries with it special responsibilities to the public at large, and to the specific communities and agencies in which recreation and park services are offered. As a member of the National Recreation and Park Association, I accept and agree to abide by this Code of Ethics and pledge myself to:

- Adhere to the highest standards of integrity and honesty in all public and personal activities to inspire public confidence and trust.

- Strive for personal and professional excellence and encourage the professional development of associates and students.

- Strive for the highest standards of professional competence, fairness, impartiality, efficiency, effectiveness, and fiscal responsibility.

- Avoid any interest or activity that is in conflict with the performance of job responsibilities.

- Promote the public interest and avoid personal gain or profit from the performance of job duties and responsibilities.

- Support equal employment opportunities. (p. 40)

In addition to striving to meet the code of ethics of the profession, leisure services leaders may wish to be guided by the code of ethics developed for citizen board members. The following code of ethics may be useful in working with town boards, staff, subcommittees, or other special groups that provide leadership to some aspect of leisure services. The Code of Ethics for Parks and Recreation Board Members is as follows:

As a Park and Recreation Board member representing all of the residents, I recognize that:

1. I have been entrusted to provide park and recreation services to my community.

2. These services should be available to all residents, regardless of age, sex, race, religion, national origin, physical or mental limitation.

3. While honest differences of opinion may develop, I will work harmoniously with other Board members to assure residents the services they require.

4. I will invite all residents to express their opinions so I may be properly informed prior to making my decisions. I will make them based solely upon the facts available to me. I will support the final decisions of the Board.

5. I must devote time, study, and thought necessary to carry out my duties.

6. The Board members establish the policy and the staff is responsible for administering the policies of the Board.

7. I have no authority outside of the proper meetings of the Board.

8. All Board meetings should be open to the public except as provided by law. (Clark, 1995, p. 41)

These two codes of ethics may serve as guideposts for leisure services leaders in their efforts to work with and provide services to a variety of publics. It remains up to the individual leader, however, to act in ways that are above reproach and serve the needs of the participants. Developing and articulating one's values and moral base is the first step to utilizing ethics in such a way as to benefit not only the leader, but those she or he serves. The remainder of this chapter presents a series of ethical dilemmas typical of the type faced in the practice of leisure services leadership. You are encouraged to read them through, determine the ideals and obligations, and then work through the issues based upon the highest ethical standards.

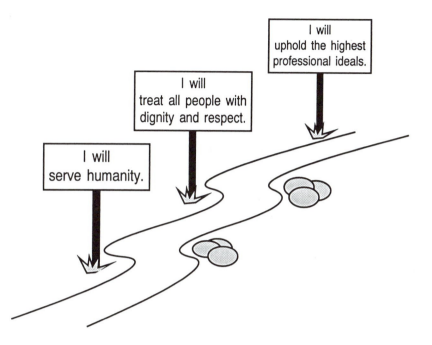

Figure 10.5 Codes of ethics serve as guideposts for a profession.

Case Studies

No Form, No Trip

You are the leader responsible for gathering children who are attending a summer recreation program and preparing them for an off-site field trip. You sent home parental permission forms last week and again yesterday, informing the youngsters in no uncertain terms that they would not be able to go on the trip without a signed form. It is agency policy—no form, no trip. A child walks up to you, who you know is from a struggling single-parent family, and tells you the form was lost, but "Dad said I could go." By now 26 of the 29 children in the program are on the bus having handed in their signed forms. The youngster without the form begins to cry asking, "Why won't you let me go? My dad said I could go." It is time for the bus to leave, what is your decision relative to this youngster going on the trip?

Wiped Out?

You are responsible for the supervision of a weight room where adults are free to drop in and work out on the various weightlifting machines. Agency policy is that everyone must have a towel in the facility and lifters are asked to wipe down the machines after use to clean their sweat off the machines. If it is determined that lifters have not been wiping down the machines, they can be denied access for a period of time. This is the second day in a row that a participant (Caucasian) has sought you out to complain that another weightlifter (African American) is not wiping down the machines after use. The complainant asks you to deny weight room access to the other lifter as per the rules. You spot check the use of the room and every time you have been in the weight room you have observed the African American participant clearly wiping down each machine. You suspect the accusations are racially motivated. How do you handle this situation?

Just Toughening 'Em Up

You are responsible for the youth soccer league; part of your job duties include recruiting and training volunteer coaches. You also visit various fields as games get underway to ensure that things are running smoothly. One team has been overwhelming other teams throughout the season, and you go to one of their games. While at the game you observe the coach yelling and shouting at the players, grabbing the youths by their shirts and shaking them when they do not perform well. At halftime the coach spends the first ten minutes berating the youngsters for their sloppy work. You ask to see the coach off to the side and you indicate that yelling at the children in this manner is not appropriate—this is an educational/recreational league. The coach responds by saying, "I've been doing this all year. It toughens 'em up—this is why we are the best team in the league." The game and the coach's behaviors resume. How do you handle this situation?

The Old Folks

You are a counselor at an senior camp where people over the age of 55 attend a residential camp for a week in May. Activities include horseback riding, arts and crafts, aquatics, archery, other sports, and fine arts. It has been made clear in all of the literature, as well as on the first day of camp, that because the camp was outdoors and people would be sleeping in wooden cabins, smoking materials would be allowed in only one designated area. The designated smoking area is away from the other buildings to minimize fire hazard, and somewhat out of the way of camp activities. By registering, people agreed to abide by the restricted smoking policy. You return to a cabin after lunch on the third day and discover two of the participants smoking in a "no smoking" area. You remind them of the policy and they tell you, "We've been smoking all of our lives and aren't going to stop now. The smoking building is too far away and we will not be shunned to some far corner of camp. We've been smoking here every day since we got here and nothing has burned down." How do you handle this?

What Are Friends For?

You work at a very popular theme park. As an employee you receive one free guest pass after every eight months of employment. You have been with the company just over nine months. You, of course, can get into the park with your employee badge at any time. Three of your best friends are in the area to visit you and want to get into the park, but they don't have enough money. One of these friends has lent you her car on numerous occasions and reminds you of this as the three ask you to use your guest pass to get them in free. They want you to say that they are potential employees who are here checking out the opportunities. The friends have driven 375 miles to visit you and are in the area for only four days. How do you handle this situation?

Summary

Values and ethics define a person; the role she or he fills serves as the medium through which those values and ethics are lived. Followers expect and look for high standards, clear ethics, and appropriate values in leaders. There are four primary avenues through which people learn ethics; modeling, discipline and training, socialization, and social interaction. Parks, recreation, and leisure services leaders can be involved in all of these functions.

Ethics serve as guides for behaviors—they explain and describe how things ought to be. Everything a leader does, says, and wears influences the perception of others about that leader. Ethics are the guideposts that help people make decisions, promote positive social values, and explain how to interact with others. In these interactions there are two basic approaches: an ethic of care, and an ethic of rights and justice. Different leaders take different approaches based on their own knowledge, style, and values system. An individual who has a clear values system and who has great personal integrity in working with others is identified as a highly principled leader. To aid in subscribing to strong ethics in the course of one's career, oftentimes professional associations develop a code of ethics. In this chapter, the code of ethics for parks, recreation, and leisure services professionals (and board members) was presented as models of what professional ethics look like.

The Front Line

Environmental ethics are those actions we take that relate to the state and conservation of natural resources. While not directly related to leisure services leadership, there is quite a bit that leisure services leaders can do to help maintain healthy parks, other open spaces, and living spaces (e.g., rural, suburban, urban). If all leisure services leaders engaged in some of the following behaviors and encouraged participants to do so when appropriate, as a profession, we could make a difference:

- reuse paper in the office (write notes and lists on the back side of used paper);
- keep a scrap paper box next to the copy machine and use that paper on which to write internal memoranda;
- use recycled paper for agency flyers and announcements;
- only make the number of copies necessary for the job;
- use a rag rather than paper towels to clean up messes;
- reduce the use of the air conditioner in your car (and the agency's vehicles)—roll down the windows;
- only drive when absolutely necessary (try walking or riding a bike for the shorter distances);
- turn off lights when leaving a room for longer than three minutes;
- turn off computers overnight;
- recycle as much as possible—the following items are recyclable in most towns: aluminum (e.g., soda pop cans), plastic (e.g., cleaning supply bottles), paper (use it up on both sides, first), newspaper, cardboard (e.g., supply boxes), magazines, and glass;
- plant trees on agency property—make it an annual event;
- plan, conduct, and promote environmentally friendly activities for all participants;

- encourage (through small incentives) participants to use nonmotorized transportation to your center (e.g., walking, biking, in-line skating, cross-country skiing); and

- compost any organic waste, whether it be from employee lunches or participants treats.

References

Bass, B. (1990). *Bass and Stogdill's handbook of leadership* (3rd ed.). New York, NY: The Free Press.

Bee, H. (1992). *The developing child* (6th ed.). New York, NY: HarperCollins Publishers.

Bethel, S. (1990). *Making a difference: 12 qualities that make you a leader.* New York, NY: Berkley Publishing Group.

Chemers, M. and Ayman, R. (Eds.). (1993). *Leadership theory and research.* San Diego, CA: Academic Press, Inc.

Clark, D. (1995). A new code of ethics for NRPA. *Parks and Recreation, 30*(8), 38-43.

Covey, S. (1991). *Principle-centered leadership.* New York, NY: Summit.

Edginton, C., Jordan, D., DeGraaf, D., and Edginton, S. (1995). *Leisure and life satisfaction: Foundational perspectives.* Dubuque, IA: Brown & Benchmark.

Goodlad, J., Soder, R., and Sirotnik, K. (Eds.). (1990). *The moral dimensions of teaching.* San Francisco, CA: Jossey-Bass Inc., Publishers.

Harris, C. (1987). *Applying moral theories.* Belmont, CA: Wadsworth Publishing Company.

Hitt, W. (1990). *Ethics and leadership.* Columbus, OH: Batelle Press.

Hughes, F., and Noppe, L. (1985). *Human development across the lifespan.* St. Paul, MN: West Publishing Company.

Hunt, J. (1991). Ethics and experiential education as professional practice. *Journal of Experiential Education, 14*(2), 14-18.

Kouzes, J. and Posner, B. (1987). *The leadership challenge.* San Francisco, CA: Jossey-Bass Inc., Publishers.

Manning, R. (1992). *Speaking from the heart: A feminist perspective on ethics.* Lanham, MD: Rowman & Littlefield Publishers, Inc.

McGrath, E. (1993). *The art of ethics: A psychology of ethical beliefs.* Chicago, IL: Loyola University Press.

Phipps, M. (1993). Ethical decision making. Presentation at the Wilderness Education Association National Conference, Fall Creek Falls State Park, TN.

Robbins, A. (1992). *Awaken the giant within.* New York, NY: Fireside Books.

Sonnenberg, F. (1994). *Managing with a conscience.* New York, NY: McGraw-Hill Publishing Company.

Chapter Eleven
Learning Opportunities

Through studying this chapter students will have the opportunity to:

- understand the four elements of negligence.
- evaluate levels of required supervision for various situations.
- describe and identify the components of a supervision plan.
- relate the conduct of an activity to personal leadership skills.
- select the appropriate forms for managing leisure services risks.

Photo by Debra J. Jordan

Risk Management in Direct Leadership

A typical configuration of a recreation or leisure activity consists of one or more participants, the environment in which the activity is held (e.g., indoors or outdoors), and the leisure services leader or leaders who conduct or facilitate the activity. Any time people are involved in an activity whether alone and self-led or supervised and led by others, illnesses, injuries and mishaps can be expected to occur. Therefore, in leisure services settings of all types there is potential for injury or illness. Examples of common situations where injuries or illnesses arise include when an individual looks away at the moment a ball is being thrown to her or him, a player falls as she or he runs, a participant has an epileptic seizure and hits her or his head on a hard surface, and an individual suffers from heatstroke at an outdoor event. As can be imagined, the potential injuries from these unexpected incidents may range from the very minor to extremely serious.

United States society has become very litigious over the past 15 to 20 years. This means that when people are injured or personal property is damaged, the tendency exists to sue an individual or organization for medical and other costs. Parks, recreation, and leisure service entities are not immune from this litigious state of mind. An increase in lawsuits in the field is due to several reasons: increased participation in leisure; greater awareness of better and safer ways to play; an increase in year-round activities; new technology and more sophisticated equipment; and increased accessibility to legal services (Baley & Matthews, 1989).

Minimizing the likelihood of injuries, and thus lawsuits, is important for several reasons. First, being named in a lawsuit can be devastating (both personally and professionally) for the individuals named as well as financially draining for the agency or organization involved. In addition to this, it seems as though lawsuits beget lawsuits—if an individual or agency is successfully sued once, it appears likely that other lawsuits will follow. Furthermore, recreation and leisure service professionals have an ethical and professional responsibility to maintain safe environments and activities for participants involved in programs and those using facilities.

This chapter is designed to assist the reader in understanding basic concepts related to legal liability and in managing the risks typically involved in direct leadership settings. Because laws and the interpretation of laws differ from state to state and between nonprofit and commercial entities, this chapter provides a general understanding of negligence and related concepts only. Recreation and leisure services professionals would be wise to check with a local attorney for information related to their particular situation in their home state.

Tort Law and Criminal Law

There are two basic types of law: *tort law* and *criminal law*. For the most part, *criminal law* deals with intentional acts against the public at-large which are addressed in the state and federal penal code (i.e., law books). Incidents that fall under criminal law are followed up in the criminal court system—someone is arrested and punishment is meted out by the state or federal government. Examples of violations of criminal law include theft, sexual assault, and driving violations (e.g., speeding tickets).

Tort means wrong or twisted (Baley & Matthews, 1989; Kaiser, 1986; van der Smissen, 1990). *Tort law* is law that deals with civil issues; those issues that arise out of living in a community. It involves both intentional and unintentional acts based on a breach of some type of contract. Because tort law involves the civil system, issues that arise out of tort law lead to lawsuits through which people seek to be compensated for losses they have incurred (van der Smissen, 1990).

Often, parks, recreation, and leisure services leaders are surprised to learn that in tort law *a person may be sued by anybody for anything at anytime* (Baley & Matthews, 1989; Kaiser, 1986; van der Smissen, 1990). This means that the possibility for being sued exists for all of us, whether we are leisure service professionals, business people, or homeowners. For instance, a person could be sued for having a hair color and style (e.g., magenta, bowl cut) that distracted someone who, as a result, collided with a fence and was injured. This type of lawsuit may not hold up in court, but the damage of initiating the lawsuit may have already been done. By being named in a lawsuit, one's name might be in the newspaper, an attorney would need to be engaged (and paid), and the time necessary to address the lawsuit could interfere with one's work, family, and other obligations.

Leisure service professionals, then, must attend to all aspects of programs and services to minimize the risk of being sued (and to remain safe). To accomplish this, an understanding of legal concepts and their impact on leisure services leadership is necessary. This chapter will discuss negligence, supervision, conduct of an activity, and the use of forms in minimizing risks.

Negligence

Negligence is the term used to describe an act which results in personal injury to another (or her or his property) (Baley & Matthews, 1989; Kaiser, 1986; van der Smissen, 1990). It is the legal term with which most people are familiar and typically refers to a situation where an individual was careless in the course of her or his job duties resulting in injury to another party. For negligence to exist, four elements must be present: *duty, an act or standard of care, proximate cause,* and *injury/ damage.* If any one of these four elements is not found, there is no negligence (and no standing for a lawsuit).

Duty

The term *duty* refers to an obligation to another individual based on a legal relationship between that individual and another (Baley & Matthews, 1989; Kaiser, 1986; van der Smissen, 1990). For negligence to exist there must be a violation or breach of that duty or obligation. Typically, in leisure services settings a leader and participants are involved in the conduct of a leisure or recreational pursuit. In this case there is a legal relationship (duty) between the leisure services professional and the participant. The leisure services leader has a duty, or obligation, to provide reasonably hazard-free activities and facilities to all participants and other staff.

Any time there is a legal relationship whereby one person owes a responsibility or has a legal obligation to another person, a duty exists. Other examples of legal duty may be found in the following relationships: teachers and students have a relationship whereby the teacher is responsible for the students; parents are responsible for children; lifeguards owe a responsibility to swimmers; coaches have obligations to players; and leisure services leaders owe a level of duty to participants. If there is no special relationship, and thus no duty, there is no negligence.

In direct leadership positions the duty owed an individual includes a responsibility to act in a safe and prudent manner, to warn of hidden and visible hazards (e.g., wet floor), and maintain a safe environment (e.g., use reasonable care)—this duty is owed when participants are using leisure facilities, in the conduct of activities, and in the general provision of leisure services.

Act/Standard of Care

The *act* refers to the actions of a person (leisure services leader) in light of the duty owed to participants. A certain *standard of care* is required to maintain a hazard-free environment for all participants. In legal terms, in an assertion of negligence, a leisure services leader will be held to the same standard that a reasonable and prudent (careful) professional maintains. This standard of care:

> would be measured by the moral qualities, judgment,
> knowledge, experience, perception of risk and skill that
> a person in the capacity of a professional would have.
> (van der Smissen, 1990, p. 43)

In other words, a leisure services leader must act in the same way that another person competent for the position would do. If a leader does not meet these expectations duty has been breached (or violated) and negligence could be found. It should be noted that, in most cases, interns and volunteers are held to the same standard of care as a professional.

What is reasonable is determined by three elements: the activity, environment, and participants. These are discussed in further detail later in this chapter. In addition to examining these elements, reasonable care is measured, in part, by foreseeability. *Foreseeability* refers to the responsibility of the leader to foresee, or anticipate, that a dangerous situation might arise if "X" were to occur. If an event is not foreseeable (by a reasonable, prudent professional) then the conduct of that activity is not unreasonable. For example, it is usually foreseeable that where water exists (e.g., pond, lake, swimming pool) and participants have low levels of swimming abilities, drowning may occur. In the game of dodgeball where a small playground ball is hurled at opponents it is similarly foreseeable that someone will be hit in the face. On the other hand, it is *not* generally foreseeable that in the excitement of playing a board game an adult would fall out of her or his chair resulting in injury.

Negligent acts may occur due to *acts of omission* where a leader does not do something she or he should do; and by *acts of commission*, where a person does something she or he should not do, or does something she or he is supposed to do, but does it incorrectly. There are three ways that a leader might behave or act inappropriately in her or his position; through *malfeasance, nonfeasance,* and *misfeasance.*

Malfeasance

Doing something that one ought not to have done (which may also be illegal) is considered malfeasance. For instance, malfeasance would have occurred if a leisure services leader slapped a participant who was using foul language. Striking any individual is an unacceptable practice, is unlawful, and should not have been done. It is an act of commission for which the leader could be held liable.

Nonfeasance

Nonfeasance is the neglect of duty; it is often perceived as passive negligence because it results out of uninvolvement (van der Smissen, 1990). An example of nonfeasance would be failing to maintain a facility by passively allowing it to age without regular maintenance or upkeep. If, due to this neglect of duty an individual were to become injured (on run-down and weak stairs, for instance), nonfeasance might be the claim and leader negligence the result.

Misfeasance

Those acts whereby a leader did not exercise due care for the rights of the participants are termed misfeasance (van der Smissen, 1990). This type of breach of duty includes both a failure to act as well as the improper conduct of an act. As an example of misfeasance by omission, in one situation that arose in a resident camp several youth were involved in a fist fight while two adult leaders rested nearby—aware of, yet choosing to ignore the events. The youth being beaten suffered eye damage from a fist to the face.

This act of omission, standing idly by while a youngster was being beaten, was an act where the leaders failed to exercise due care for the rights of the participant and is thus malfeasance. The leaders justified their inaction in stopping the fight based on the fact that the youth receiving the beating had been teasing and picking on the other youngsters earlier, and in their words, "He deserved it [the beating]." This was evidence of very poor judgment by the leaders.

As an example of misfeasance by improper conduct, a recreation therapist was helping to transfer a person who used a wheelchair to her bed. In the course of the transfer, an incorrect technique was used and the individual with the disability fell to the floor, suffering a broken leg. The transfer act was appropriate, but it was done incorrectly. This was misfeasance during an act of commission.

Proximate Cause

In addition to duty and a breach of that duty the third element that must exist for negligence to be proven is *proximate cause*. Proximate cause refers to the actual cause of the injury or damage. For negligence to be attributed to an action, it must be shown that the injury was the direct result of the action (remember, actions may be acts of omission or commission). Often a defense attorney will attempt to prove that there was an *intervening act* that came between a negligent act and the injury. If an intervening act was found, the negligent act would have been found to have had no proximate cause, and there would be no negligence.

In the second example of misfeasance above, the incorrect technique used during the transfer was what caused the fall, and thus the injury. It was the proximate cause of the broken leg. Imagine the same staff member doing the same incorrect technique, but rather than dropping the person with the disability, the brakes on the bed failed causing it to move, and *that* was the reason the person fell to the floor breaking her leg. The bed brakes failing would have been the proximate cause of the injury and not misfeasance (i.e., using the incorrect technique) on the part of the recreation therapist.

Injury/Damage

The fourth element that must exist for negligence to be found is actual injury (to a person) or damage (to physical property) (van der Smissen,

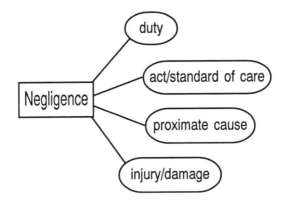

Figure 11.1 *For negligence to be found, all four elements must exist.*

1990). The injuries might be physical (e.g., fracture, sprain, head injury), emotional/mental (e.g., anguish, humiliation and embarrassment, emotional trauma, psychogenic shock), or economic (e.g., replacement cost for equipment, loss of one's job, future medical bills). Interpretation of injury or damage differs by state with some more loosely defined than others; it is wise to become familiar with the guidelines in one's home state.

Understanding the four necessary elements of negligence is critical to beginning the process of reducing and minimizing risks and hazards. Duty, an act, proximate cause, and injury/damage must all be found to exist for a claim of negligence to be made. Duty is established based on relationships, and proximate cause and injury/damage are "after the fact" constructs. To best minimize risks, the area in which parks, recreation, and leisure professionals might choose to focus is on the act/standard of care. There are many components that fit within this element of negligence and they are addressed in the remainder of this chapter.

Types of Supervision

Leader supervision of leisure services events is a very important element in managing risks related to standard of care. Van der Smissen has noted that, "a lack of or inadequate supervision is the most common allegation of negligence in recreation and leisure services" (1990, p. 163). The duty to supervise is determined based on the relationships or

duty owed between the person supervising (the leader) and the participants. In the delivery of recreation and leisure services supervision is
inherent in most activities. Whenever a leisure services agency or
organization sponsors and conducts a leisure activity, supervision is
required. The supervision is usually performed by an activity or
program leader.

There are various elements of a recreation or leisure activity that
help to determine the nature of the required supervision. It is important
to recognize generalities that impact the type of supervision required
(see Table 11A) so as to make wise decisions relative to appropriate
level of supervision. In parks, recreation, and leisure services settings
there are times when the leader (employee) is considered *in loco
parentis*. In other words, the leisure services leader is acting in the place
of the parent or guardian in the care and safety of a minor (i.e., a youth
under the age of 18 or 21, depending upon the state in which one resides).
It is important to note that acting *in loco parentis* actually demands of
the leader a level of care and supervision of the child **greater** than that
owed to the child by her or his parents.

As an example, a family with two youth ages 13 and 14 years might
go camping at a state campground. They set up the family tents well
away from the shower house/bathroom to better enjoy the natural
surroundings. Most parents would consider the ages of their young
teenagers and allow the adolescents to walk to the shower house without
being accompanied by parents. The parents' judgment seems reasonable; to allow young teens to walk to the shower house in this type of
setting without being escorted is not uncommon.

Now imagine the same situation, but rather than with parents a
group of young teenagers are on a camping trip sponsored by the local
YMCA. The counselors would be acting *in loco parentis*, yet in this
instance, it would be best if the adolescents were accompanied to the
shower house. The many possible ways for young people to get into
mischief remain the same in both situations: the teenagers might decide
to tour the campground and see what "fun" they might induce, a stranger
might interfere with the safety of the teens, or the youth might get
temporarily misplaced (lost). In the first scenario the parents would
likely be distraught over the incident, yet no legal or civil action would
likely be undertaken for their failure to properly supervise their children. In the second scenario, however, if an injury should occur to one
of the teens the counselors would be legally responsible for that
incident.

Table 11A   *Specificity of Supervision: Many factors influence the type of supervision needed to be effective in direct leadership.*

		highest specificity of supervision ⟷	lowest specificity of supervision
Participants	age	very young	teen	adult
	developmental abilities	low	moderate	high
	skill level	low	moderate	high
	previous exposure	none	some	lots
Activity	complexity	high	moderate	low
	difficulty	high	moderate	low
	inherent risk	high	moderate	low
Environment	maintenance & condition	poor	good	excellent
	participant familiarity with space	none	some	lots
Leader	skills	low	moderate	high
	maturity	low	moderate	high
	experience	low	moderate	high
	competence	low	moderate	high

In direct leadership situations, whether *in loco parentis* or as a professional, there is an inherent duty to supervise—the activities are sponsored and led by agency personnel; this results in an expectation of safe conditions. To ensure these safe conditions there are three types of supervision which are utilized in situations dependent upon various elements. The types of supervision are: *general, transitional,* and *specific.* It is necessary to fully understand the three types of supervision and the activity being supervised to know which type of supervision is required when. Failure to afford participants the appropriate type of supervision may result in increased risk of injury to participants and lead to claims of negligence.

General Supervision

General supervision describes situations where a leader oversees a broad area. The focus of general supervision is on the conduct and demeanor of individual participants or on the physical environment itself. For example, a leisure services leader might provide general supervision to adults who are playing beach volleyball. When focused on player conduct and demeanor a supervisor would notice if a player was playing overly aggressively, or who appeared to mentally "check out" of the activity. In either case, the supervisor might wish to visit with the individual and ask her or him to settle down, or to pay closer attention so as to avoid injury. A supervisor focused on the physical environment would watch the court and nearby areas for potential hazards. If another ball, Frisbee, or other object were to enter the playing area the supervisor would halt play to remove the hazard.

In general supervision, visual and voice contact are easily maintained with participants in the area being supervised, and the ratios of leaders to participants can be quite low. Examples of general supervision include the supervision teachers provide on playgrounds, coaches supervising an athletic practice, leisure services leaders supervising an open gymnasium period, and a docent supervising a museum visit. In all of these instances the ratio of leader to participants might be 1:20 or more.

Transitional Supervision

Transitional supervision is defined as it sounds; it is the supervision one uses when shifting from general to specific supervision and vice versa (van der Smissen, 1990). In the conduct of an activity many situations may arise which demand a change in the level of supervision: the teaching of new skills, the introduction of new (unknown) participants, or a change in environmental conditions. For example, moving from warming up in an athletic practice to learning and practicing new drills would require a change from general to specific supervision. A change in weather conditions might warrant more specific supervision as might participant fatigue, participant attention levels, activity difficulty, and familiarity with the play space or activities.

Photo by Lattin Photography; Courtesy of the Family YMCA of Black Hawk County

General supervision is usually sufficient in large group and team sports activities.

Specific Supervision

Leisure services leaders are required to engage in specific supervision when there is instruction involved, participants are low skilled, and when participant behaviors so indicate (e.g., participant unpredictability). *Specific supervision* is defined as supervision where direct contact with participants is made by the supervisor (van der Smissen, 1990). Direct contact does not necessarily indicate physical contact; close visual and voice contact are elements of specific supervision, as well. There are times, however, when physical contact by a supervisor is necessary (e.g., spotting in gymnastics, spotting individuals on a ropes or teams course, or in rock climbing). Any time the risk of injury increases, the level of supervision (i.e., specificity) owed to participants increases. See Table 11A (page 379) for examples of the impacts of change in participants, activity, and environment on the needed type of supervision.

Photo courtesy of the Family YMCA of Black Hawk County

Leisure service leaders would be wise to utilize specific supervision in activities with inherent risks.

Leaders as Supervisors

Whenever a leisure services professional leads a sponsored activity, she or he owes a legal duty to the participants to conduct activities in a safe and conscionable manner. As described in the above explanations of the various types of supervision, leisure services leaders are viewed as supervisors of participants, activities, and areas. As supervisors, if a question of negligence arises the leader will be measured against a standard of a reasonable and prudent professional. Reasonable and prudent professionals are competent and are positioned in appropriate locations relative to participants and potential hazards.

Competency

Competency refers to the quality or condition of being qualified to perform an act. Leisure services leaders are expected to be competent in a variety of areas such as direct leadership techniques, behavior management, human development, emergency care, and others. Van der Smissen (1990) has indicated that the competence of a supervisor is measured by several components which include, but are not limited to, the following.

Knowledge

To minimize liability, it is important for supervisors to be knowledgeable about the participants, the activity, and the environment. This knowledge must extend to include the proper ways of conducting activities as well as to ascertain potential hazards. More will be said about the three areas of knowledge in a later section which discusses the conduct of an activity.

Age

It is important that the age of the leader be appropriate to the activity requirements. Age is considered to be correlated to maturity level, and is very important in many situations. In some instances, leader age is mandated by certification or accreditation standards. For instance, to be an American Red Cross Canoe Instructor an individual must be a minimum of 21 years of age. Another age consideration is based on the difference between the ages of the leader and participants. This often is an issue when participants are adolescents and leaders are in their late teens/early twenties—the age difference is minimal and difficult supervisory issues can arise as a result of this.

Experience

Previous experience and level of experience are other important factors when selecting the appropriate supervisor or leader for a particular task. If leader experience level is weak and the situation requires a good deal of attention it might be best to pair that supervisor with a more experienced person until the less seasoned leader develops the necessary skills and judgment.

Credentials

If national or industry standards require certifications or licensure for particular positions, it would be wise for those filling those slots to hold those documents. *Industry standards* are those that are not mandated by any national entity, but are commonly accepted as minimum standards for a person filling a particular position or job. As an example, in the 1990s it is common practice (i.e., industry standards) for those individuals who work with youth in youth-serving and leisure services agencies or organizations to hold certificates of completion for training in universal precautions (e.g., blood borne pathogens) and mandatory child abuse reporting. Competent supervisors would have and maintain these and other certifications.

Attentiveness to Duty

Any time an injury occurs, questions will be raised about one's attentiveness to the situation. For instance, a lifeguard on duty should have her or his attention on the swimmers and others at the waterfront at all times. An inattentive lifeguard (perhaps visiting and talking to people) may miss potential hazards resulting in unsafe conditions for participants. Being attentive to one's responsibilities is important for all parks, recreation, and leisure services leaders. Attentiveness is equally important whether one is leading or supervising a gymnasium, childcare center, nature center, or amusement ride.

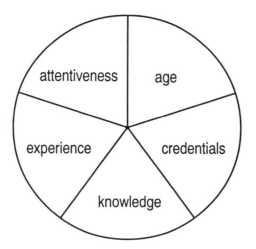

Figure 11.2 *In supervisory roles, leisure services leader competence is defined by many traits.*

Supervisor Location

Supervisor location is as important as supervisor competence in minimizing risks. Supervisors *must* be accessible to participants and the area they are supervising to meet expectations of their jobs. A well-located supervisor can manage problems and foresee potential hazards more easily than one who is in the wrong place, too far away, or out of view. When considering placement, one should think about proximity; that is, the relative closeness of the leader to potential trouble spots, and to initiating emergency systems. Being in the right place at the right time should not be an accident. Rather, supervisor and leader location should be purposeful and deliberate relative to participant, activity, and facility needs.

In addition to physical proximity, being able to make visual and voice contact with participants in all corners of the environment is important to be able to act promptly and appropriately. Being within visual contact allows the supervisor to see not only what is currently going on, but also to foresee or anticipate what might occur next. Voice distance without visual contact is limiting as the supervisor is unable to glean all the necessary information to make decisions regarding a particular situation.

Depending upon the activity, the environment, and the participants, the location of the supervisor may vary. Supervising with a focus on participants requires a level of visual contact with participants so as to be able to make judgments relative to their actions. Focusing on the area or physical environment necessitates a leader being within eye view of the area to be supervised.

There are occasions in these situations when the visual contact should be continuous (such as at a waterfront) and other times when it need not be continuous and uninterrupted. For instance, if a leisure services leader were supervising an open gymnasium or arts-and-crafts room *being able to see* and *checking in* on the participants is what is necessary.

Supervisor Functions

In addition to being competent, in the appropriate location, and determining and applying appropriate types of supervision to participants there are additional functions of an activity supervisor (i.e., direct leadership). According to van der Smissen (1990), the role of supervisor has five primary functions:

- to manage participant behaviors;
- to render emergency care;
- to enforce rules equitably;
- to be alert to dangerous conditions; and
- to maintain responsibilities for participants off premises.

Behavior Management

It is the responsibility of the supervisor to maintain control of a group through appropriate behavior management techniques. Through appropriate behavior management a leader helps to maintain safe activity conditions; people-generated hazards can be minimized and participant safety and enjoyment maximized.

Render Emergency Care

Should something go awry and a participant require emergency care, it is the responsibility of the supervisor, or direct leader, to provide that aid. This is not to say that the supervisor must physically provide first aid, but rather she or he is responsible for enacting the emergency medical system (EMS) (i.e., calling 911) if necessary and protecting the individual from further harm. Many leisure services agencies require first aid and CPR certifications as prerequisites to employment. These two certifications are quickly becoming industry standard in all aspects of parks, recreation, and leisure services.

Enforce Rules Equitably

A third responsibility of a supervisor is to establish, communicate and enforce all rules equitably. Establishing, communicating, and enforcing rules equitably allows for differences in participant skill levels, developmental stages, and in environmental conditions while maintaining a safe environment. If a rule is not enforced in one instance because the situation involves a friend or because the leader is simply trying to be "nice" difficulties could arise that might result in a claim of negligence.

Be Alert to Dangerous Conditions

It is a function of a supervisor to always be alert to dangerous conditions. Dangerous conditions might arise out of participant behaviors (e.g., inattentiveness, acting out), staffing situations (e.g., not enough staff, or improperly located staff), the activity (e.g., some activities may be inherently dangerous, others are improperly conducted, or overly difficult), and the environment (e.g., indoor or outdoor conditions such as wet floors or extreme temperatures might compromise safety). Leisure services leaders are expected to be constantly on the watch for changing conditions, and to foresee and avoid potential hazards.

Have Responsibilities for Participants Off Premises

Leader responsibility for participants exists whether one is on agency premises or off-site. Whenever participants are off-premises and involved in a sponsored activity, a supervisor has a responsibility to minimize hazards and present activities in a safe fashion. Trips to the pool, to the ball field, or to the concert hall all demand ongoing supervision while in transit and at the new location.

◆ Manage participant behaviors

◆ Render emergency care

◆ Enforce rules equitably

◆ Be alert to danger

◆ Maintain responsibilities off-site

Figure 11.3 Supervisors are expected to engage in tasks related to five functions.

Having a Supervision Plan

To supervise well and minimize risks it is wise to develop and follow a *written* supervision plan. A written plan may serve to educate and train new leaders and supervisors, as well as remind existing supervisors of proper procedures. A written plan can minimize the confusion over when to use what type of supervision, where to locate, and should serve to identify necessary supervisor credentials. According to Kaiser (1986) and van der Smissen (1990), a plan for supervision should answer the following questions:

- How many supervisors are required for what types of events? What are the qualifications of a supervisor (e.g., age, certifications, experience)? How will appropriate supervisors be identified?

- What types of supervision are required? This is an explanation (in global terms) of when general, transitional, and specific supervision should be practiced.

- Where should supervisors be located? Being specific about approximate or relative locations helps to minimize confusion for supervisors. Location might be defined in relation to participants, the activity, or the area. For example, when leading young children in a pool area, activity supervisors (not lifeguards who remain at their posts) might be directed to be located in the midst of the children. When supervising participants on a softball field, leaders might be directed to walk around the facility in a particular pattern so that their location is fluid.

- When should a supervisor intervene? Knowing when to directly interfere and when not to do so is something that is learned through experience and, often, is part of agency policy. When in the learning stages a leader may find that while stepping into a situation might irritate participants, it is generally wiser to interfere than not.

- What are the expectations of a supervisor? All supervision plans should articulate and describe the expectations of a supervisor. For example: Are supervisors expected to physically break up an altercation, perform first aid, deal with the media, expel participants, call their supervisor when…, clean bathrooms, and lock or unlock doors?

Having a written supervision plan will help not only as a training aid for supervisors, but it also provides a guide for understanding leader expectations should a participant be injured. As long as the supervision plan is followed appropriately, the risk of liability is minimized. Having a written supervision plan and not following it, however, may lead to additional concerns related to claims of negligence.

Conduct of the Activity

The conduct of an activity is the very essence of recreation and leisure services leadership. Leisure services leaders conduct a large variety of activities for all types of people. The manner in which activities are conducted (and supervised) has a tremendous impact on the safety, well-being, and enjoyment of the participants (and the leader!). Conducting an activity improperly can lead to injury and lawsuits.

It is absolutely critical for recreation and leisure service providers to remember that *there is no compromise for safety*. There are times when leisure services leaders find themselves in situations where they feel as though they have to play the "bad guy" by enforcing sometimes unpopular safety rules; this can be an uncomfortable feeling, particularly when leading a group of one's peers. It must be understood, however, that the leader has ultimate responsibility for the safety of each participant in the group. If safety rules or guidelines are not followed consistently and a participant is injured, the leader could be at risk for negligence.

If, for instance, people were allowed to stand on an earth ball (a large four- to six-foot diameter ball) "just this once," and an individual was injured during that play, the leisure services leader could be held liable—negligence could be found for failure to follow safety rules. Leisure services activities have safety rules and guidelines to minimize risks, not to constrain participants from having fun. If activity rules seem overly stringent, perhaps they warrant a review in a staff meeting, but activity leaders should not feel free to disregard rules because some participants complain. Remember, *there is no compromise for safety*.

In the process of leading activities, leisure services leaders have a responsibility to follow professional standards and practices to keep participants safe and free from harm. As mentioned earlier the safe conduct of an activity requires a knowledge of participants, the activity, and the environment in which the activity is held (van der Smissen, 1990).

Knowledge of Participants

To conduct an activity safely, leisure services leaders must have a solid understanding of the participants and their level of readiness for the upcoming activity. It is necessary to learn and understand the differences in people based on their developmental abilities, previous experience with the activity, physical condition, and their physical and emotional capabilities. While this type of information often results in generalizations about people, it is wise to remember many individuals fall well-above and well-below the norm of a particular group. Therefore, leaders are cautioned to avoid making stereotypical judgments about participants; information should be gathered to support all evaluations made of participants.

Once this information is gathered a competent leisure services leader will use it in her or his decision making related to types of equipment (e.g., Nerf ball or Whiffle ball, safety scissors or "regular" scissors), the selection of teammates and opponents (e.g., to help balance skill, physical size, and maturity levels in opponents), and the nature and enforcement of activity related rules (e.g., younger children generally require more explicit and clearly stated rules than do older individuals).

Developmental Abilities

Generally, development abilities are defined by considering a combination of information: participant age, maturity, coordination, and physical size. Age alone can provide some information about the probable maturity level of the participants, but combined with observations of actual maturity, kinesthetic awareness, and physical size, developmental abilities provide a much more accurate assessment of what can be expected of participants. For example, when working with adults who are mentally retarded, knowledge of their developmental abilities (i.e., what cognitive, emotional and physical capabilities they have) tends to be a more accurate assessment of actual ability than age or physical size.

Previous Experience and Skills

Leisure services leaders are expected to have knowledge of participants' general intelligence, experience, and knowledge base related to the planned activities. Knowing these things can be helpful in deciding how to conduct an activity—which rules to state when, whether to run

- developmental abilities
- previous experience
- skill level
- physical condition
- emotional state

Figure 11.4 A thorough knowledge of participants is required of leaders in a supervisory role.

or walk, and the type of supervision required. It is not always wise to accept participants' statements about their skill levels, however. When faced with embarrassment many participants will exaggerate their skills and previous experience with a particular activity.

For example, when asking a group of individuals at a pool if they can swim, almost every one will either answer in the affirmative or remain silent. However, when those individuals are swim-tested, it is highly likely that a leader will discover that at least one of them does not know how to swim. Therefore, while it is appropriate to solicit a verbal self-report as to previous experience and skill level from participants, in activities with inherent risk a physical test of abilities should be conducted.

Physical Condition

It is the leisure services leader's responsibility to know about obvious and hidden physical limitations of participants which might interfere with full or safe participation in the activities. This includes a general knowledge of physical conditions such as obesity, recent illnesses, and pertinent previous injuries. Obviously, one should use her or his judgment; it is not necessary to know if someone has a bad knee if the activity is a card game, but the leader should know about joint injuries if the activity is a walk or hike of some type. For day-to-day drop-in types of activities, a standard medical information form completed at registration and kept on file is usually sufficient. This way, if an injury should occur, a general medical history is available for those who will be treating the participant.

Physical and Emotional Capabilities

Again, for safety as well as for maximum enjoyment it is helpful to know about the physical and emotional capabilities of group members. If an activity results in emotional stress and that stress might negatively affect one's mental or physical health, that activity should be avoided.

Leisure services leaders are expected to have a general knowledge of the emotional states of participants. For instance, participants who are involved voluntarily often have a more positive and alert emotional state than do those who are "forced" to participate (e.g., children are sometimes "forced" to participate by parents due to a need for childcare). Furthermore, it is helpful for leaders to be alert to any participants who might have a propensity for violence or are especially agitated during the session.

Knowledge of the Activity

In addition to having a solid knowledge of the participants, a leisure services leader is expected to have knowledge of the activity to be conducted. Knowledge of the appropriate equipment, activity objectives, rules, and safety concerns will aid a leader in making decisions as to the appropriate timing of the activity, and will help her or him to foresee hazards and take protective action.

Rules and Level of Skills Needed

Knowledge of the activity rules and level of skills needed to safely participate allows the leader to select activities which match the needs and skill levels of those who wish to engage in such activity. Furthermore, a leader who knows the activity rules can ensure safe practice by communicating and enforcing those rules to all participants.

Actual Instruction and Safety Needs

A leader has a responsibility to teach *safely*, teach *safety*, and to *warn* of hazards in the conduct of an activity. To safely conduct an activity a leader needs to know how to provide directions (e.g., differences in giving directions based on the development level of participants) and the potential safety concerns. This is particularly the case if an activity has been modified. For instance, the children's game of "duck, duck, goose" can be very hazardous if children are not instructed in how (and how not) to tap another child on the head or shoulder. Potential safety concerns of this activity include slipping while running, twisting one's ankle, and physical roughness in tapping. Neglecting to inform participants about potential hazards could lead to liability problems.

Sequencing and Progression

Sequencing activities appropriately and developing a sound progression of activities are the responsibility of the leader. A competent leader will know when to introduce new skills within an activity and when not to. If a group is struggling to grasp basic skills, moving on to the next skill level is not a wise choice. For example, one would not introduce dive rolls to people who cannot yet do forward rolls (i.e., somersaults). It is best if activities are led in a progression with activities that are complex and rigorous following those that are simpler and easier to grasp. An example of this would be teaching Newcomb prior to learning volleyball.

Knowledge of the Environment

In addition to understanding participants and having a solid knowledge of the activity, knowing about the environment (advantages and disadvantages of the space, hazards and layout) in which one is playing is necessary. It is important that the environment be appropriate for the activity being conducted. For example, playing rugby on an asphalt surface would not be appropriate because it could lead to severe injury. While most activity instructions do not include information about preferred playing surfaces, leaders should consider the requirements of the activity and make an appropriate judgment about environmental requirements.

Playing Area

If indoors, a leisure services leader should be knowledgeable about the playing area; if outdoors, the leader should be knowledgeable about the grounds and surrounding area. Ascertaining this information usually requires a walking tour of the area to look for hazards and potential hazards. Omitting this physical inspection of the environment could lead to unsafe leadership situations. It is expected that leaders will ensure playing areas safe from hazards and potential dangers. This includes avoiding such things as wet surfaces, litter and broken glass, hanging branches from trees at eye level, extraneous equipment lying about, and poor lighting.

Photo by Fratzke Photography; Courtesy of Hartman Nature Reserve

Checking the environment for hazards can lead to interesting finds.

Equipment

Typically, the conduct of leisure activities involves some type of equipment (e.g., balls, hoops, paint brushes) and structures (e.g., goal posts, fences, playground structures). As with the grounds, it is necessary to conduct an inspection of these items prior to the conduct of an activity. In addition to being free from defect, the leader should be sure that the items are being used in the way in which they were intended. For instance, using a jump rope as a bull whip could lead to injury and to claims of leader negligence. Using defective equipment may also be cause for claims of negligence; leaders are expected to be aware of (and take action to remove) any defect in all equipment used in leisure services activities.

Safe and responsible conduct of an activity demands that leisure services leaders be aware of three activity elements: knowledge of participants including developmental stage, skills, and previous experience; knowledge of the activity including rules and potential safety issues; and knowledge of the environment including the playing area and equipment. With this knowledge leaders can make appropriate judgments related to activity selection and appropriate direct leadership techniques.

Facilities and Environment

Legal concerns about leisure services facilities and environment fall into two general categories—agency liability for maintenance of facilities and leader liability for conducting an activity on unsafe premises. Parks, recreation, and leisure services agencies and organizations owe a duty to their constituents to maintain safe properties. For instance, in city parks one would expect picnic pavilions to be free from dangerous structural problems (i.e., wooden picnic tables free from splinters, concrete flooring free of large cracks and uneven surfaces). If these expectations are not met, issues of legal liability (e.g., negligence) could be the result.

An activity leader is liable for the conditions of premises being used in the conduct of an activity. This is true whether the area being used is public (e.g., a city park) or privately owned (e.g., fitness trails on commercial property). A leader is responsible (and expected) to avoid placing or leading activity participants in an unsafe situation. If a hazard is found, either in the facility or environment, a leisure services leader is responsible to first report and document the hazard (van der Smissen, 1990). *Once discovered, a leader must avoid conducting an activity in the vicinity of the hazard.* In an unsafe area a leader's choices related to conducting the activity are to:

• stop the activity;

• modify the activity so the hazard is not an issue; or

• make a temporary repair, warn the participants, and continue.

This last option is viable only if the leader knows how to (and is capable of) making a safe and appropriate repair.

To minimize risks to participants and to minimize risks of negligence to the leaders, it is important to hold periodic and scheduled inspections of facilities and outdoor environments. Furthermore, it is critical to *inspect a site immediately prior to its being used for the conduct of an activity.* This is particularly true if a leader has any reason to suspect that the nature or care of the facility has changed since the most recent inspection.

For example, a day camp utilizes a public park area for its programming and activity efforts. Camp runs daily, Monday through Friday, and grounds inspections are performed every Monday morning before the campers arrive. The Fourth of July holiday occurs on a Wednesday and the park is a favorite spot for celebrations. On Thursday morning the camp director and all the counselors should conduct a thorough grounds inspection because soft drink and alcoholic beverage containers (among other trash) likely would be found throughout the park. This type of litter can pose hazards to participants in the pursuit of leisure.

In addition to having a basic understanding of legal issues related to negligence, leisure services leaders may wish to use forms and records to minimize risks. While the use of various forms, particularly releases and waivers, has been questioned recently, there is value in their appropriate use (Baley & Matthews, 1989; Kaiser, 1986; van der Smissen, 1990). This next section will provide an introduction to the more common forms used in recreation and leisure service settings as elements of a risk management plan.

☑ modify the activity to avoid hazard

☑ make a temporary repair, warn & continue

☑ stop the activity

Figure 11.5 *Once a leader discovers a hazard related to a facility or play area, her or his choices to continue the activity are limited.*

The Use of Forms in Risk Management

The purpose in using most forms for risk management is to limit the liability of individual employees (i.e., leisure services leaders) and of a particular agency. While questions have arisen over the effectiveness of waivers and release forms, the courts have found them to be useful in determining participant understanding of the risks involved in the activity (Baley & Matthews, 1989; Kaiser, 1986; Niepoth, 1983; van der Smissen, 1990). In other words, at times, risk management forms are used for informational and public relations purposes. It is suggested that all forms being developed by an agency be examined by an attorney or risk management specialist prior to use. This will help to ensure appropriate language and that the content of the forms is not contrary to state or local laws.

All risk management forms should be legible (e.g., type written or printed on a computer printer) and written in clear, unambiguous language. To be valid, forms should be dated and signed by the participant; it also must be shown that the forms were understood by the person signing them. In this effort it may be best to not only have the participants read the forms before signing, but have the leader read the content of the forms aloud to participants and provide an opportunity for participants to ask questions.

With all risk management forms it is important to note that while parents or guardians are usually requested to sign forms for their minor children, *parents or guardians may not sign away their children's rights* (van der Smissen, 1990). This means that although a parent may sign a form waiving the right to collect monetary damages in the case of injury to her or his child, once the minor child reaches the age of majority, that child may sue on her or his own behalf. Therefore, leisure services agencies should save forms and records for a minimum of five years, and it would be wise to save those that involve minors for five years past the year the child reaches the age of majority.

Types of Forms

There are a variety of forms commonly used by parks, recreation, and leisure services agencies of all types in efforts to inform participants of potential hazards and to minimize risks of negligence to the agency. Some forms are primarily used to inform, while others ask signees to voluntarily relinquish their right to sue in the event of an injury due to the negligence of the leader.

Parental (Guardian) Permission

Parental or guardian permission forms are used to solicit permission from parents and guardians for their child to engage in particular activities. Commonly, these forms are used as public relation tools to inform parents or guardians about upcoming events. Often, a generic permission form is used, but there are times when it is necessary to utilize activity-specific forms. For instance, when a child is to be transported away from the primary location for a field trip, to engage in aquatic activities, or in an activity which might be physically or emotionally trying for a youngster specific forms identifying the particulars should be used. Other times a more generic parental permission form is all that is required; this form typically states that the named child has permission to engage in common center activities.

Medical History

A medical history form is an important form to have on hand for extended sponsored activities (e.g., day camp, adult softball leagues, open gymnasium time where minor children participate without parents or guardians), which require agency provided travel (e.g., field trips), and for activities where the participants have special needs (e.g., health concerns, physical/developmental disabilities).

In addition to the expected medical history, these forms commonly include a physician's signature (indicating good overall health), medical insurance information, and a "Permission to Treat" statement. A "Permission to Treat" statement usually is worded in such a way as to indicate that should the participant be unable to speak for herself or himself, permission for medical treatment to begin is authorized.

In the case of minor children, parents or guardians indicate their permission to have their child treated should they be unavailable for immediate consultation. For these forms to be effective, they must be readily available and should remain within the vicinity of the participant. This means that if a field trip is planned, the medical history forms should go with the group on the trip; if the group is on agency property, the forms are located in a nearby office.

Accident/Incident Report

Accident/incident reports are used for several reasons: to document treatment of an injury as documentation for insurance needs, to provide agency statistics, and to assist in legal situations. This report form is one of the most important forms utilized by recreation and leisure service personnel. It is the actual documentation of an accident or incident where an individual was hurt or property damaged. To be useful, accident/incident reports must be completed within a short time of the event, should be thorough and free from speculation. A "just the facts, ma'am" approach should be taken with all legal forms, and in particular, this form.

Therefore, when describing an accident or incident, the leader completing the form should use "dry," objective language. In response to "What led up to this incident?" Rather than stating on an accident/incident report, "people were goofing around when they shouldn't haven't been...," one would write, "horseplay occurred between several participants and they were told on three occasions to stop." The second statement is factual without being subjective, and limits speculation.

Well-designed accident/incident reports will have a space for the person completing the form to illustrate or draw the scenario, body part injured, or physical layout of the environment in which the incident occurred. In addition, information about the environment, participants and witnesses, a factual description of what occurred, and the disposition of the incident should be provided (e.g., the participant was sent home, EMS was activated, damaged equipment was removed from the area).

Assumption of Risk/Agreement to Participate

An assumption of risk or agreement to participate form is used to document that participants know and understand the inherent hazards and possible injuries of an activity. All activities have risks and many are so common as to not warrant such a form. For instance, many sports, playground activities, swimming pool use, and attendance at athletic events are so common in society, that it is considered that there is little chance that an individual would not know and understand the risks involved in participation. There are other activities, however, of which the common person would not be expected to know and understand the inherent risks. In these instances, an agreement to participate or assumption of risk (AOR) form would be desirable.

To be useful an AOR should *describe in detail the nature of the activity, the expectations of the participants, and information about potential hazards.* If one is going on a canoe trip and death by drowning is possible, it is best to include that information on the form. Some parks, recreation, and leisure services professionals have expressed concerns that identifying the extreme physical hazards of an activity might drive participants away, but this has not been the case (van der Smissen, 1992). A failure to describe and articulate all risks could limit the usefulness of this form.

In addition to describing the nature of the activity and all of its potential dangers, information about the *expectations of the participants* should be included. In this statement, participants are informed that they will be expected to follow rules of the trip, and respond to the activity leader when called upon to do so. If participants are expected to provide written documentation of previous experience or skill level, it would be wise to include this requirement in the AOR.

Another necessary element of an agreement to participate form is a statement about the *condition of the participants.* If participant skill levels are varied, this should be so stated; if participants are expected to be in good physical health, this should also be stated.

Release/Waiver

In common usage the terms *release* and *waiver* are used interchangeably, and while the law makes a technical distinction between the two, for purposes of this text, the terms will be used as one. A release or waiver is based in contract law; essentially by signing such a form the participant indicates that she or he knows and understands the risks involved in an activity, chooses to engage in the experience in spite of those risks, and then through this contract, agrees not to hold the leader and agency liable for negligence. In most cases, as long as the contract was entered into legally and the language was clear and unambiguous the waiver or release will be considered valid.

Photo Release

The last form that will be discussed here is a photographic release form. The purpose of this type of form is slightly different from the ones described above as it is used primarily to protect privacy and property interests. Particularly in the field of therapeutic recreation, issues of privacy are paramount. Permissions must be gained prior to publishing any client photographs where individuals might be identifiable. Failure to do so could result in a lawsuit based on invasion of privacy.

Property rights relate to photographs in that it is plausible that a photograph could be sold to a publisher resulting in a financial gain for the seller. Generally, the subject of the photo has rights to the use of her or his likeness in money making ventures. It is always wise to gain permission from the subjects for use whether it be issues of privacy or property.

Summary

Understanding the basics of legal liability is critical to being a successful leader. Sound knowledge helps to minimize problems and increases enjoyment of leaders and participants. One of the primary tenets of legal liability is that anyone can sue anybody for anything at any time. In this light, leisure services leaders should strive to minimize leader negligence. Negligence is based in tort law and in order for negligence to exist four elements must be present: duty, act/standard of care, proximate cause, and injury.

A lack of supervision is the primary complaint identified in lawsuits. To be effective, leisure services leaders need to know when to use general, transitional, and specific supervision. The nature of the participants, activity, environment and leader combine to determine which level of supervision is required in what instance. Supervisors have five basic functions and are expected to be competent and in an appropriate location relative to the participants and area being supervised. A comprehensive supervision plan will go a long way in minimizing risks.

In conducting an activity, a leader is expected to have solid knowledge of the participants, activity, and the environment. With this knowledge, activity selection is easier, site inspections are focused, and the leader can make sound (and safe) decisions. There are many forms available for use in the efforts to minimize risk to an individual leader and agency. These include parental permission forms, medical history forms, accident/incident reports, assumption of risk forms, releases/waivers, and photographic release forms.

This chapter has merely introduced the concepts surrounding leadership and liability. Recreation and leisure services students and practitioners are encouraged to seek additional information pertinent to their own state and country, and continue to study this area.

The Front Line

The following risk management checklist is provided for use in direct leadership situations to help ensure the safety and enjoyment of participants. Prior to beginning any leisure services activity, leaders should conduct a visual (and, if necessary, tactile) check of the facility and structures, grounds, and equipment. In addition, summarizing one's knowledge of the activity, participants, and staff involved is helpful to illustrate competence and concern for safety issues.

Risk Management Checklist

Facility/Structure

Are the lights in working order throughout the facility?
Is the floor clear of debris (e.g., paper, trash, broken glass, dirt)?
Is the floor clear of water?
Are obstacles clear from the playing area (e.g., unused equipment, tables, chairs, benches)?
Do you have a clear view of all playing areas?
Is the area secure from unauthorized visitors?
Does the structure have any inherent hazards (e.g., exposed bolts, splinters, rough surfaces)?
Where is this facility/structure in relation to potential danger zones (e.g., roads, water, electrical wires)?
Are the facilities appropriate for the weather conditions?
Is the facility clean?
Is the structure in good working order?
Where is the nearest emergency telephone?

Grounds

Is the ground surface smooth and free from holes and divots?
Is the ground clear of debris (e.g., paper, trash, broken glass)?
Is the ground clear of water?
Is the ground surface slippery?
Is the ground the appropriate surface for this activity?
If playing at dusk or dark, is the area well lit?

Do you have a clear view of all playing areas?

Is the area secure from unauthorized visitors?

Where are these grounds in relation to potential danger zones (e.g., roads, bodies of water)?

Where is the nearest emergency telephone?

Is there indoor access in case of inclement weather (e.g., humidity, lightning)?

Equipment

Is the equipment in good working condition?

Is the equipment being used as it was intended?

Is the equipment appropriate for this activity and age group?

Does this equipment have inherent hazards (i.e., earth ball, scuba gear)?

Is it possible that this equipment will break or stop functioning in the middle of an activity?

What are the possible misuses of this equipment?

Is it appropriate for participants to play on or with this equipment unsupervised?

Is a first-aid kit available?

Is water available?

Activity

Is the activity developmentally appropriate?

Does the activity require general or specific supervision?

Do you have the appropriate numbers of staff needed for this activity?

Has the activity been presented or taught in sequential order?

Do you have enough materials to offer the program safely?

Is there potential for participant-induced hazards (e.g., fights, horseplay)?

Is this activity being conducted on or in suitable facilities/grounds?

Is safety emphasized in giving the activity instructions?

Is water or access to water provided?

Have potential activity-associated risks been identified?

Staff

Is the staff mature, responsible, respectful, and professional?

Does the staff know and understand emergency procedures?

Is the staff certified and/or properly trained to conduct this activity?

Does the staff have good judgment ("know what they know and know what they don't know")?

Do staff members always put the safety of participants first?

Do staff err on the side of safety?

Do the staff provide proper supervision to all activities/participants?

Are the staff attentive to the program and participants?

Has the staff played, "What if?"

Do staff members have access to medical forms?

Participants

Do the participants have a sense of self-care?

Why are the participants in attendance?

Do participants understand the importance of safety?

Do participants follow instructions?

What is the group atmosphere like (e.g., respectful, careless, wild, calm)?

What are the group norms with regard to treatment of group members?

Do you have participants who abdicate self-responsibility? consider themselves immortal? are seemingly disembodied?

Do participants have previous injuries or medical conditions that warrant consideration (e.g., epilepsy, allergic reaction to bee stings, bad knees)?

Does each participant have on file a medical history form, release for treatment form, and release for participation form?

Are participants properly attired for the activity and weather conditions?

References

Baley, J. and Matthews, D. (1989). *Law and liability in athletics, physical education and recreation* (2nd ed.). Dubuque, IA: Wm. C. Brown Publishing.

Kaiser, R. (1986). *Liability and law in recreation, parks, and sports.* Englewood Cliffs, NJ: Prentice Hall.

Niepoth, E. W. (1983). *Leisure leadership.* Englewood Cliffs, NJ: Prentice Hall.

van der Smissen, B. (1990). *Legal liability and risk management for public and private entities.* Cincinnati, OH: Anderson Publishing Company.

Chapter Twelve
Learning Opportunities

Through studying this chapter students will have the opportunity to:

- describe the many steps of preparing for leadership;
- understand the importance of knowing demographic information about the group one is about to lead;
- learn about four different levels of recreation goals;
- practice writing goals and objectives; and
- outline a method of game and song leadership.

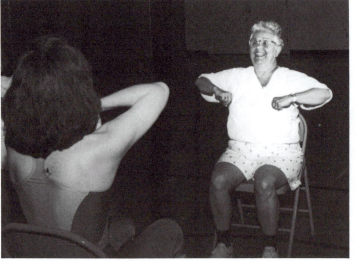

Photo courtesy of the YWCA of Black Hawk County

CHAPTER

Direct Leadership Techniques

One of the most exciting and enjoyable aspects of leisure services leadership is the putting into practice all of the leader competencies one has learned. Being in front of a group, sharing one's skills and enthusiasm, teaching new skills, and helping people to achieve a higher quality of life is the highlight of the profession for many leisure services leaders. Direct leaders have a tremendous impact on the groups and individuals they lead. A leader's personality and leadership style can incite people to stretch themselves and truly enjoy all of their leisure experiences—this is accomplished through direct leadership.

Direct leadership techniques are those methods and approaches used when leading individuals and groups in parks, recreation, and leisure settings. Direct leadership involves the act of working with a person or persons directly in a face-to-face situation. In the delivery of leisure services, examples of direct leadership include game and song leading, facilitating a leisure education session, giving a guided tour, coaching a youth sport, and leading exercise classes.

To be successful in leisure services, direct leadership skills are necessary. Understanding what goes on "in the trenches" and being successful at working directly with people are two of the most important aspects of success for leaders in the leisure services field. These techniques and skills are used in all leisure settings and with all ages of people.

Being responsible for direct leadership involves establishing the environment, leading people in a variety of recreation and leisure activities, examining differences in leading based on style, and applying theoretical concepts to situations that exist in the provision of leisure services. Successful leadership consists of four phases: *preparation, priming the group,* and *delivery.* Each of these phases will be discussed in this chapter.

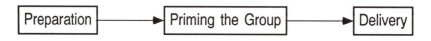

Figure 12.1 *Direct leadership involves three distinct phases.*

Leadership Preparation—Phase I

Leadership and being an effective leader do not simply happen, a leader must make them happen. Every leader has her or his own style, methods, and competencies which make leadership work for her or him. Yet, within those personal styles, methods, and competencies common elements of leadership can be identified that help prepare a leader for successful face-to-face leadership.

Everyone has been in situations where ineffective leadership was recognized (e.g., the activity flopped, was disorganized, the environment was chaotic, people were bored), yet few have gone the next step to determine exactly what it was that led to this evaluation. If the leadership presentation and interactions were closely examined, one would likely notice that a hallmark of a good leadership was lacking—being prepared.

It becomes evident very quickly when a leader is ill prepared for an activity or session. Whether it is facilitating a staff meeting, leading a group of senior citizens in low-impact exercises, or leading songs while waiting for an overdue bus, effective and ineffective leaders can be spotted easily. The ineffective leader comes in, sits down, and says, "So, what are we here to talk about?" An effective leader has an agenda prepared and a copy at each place. An ineffective leader fumbles about trying to decide how she or he wants the room to be set up, an effective leader has the chairs and room arranged prior to participant arrival. An ineffective leader does not know any songs and is trying in vain to maintain order, an effective leader is one around whom the children flock as they take turns leading songs.

This section of the chapter will help set the stage for effective leisure leadership. Setting the stage is about being prepared. Among other things, good leaders are prepared for *the people, the activities,* and *the unexpected.* Leaders interact with people; most recreation leaders work primarily with groups, although there are situations where a leader works with only one or two leisure participants. As a part of leader preparation, understanding something about the participants and the group will help ensure effective and upbeat leadership.

Photo courtesy of the University of Northern Iowa Public Relations Department

Leadership preparation involves preplanning, some of which may be paperwork.

Group Composition

Knowing something about the group one is about to lead makes direct leadership much easier than when going in without any information whatsoever. The more a leader knows about a group, the better decisions she or he can make relative to appropriate leadership styles, type of communication, potential difficulties, and the probable needs and desires of the participants. People of different ages, physical and/ or mental abilities, sex, gender, sexual orientation, and racial or ethnic background respond differently to different styles and techniques of leadership. To be best prepared, leisure services leaders might want to ask and answer several questions about the group composition prior to beginning. Questions might include:

How large is the group?

Group size will impact preparation, implementation, and leadership style. Typically, large groups require more structure than small groups for a leader to maintain control. They also require additional equipment, time for breaking into smaller groups (if needed) and receiving instructions. On the other hand, smaller groups tend to complete activities more quickly than do larger groups.

What is the approximate percentage of females and males in the group?

This information is sometimes helpful in determining attitudes and comfort levels of participants. As previously discussed, females and males are socialized differently from one another, communicate somewhat distinctly, and have differing expectations of leaders. The effects of socialization last a lifetime and this knowledge combined with other information about a group may give the leader a fairly good picture of what to expect. For instance, if there is a large percentage of boys in a group of eight-year-olds to ten-year-olds, a leader may expect an overall desire for highly active games. On the other hand if the group consists of women over fifty years old, there might be a stronger desire for socially-oriented activities.

What is the mix of ages of participants?

Knowing the approximate ages (or age cohort) of group members helps a leader select appropriate leadership techniques based on knowledge about developmental stage, level of sophistication, types of preferred activities, and appropriate complexity of rules. It has already been noted that leading children is different than leading teens and adults. A wide range of ages in one group presents special challenges for a leader to strive to fully engage all participants as much as possible. For example, how a leader presents activity instructions, approaches behavior management, makes decisions, and manipulates an environment all vary depending upon the ages of the participants.

Do any group members require special considerations due to physical or mental ability differences?

Full involvement of all group members should be a goal of parks, recreation, and leisure services leaders, and while a leader should always be prepared to adapt activities for someone with special needs, it is helpful to know of any specific needs in advance. This information is not always available, however, and simply because one hears that none of the participants have special challenges does not negate the need to be prepared to adapt or change activities and leadership techniques. For instance, if a leader knows in advance that one group member has poor hearing, she or he can prepare to present activity instructions through physical demonstration as well as verbally. In addition, it may be important to minimize all potential noise distractions (e.g., poor acoustics, music playing over the loudspeaker).

How experienced are the participants with the planned activities?

A leisure services leader can be much more effective if she or he knows whether participants are beginners, experts, or the group is of mixed abilities. With this knowledge leadership techniques and activities can be modified appropriately to match skill levels and participant goals. As an example, novices may require closer leader supervision, more repetition, and more structure than those who have more expertise in a particular activity.

What are the group members' reasons for participation?

People participate in leisure activities for a variety of reasons: because they were invited to participate, parents desired it, peer pressure, or they wanted to participate (also for a variety of reasons). Each reason has different implications for the level of readiness of participants and approaches leaders may take in their leadership efforts. If, for instance, a child has been forced to attend because her or his parents needed the supervised childcare, the child may not be positively motivated to participate. She or he may require much leader intervention to partici-pate in an appropriate manner.

Do group members know one another?

Group members who know one another have likely established some elements of group dynamics. Levels of trust, group roles, decision-making processes, and norms have probably been developed to some extent. This may be an advantage or disadvantage for the leader, depending upon the goals of the group, leader, and agency. In previ-ously formed groups the leader may be perceived as an outsider and may have to work to gain influence and be fully effective. In groups not yet formed, the leader often is influential in deciding the norms and internal processes.

Are medical histories available to the leader?

The importance of this information may depend upon the nature of the organization and activity. In a therapeutic recreation setting knowing medical histories could be critical to successful leadership. In all settings, medical history forms for participants and staff members should be a prerequisite to field trips and other off-site trips or activities. A leader who has access to medical background (as necessary) would be able to make decisions about both activities and leadership approaches to be most effective and safe.

Learning about a group prior to leading leisure service activities is one step to effective and successful leadership. A concerned leader will gather information about group composition and weigh it in relation to her or his own abilities and limitations to determine appropriate styles and techniques to utilize. The more a leisure services leader knows about the people she or he is about to lead, the easier, more enjoyable, and successful she or he will likely be.

Risk Management Considerations

In addition to understanding as much as possible about the participants one is about to lead, it is very important to consider and address issues of risk management. Knowing about the group can help a leader understand concerns of risk management related to the participants, the

group size
age mix
gender mix
any special needs
skill levels
why members are participating
degree of member familiarity

Figure 12.2 Information about the group helps a leader in selecting appropriate leadership techniques.

environment, and her or his own leadership skills and approaches. Effective risk management will protect not only the leader, but also the participants, equipment, and facility.

As a competency of direct leadership, effective risk management begins with the development of policies and procedures designed for the safety of everyone and everything. Addressing the considerations listed below prior to engaging a group in leadership will help a leisure services leader ensure safe leisure activities.

> Have you gone through the risk management
> checklist?

An example of a risk management checklist is presented in The Front Line of Chapter Eleven. To be fully prepared as a leader, all areas should be checked for and cleared of potential hazards. Both a visual and hands-on check should be conducted on a periodic basis as established by agency policies, and a visual check should be conducted in an activity area prior to each and every activity session.

> Are the staff assigned to this direct leadership
> opportunity right for the job?

As a direct leader, knowing about the skills, temperament and limitations of oneself, as well as peer leaders, is vital to the safe conduct of activities. Utilizing individual strengths and managing limitations helps to spur staff growth and maintains a level of quality and safety to which all parks, recreation, and leisure services leaders should all strive.

> Do you know enough about the participants to
> be safe?

Learning about group composition not only makes a leader's job easier, but it is an important risk management tool because it helps in activity selection and sequencing, decision making, behavior management, communication, and so on.

> Are the activities appropriate for the group?

Once learning about the group composition and having checked safety issues, a leader may now turn her or his attention to the activities. Effective leaders will want to be sure that activities are age and developmentally appropriate, sensitive to differences in group members, and meet the goals of the session.

Risk management is an area in which leaders can never be overprepared. Instilling an appreciation for risk management, and being aware of potential hazards and dangers are two of the most effective steps to minimizing injuries and accidents while engaged in leisure. An effective leader is one who always is on the lookout for ways to make activities more enjoyable and safe.

What If...?

If done thoroughly, the preparation phase of direct leadership can be a lengthy process. With experience and practice, however, solid preparation can become second nature. In addition to addressing preparation issues already mentioned, another aspect of direct leadership that is critical to being well-prepared is playing "what if?" "What if?" is an activity process that helps a leader to prepare for the unexpected.

Brainstorming questions, scenarios, and potential issues before they happen is a key to facilitating enjoyment, maintaining safety, and managing participant behaviors. Until one is practiced at it, it is best to engage as many people as possible in the generation of "what if?" questions and related issues. In addition to generating those questions and issues, it is important to define the answers. Simply raising the questions without appropriate answers does little for leader readiness. There are many "what if?" questions to be asked in preparation for the delivery of leisure services. For instance:

- *what if* someone has to go to the bathroom? It is fairly common for every child to have to go to the bathroom when one child expresses the need. Will the entire activity be stopped for the whole group to go? Does the child have to be escorted to the restroom? (If it is a public setting this would be wise.) Is it possible for participants to come and go as they need? Where is the bathroom in relation to the activity space (e.g., distance, street-crossing hazards)?

- *what if* a participant forgets her or his lunch (at an all day event)? If an activity is a full-day activity and a lunch is forgotten, the leader should be prepared to assist the hungry participant. Do the leaders bring extra fruit and bread to share? Does the agency provide emergency money for such contingencies? Will all participants be asked to share? Or is the participant left to go hungry?

- *what if* a child does not bring a completed parental permission slip for a field trip? Agencies usually have strict policies on this issue. Permission slips are required for liability reasons and allowing a child to participate without one can put the leader and agency at risk. What is your agency policy? Is the child sent home? What if parents are not at home? Does the child stay at the agency? Is there someone available to watch the child?

- *what if* a participant arrives early or late? Participants arrive at structured leisure activities at various times; some arrive 15 to 20 minutes early, others arrive 15 to 20 minutes late. What do the early or late arrivals do? Are staff assigned to assist them? How long will an activity be postponed while waiting for latecomers?

- *what if* someone is not wearing appropriate footwear? What are the safety and participation implications?

- *what if* someone refuses to participate? Should she or he be "forced" to participate?

- *what if* someone gets injured or becomes ill? Is the emergency medical system in place? Do all leaders know what to do?

- *what if* a fight starts? Do the leaders break it up, call police, or report it? To whom?

- *what if* it begins to rain on an outdoor activity? Is the activity over? Is the activity moved? If so, to where? How will this be accomplished?

- *what if* the equipment breaks? Are there replacements available? Can it be repaired? Are repair materials and tools handy?

- *what if* the power goes out? What are the safety and participation implications?

- *what if...?*

Asking and answering "what if?" questions will help to minimize hazards, maximize participant satisfaction, and make leadership easier and more enjoyable. After learning everything possible about the group, going through the risk management checklist, and playing "what if?" the next element of preparation is to consider and develop goals and objectives for the leadership session. Understanding participant goals and articulating leader goals and objectives will provide the focus and direction for the leisure experience.

Figure 12.3 *Playing "what if?" can help a leader clarify areas of concern and their management in activity leadership.*

Goals and Objectives

Articulating and putting on paper goals and objectives for leisure services activities are two of the most underused skills of direct leaders in leisure services. For many years now, school teachers have been articulating and writing goals and objectives for their students, but in the leisure services field the connection between effective teaching and effective leadership is often missed. Many believe that just as effective teaching is effective leadership, effective leadership involves effective teaching. Parks, recreation, and leisure services leaders may teach participants songs, games, or new leisure skills; teaching, then, is integral to leadership.

Goals and objectives are the bedrock of effective and sound leadership. They provide the structure around which leisure activities are built and help leisure services leaders to define their tasks. An effective and well-prepared leader knows what she or he hopes to accomplish through leisure *prior* to engaging in the leisure experience. This knowledge influences participant involvement, how instructions are given, and what group leadership techniques are used.

Goals

A goal may be short-term or long-term; it is a course of action that one intends to follow—an aim. Objectives are the steps to reaching the goal. A well-prepared leader is one who has a solid sense of the goals and objectives she or he hopes to accomplish. A lack of goals and objectives may result in aimless activities, unsatisfied participants, and ineffective leadership. There are four general levels of goals: *societal, agency, leader,* and *participant* (Russell, 1986).

Societal Goals. Societal goals are aims or ideals of a community. These goals tend to be culturally relevant (meaning they change with the times), and may or may not be in the best interest of all community members (i.e., citizens). Examples of societal goals include the goals of stopping child violence, preventing teenage parenthood, and maintaining a litter-free neighborhood. These goals may directly or indirectly impact the provision of leisure services. In fact, it is quite common for leisure programs to follow in the wake of articulated social goals. An example of this is the rise in midnight basketball games as a response to preventing teen violence. Typically, societal goals exist at the agency level.

Agency Goals. Agency goals are those espoused by the agency or organization. Often, these goals are identified in the agency mission statement, or a statement of purpose. Agency goals might include things such as to make a profit, to provide the highest quality services at the lowest price, and to see that all people no matter their socioeconomic status receive the benefits of leisure services. As an example, one goal of Special Olympics International (SOI) is to provide sports training to help develop physical fitness for people over eight years of age who are mentally retarded. This goal drives the specific program goals and objectives. If an agency is tax supported, its goals typically will be in line with the prevailing societal goals and norms of the local geographic area.

Leader Goals. Leader goals might mirror those of the agency, but usually other elements exist as well. A leader might have as a personal goal to be promoted, to make a lot of money, or to make a real difference in the lives of others. If goals of the leader are synchronous with those of the agency, the greatest compatibility and leader satisfaction occurs. If agency and leader goals are antithetical to one another, one or the other will be unsatisfied and leader effectiveness could be negatively affected (Jordan & Mertesdorf, 1994). Leaders also have goals for specific programs and participants that often mirror the agency goal. For instance, a leader in SOI might have as a goal to increase the cardiovascular fitness of all athletes in her or his program.

Participant Goals. Participant goals are quite diverse. People may desire to participate in leisure to exercise, to learn a new skill, to be with others, to do something different, to have excitement, to respond to peer or parental pressure, and for many other reasons. When developing and leading programs and activities, it is important for a leader to bear in mind that people have many different goals. As the leader, it usually is best to focus on one or two participant goals in the planning and leading of programs. As an example, an SOI participant may have as a personal goal to improve skills specific to a particular sport—in order to address this participant goal, a leader will first have to be aware of the participant's desire.

To provide structure and focus to leisure experiences an effective leader identifies the goals and objectives of each activity. Oftentimes goals and objectives are established for an entire day, week, or session. As mentioned earlier, it is important that a direct leader's goals and objectives be compatible with the goals and objectives of the agency for which she or he is working. Goals are broad statements that describe the intent of a particular program or leadership techniques; common leisure goals include the following:

- *skill development* (e.g., throwing, drawing, jumping, painting) and *knowledge development* (e.g., history of the area, rules of the game, factual information about natural phenomena such as star gazing or plant development). A session or activity that has skill or knowledge development as a goal will encourage teaching and practice sessions. A skill and/or knowledge development goal will tend to dictate that information and activities be presented in such a progression as to allow participants time to develop an understanding of basic material and competencies prior to moving on to more complex skills and knowledge;

- *interpersonal skills* (e.g., decision making, problem solving, communication) and *social goals* (e.g., being with others, sharing, helping) are common reasons people participate in a wide variety of leisure experiences. Enhancing the likelihood that these types of goals will be met is often a secondary aim of leisure services leadership. This may be accomplished through manipulating the physical environment and purposefully planning activities that will enhance this goal;

- *democratic living skills* (e.g., cooperation, ideals of fair play, equality) often are the focus of leisure activities, particularly for young people. Through leisure, where fun and enjoyment are the primary foci, lessons about being a good sport, how to win graciously, lose with dignity, and how to work together are learned;

- *to have fun and serve as diversionary (nonutilitarian) activity* is a perfectly legitimate goal of recreation and leisure activities. In fact, many participate in leisure experiences with having fun as the primary goal; and

- *health benefits.* Many people engage in leisure for the physical exercise and mental health benefits derived from it. Physical exercise makes participants feel better physically, emotionally and mentally. The health and wellness benefits of many leisure activities are tremendous. Physical exercise is seen as a secondary goal of leisure participation by many participants.

People engage in leisure for a variety of reasons and have a variety of goals for which they aim. As a leader, it is perfectly acceptable (although it can be confusing, initially) to work toward more than one goal at one time. For each goal, leisure services leaders develop objectives, which are the stepping stones to achieving goals, to identify how the goals will be reached.

Objectives

Objectives are the steps to reaching goals. If one were to picture a staircase, objectives would be the individual steps and the goal would be at the top of the stairs. Each step can have three different types of objectives: *cognitive, behavioral,* and *affective* (Bloom, 1956). *Cognitive* objectives are those that deal with thinking, *behavioral* objectives deal with physical actions and skills, and *affective* objectives deal with feelings and emotions.

In leisure services all three objectives are addressed through direct leadership although one may be more emphasized than another. For instance, in working with the frail elderly one might focus on cognitive objectives dealing with mental stimulation and memory retention; participants in rehabilitation may focus on objectives such as coordination and strength; and when working with children with developmental disabilities a leisure services leader might focus on affective objectives such as sharing and cooperation.

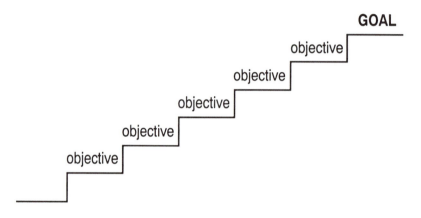

Figure 12.4 *Objectives are the steps to achieving articulated goals.*

As steps to goals, objectives are statements that indicate very specific actions to be taken to help meet the goal. In leadership, first articulating the goal or general purpose of what one does is important for structure; knowing the related objectives helps to meet those goals.

Writing objectives can be a confusing and difficult process. To those just learning how to write objectives, it may seem as though the goals and objectives are quite convoluted. In essence, however, objectives may be defined as specific, measurable statements needed to reach a goal. In that light, objectives must be related to goals.

Thinking SMART helps a leader to remember that objectives are:

S = Specific,
M = Measurable,
A = Achievable,
R = Realistic, and
T = Trackable.

If any one of these individual components is missing or weak, however, the objectives will not be as effective as they need to be. Writing down objectives as they are developed aids in focusing the leader, and provides a framework and reasoning for leadership actions taken. The aim of writing objectives, whether they be cognitive, behavioral, or affective, is to design them in such a way that if they were turned into a question, an individual could answer without hesitation, "yes" or "no." If the best answer is "sort of," the objective is not written as specifically as needed.

ABCDs of Writing Behavioral Objectives. To aid in the development and writing of objectives it might be helpful to follow the ABCD method. Objectives go hand-in-hand with goals. Prior to writing objectives, one must know the goal for which one is striving. Objectives are the steps to achieving goals. To be effective and useful, then, objectives *must* be specific, measurable and meaningful. Objectives are used to serve as guideposts to measure whether or not an individual has done the action named in the objective.

Writing an objective is much like writing a sentence—there is a subject, verb, object, and modifier—and every objective must have all these components. In this case, the subject is *who* will do the behavior, the *what* is the verb (or behavior the subject will be doing), the *how* is the object that explains the behavior to be done, and *how well* is the modifier. These elements are the ABCDs of writing objectives which are further defined below:

A = Audience

The *audience* identifies who is doing the action (i.e., behavior) described in the objective. The audience should be identified as specifically as possible. Audiences commonly found in leisure and recreation objectives include campers, children, participants, swimmers, clients, runners, players, adults, guests, customers, teens, and other terms that describe a group of people. For example,

The participant....

B = Behavior

The *behavior* is the action the audience must do (i.e., verb in the sentence), and it is required in a behavioral objective. There should be only *one* verb or behavior in each objective; otherwise, the objective is extremely difficult to measure. Common behaviors in leisure and recreation objectives include throw, hop, jump, count, answer, demonstrate, build, run, lift, read, speak, introduce, play, sing, take initiative, control her or his emotions, collaborate, and other actions or behaviors common to the accomplishment of a particular leisure task. For example,

> *The participant will introduce three group members to the rest of the group....*

C = Condition

A *condition* helps to describe the behavior in specific terms. Anything that serves to further identify the behavior in the objective is considered a condition. Often, a condition can be recognized by the way it describes *how* or *when* an action is to be accomplished. For instance, if an objective specified that the audience was to throw a ball, *how* would they throw it (e.g., overhand, underhand, with two hands)? In addition, what kind of ball must they throw (e.g., a football, basketball, playground ball, tennis ball, Nerf ball)? When will the throwing occur (e.g., by the last session, before the session is over, by the end of the season, at the beginning)? For example,

> *The participant will introduce three group members to the rest of the group by saying each person's name and identifying her or his favorite leisure activities....*

D = Degree

The *degree* in an objective describes *how well* the behavior will be accomplished. To what degree of competence will the audience be held? Various ways of stating degrees include such things as 90% of the time, with fewer than four errors, without any leader prompts, without falling over. The degree *must* match the behavior—it should answer the question, *how well* must the audience do the behavior? Therefore, if the action is throwing, *how well* must the person throw (e.g., hitting the target eight out of ten times)? If singing is the behavior, how well must the individual sing (e.g., without any mistakes)? If playing jacks and the goal is improved social skills, the degree might be without arguing over lost points. For example,

> *The participant will introduce three group members to the rest of the group by saying each person's name and identifying her or his favorite leisure activities without making a mistake.*

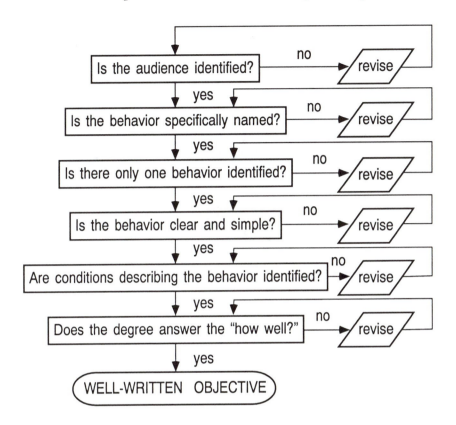

Figure 12.5 *To determine if an objective is well-written and meets needed criteria, ask these questions.* Adapted from Mager, R. (1984).

Manipulating the Environment

When people hear the term *manipulate* many think of negative connotations where *to manipulate* means to be devious or underhanded. In leisure services leadership however, leaders manipulate situations, people and activities all the time. In fact, those who are highly skilled at positive manipulation are often very successful leaders; participants seem to lead themselves. Positive manipulation, then, is the artful handling of a situation.

An effective leader manipulates the environment to set the mood, to encourage participation, and to make leadership easier. Purposefully arranging the physical environment can enhance or detract from the socioemotional and psychological elements of leisure settings. The *socioemotional element* is concerned with individuals' feelings of belonging, affection, comfort, and acceptance. All of these elements are very important to successful leisure service experiences. Positive affect is developed through manipulating the physical and activity environment (examples are provided below). The *psychological environment* involves feelings of identity, achievement and mastery. By changing the physical environment, leaders can meet the needs of participants.

An effective leader might consider altering the physical environment in the following ways:

- *the use of color in leisure settings* is a subtle, but highly effective way to manipulate the physical environment for social and psychological purposes. "Hot" colors (e.g., red, orange, yellow) tend to increase both cognitive and behavioral activity levels while the "cool" colors (e.g., blue, green, violet) tend to induce a calmer, more quiet response. In addition, bright colors tend to excite participants while pastels and muted colors help in maintaining a calmer atmosphere. Leaders would be wise to decide on what is appropriate to meet the desired goals and objectives, and manipulate the environment to meet them;

- *lighting* is another physical element that can be manipulated; it is often used to enhance socioemotional responses in participants. Bright, white lights set a mood of excitement and alertness while softer lighting can set a mood for intimacy and group closeness. For example, we rarely see bright fluorescent lights at dance clubs—it makes more sense to have bright lights for a crafts project;

- *noise, sounds, and music* also affect the mood and atmosphere of a leisure setting. Amusement parks, malls, and eating establishments have been using various types of sounds, noises, music, and colors to enhance our buying and eating habits for years. Loudness, style of tunes, and tonal quality all impact how people feel about others, the activity, and the situation;

- *artwork, murals, posters, pictures, and the use of various media* contribute to the atmosphere as well. Involving participants in the creation of wall hangings can enhance a variety of feelings and, at the same time, create an atmosphere of ownership. Often, leaders cannot change the color of the activity space, but the effect can be accomplished through the use of colorful artwork, posters, and wall hangings;

• *arrange the space for maximum safety.* This involves following the risk management checklist and putting away or guarding hazards (e.g., benches or chairs in the gymnasium). Separating incompatible structures and activities is an important consideration in arranging space for safety;

• *arrange space for maximum efficiency* by having equipment and structures to be used in a convenient location. Has the needed gear and equipment been arranged nearby, yet is out of the way of other activities?;

• *arrange activity space for maximum effectiveness.* It is not particularly effective to have an activity that utilizes loud music next to an area to be used for individual skill instruction (this seems to happen all too frequently). A tip for leisure services leaders is when giving instructions (or simply trying to talk to an individual) for an activity in an area where there are many potential distractions, arrange and focus the group on the leader—turn the participants to face into a corner or other constrained space where the leader can stand to give instructions; and

• *consider the type, size and shape of the open space.* How will it be utilized to its maximum benefit and usefulness?

As one can see, from manipulating the physical environment, to articulating goals and objectives, playing "what if?" attending to risk management concerns, and learning about the group one is about to lead, there is quite a bit to do prior to ever meeting the group. This preparation phase is essentially the first contact a leader has with a group and is very important to the overall success of the leader. Once well prepared, a leader is now ready to meet the participants and engage in the second phase of direct leadership—*priming the group.*

Photo courtesy of the Western Home

Involving participants in helping to decorate walls is a way of manipulating the environment, and can help set the mood for what is to come.

Priming the Group—Phase II

Phase II of leadership in parks, recreation, and leisure services is priming the group for an activity, song, or other type of leisure session. Completing preparation steps first will provide the information a leader needs for selecting the types of leadership techniques that will be most effective in the anticipated situations. Priming the group includes *getting a group's attention, dividing a group into subgroups,* and *learning participant names.*

In general, it is best to think of ways to accomplish the priming tasks that are fun, experiential (i.e., active and interactive), and are integrated into the actual activity. This will help to keep things from feeling choppy, thereby increasing leader effectiveness and participant satisfaction. The examples for the various priming elements provided below are appropriate for adults, children, and people of different physical and mental abilities. Leaders would be wise to remember that it is during these initial minutes that the tone is set for the remainder of the leadership interaction. In addition, it is during this phase that leaders will make an impression (first, and often lasting) on participants; this is a critical phase for successful leadership.

Getting a Group's Attention

Prior to beginning an activity with a group, it is part of the leader's role to get the group's attention. Initially, getting a group's attention may be a bit chaotic. Particularly in large groups, there is much noise, fidgeting, and movement as people expectantly await the start of an activity. An effective leader strives to use this excitement as the group moves into the conduct of the activity itself.

Recreation and leisure activities should be fun and enjoyable for all; fun is one of the defining elements of leisure. Therefore, techniques where a leader stares a group into quiet submission, incessantly blows a whistle, or berates individuals with voice tone and, "Quiet please," are antithetical to meeting the goal of having fun and promoting the leisure ideal.

Basic principles for activities used in priming a group include:

- being fun,
- respectful,
- unexpected, and
- experiential (i.e., active and interactive).

Making some type of loud noise is a very common method of getting a group's attention. If this is the leader's preferred technique, it should be as fun and unique as possible. One noisemaker to avoid is a traditional whistle; a traditional whistle is loud, piercing, and reminds many people of authority figures (e.g., referees, police officers) for whom they do not necessarily hold positive leisure connotations. Using a nontraditional noisemaker such as a party horn, a drum, or a dinner (or cow) bell maintains a level of fun, is unique, and is usually unexpected. It is best to use a noisemaker that utilizes low tones and pitches; high-pitched whistles and horns are difficult to hear for some people. In addition, the louder high-pitched whistles are, the more shrill and displeasing they sound. Leisure services leaders will want to experiment with a variety of noisemakers, and use them sparingly; frequent use of a noisemaker may lessen its effectiveness at getting a group's attention.

Another method of getting a group's attention is to start clapping (applauding) or stomping feet. Often, others will join in (in fact the leader may suggest that as people hear the applause, that they too begin to clap). The thunderous applause will quickly drown out other efforts to talk or make noise. When the leader stops clapping, the group usually stops and is now ready for words from the leader.

A variation on group clapping is for the leader to say, "Clap once if you can hear me." Those who hear, clap once. "Clap three times if you can hear me." Those who hear clap as directed. The leader continues with four or five variations until all members appear to be involved. When the leader stops the clapping, all attention is on the leader and the group is prepared for the next step.

A variation of "clap once…" is to direct participants to do a variety of actions in addition to clapping. In a "regular" tone of voice and volume the leader says, "touch your knee if you can hear me." Those who can hear do as directed. "Touch your head if you can hear me," "put your hands over your mouth if you can hear me." This technique requires no shouting by the leader, warms up the group, and is quite successful at getting a group's attention.

Dividing Groups

If a leader is working with a group of more than 13 to 15 people, for some activities it may be necessary to divide the group into smaller subgroups. Again, remembering that leisure settings should have an element of joy and fun when dividing a group can be a bit of a challenge.

Positive Methods for Dividing a Group

Following the same guidelines as mentioned above *dividing a group should be fun, enjoyable, experiential, and leave people with their dignity*; this requires conscious thought on the part of the leader. It is particularly helpful if the methods used for dividing a group relate to the goals and objectives of the session. If a primary goal is to enhance social skills, the leader will want the group to divide in such a way as to facilitate social interactions. If skill development is a goal, dividing a large group into groups where skills can be developed (e.g., people of like skills and abilities together in one group) will be important. Likewise, if maximum participation is a goal, then subgroups should reflect that need.

If it is important that subgroups consist of people who are similar in physical size, a leader could first have the entire group line up by height (adding elements such as lining up by height without speaking, while blindfolded, or both may add fun and excitement to the effort). Once a group is lined up by height, have every other person step forward—this will result in two groups (one front and one back) which are divided relatively evenly by physical size.

If social interaction is a key goal, a leader might consider dividing a group by playing an activity such as Animal Call. When playing Animal Call each person is given a name of an animal that is unknown to others. The goal is to find one's species-mates by only making that animal's noise and gestures. This activity is enjoyed by all ages and serves to warm people up in a fun, unique fashion. A variation of this is to match people up by lines of songs and have them find the rest of their song lines through repeatedly singing their line.

Crazy Handshake is another technique to encourage social inter-action. Each person is given a number between one and ten. They are then directed to be mute and to find their teammates by moving about the space and silently shaking hands the number of times as the number they were given. People with the same number of handshakes make a team.

Other techniques that work well in dividing groups randomly is to distribute colored pieces of paper as group members arrive and divide the group based on who has what color. Or, give each person a card from a deck of playing cards and call groups based on numbers, colors, or suits, for example.

Figure 12.6 Animal Call is one of many positive methods to divide a group.

There are many ways to divide a large group into smaller groups which are creative, equitable, and do not negatively impact participant self-esteem. It is the leader's responsibility to learn, practice and select methods which enhance, rather than detract from, the larger leisure experience.

Methods to Avoid

There are several techniques for dividing groups that should be avoided in most leisure settings: *team captains, counting off*, and *dividing by sex*. At one time in most people's lives they have experienced someone dividing a group by using team captains. As a child (or adult) being the last one chosen can be a hurtful and humiliating experience. There are few, if any, circumstances in leisure services that warrant using this method to divide a large group into smaller ones.

Another undesirable technique used to divide a large group is by counting off. This is commonly used in school systems, and when used with children often will evoke a flurry of activity as youngsters quickly try to realign so as to be in the same group as their best friends. Used with adults, counting off may be viewed as childish and paternalistic. An advantage to counting off when dividing a group, however, is that it is a time-efficient way to break a large group into smaller ones. If time is running short, counting off may be an acceptable technique to dividing a group; it should be used sparingly.

Yet another less than desirable technique of dividing a large group into several small groups is to divide by sex—females in one group, and males in the other. Unless for an activity-based purpose, this method of pitting females and males often perpetuates stereotypes of "us versus them" and may establish a negative tone within the group.

Learning Names

Success in leadership is a combination of many things, one of which is earning the respect of participants. People like and respect those whom they believe like and respect them. One way to show this is by using people's names, and by using and pronouncing names the way people wish to be called. An individual who introduces herself as Tomika should be called Tomika, not Tommi or some other derivative that the leader feels is cute, nice, or easier to pronounce.

Learning names is a task often overlooked (it is assumed it will simply happen) or completed very quickly and without a lot of innovation. This may be due to time constraints, inappropriate assumptions, or inexperience on the part of the leader, but learning names of individuals is vital to the enjoyment and productivity of the group. Calling, "Hey, you in the green striped shirt," is both disrespectful and oftentimes ineffective in actually getting that person's attention. Leaders facilitate the learning of participants names for themselves as well as other participants. Leaving the learning of names up to individual participants may result in group members who are uncomfortable, lack trust among themselves, and are slow to come together; this may result in the leisure environment feeling somewhat stilted and uncomfortable. A leader can remedy this situation through planning and use of creative activities to facilitate the learning of everyone's names.

Name Games

Name games are those activities that have as a primary purpose the learning of individual names by other group members as well as the leader. The leader may wish to play these activities at every session until everyone feels comfortable with other people's names. The activities tend to be light in tone, range from semiactive to very active, and once going, move fairly rapidly.

Most name games are played with the group in a circle formation and there are several reasons for this. First, a circle brings people physically close together, yet is fairly nonthreatening. Second, everyone can see everyone else when a circle is formed, thus the chance of subgrouping or cliques developing is minimized. Third, the leader can be an active participant without losing the ability to provide adequate supervision. Lastly, circles are preferred because they bring people together on an equal footing; one individual is not sitting or standing higher, ahead of, or behind another. With a minimum of adaptations, name games are accessible to all potential group members.

Stuffed Sock Toss

The Stuffed Sock Toss teaches participant names through rapid and repetitive naming of group members. The group stands in a circle, facing center. The center of the circle is left empty as it soon will be filled with flying socks. Everyone goes around the circle and says her or his name loud enough for all to hear; this occurs twice and should be done slowly. The leader then calls out an individual's name and tosses a sock, stuffed with soft material, to the named individual. That person calls out another's name and tosses the stuffed sock to that person. Each group member quickly becomes involved as names are called out and the sock is tossed to new individuals.

As participants become more proficient and naming/tossing speeds up, the leader may introduce a second sock so that two names are being called out and two socks are tossed simultaneously. The leader can add as many socks as desired to maintain a certain level of challenge and excitement. As an alternative to stuffed socks the program leader may use a Nerf (or other soft) ball. There are several soft baseballs and softballs on the market which work very well for this activity.

Name Charades

Another suggestion for learning the names of groupmates is for group members to combine some type of nonverbal gesture with their name and share that with the entire group. Name charades allows individuals to personalize their names with a physical movement that in some way characterizes themselves. The group stands or sits shoulder-to-shoulder in a loose circle, facing center. One at a time, each person steps or leans into the circle, and, saying her or his name, makes a physical gesture.

*Figure 12.7 Priming a group is an important element for success-
ful direct leadership.*

The gesture may be small or involve the entire body. The leader may encourage participants to add style, vivacity, and flair to their movements. The entire group then mimics the motion and repeats the name.

This naming, gesturing, and imitating continues around the circle until each has shared her or his body gesture. A grand finale is done with everyone at once saying her or his own name and gesturing. A variation of this activity is for each succeeding person in the circle to repeat all of the previous names and motions before doing her or his own.

At this stage the leisure services leader has completed preparation for the leadership session and has primed the group. It is now time to provide activity instructions or directions to participants. Leaders are reminded that throughout this process, considerations and modifications should be made to accommodate the needs of the group based on the characteristics of the participants.

Delivery—Phase III

Once the preliminary tasks of being prepared, getting a group's attention, dividing a group, and learning names has occurred, it is time to move into the delivery of the activity. *Delivery refers to the aspects of activity and song leadership that involve introducing an activity and giving directions or instructions to participants.*

Leading games and activities is part art and part science. The art of leadership includes the intangible qualities of leadership that are critical to success such as using sound judgment, integrating one's personality into activity leadership, and having a positive and upbeat attitude. These leadership elements are difficult to teach and are acquired and internalized over time.

The science aspect of activity leadership can be readily taught. It involves following certain steps and much proper planning. Children and adults can be taught these steps as they begin to lead others in a variety of games, sports, arts and crafts, and drama events.

Introducing an Activity

Introducing an activity, song, or leisure experience continues to refine the tone that was established when the group was learning names and dividing into smaller subgroups. Typically, a leader does four things when introducing an activity: *identifies herself or himself, identifies the*

Photo by Lattin Photography; Courtesy of the Family YMCA of Black Hawk County

Direct leadership is characterized by one-on-one relationships with leisure participants.

activity, explains the object or goal of the activity (e.g., to score goals, to cooperate, to run from here to there), and *tells a short story* (fact or fiction) *to help set the mood of the activity.*

Leader Introduction

An oversight of many leisure services leaders is not to introduce and reintroduce themselves every time they work with participants. Staff members who have worked at a particular agency for a long time often have the mistaken belief that everyone knows their names. In most leisure settings, however, participants continuously change; therefore it is always best to introduce oneself at the beginning of every session.

Name the Activity

After introducing one's self to participants most leaders will then tell participants the name of the activity or song. This is to help participants understand and put into context what is coming next. Bear in mind that although some people might say that they have played this game all of their lives, they may know a version different from the one you are about to introduce. Leaders should not assume people know how to play even "standard" activities or sing common songs. There are many local variations in activities, and various tunes and melodies to common songs.

Identify the Goal of the Activity

Prior to beginning an activity, it is best to remind or tell participants about the aim of the activity. This serves to ensure that everyone is aiming for the same goal. While the leader may have as a goal to enhance social interaction among participants, the goal that is shared with participants at this point is the *goal of the activity*. For example, although a leader may select checkers as an appropriate activity to increase fine motor control in the hands, in this place participants would be told that the goal of checkers is for one player to take all of her or his opponent's pieces before the opponent takes her or his pieces.

Tell a Story

After clearly stating the goal of the activity, it becomes important to further establish the mood (the leader has already altered the physical environment to maximize the desired activities and affect). This is often accomplished through telling a short story (60 seconds or less). The story might be fact or fiction, and its purpose is to engage participants, to draw them in, to get them "psyched." Using all of her or his enthusiasm, a leader might personalize the story ("I used to play this when I was younger," or "My great-great grandmother taught me this…"), make it pure fantasy ("Picture the days of long ago, when humans were just beginning to walk," or "A UFO landed in a field and creatures I had never seen before got out of the space ship"), or teach with the story ("This game originated in Africa and was played by people of all ages"). The story helps to set the mood and accomplish the leader's goals for the day.

Giving Directions

Once the activity has been introduced it is time to give the participants the directions for how to play. As stated earlier, a leader should be careful not to assume, and not to allow others to assume, that they know how to play a particular activity. Games, activities, and songs have many variations and it usually is important for participants to be playing by the same rules. In stating directions or guidelines for an activity, a leader might remember the following acronyms: KISS, KIP and PLAY.

KISS

Keep It Short and Simple is the most important guideline for giving directions for activities and songs. An effective leader will speak in clear, unambiguous language; say what she or he means, then stop. This of course, requires that a leader be very familiar with the activity prior to beginning. A leader who is unfamiliar with the activity instructions often will hesitate, give contradictory instructions, and otherwise confuse the participants.

KIP

Keep It Positive is another guideline for effective leadership. This refers to stating the rules of an activity in a *do* rather than *do not* fashion. For example, pools and aquatic facilities have well established rules about horseplay around the water (with good reason). Often, a list of what *not* to do is posted, for example, no running, no horseplay, no dunking, no diving, no food or drink beyond this point. Creative youngsters are left thinking about the alternatives. No running leaves room for skipping, hopping, cartwheeling, and walking "really fast."

Without explicit directions about the desired behaviors, people will generate their own ideas. In addition, constantly being told to *not* do things may leave a person feeling small and powerless. If leaders state rules in a positive fashion they will likely be better respected and, therefore, effective. Leisure services leaders should get into the habit of telling people what they *can* do when leading activities.

PLAY

PLAY means just what it says; once giving enough instruction to participate safely and within necessary guidelines, leaders should *stop talking and allow participants to play, sing, experience, or otherwise participate.* Whether it be a crafts class for senior citizens, sports in a youth league, or aquatic movement in a rehabilitation unit, leisure services leaders need to get out of the way and let people play. Play is when participants are engaged in the leisure experience, it is when objectives and goals are being met.

Leading Songs

Leading songs is much like leading activities in that the techniques described above work equally well with either event. The important thing to recognize about song leading is that one does not have to know how to sing (e.g., be able to carry a tune) to be an effective song leader. Many great recreational song leaders are not at all musically inclined.

Music, particularly singing, is an element that in and of itself is joyful and uplifting; it is difficult to sing and be somber. Singing can be a magical element in any setting and with all ages. Singing can be used during down time, as a start up, and as part of closing an event or day. It can help get participants energized, calm them down, or get them in a particular mood.

As with activity leadership, when leading songs, leaders should begin with a leader introduction, name the song, tell a story, and then give directions. If a round is to be sung, it will be necessary to divide into a number of groups. Leaders may choose to divide the group into subgroups after learning names or after singing the entire song through once.

Sing the Song Through Once in Its Entirety

So that participants have a context, it is usually best for the leader to sing the entire song through once, using hand and body motions. This might be done alone, or with the assistance of participants from the group; more than three assistants makes it difficult for listeners to make out the words of the song.

The ability to carry a tune is not necessary to be an effective song leader.

Photo courtesy of the Conestoga Council of Girl Scouts

Steps to Song Leading

If analyzed step-by-step, song leading commonly follows the steps listed below:

- Once the participants have heard and seen the song (and motions) the leader sings one verse and has the group repeat line-by-line.
- Depending upon the length of the song and the abilities of the group, the leader may wish to sing two lines at a time and have the group repeat.
- Sing the entire song through with the participants.
- If there are hand or body motions in the song, the leader goes through the song again, using the motions. Making one motion at a time and having the group imitate it allows for learning by demonstration (depending upon the length of the song and the abilities of the group, the leader may wish to sing two lines at a time with the motions and have the group repeat and imitate).
- Sing and act out the entire song. The song should be sung a minimum of twice through to help all participants to best learn the song.

Teaching a song in a round

There are a few extra steps to teaching and leading a song to be sung in a round:

- A round is usually sung as many times as there are groups. This evens things out so that every group has an opportunity to sing the song through the same number of times.
- Follow the steps listed for song leading.
- Once the entire group has "a handle on" the song, divide the group into appropriate numbers. Three groups are most common, but depending upon the age group this may be adjusted up or down.
- It is the leader's job to engage all participants in singing their part of the round at the appropriate times. An engaging leader will use her or his entire body to engage the

group. By physically moving from group to group, using large hand gestures, and mouthing the words in front of each group so the members are sure when it is their turn to sing, a leader can enthusiastically engage the subgroups.

Transitions

Transitions are psychological links between two or more different experiences which help smooth out leadership and interactions with the group. *Transitions provide the connection between activities, programs, or sessions in a leisure setting.* They serve to maintain momentum in activities, help to reassert leader positioning, and provide a psychological bridge so participants feel comfortable with where they are and where they are going. Transitions are verbal links made by the leader; they occur between the phases of activity leadership and between activities themselves.

Transitions often link activities together by what is similar between them. For instance, if the group was moving from playing wallyball to playing crab soccer a leader might make a transition by commenting on the use of the ball—"We just finished playing a game that used a small ball, now we are going to play an activity that uses a large ball." Transitions also may comment on what is different between activities—"We just finished playing a game where we used our hands, now we are going to play an activity where we use our feet." Some transitions use a combination of commenting on similar and dissimilar elements—"We just finished playing a game that used a small ball and where we got to use our hands. Now we are going to play an activity that uses a large ball and instead of our hands, we'll use our feet."

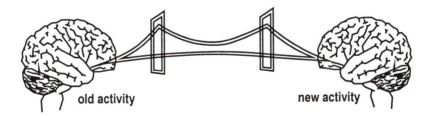

old activity   new activity

Figure 12.7 Transitions serve as psychological bridges between steps of an activity and between different activities.

Whatever the preferred technique, transitions are important to the effective leadership of any activity or session. Transitions are used within activities, between activities, and even between activity sessions. Effective use of transitions will lead to increased participant satisfaction.

Concluding a Leadership Session

Some activities come to their own natural conclusion with very little effort on behalf of the leader. Others require the leader to provide direction to the wrap-up of the activity or session. Usually, it is best to *stop playing while people are still having fun.* This way participants will want to reengage in that leisure experience at another time. A solid and well-planned method to conclude activities or leisure sessions is just as important as is a strong beginning to the activity. Poor conclusions occur when there is a lack of planning and a lack of focus by the leader. Weak conclusions are endings that leave participants hanging, wondering if the session is really over, or if there is more yet to come.

The conclusion is a leader's last opportunity (at this session) to influence the leisure experience. It is a time that can be used to *bring people together, to summarize, to leave people with positive feelings,* and *to leave participants wanting more.* If the event or day has been competitive and individuals are feeling less than friendly and supportive toward one another, at the conclusion the leader might emphasize how the group worked together. In addition, the leader can guide the group into summarizing the events of the day and do a quick review of how things went.

Furthermore, a conclusion serves as an opportunity for participants to leave the experience on an upbeat note. It is fine to acknowledge difficulties, whether they be leader or participant generated, but speaking in positive terms will leave participants feeling good about the experience. "I know we had a difficult time getting started, but once we got going, the group came together and...."

One of the more critical elements of a successful conclusion is that it be *definitive.* People need to know something is over when it is over. Whether the leader leads the group in a rousing cheer or comments about things accomplished, a concluding statement should be made which leaves no room for doubt about the session being over.

Conducting Meetings

In addition to leading activities and songs, leisure services leaders will often be asked to lead or facilitate meetings. Meetings might be held with sport league coaches, peers, programmers, front desk personnel, and the public, among others. Having appropriate leadership skills to facilitate a meeting in a firm task and people-focused fashion is necessary for effective and efficient meeting leadership. Time, resources, and people are much too valuable to waste in disorganized or unnecessary meetings.

Both leisure services leaders and participants are often involved in multiple tasks simultaneously; therefore, it is desirable to have meetings which are purposeful, succinct, and held only when necessary. Leaders should avoid holding meetings when there is no agenda (nothing to talk about)—even if a meeting is regularly scheduled for that date and time. Announcements often can be made quite efficiently via written memoranda or through electronic postings.

Generally, meetings are either formal or informal in structure. Formal meetings commonly follow Robert's Rules of Order to maintain flow and an organized structure. These meeting rules control who speaks when, how to make and decide a motion, what material may be considered at what time during the meeting, and it serves to manage other meeting functions in an organized and predictable manner. There are several good resources available in local libraries and bookstores that explain Robert's Rules of Order in an easy-to-follow format. Informal meetings are a bit more free flowing and allow people to freely interact as needs arise. Many leaders prefer to conduct meetings by loosely following Robert's Rules of Order, while maintaining an informal atmosphere.

Prior to the Meeting

There are several tasks that a leader of a meeting is expected to accomplish—some are addressed prior to a meeting being held, other tasks occur during the meeting, and there are follow-up tasks to attend to, as well. Prior to a meeting an effective and efficient leader plans ahead. During the planning phase the leader decides the *purpose* of the meeting, *who* is to be in attendance, *where* the meeting will take place, how the *room* is be arranged, *when* the meeting is to be held (and for how long) and *how* the meeting is to be conducted. In addition, a leader will provide meeting participants with needed information or supplies and an agenda.

Bearing in mind that people are very busy, an effective and efficient leader will notify participants of a meeting at least seven working days ahead of the meeting date. This notification should include the meeting *date, time, location,* and *general purpose.* It is also common at this phase to *include a tentative agenda* and request additional agenda items. An agenda serves to provide enough information so that meeting participants arrive at the meeting prepared to address the issues. By sending this out well ahead of the meeting time and date, participants can prepare and be conscientious in their treatment of each item.

The Meeting Agenda

A final agenda should be received by all invited participants a minimum of two days ahead of time unless an emergency meeting is being called. When developing the agenda it will be necessary to make an educated guess regarding the length of time needed for each item during the meeting; the leader will strive to select material to fit within the allotted time period without rushing through agenda items.

An agenda typically includes the following information:

- the heading: AGENDA.
- the name of the group that is meeting: centered and at the top of the page.
- date of the meeting: centered and at the top of the page.
- time of the start of the meeting: centered and at the top of the page.
- location of the meeting: centered and at the top of the page.
- purpose statement: the general purpose of the meeting. This provides a sense of focus to the meeting and helps to keep participants on track.
- old business: any business not finished from a previous meeting is placed on the agenda. This includes items that were tabled, which required additional discussion or fact finding, or were not completely addressed at the last meeting. If this is the first meeting of a group, there will be no old business.

- acceptance of minutes: at the beginning of each meeting it is common to review and accept the minutes from the previous meeting. Oftentimes, corrections are made, noted in the current minutes, and then the old minutes are accepted.
- new business: this includes any material to be addressed in the current meeting, not previously discussed.
- other items: miscellaneous items that do not fit well in another above category.
- announcements: information to be shared, for which discussion and group decisions are not needed. Typically, dates and times of upcoming events, due dates, and factual information (e.g., the location of the policy manual) are listed as announcements.

During a meeting the agenda is used as a guide to help participants (and the leader) focus on the tasks to be addressed in the meeting. While agendas can be extremely helpful when used in this fashion, leaders would be wise to remember that flexibility remains important. A change in the agenda or flow of the meeting does not mean the meeting is being run poorly—it may simply indicate a responsiveness to the needs of those in attendance. See Figure 12.8 (page 444) for a sample agenda.

During the Meeting

The leader sets the tone for each and every meeting. As with activity and song leadership, some of this tone setting may be accomplished through the physical environment. The *arrangement of the meeting room* serves to direct communication and reinforce the nature of the meeting. Many meetings are held sitting at a long rectangular conference table, with the leader seated at one end (the head of the table). This arrangement directs communication and attention to the leader and minimizes, but allows, conversations between participants. A meeting held at a round table, on the other hand, encourages equal participation between all those in attendance. Other meetings that have a strong one-way information sharing purpose (the leader has information to pass on to participants) may be held in a room arranged like a traditional classroom with the leader at the front of the room and participants in desks or chairs, all

American Humanics, Inc.
Humanics: The Journal of Leadership for Youth and Human Service
Editorial Advisory Board Meeting

AGENDA
8:00 a.m. – 4:15 p.m.
10 February 1995
Wyndham Warwick Hotel
Houston, TX

Purpose Statement: The purpose of this meeting is to continue development of editorial policies and procedures related to the business of the *Humanics* journal. In addition, discussion will involve the future of the Journal.

1.0 Call to Order
    1.1 Welcome
    1.2 Introduction of Board Members
    1.3 Introduction of Guests
    1.4 Acceptance of the minutes
    1.5 Changes in/adoption of agenda
2.0 Old Business
    2.1 Reports of Action Items
        2.1.1 Solicitation of photographs
        2.1.2 Solicitation of manuscript
        2.1.3 Revised purpose statement
        2.1.4 Funding options for future issues
    2.2 Upcoming Issues
        2.2.1 Content
        2.2.2 Solicitation of manuscripts, issues of critical concern, student reflections of AHMI, photographs
    2.3 Operating Procedures
        2.3.1 Review and accept purpose statement
        2.3.2 Review and accept article review process
        2.3.3 Review and accept EAB membership process
        2.3.4 Review and accept job descriptions
        2.3.5 Identify Review Panel Members
    2.4 Distribution Plan
        2.4.1 Who should receive the journal?
        2.4.2 Mailing/distribution mechanism
3.0 New Business
    3.1 Future of the Journal
        3.1.1 Report from AH (Phil)
        3.1.2 New managing editor
        3.1.3 Development of new contract for publication
        3.1.4 Budget
        3.1.5 Timing of movement/transfer

Figure 12.8 Sample Agenda

facing the leader. The purpose of the meeting, leader style, and desired participant involvement combine to influence meeting room arrangement.

In addition to determining room arrangement, a meeting leader also sets the tone with regard to punctuality, staying on task, and developing and maintaining an atmosphere of friendliness and respect. To help establish an atmosphere of trust and participation, it is useful to *begin with introductions*—even if it is believed that everyone knows one another. Next, *go over the agenda* and ask for changes or additions to it. Establish or reiterate the meeting ground rules—the need to stay on task and the mechanism in place to assist that occurrence, a reminder that the leader's job is to facilitate movement in thoughts and ideas, the use of Roberts Rules of Order, and so on.

It might be helpful to set aside time at the beginning of a meeting to *socialize.* By allowing the first five to seven minutes of a meeting for socializing, participant need to visit and catch up with one another is addressed. It is necessary to be clear about the intent of this time so that the actual business component of the meeting can *begin on time.* For many, beginning a meeting late is an indication of a lack of respect for the participants and the value of their time. For these individuals nothing is worse than to have to wait for latecomers. Leaders might begin with a reminder about announcements (found on the agenda), and make it clear that everyone is responsible (for themselves) to know what occurs at meetings once a meeting is scheduled to begin.

Prior to beginning the actual conduct of the meeting it is necessary to identify an individual to record minutes. This individual may be an agency secretary or a member of the group—it is common for individuals in meetings to rotate turns in taking minutes. Minutes are the official record of what occurred during the meeting and will serve to inform others of those events.

During a meeting the leader's job is to facilitate communication and complete the agenda. To accomplish this it is necessary to direct and manage the flow of conversation and the tone of the meeting. The agenda will help to focus participants on the meeting tasks, and as much as is reasonable, it should be followed. Having an agenda and not following it at all can leave meeting participants feeling unsettled and confused.

In addition to allowing the agenda to serve as a meeting guide the leader will need to have control over the individuals in attendance. This does not mean that a leader must use an autocratic leadership style, rather it means that the leader controls the flow of the meeting. To accomplish this there are times when the leader will be required to *interrupt others while they are speaking*. The leader owes a responsibility to each member of the meeting team to encourage equal involvement, and so must strive to prevent any one individual from monopolizing the meeting.

If it is necessary to interrupt someone who is transgressing into an unrelated tangent, repeating thoughts already heard (unless done so for clarification), or rudely addressing other meeting participants, a leader should do so with respect. For example, "Excuse me, I appreciate your participation in this meeting, but we need to return to the agenda" may serve to get things back on track. If necessary, the leader may call a short recess and speak to the offending individual away from others asking her or him to allow for other voices to be heard.

Part of the responsibility owed to each person in the meeting is to include everyone in the meeting activities. A meeting leader may need to draw certain individuals into the meeting by asking for their opinions directly or by taking turns around the room voicing opinions or sharing information. By playing the role of gatekeeper, the leader can be sure that each person is heard on each agenda item. Once agenda items are discussed, information shared, and motions and decisions made, the leader should move the group on to the next agenda item. By moving through each agenda item this way, the meeting can end at its scheduled time.

Most meetings have a definitive meeting time and many standing meetings (e.g., staff meetings) are slated to last 60 minutes. Whenever the meeting is scheduled to end, the meeting leader should make all attempts to *end the meeting at that time*. Participants will have planned other tasks and meetings around this one and this should be respected. If people do not trust that the leader is going to end the meeting on time, they may act out in a variety of ways. To conclude a meeting on time it is not uncommon to have to eliminate some items from the agenda; a good deal of leader flexibility is needed throughout the meeting. If there is ample reason to run overtime, the leader should alert meeting participants as soon as this becomes apparent so that arrangements may be made to either move items up on the agenda, or for people to change their schedules. In any event, the leader should strive to end the meeting on an upbeat note.

After the Meeting

Once the meeting has ended and the next meeting time scheduled, stop conducting business and socialize for a few moments. To continue to discuss issues after the meeting has ended and some people have left can cloud the issues and cause hard feelings. *Enjoy one another's company* and save additional business-related concerns for the next meeting.

Periodically leaders will want to evaluate the meetings; particularly regularly scheduled meetings. This may be done verbally, in writing, or both. By asking staff members how they think meetings are going the leader receives valuable participant input and can make adjustments in future meetings. Ask participants to respond to such questions as: What are we spending too much time on? not enough time on? What types of things should be covered that we are not covering? Are people satisfied with the meetings? why/why not? Do individuals feel that their voices are heard? that they are treated with respect? By involving meeting participants in developing evaluation questions and conducting an evaluation every fourth or fifth meeting a leader can improve her or his own meeting leadership.

Minutes

Minutes are the official record of what occurred during the meeting. To be as useful as possible, minutes should be distributed to meeting participants, as well as those who were unable to attend the meeting, within two to three working days after the meeting was held. It was stated earlier that minutes are recorded during the meeting by either a secretary or a participating group member. This individual takes notes throughout the meeting and after the meeting summarizes them in a concise fashion. The intent is to provide minutes that are detailed enough so that an absent person can understand the gist of what occurred and what actions were taken; yet succinct enough so as not to be overwhelming.

Typically minutes mirror the agenda and include the following items:

- the heading: MINUTES.
- the name of the group that met: centered and at the top of the page.

- date the meeting was held: centered and at the top of the page.
- time of the start and end of the meeting: centered and at the top of the page.
- location of the meeting: centered and at the top of the page.
- roll call: list the names of those present, those absent, and those excused.
- list names of guests in attendance: a guest is any invited or drop-in individual who is usually nonvoting, yet has a particular interest in the meeting information.
- action items: action items are identified throughout the minutes and stand out from other material. They serve as reminders to participants to complete a task. Action items are tasks that need specific action by participants by a specific date (often prior to the next meeting). For instance, "ACTION ITEM: Each group member will develop a team roster and bring enough copies of it to share with other coaches at the next meeting."
- acceptance of minutes: at the beginning of each minutes it is common to indicate that the previous minutes were reviewed and accepted. Minutes are either "accepted as is" (with no corrections), or "with corrections (as noted)."
- old business: a summary of information identified as old business on the agenda. If a lengthy discussion occurred over a particular item, it is common to record it as, "A lengthy discussion ensued surrounding risk management around the pool area. It was decided that...." If, for example, two or three major issues or viewpoints were discussed in the meeting, those might be summarized here.
- new business: as with old business, this section of the minutes includes discussion and decisions that were raised in the meeting under this heading.
- other items: a summary of the miscellaneous items that did not fit well in another category.
- announcements: a reminder list of announcements from the agenda, plus any new announcements are added here.

- next scheduled meeting: commonly listed at the bottom (and in the same place on every set of minutes) is the date, time, and location of the next meeting.

- submitted by: whether minutes were recorded by agency personnel or a meeting group member, it is important to identify who the recorder was. In this way, should a question or need for clarification arise, the appropriate individual might be found easily.

To share in ownership of meetings, some meeting leaders like to *rotate responsibility for facilitating meetings*. To accomplish this the leader works in conjunction with the meeting facilitator in developing the agenda and in establishing meeting protocols and ground rules, but allows that individual to facilitate the business of the meeting. This helps others to understand the importance of staff meetings and to appreciate the work that goes into them. Another technique is to delegate certain components of the meeting to individual participants so that several people are actively involved in the meeting process. The leader should bear in mind that, ultimately, it is her or his responsibility to facilitate the meetings efficiently and effectively as possible. It is not always wise, therefore, to delegate meeting leadership to others. Sample minutes appear on pages 450-451.

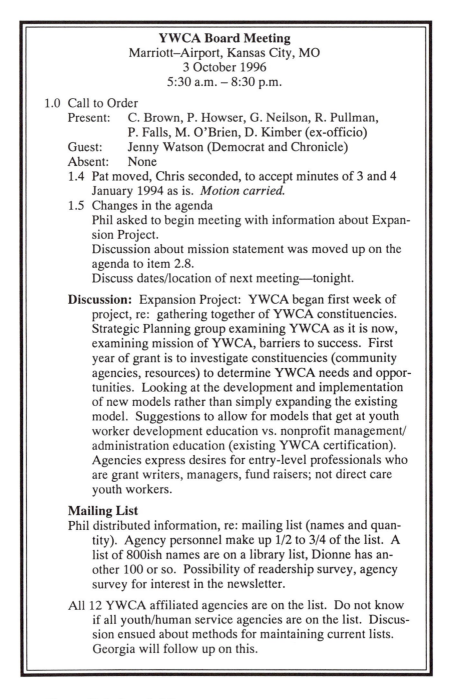

YWCA Board Meeting
Marriott–Airport, Kansas City, MO
3 October 1996
5:30 a.m. – 8:30 p.m.

1.0 Call to Order
Present: C. Brown, P. Howser, G. Neilson, R. Pullman,
            P. Falls, M. O'Brien, D. Kimber (ex-officio)
Guest: Jenny Watson (Democrat and Chronicle)
Absent: None

1.4 Pat moved, Chris seconded, to accept minutes of 3 and 4
     January 1994 as is. *Motion carried.*

1.5 Changes in the agenda
     Phil asked to begin meeting with information about Expan-
     sion Project.
     Discussion about mission statement was moved up on the
     agenda to item 2.8.
     Discuss dates/location of next meeting—tonight.

Discussion: Expansion Project: YWCA began first week of
     project, re: gathering together of YWCA constituencies.
     Strategic Planning group examining YWCA as it is now,
     examining mission of YWCA, barriers to success. First
     year of grant is to investigate constituencies (community
     agencies, resources) to determine YWCA needs and oppor-
     tunities. Looking at the development and implementation
     of new models rather than simply expanding the existing
     model. Suggestions to allow for models that get at youth
     worker development education vs. nonprofit management/
     administration education (existing YWCA certification).
     Agencies express desires for entry-level professionals who
     are grant writers, managers, fund raisers; not direct care
     youth workers.

Mailing List
Phil distributed information, re: mailing list (names and quan-
     tity). Agency personnel make up 1/2 to 3/4 of the list. A
     list of 800ish names are on a library list, Dionne has an-
     other 100 or so. Possibility of readership survey, agency
     survey for interest in the newsletter.

All 12 YWCA affiliated agencies are on the list. Do not know
     if all youth/human service agencies are on the list. Discus-
     sion ensued about methods for maintaining current lists.
     Georgia will follow up on this.

Figure 12.9 Sample Minutes

Newsletter is being developed from YWCA; the first one being sent out this month. It will include information updates, new Board members, article on conference, update on YWCA happenings, article on planned giving opportunities. Readership consists of: 5-year donor list, alums, members. Intent is to distribute the newsletter quarterly (perhaps only 3 this year). Suggestion to focus each issue on different concerns.

Newsletter should:

Include (1) information to explain the mission of the YWCA, (2) promulgate knowledge that influences profession practice (how-to material), (3) promote the advancement of knowledge through research—practitioner friendly, i.e., implications for professional practice.

Use regular columns to meet needs of short information needed now. Layout will help with catching, drawing in leaders, telling them "this piece is readable."

The purpose statement of the Newsletter is being revised to reflect the following thoughts: the Advisory Board will seek to encourage a free exchange of ideas from a variety of perspectives. The submission and equitable treatment of all material submitted. Within the editorial content of the newsletter freedom of press, intellectual discourse, dialogue, breadth of ideas, inquiry must be allowed. The newsletter will seek to address a variety of issues, perspectives, and view points without bias. The newsletter will serve as a forum to discuss issues, concerns, concepts that reflect a diversity of ideas, perspectives and viewpoints.

Once accepted by the YWCA Board, this statement will be included on the first page.

There is a need to conduct a reader survey—who reads, why, what they get out of it, etc., could use focus groups. A thorough and useful survey would take a year of development. Reconsider in the future.

ACTION ITEM: Potential dates for next YWCA meeting: February 3, 4, 5 or 10, 11, 12. Fly in Friday evening, meet all day Saturday, leave Sunday morning, Phil is checking on dates/location.

Meeting adjourned 8:25 p.m.
Minutes submitted by D. Kimber

Figure 12.9 *Sample Minutes (continued)*

Summary

This chapter has established the groundwork for direct leadership techniques. There are three phases to direct leadership skills: preparation, priming the group, and delivery. An effective leader is one who is prepared, knows the group with which she or he will be working, and has followed risk management procedures. In addition, preparation entails establishing goals and objectives, and setting the mood by manipulating the environment and playing "what if?"

Once having taken care of preparations, a leader primes the group. Priming the group involves using fun, experiential and unique techniques or activities to get the group's attention and divide the group into smaller groups. It is best to avoid using team captains or counting off as ways of dividing a group because of negative effects. Learning names is very important to group satisfaction and is part of the priming stage.

The delivery phase of direct leadership includes the leader introducing both herself or himself and the activity, identifying the goal of the activity, telling a story and giving directions. When giving directions it is best to follow the KISS, KIP and PLAY methods. Within and between activities, transitions are used; transitions are psychological bridges used both within and between activities. Conclusions are as important as beginnings in leisure experiences and may be used to maintain positive affect and to bring individuals back for more.

Finally, meeting leadership was discussed as a role and responsibility of many direct leaders. What to do in the preparation of a meeting was discussed as was the actual conduct of a meeting, and what to do upon the completion of a meeting. The importance of developing and distributing agendas and minutes were also presented.

The Front Line

Helpful Hints for Effective Leadership

- Do unto others as they would want to be done unto.

- Involving participants (especially children) in decision-making processes takes extra time; do it anyway.

- Ask questions that will require more than a yes/no response.

- Never ask a question for which you are not prepared for the answer.

- If out-of-doors, let the group face the leader; the leader faces the sun.

- Never wear sunglasses (unless for safety), it hides your eyes from participants.

- Flexibility and being able to respond in ambiguous situations are hallmarks of good leaders.

- Always end an activity while the participants are having fun.

- Safety should never be compromised, nor negotiated.

- End an activity on a positive note, even if the participants were not always positive.

- Always love the person, dislike the behavior.

- Provide structured choices.

- Power is like love, the more given away, the more one has.

- Do not treat children like miniature adults.

- Be aware of your surroundings, arrange participants to minimize outside distractions.

- All children need to run, jump, and scream—let them.

- Always be honest with children (and others).

- Adult logic and reasoning does not always make sense to a child.

- Participants will be excited about things leaders are excited about.
- Remind yourself (and other adults) to PLAY every once in a while.

References

Bloom, B. (1956). *Taxonomy of educational objectives.* New York, NY: Longmans.

Jordan, D. and Mertesdorf, J. (1994). The effects of goal interdependence between leisure service supervisors and employees. *Journal of Applied Recreation Research, 19*(2), pp. 101-116.

Mager, R. (1984). *Measuring instructional results* (2nd ed.). Belmont, CA: Pitman Learning, Inc.

Russell, R. V. (1986). *Leadership in recreation.* St. Louis, MO: Times Mirror/Mosby.

Chapter Thirteen
Learning Opportunities

Through studying this chapter students will have the opportunity to:

- understand the impact of social and professional issues on leisure services leaders;

- describe the signs of child abuse and explain the role of the leisure services leader in reporting suspected abuse;

- examine the importance of taking universal precautions when dealing with blood borne pathogens;

- discuss the nature of the C.L.P. and C.T.R.S. certifications; and

- identify various certifications and professional memberships a leisure services leader may obtain.

Photo courtesy of the YWCA of Black Hawk County

CHAPTER

13

Selected Social and Professional Issues Affecting Leisure Services Leaders

To reach their professional potential, leisure services leaders need a solid awareness and understanding of the social and professional issues facing the field. Social issues are those issues and concerns that exist in society and have an impact, both good and bad, on the quality of life and social mores. Social issues include forces acting both out of and on society such as poverty, homelessness, crime and violence, and the decline in national fitness levels. Professional issues are those concerns that affect the professions of parks, recreation, and leisure services. Professional issues include such things as developing a set of professional ethics, becoming increasingly professional (with licensure, degree requirements, and the prestige and respect of a profession such as law or medicine), and understanding the role leisure plays in quality of life issues. All of these concerns affect leadership in parks, recreation, and leisure services.

Leisure services settings are microcosms of society. This means that what occurs in larger society, both positive and negative, also occurs in or affects leisure services settings. Social issues such as unemployment, HIV/AIDS, child abuse, and violence all impact on leisure in some respect. Higher rates of unemployment affect individuals' ability to purchase leisure services, and reduces their quality of life; HIV/AIDS impacts the way leisure services leaders treat small wounds and injuries and influences the participation of some people. In addition, leisure services leaders need to be aware of concerns surrounding child abuse to avoid accusations and to serve as modes of intervention; other forms of violence impact leisure services in the need for conflict resolution and in addressing participant safety.

Professional issues such as certification and accreditation also impact the ongoing growth and development of leisure services leaders. Working with a variety of people in different types of situations may require leisure services leaders to fulfill many roles: instructor, information provider, mediator, facilitator, mentor, director, entertainer, counselor, problem solver, presenter, and authoritarian, among others. In filling these many roles, a breadth of knowledge and a variety of skills are needed. Continuing education and certification help to ensure knowledge and skill levels in these areas.

Effective leaders become aware of the impact of both social and professional issues within the profession as well as on leadership situations and their personal leadership styles. In increasing their awareness, leaders can direct their own continuing education to meet personal needs as well as the needs of constituents and the profession as a whole. This chapter will address a selection of social and professional issues that influence leader effectiveness: child abuse, blood borne pathogens, leader certification, and professional memberships.

Child Abuse

Child abuse is an issue facing all parks, recreation, and leisure services providers who work with, have contact with, or provide services for children. Child abuse affects leisure services professionals in two ways—first, leaders must be aware of the impact they have on children in the provision of services, managing behaviors, and leading activities (to avoid being perpetrators of abuse); and second, the children involved in leisure services activities may be victims of abuse and require leader intervention (as a mandated or volunteer reporter).

According to the federal law, Child Abuse Prevention, Adoption and Family Services Act of 1988 (P.L. 100-294), child abuse (child maltreatment) is defined as:

> The physical or mental injury, sexual abuse, or exploitation, neglectful treatment, or maltreatment of a child by a person who is responsible for the child's welfare, under circumstances which indicate that the child's health or welfare is harmed or threatened thereby, as determined in accordance with regulations prescribed by the Secretary of the Department of Health and Human Services. (Gustavsson & Segal, 1994, p. 75)

The regulations indicate that *child maltreatment* includes physical, emotional and sexual abuse, while *neglect* is the failure to care for a child's basic needs which may include physical needs, emotional needs, or both. In leisure services, child abuse may be passive where a child observes another child being abused, or active when abuse is directed at a particular child.

Types of Child Abuse in Leisure Services Settings

There are several types of abuse which may be imposed on youngsters: verbal, physical, emotional, and sexual. *Verbal abuse* is the most commonly occurring type of abuse and includes such things as name calling (e.g., "you jerk," "what a baby"), hurtful comments regarding performance (e.g., "you couldn't hit that ball if you tried," "you stink at this"), swearing at participants, and comments designed to demean a child's integrity (e.g., "you are a liar—I've never heard you tell the truth," "the only way you ever win is when you cheat") (Parents and Coaches in Sports, n.d.). *Physical abuse* arises out of any physical touch that is hurtful, or activities purposefully designed to cause pain to the participant (Parents and Coaches in Sports, n.d.). Grabbing, shoving, slapping, and excessive exercise (e.g., 50 push-ups) as a method of discipline could all be considered physical abuse. *Emotional abuse* of children often involves having unrealistic goals and expectations for them (Parents and Coaches in Sports, n.d.). Examples of this type of abuse include pushing a child to win every activity, aggressively urging a youngster to score the most points, and not allowing children to make mistakes. *Sexual abuse* may be any form of sexual contact or implied sexual contact between an adult and child (Parents and Coaches in Sports, n.d.). Any type of sexual harassment, implicit or explicit sexual comments and innuendoes, and sexual touch are all examples of this type of abuse.

Contributing Factors

There are a variety of larger social problems that, by their existence, contribute to abuse of young people. This is to say that if the contributing factors were satisfactorily addressed, a good deal of child abuse would be mitigated. Leisure services plays a role in addressing many of these issues through various agency mission statements and the provision of services. Research has shown that social problems such as poverty, substance abuse, mental health problems, unemployment, financial difficulties, isolation and a lack of social support all contribute to higher incidences of child maltreatment (Gustavsson & Segal, 1994; Howing, Wodarski, Kurtz & Gaudin, 1993; McWhirter, McWhirter, McWhirter & McWhirter, 1993; Monteleone, 1994; Myers, 1994; Rothery & Cameron, 1990). It is also known, of course, that once child abuse begins it becomes cyclical, that is, a victim of abuse very often becomes an abuser.

Consequences

The consequences of child maltreatment are great for the individual child, siblings, and for larger society. The detrimental effects of child abuse result in an individual who has a whole host of long-lasting personal problems. These personal problems negatively influence the long-term success and life quality of the individual. Very often, victims of child maltreatment suffer from low self-esteem, depression, sleep and eating disorders, and may be suicidal at various times throughout their life. The effects of the mistreatment may be observed in severe behavior extremes, impulsiveness, social withdrawal, or excessive anxiety (Howing, Wodarski, Kurtz, & Gaudin, 1993; Monteleone, 1994; Rothery & Cameron, 1990). Leisure services leaders may be in positions to recognize and help alleviate many of these interim effects.

Other negative results of child abuse for the victim include delayed development (e.g., physical, emotional, social), an inability to concentrate, substance abuse, and sexual promiscuity (often, at a very young age). Interpersonal skills are often impacted negatively because those who are maltreated as children develop a distrust of adults and peers; this often translates into a lack of successful peer relationships (Gustavsson & Segal, 1994; Howing, Wodarski, Kurtz, & Gaudin, 1993; McWhirter, McWhirter, McWhirter, & McWhirter, 1993; Monteleone, 1994; Myers, 1994; Rothery & Cameron, 1990). It is readily apparent that the consequences of child abuse are powerful, long lasting, and highly undesirable.

Signs of Child Maltreatment

A prominent role for leisure services leaders in addressing child abuse is in the prevention, recognition, and reporting of suspected cases of abuse. As mentioned in the definition of child abuse, maltreatment may be physical, emotional, sexual, or a combination of the three. Neglect may be emotional or physical. While physical abuse, sexual abuse and neglect may manifest themselves in observable injuries, all types of abuse and neglect have some observable characteristics. Often, signs of maltreatment are in the form of victim behavior extremes. If a physical injury is apparent, a concerned leader needs to consider *first* if injury could have occurred as described; *second*, the leader must decide if the child is developmentally mature enough to have caused the injury as indicated. Patterns of injuries over time (e.g., old and new bruises) may be indications of maltreatment of a child.

Indicators of physical abuse. Injuries including bruises, fractures, and various types of wounds and burns (particularly those caused by cigarettes) can be signs of physical maltreatment (however, some injuries may also be signs of an active, exploring child). Head and internal injuries are common results of physical abuse, rather than typical childhood exploratory injuries. Behavioral characteristics of abused children may include overly passive or aggressive behaviors, a fear of physical contact such as a touch on the shoulder or pat on the back, regressive behaviors (i.e., the child reverts to acting much younger than her or his years), or a child acting frightened of her or his parent(s) or guardian(s) (Gustavsson & Segal, 1994).

Signs of emotional abuse. Emotional abuse may be the most difficult to ascertain because there is no obvious physical injury or pain. However, emotional abuse can be just as harmful to a child as physical maltreatment. Children who are emotionally maltreated or neglected may manifest a lack of trust of adults and peers, low self-esteem, and have poor interpersonal skills. An inability to cope with everyday stresses and frustrations, unexplained aggressiveness, and hyperactivity may also indicate emotional abuse. Some children may withdraw, be apathetic or unresponsive about everything, and lack decision-making skills. Many victims of emotional abuse or neglect turn to substance abuse as a means of escape or to draw attention to themselves (Monteleone, 1994).

Signs of sexual abuse. In some recreational settings leisure services leaders may observe what appear to be signs of sexual abuse. This is most often the case in situations where children change their clothes (e.g., when preparing to go swimming) in front of activity leaders, or in situations of extended contact (such as exists at a resident camp). Injuries to the genital or anal areas; torn, stained, or bloody undergarments; sexually transmitted diseases (STDs); and pregnancy at a young age are all signs of sexual abuse (Gustavsson & Segal, 1994). Children who are so abused often feel extreme rage, anger, and frustration at what is happening to them. Signs of sexual abuse may be

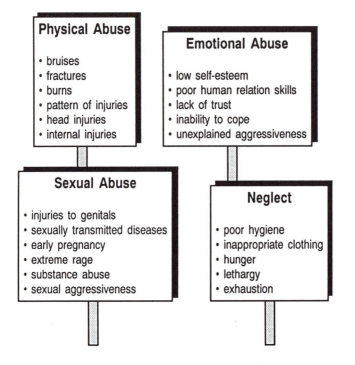

Physical Abuse

• bruises
• fractures
• burns
• pattern of injuries
• head injuries
• internal injuries

Emotional Abuse

• low self-esteem
• poor human relation skills
• lack of trust
• inability to cope
• unexplained aggressiveness

Sexual Abuse

• injuries to genitals
• sexually transmitted diseases
• early pregnancy
• extreme rage
• substance abuse
• sexual aggressiveness

Neglect

• poor hygiene
• inappropriate clothing
• hunger
• lethargy
• exhaustion

Figure 13.1 *Signs of child abuse can be quite diverse.*

manifested in feelings of humiliation, a sense of a lack of control over self, and irrational thinking (Monteleone, 1994).

Many children who are sexually abused become sexual aggressors in inappropriate fashions. They may project sexual desires onto a leisure services leader, their own peers, or younger children. Sexual promiscuity and substance abuse are also signs of being victimized in this fashion.

Signs of neglect. Leisure services leaders are often aware of various issues of child abuse, but may be less aware of the impact of child neglect on the healthy development of young people. Being alone for long periods of time without adult supervision is commonly perceived as neglect. Neglect may also occur with adults present in the household (e.g., they ignore the children). Poor personal hygiene, inappropriate or inadequate clothing, frequent hunger, and lethargy or exhaustion are common signs of neglect. In addition, poor academic performance, a high rate of school absenteeism, and delinquent behaviors also may be indications of child neglect (Gustavsson & Segal, 1994; Monteleone, 1994).

Characteristics of Maltreating Adults

Often, one can make a determination of child maltreatment by combining knowledge of injuries to a child and information about the adults involved. Because child maltreatment tends to be cyclical, a history of abuse or neglect as a child is a common characteristic of an abusing or neglectful adult. The use of excessively harsh discipline (e.g., screaming, hitting with an object, overreacting to minor mishaps) is quite common, as is a history of mental illness, alcohol and/or drug abuse, and a chaotic home life. Another characteristic of maltreating adults is social isolation—they may have little or no contact with others, either purposefully or by the nature of their geographic or financial predicament (Myers, 1994; Rothery & Cameron, 1990). Adults who experience undue stress related to finances and other contributing factors are more likely to engage in child maltreatment than adults who do not experience such stresses (Gustavsson & Segal, 1994; Monteleone, 1994).

Certainly, being aware of the potential for child abuse and recognizing the signs and indications are important for leisure services leaders. Once maltreatment has been observed or is suspected, leisure services leaders must then take the next step—reporting the suspected abuse. Reporting suspected child abuse can be one of the most wrenching situations in which leisure services leaders find themselves. An overriding concern for the safety and well-being of the child is often tempered with the question, "what if I am wrong?" To aid in the decision-making process many states have passed laws dictating who must report suspected child abuse, to whom, and when. These laws are designed to protect the child and to afford some liability protection to the individual making the report, should an error be made.

Mandatory Reporters

According to Gustavsson and Segal, "mandated reporters are professionals who, in the course of their work, may discover child maltreatment" (1994, p. 79). Individuals designated as mandatory reporters are determined by each state and may include teachers, physicians, police, and other social service professionals including those in leisure services. *Each state has reporting laws and legislation which identify the definition of child abuse, and standards and procedures for reporting it.* Therefore, leisure services leaders should be cognizant of the specifics relative to their own state. Each state has laws regarding the following:

- what must be reported;

- who must report (usually teachers, physicians, and police; many states list any childcare provider and twenty states name "any person");

- when it must be reported (e.g., immediately by phone; when a reporter has "reason to believe" or "reasonable cause to suspect" maltreatment);

- reporting procedures and to whom to report (the most common child protection agencies that receive child abuse reports include social service agencies, police departments, health departments, and juvenile court systems);

- the existence and operation of a central registry (i.e., names of accused individuals are entered into a central registry for ease of intervention and follow-up);

- rules regarding protective custody for children and immunity for good faith reporters (e.g., immunity from civil and criminal prosecution); and

- sanctions for failure to report (in many states, a failure to report is a misdemeanor with a fine and/or jail time) (Monteleone, 1994).

In trying to determine the reasons behind mood swings, extremes in behavior, or participant difficulties, a leisure services leader may engage in conversation with a youngster which results in the knowledge that the youth is being or has been maltreated. The child might begin to share this information by asking the leader to promise not to tell anyone. Leaders must recognize and tell the child that this type of promise is not possible. For the safety of the child and by law, once abuse is suspected or known, a report *must* be made. Leaders should be very careful of promises (which cannot be kept) made to young people when faced with this issue. A lack of trust and feelings of humiliation and shame often accompany such revelations and leaders need to be very cognizant of the long-term impacts on and the feelings of the young person involved.

The Process of Reporting

Once an individual has determined that suspicion of child abuse exists a report must be made. While the procedure in each state varies somewhat, the typical reporting process is as follows:

(a) a report is made by a volunteer or mandated reporter who has "reasonable suspicion" of abuse occurring;

(b) the report is screened through an intake process by child protective services (CPS) agency personnel;

(c) a decision is made to send out an investigator (this usually occurs within 24 hours of the initial report);

(d) a case record is made;

(e) findings are recorded; and

(f) case and intervention plans are developed and implemented.

To initiate legal action, should it be deemed necessary, CPS personnel must first substantiate the claim of maltreatment (McWhirter, McWhirter, McWhirter, & McWhirter, 1993).

The ultimate goal of many state CPS agencies is to maintain the integrity of the family unit; therefore, disposition of child maltreatment cases may include parental support classes, family counseling, and temporary removal from the home. Ultimately, if no other intervention works, a child may be permanently removed from the home and put into the foster care/adoption system (Howing, Wodarski, Kurtz, & Gaudin, 1993; McWhirter, McWhirter, McWhirter, & McWhirter, 1993; Myers, 1994).

After Making the Report

Once a report has been made, a leisure services leader should strive to treat the child as before—with respect and understanding. Once the child knows that an adult is aware of the "secret," she or he may increase in acting out or engaging in inappropriate behaviors; this is often a result of the fear and anxiety of what will occur as CPS becomes involved. A leader will want to be as sensitive as possible to the needs of the youngster, whether it be a need to be alone, to talk, or simply to be in the company of supportive and caring adults. Talking about and sharing

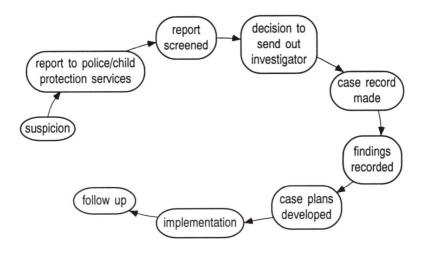

Figure 13.2 *Once a mandatory reporter of child abuse reports a suspected case, the process moves forward.*

accounts of abuse should be initiated by the young person, not by leisure services leaders. Very few leisure services leaders are trained as psychiatrists or therapists and are limited in how they can help the youngster. Leaders *can*, however, be good listeners and establish opportunities for the abuse victim to feel in control, as well as experience success in recreational activities.

Other ways in which leisure services leaders can have a positive impact with children who have been maltreated is to design and lead activities to help rebuild a sense of trust in others. To initiate this, leaders will need to be consistent, dependable, and reliable for those youth (all participants respond well to leader consistency). Active listening and responding to stated needs—a genuine caring about the child—is vital for reengaging wholesome child development. Designing activity and leadership opportunities so that youth have a high likelihood of success and are *not* judged by how well they perform is also important. Effective leadership techniques for victims of child abuse usually require heightened awareness and sensitivity toward the participant. Efforts to improve leadership techniques for victims of neglect and abuse are usually beneficial to *all* participants.

The realization that children who are maltreated often suffer in terms of appropriate interpersonal skills should direct leisure services leaders to model and design opportunities for the development and practice of social skills (e.g., sharing, coping with disappointments and frustrations, decision making, communication). Basic life skills such as self-esteem, communication, conflict resolution, decision making, stress management, and leisure education are all needed skills for children from abusive backgrounds. By providing a wide variety of opportunities for those youth (in fact, all youth) to construct and try out their own ideas, leisure services leaders can begin the process of empowering abuse victims to stand up for themselves (Monteleone, 1994).

Leader Caveats

Caveats are warnings or messages to be careful. When addressing and considering the concerns surrounding the issue of child abuse, there are several caveats for leaders. By their positions (e.g., camp counselor, locker-room attendant, playground supervisor, trip leader), leisure services leaders are often in *situations* where their actions could be perceived as suspicious by those observing. In addition, by their *actions* (e.g., some behavior management techniques, motivational methods, specific supervision), leisure services leaders may come under scrutiny for allegations of child maltreatment.

To avoid any claim of misconduct, yet still maintain safe and effective leadership, leaders should continually examine their own behaviors with children. It may be helpful to imagine what a behavior or situation might look like to someone out of earshot and across the room. No matter how innocent a particular behavior is (e.g., hugging a crying child), from across the room it may look very different. Therefore, leaders should be very aware of their actions, words, and intentions at all times (and crying children may still need to be hugged).

Reaching out and touching children (and adults) is one aspect of leadership that has a tendency to draw attention from observers. Children now are taught about "good" touching (e.g., nonsexual hugs, pats on the back, high fives) and "bad" touching (e.g., sexual or hurtful) in schools. Leaders, too, need to know what constitutes good and bad touches.

Touching, of course, should be appropriate for the situation. That is, it is generally acceptable for a hug to follow bandaging a scraped knee and a pat on the back to be given as congratulations for a job well done. Many times it is best to ask an individual for permission to touch her or him before doing so—"Would you like a hug?" "Is it okay if I give you a pat on the back?" This way, if such touching is not comfortable for the child she or he can tell you so—allowing children to define the boundaries of touching will help to minimize misinterpreted intentions.

When in public settings different from the usual recreational setting (e.g., on a field trip, at a local waterpark), it is often necessary for safety and liability reasons, to accompany small children to the restroom or locker room. To protect oneself from perceptions of impropriety, it is usually wise to either accompany multiple children simultaneously or ensure that other adults are nearby. In this way, if a child must be assisted with dressing or attending to personal needs, witnesses are available to observe and confirm leader actions.

Other situations raise concerns and awareness of child abuse: when engaged in behavior management with children (e.g., when using touch or physical intervention) and any time one is alone with a child (e.g., in the office, equipment room, vehicle). To minimize concerns about child maltreatment in these situations, it would be wise to be aware of who is doing what where, the setting itself, and who is around. These concerns are valid because Myers (1994) indicated that recent research shows that, while it is uncommon, there are times when children *will* lie about maltreatment. To be effective and still meet the human needs of young people, then, leaders will want to do what they can to protect themselves and their young charges from any perception of wrongdoing.

Blood Borne Pathogens and Universal Precautions

In addition to a concern about maltreatment of children, leisure services leaders need a basic awareness of the prevention of transmission of blood borne pathogens to help keep themselves and participants safe. Diseases such as hepatitis B, tuberculosis, and HIV/AIDS are considered blood borne pathogens. This means that these diseases are transmitted through contact with an individual's blood or other bodily fluids (e.g., mucous from sneezing, spittle from coughing, urine or feces). In leisure services settings there are many instances when contact with another person's bodily fluids may occur such as when a child wets the bed at camp, a participant gets a bloody nose from being hit with a ball, or an individual sweats profusely onto weight machines.

Leisure services leaders commonly provide minor first aid to slightly injured participants, thereby being exposed to blood. Those in therapeutic recreation settings may deal with many bodily fluids in the normal course of their work. Many blood borne pathogens are impossible to detect simply by looking at someone, and the diseases have varying degrees of danger to those exposed to them (e.g., hepatitis B can be debilitating over the life course, HIV/AIDS is fatal; both of these diseases are incurable). The possible transmission of HIV frightens many, however, other communicable diseases such as hepatitis B and tuberculosis are much easier to transmit from one individual to another than is HIV. Therefore, while we may attribute an increase in awareness of blood borne pathogens to the rise of HIV and AIDS, the resulting precautions make tending to ill, injured, or needy persons safer for everyone.

To protect oneself as well as other participants from all blood borne communicable diseases a leader will want to take *universal precautions* when providing assistance. Universal precautions are those actions taken by a person who is handling bodily fluids in any situation (such as cleaning up after an incident or rendering aid to another) to protect herself or himself against unknown (and often invisible) diseases. It is important to remember that HIV, hepatitis B, and tuberculosis infections are nondiscriminatory. Children and heterosexual women, in fact, constitute the fastest growing group of individuals infected with HIV. Heterosexual teenagers are also becoming infected with HIV (and other sexually transmitted diseases) at alarming rates (Land, 1992).

It is best to presume that everyone is contagious and capable of infecting others. Following universal precautions ensures the same treatment of everyone—use of rubber gloves, a medical mask, and care in disposing of soiled bandages and other materials. The Occupational and Safety Health Act (OSHA), provides guidelines for managing blood borne pathogens in various situations. Summarized from Skaros (1995), the guidelines include:

- educating staff and participants about the identity and proper disposal of contaminated materials;

- removing from any activity any individual who has evidence of bleeding or blood on herself or himself (or clothes) until it can be cleaned up;

- ensuring that any area used for first aid is *not* used for eating, smoking, applying cosmetics, inserting contact lenses, or any other activity that could increase the risk of infection;

- ensuring an adequate supply of disposable personal protective gear for use during first aid;
- encouraging hepatitis B vaccinations of all staff who are likely to come into contact with bodily fluids of any sort; and
- establishing a thorough record-keeping process to document all levels of exposure.

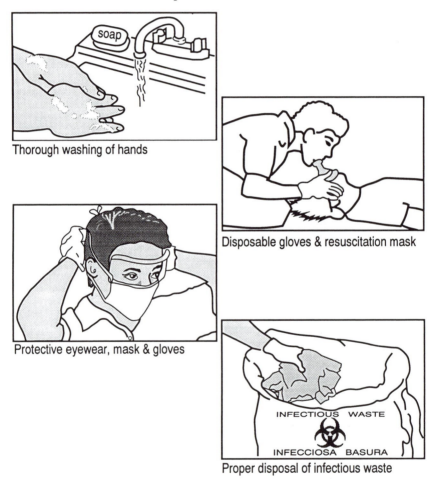

Thorough washing of hands

Disposable gloves & resuscitation mask

Protective eyewear, mask & gloves

Proper disposal of infectious waste

Figure 13.3 Universal precautions are just that—they apply to everyone in all situations where bodily fluids might be transmitted.

Professional Issues

Professionalism includes a knowledge of the impact of social issues on leisure services participants, the leader, and the profession. In addition, a leisure services leader who strives to be the best leader possible seeks out professional contacts and is involved in continual personal education. Competence requires remaining involved in the evolution of the profession and a commitment to learning as new things are discovered. One way to demonstrate a commitment to the profession and ongoing learning is through professional certifications and membership in professional organizations.

Certifications can be sought in two general areas—one's area of professional expertise, and those certifications related to health and safety issues. Many entry-level and mid-level positions in leisure services require a minimum of certifications in various health and safety issues (e.g., CPR and first aid). Other certifications enhance a leader's competence and verify a commitment to the profession—employers often look for individuals with certifications to fill positions. All certifications require testing; some require written tests which examine knowledge and understanding of material while others require both written and physical skill tests.

Certification is a term that describes the process whereby an individual voluntarily submits her or his credentials for review based upon clearly identified competencies, criteria, or standards (Edginton, Jordan, DeGraaf & Edginton, 1995). The primary purpose of certification is to ensure that staff employed in leisure services meet high standards of performance. In addition, certifications often help when liability and negligence concerns arise. Certifications have, in many instances, become industry standard; this means that the standard or norm in the profession is for staff to be certified. Generally, certifications in basic first aid and CPR are required of direct leadership staff and are considered industry standards for leisure services leaders.

Becoming certified assures employers that certified applicants meet prescribed education, experience, and continuing education requirements and have shown dedication to profession through voluntary certification. Certification is *not* a guarantee of a particular level of performance, however. There is great variation in ability and performance of certified individuals. Certifications are awarded by a wide variety of national agencies and organizations as well as local entities.

Certifications

The National Recreation and Park Association (NRPA), in conjunction with the American Association of Leisure and Recreation (AALR), certifies leisure services professionals indicating that certified individuals have been exposed to a basic body of knowledge through formal education and experience.

In 1981 NRPA/AALR developed a National Certification Board consisting of professionals who provide guidance to the dual organization certification program. Through NRPA/AALR a leisure services professional may be certified as a Certified Leisure Professional (C.L.P.) or a Certified Therapeutic Recreation Specialist (C.T.R.S.). The certification process is designed to: (1) formally recognize individuals who fulfill requirements of certification; (2) encourage professional growth and individual study; and (3) provide a standard of knowledge desirable for leisure services professionals. Many employment positions in parks, recreation, and leisure services now indicate that the C.L.P. or C.T.R.S. certification is required or desirable prior to employment.

Certified Leisure Professional (C.L.P.)

An individual who is certified as a C.L.P. has graduated from an accredited university and passed a written test in several core knowledge areas of job-related tasks common to entry level professionals. The core areas tested include leisure services management, leisure and recreation program delivery, natural resource and facilities management, and therapeutic recreation. The certification is valid for two years during which time a certified individual needs to earn 2.0 continuing education units (CEUs) to maintain certification. Exams are given in various cities around the country and are typically offered twice a year.

Certified Therapeutic Recreation Specialist (C.T.R.S.)

The National Council for Therapeutic Recreation Certification (NCTRC) was formed in 1981, and follows the credentialing process utilized by the Council for Advancement of Hospital Recreation and the National Therapeutic Recreation Society. It is designated as a certification program for individuals desiring to work in the field of therapeutic recreation. NCTRC establishes and tests on the acceptable standards for therapeutic recreation personnel. NCTRC is recognized by healthcare accrediting bodies, and state and federal regulatory groups, as the credentialing authority for therapeutic recreation personnel in the

*A Certified Therapeutic Recreation Specialist—many work with
seniors in activities such as pet therapy.*

United States. Individuals who are eligible to sit for and pass the written
exam receive a C.T.R.S. certificate.

According to the NCTRC mission statement, the NCTRC exists to
protect the public and promote the provision of quality therapeutic
recreation services. This is accomplished through: (1) establishing
standards for certification and recertification; (2) granting recognition
to individuals who voluntarily apply and meet established standards for
certification and recertification; and (3) monitoring adherence to the
standards. NCTRC evaluates the educational and experiential qualifications of therapeutic recreation professionals as part of the certification process.

To be eligible to sit for the C.T.R.S. exam an individual must hold
a baccalaureate degree from an accredited college or university and
have successfully completed a minimum of a 360-hour, ten-consecu-
tive-week internship under the supervision of a C.T.R.S. The C.T.R.S.
exam covers the following material: background information, diagnostic groupings and populations served, assessment, planning programs
and treatments, implementing programs and treatments, documentation
and managing services, organizing and managing services, and professional issues. Initial C.T.R.S. certification is valid for five years; to
renew, one needs a combination of professional experience, continuing
education credits, and reexamination.

Certified Recreational Sports Specialist (C.R.S.S.)

In addition to the two professional certifications offered by the NRPA/ AALR, the National Intramural–Recreational Sports Association (NIRSA) offers a certificate to professionals working in the field of recreational sports. The certification was developed in 1979 to help maintain a high quality of professional competence of recreational sports specialists; to provide a means of identifying individuals who possess the necessary knowledge and expertise required in the field; to promote the educational standards set forth for recreational sports professionals; and to encourage professional growth and development of recreational sports personnel. A written examination is required which covers the following knowledge areas: programming, management and operations, risk management and legal concepts, program evaluation, participant's rights, history and philosophical foundations, and professional ethics. There are several categories of eligibility to sit for the exam, and interested individuals are encouraged to write for additional information (see page 489).

Specialty Certifications

Several different types of certifications exist that enhance the leadership skills and professional commitment of entry-level leisure services personnel. Individuals may be certified as youth coaches, sports officials, Special Olympics coaches and officials, aerobics instructors, ropes course facilitators, and others. In addition, leaders may be certified as having received instruction in reporting child abuse and universal precautions.

Youth Sports

Individuals interested in working in youth sports as coaches, directors of coaches, or officials may wish to be certified as a youth sports coach or official. These types of certification are offered nationally through the YMCA of the USA, many local organized youths sports programs, and the National Youth Sports Coaches Association (NYSCA). The NYSCA promotes national standards for youth sports. They include:

- selecting the proper environment for each child (i.e., considering age, developmental stage, type of sport, rules in the sport, and level of physical and emotional stress);

- selecting youth sports programs that are designed to enhance the emotional, physical, social, and educational well-being of children;

- encouraging a drug, tobacco, and alcohol-free environment for children;

- recognizing that youth sports are only a small part of a child's life;

- insisting that coaches are trained and certified;

- being positive role models exhibiting the ideals of fair play;

- insisting on safe playing facilities, healthful playing situations, and proper first aid;

- providing equal sports play opportunities for all youth regardless of race, creed, sex, economic status, or ability; and

- involved adults must be substance free at all youth sports activities (NYSCA, n.d.).

Youth sports coaches training programs vary in length from clinics of six hours to full-training programs up to 20 hours. Information usually covered in such training includes youth sports philosophy, rules of the game, developmental characteristics of youth, working with officials, substance abuse, and ideas for planning practices. By contacting the national offices, leisure services leaders can find information about state contacts and local certification programs:

National Youth Sports Coaches Association
2050 Vista Parkway
West Palm Beach, FL 33411
(407) 684-1141 or (800) 729-2057

Officials training is commonly offered through the regulating body of particular sport (e.g., Amateur Softball Association of America [ASA], United States Volleyball Association [USVBA]) and interested leisure services leaders are encouraged to seek additional information from these agencies:

Amateur Softball Association of America
2801 N. E. 50th Street
Oklahoma City, OK 73111
(405) 424-5266

United States Volleyball Association
3595 East Fountain Boulevard, Suite I-2
Colorado Springs, CO 80910
(719) 637-8300

USA Basketball (formerly known as the *Amateur Basketball
    Association of the United States)*
5465 Mark Dabling Boulevard
Colorado Springs, CO 80918
(719) 590-4800

Special Olympics Coach

Special Olympics International (SOI) offers training to individuals who desire to coach Special Olympic athletes in a variety of sports programs. Special Olympics has a tier system whereby different sports receive varying levels of technical support from the international organization. Tier I core sports receive the maximum support from Special Olympics International and include aquatics, athletics (track and field), basketball, bowling, football, alpine skiing, cross country skiing, and floor hockey. These sports tend to be those in which the largest number of athletes participate. Core sports in Tier II include cycling, gymnastics, powerlifting, roller-skating, softball, volleyball, figure skating, and speed skating—these sports receive some support from Special Olympics. Tier III sports receive the least support and include the following events: equestrian, table tennis, team handball, tennis, and poly hockey.

Special Olympics International offers three levels of coaching training—a Volunteer Coach Course, a Principles of Coaching Course, and an Advanced Sport Coach Course. The *Volunteer Coach Course* is an introductory-level course designed for volunteers and professionals who wish to coach Special Olympics athletes. Volunteer Coaches Training for Special Olympics athletes is available for all sports. The training commonly includes background information about Special Olympics International and its sports program, support services available for the coach, hints for recruiting athletes and assistant coaches, safety issues, developing seasonal coaching and practice plans, teaching the skills of an activity, improving athlete performance, preparing for competition, and a ten-hour practicum.

The Principles of Coaching Course is a non-sport-specific course addressing the fundamental principles of coaching Special Olympics athletes. It includes such material as philosophy of coaching, sports psychology, sports instruction planning, injury prevention and safety, and developing physical readiness for competition. The course involves a ten-hour practicum for completion.

The Advanced Sport Coach Course is an additional 16 hours of training and includes information about competition strategies, in-depth coverage of specific sport skills, and a greater understanding of training principles. As with the other coaching trainings, this certification requires a ten-hour practicum.

In addition to coaching certifications, Special Olympics offers a Special Olympics officials certification. This certification may be obtained through clinics and practicum experience at local, area, and chapter competitions. Material covered in training sessions includes the philosophy of Special Olympics International, information related to ability grouping for competition, general medical information, and rules interpretations specific to the sport.

Special Olympics International
1325 G Street NW, Suite 500
Washington, DC 20005
(202) 628-3630

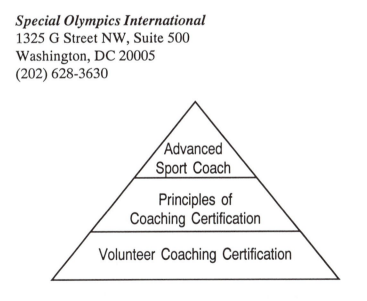

Figure 13.4 *Special Olympics International offers several levels of certifications for coaches and volunteers.*

Aerobics Leader Certification

As it becomes more evident that a qualified aerobics instructor or leader should know more than simply how to move to music, training for aerobics leaders and instructors is quickly becoming a prerequisite of employment. Certification programs are conducted by a variety of national and local agencies and hospitals, and commonly cover a wide spectrum of material. Information contained in typical aerobics instructor training include components of an exercise class, basic exercise selection, practical applications of exercise science, nutritional information, biomechanics of movement, exercise physiology, choreography, music selection, and safety and liability. Course lengths vary from 25 to 100 hours depending upon the agency or organization providing the certification. Several national agencies provide certification in aerobics leadership; several of the more widely accepted programs are listed below:

> ***Aerobics and Fitness Association of America (AFAA)***
> 15250 Ventura Boulevard, #200
> Sherman Oaks, CA 91403
> (800) 446-2322
>
> ***American College of Sports Medicine (ACSM)***
> P.O. Box 1440
> Indianapolis, IN 46206-1440
> (317) 637-9200
>
> ***American Council on Exercise (ACE)***
> 5820 Oberlin Drive, Suite 102
> San Diego, CA 92121-3787
> (800) 825-3636

Ropes Course Facilitator

While there is no one nationally accepted certification program for ropes course leaders, it is recognized that formal training and certification are highly desirable (i.e., industry standard) prior to leading groups on ropes or teams courses. In fact, there are many nationally accepted practices regarding safety and technical skills associated with a ropes course. Typically, ropes course facilitators require training in basic

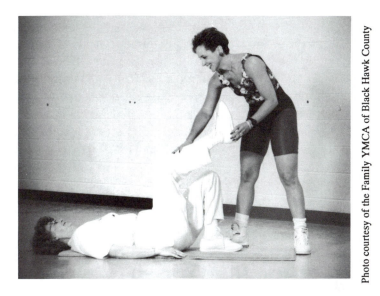

Photo courtesy of the Family YMCA of Black Hawk County

Leisure services leaders interested in fitness may wish to gain certification in one-on-one training and aerobics.

adventure programming, facilitation skills, group dynamics, safety and rescue, ropes and knots, program planning, working with people with disabilities on ropes courses, and structure maintenance. Ropes course facilitator training typically requires a practicum of some type. Length of course varies from one day to two weeks depending upon the breadth and complexity of the material to be covered. For certification and course information leaders are encouraged to contact:

Project Adventure
P.O. Box 100
Hamilton, MA 01936
(508) 468-7981

CradleRock Outdoor Network
P.O. Box 730
Lake Harmony, PA 18624
(717) 722-3500

YMCA of the USA Training Program

The YMCA of the USA offers various training at program schools across the country which lead to various certifications. All sessions are open to YMCA volunteers and staff members, and some training is open to the general public. The YMCA of the USA trains people in many diverse areas such as CPR and first aid; "Working With" programs for specific populations such as different age groups, people with disabilities, program volunteers, and military families; aquatics, camping, childcare, community development (e.g., substance abuse prevention, prejudice awareness, conflict and violence prevention and management), health and fitness (e.g., Fitness Leader, Fitness Instructor, healthy back, prenatal/postpartum exercise), youth sports, and teen leadership. In addition, the YMCA of the USA provides leadership and management training for directors in their Executive Development Program. Course hours and prerequisites vary with course sessions typically from four (e.g., the "Working With" programs) to 28 (e.g., aquatics) hours in length.

Mandatory Reporter Training

Colleges, universities, and many nonprofit organizations now offer training related to information needed by mandatory reporters of child abuse. Typical training sessions are two to four hours in length. These are noncertification courses that provide information about recognizing signs of child abuse, what to do if a child reports abuse, and identifying resources for intervention.

Universal Precautions

Similar to mandatory reporter training, several different agencies offer training and awareness sessions about universal precautions. As noted earlier in this chapter, universal precautions are those steps taken when handling an individual's bodily fluids to minimize the transmission of disease. Typical noncertification courses are two to four hours in length.

American Red Cross Community First-Aid and Safety Education

The American Red Cross is internationally known for its development of and training in health and safety standards. The Red Cross continually updates and improves its standards and educational programs. The most commonly sought certifications are related to emergency care. The Community First-Aid and Safety Education program is divided into three sections: Adult CPR, Child and Infant CPR, and First Aid.

Cardiopulmonary Resuscitation (CPR)

Leisure services leaders are often required by job position to be certified in basic life saving skills. Typically, recreation and leisure services agencies require direct leaders to be certified in cardiopulmonary resuscitation (CPR) and first aid. The American Red Cross is the primary agency that certifies individuals for CPR competency, although the American Heart Association and the YMCA of the USA provide similar certifications.

Through the American Red Cross, leaders can be certified in two types of CPR—Adult CPR, and Child and Infant CPR. Currently, the Red Cross requires certification in Adult CPR as a prerequisite to both Child and Infant CPR and First-Aid Certification. All CPR certifications are valid for one year.

Adult CPR. Initial Adult CPR training requires four hours of class time with practice on a mannequin. American Red Cross CPR training involves practicing an emergency action plan—caring for breathing emergencies, airway obstruction, cardiac emergencies—and information about how to prevent heart attacks.

Child and Infant CPR. Child and Infant CPR requires five hours of training and addresses basic life support for persons under the age of nine years. It also covers how to prevent injuries to infants and children in and around the home and play areas. Recertification may be completed on a "challenge" basis whereby within one year of initial certification individuals may be recertified after being tested on their skills and passing the written exam.

Community CPR. As a combined course, leaders may take community CPR, which is a six-and-a-half-hour course that teaches recognizing and caring for breathing and cardiac emergencies in adults, infants, and children.

CPR for the Professional Rescuer. CPR for the professional rescuer is designed as a nine-hour course for individuals who are expected to respond to emergencies as a part of their jobs. Covered in this course are principles of CPR for adults, children and infants, two-person CPR, ventilation with airbag and mask, and how to minimize disease transmission. There are no prerequisites for this course. Because of the thoroughness of course content, CPR for the professional rescuer is the course recommended for leisure services leaders. Recertification courses are four-and-a-half hours in length and must be completed prior to the one-year expiration of initial certification.

CPR/First-Aid Instructor. Beyond being certified as competent in CPR, an individual may be certified as a CPR/First-Aid Instructor; this certification is for those interested in teaching CPR and first aid. Many leisure services agencies now require at least one staff member to meet this level of certification to serve as the certifying instructor for all employees. Previous teaching and/or certifications are not required to become a CPR/First-Aid Instructor. The course is sixteen hours long and is valid for three years.

First Aid

As the third unit of its Community Safety Education program, the American Red Cross offers courses in **Community First Aid.** Bleeding, shock, broken bones, seizures, poisoning, and other emergency situations are covered in this nine-hour training program. Adult CPR and Child and Infant CPR are included in the community first-aid certification; the first-aid certification is valid for three years, and the CPR certifications are valid for one year.

First Aid—Responding to Emergencies. A more in-depth first-aid course is also offered by the American Red Cross called First Aid: Responding to Emergencies. This course is a semester-long course offered at many colleges, universities, community colleges, and technical schools. First Aid—Responding to Emergencies covers CPR for adults, CPR for children and infants, first aid, and material related to prevention of injury and illness.

Aquatics Certifications

Anyone desiring to work in or near water, whether it be a swimming pool, waterpark, or natural waterfront will be required to hold one or more aquatic certifications. As with first-aid and safety education, the American Red Cross is the most widely recognized and accepted certification program for aquatic certification needs. Aquatic safety programs range from basic "drown proofing" to teaching swimming to advanced water rescue techniques.

The American Red Cross offers a variety of aquatic certifications—a must for any leader working near water.

Community Water Safety

Community Water Safety is a four-hour course that provides individuals with general water safety information. The course is designed to create an awareness of the causes and prevention of aquatic injuries. The course includes information about staying safe while having fun, preparing for water activities, water hazards, aquatic recreation, and taking action in an emergency.

Basic Water Safety

Basic Water Safety is a nine-hour course that provides individuals with general water safety information. The course is designed to create an awareness of the causes and prevention of aquatic accidents. Course content includes: information about how to prevent water injuries; self-help skills (e.g., releasing cramps, recognition of hypothermia); reaching, throwing, and wading assists; types of life jackets and their proper use; and diving safety.

Emergency Water Safety

Emergency Water Safety is another nine-hour course specifically designed for persons in recreation, education, and public service positions who are going to be responding to various types of aquatic emergencies.

Course content includes towing a passive victim, rescue breathing in shallow water, escape techniques, procedures for handling spinal injuries, and removal of an injured or ill person from the water.

Basic Lifeguarding

Basic Lifeguarding is an 18-hour course and provides entry-level knowledge, skills, and training needed by an individual to become a lifeguard at a swimming pool. Participants must be at least fifteen years of age and pass a water skills test to enter the course. Material in this course includes preventative lifeguard skills, steps to reduce or eliminate hazards at a pool, rescue techniques including assists and proper use of equipment, and procedures for handling spinal injuries.

Lifeguard Training

Lifeguard Training is a 33-hour course designed for individuals wishing to lifeguard at all types of bodies of water. Prerequisites for this course include the requirement that candidates be a minimum of fifteen years of age and pass a water skills test. Course content includes professional rescue techniques, interacting with the public, preventing aquatic injuries, patron surveillance, being prepared for emergencies, first aid for injuries and illnesses, handling of spinal injury, and what to do after an emergency. Three certifications are provided upon completion of this course: Lifeguard, First Aid, and CPR for the Professional Rescuer.

Head Lifeguard

Head Lifeguard Training is offered by the American Red Cross to individuals who are currently certified as lifeguards and wish to learn more about supervisory positions. The focus of the course is on the roles and responsibilities of the head lifeguard, minimizing risk, aquatic injury prevention, selecting lifeguards, training, building a lifeguard team, interacting with the public, emergency response, and looking to the future. Head Lifeguard Training is a six-hour course.

Water Safety Instructor (WSI)

In the 36-hour Water Safety Instructor (WSI) program, individuals learn to teach learn-to-swim and community water safety courses. Prerequisites include: a minimum age of seventeen years, completion of a three-hour precourse session, and completion of instructor candidate training (done in the WSI class). Focused on teaching swimming skills, the content of this course includes teaching progressions, the development of lesson plans, recognition of skill errors and the ability to give corrective feedback, motor learning and hydrodynamic principles, cultural diversity, fitness and training, and disabilities and other conditions. The course begins with a preliminary written swimming and water safety skills test as a prerequisite for continuation.

Lifeguarding Instructor

In this 15-hour program, individuals learn to teach American Red Cross lifeguarding and water safety courses (Basic Water Safety and Emergency Water Safety). Contents include course administration and planning, teaching progressions for lifeguarding and water safety skills, and recognizing common skill errors and providing corrective feedback. There is a prerequisite of lifeguard training to enroll in this course.

As can be seen from the certifications mentioned here, there are many avenues for professional education for leisure services leaders. The list of above certifications is by no means exhaustive; several agencies and organizations offer other leadership level certifications which would enhance various types of leisure services positions. Entry level leisure services personnel are strongly encouraged to seek out appropriate certifications and training to enhance their sense of competence and professional growth. In addition to certifications for enhancing one's direct leadership skills, joining professional organizations and associations is another indication of one's commitment to the profession and continued personal and professional education.

Professional Associations

Membership in professional organizations provides an opportunity to network with practitioners and educators, gain new information, and promote one's own organization or agency. Like gaining appropriate certifications, a membership in one or more professional associations is indicative of a commitment to the profession and an interest in personal growth and development. There are national associations for all interest areas in the leisure services profession. This diversity in professional associations allows one to join and network with other professionals who share interests and concerns specific to one (or many) leisure services specialty. This networking provides opportunities for individuals to share problems, solutions, issues, and success stories with one another.

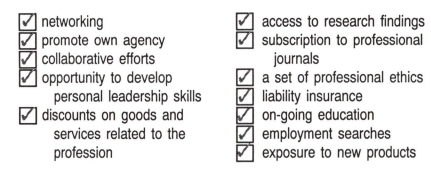

Figure 13.5   The benefits of joining and participating in professional associations are quite varied.

In addition to networking with other professionals, many professional organizations develop and promote standards of practice. This is evidenced in the various certification and accreditation programs offered by professional associations such as the C.L.P. and C.T.R.S. certifications offered by NRPA/AALR. The certification programs are one method of continuing education. In addition to this, many professional associations offer periodic conferences where educational sessions are offered to delegates. It is common for individuals to gain CEUs (continuing education units) during these conferences to maintain certification.

Other benefits of joining professional associations include access to research findings about practical issues; access to liability, health, and retirement benefits; subscription to a professional journal or magazine, and the opportunity to become involved in developing the profession through association leadership. Furthermore, many professional associations offer educational scholarships to college students.

As mentioned, there are a large number of professional organizations to represent the varying nature and character of the profession. Many of these organizations are commonly referred to by their acronyms. Thus, the Association for Experiential Education is more commonly known and referred to among its membership as AEE. Some of the more common professional organizations that employ individuals in the leisure services field include the following:

American Alliance for Health, Physical Education, Recreation and Dance (AAHPERD)
1900 Association Drive
Reston, VA 22091
(703) 476-7300
Internet: aalr@aahperd.org

AAHPERD is dedicated to promoting those who have interests in health and safety education, intramurals, aging, fitness research, physical education, adapted physical education, sport, dance, leisure and recreation, and outdoor education and recreation. The major publication of AAHPERD is the *Journal of Physical Education, Recreation and Dance*. AALR is the substructure of AAHPERD dedicated to promoting the field of leisure and recreation within the membership of AAHPERD. NRPA and AALR work in collaboration with one another to accredit colleges and universities and to certify individual professionals.

American Camping Association (ACA)
Bradford Woods
5000 State Route 67N
Martinsville, IN 46151
(317) 342-8456

The American Camping Association is concerned primarily with increasing and assuring the quality of organized camping and conference centers. Membership in ACA is open to individuals and organized camps that promote camping activities, including those involved in providing camping programs at private, youth-serving, church, and in agency/nonprofit organizations. ACA holds an annual convention, manages and publishes camping related books, and produces its primary publication, *Camping Magazine*, on a bimonthly basis. In addition, ACA conducts an internationally recognized accreditation process for camps and conference centers.

Association for Experiential Education (AEE)
2885 Aurora Avenue, #28
Boulder, CO 80303-2252
(303) 440-8844
Internet: aaemikal@nile.com

The AEE has its roots in adventure education and is committed to furthering experience-based teaching and learning in all settings. AEE has several professional and special interest groups within it including: experience-based training and development; schools and colleges; women in experiential education; therapeutic adventure; and Natives, Africans, Asians, Latinos(as) and Allies of AEE. Members include people involved in schools, recreation programs, human service providers, correctional and mental health institutions, youth service agencies programs for people with disabilities, environmental centers, outdoor adventure organizations, and universities.

AEE provides program accreditation and peer review for adventure education and experiential education programs internationally. AEE publishes and sells several books and other publications for those interested in outdoor and experiential education. Membership benefits include receiving the *Journal of Experiential Education* (three times a year), newsletters, and discounts on AEE publications and conferences. A listserv (or electronic mail list) is available on the Internet for those interested in learning more about the issues affecting experiential education. To subscribe to this listserv send an e-mail message to *listproc@lists.princeton.edu*. The e-mail message must be sent from your account (the list pulls your e-mail address from the header). Leave the subject line blank and in the body of the message type: subscribe aeelist (your name).

American Therapeutic Recreation Association (ATRA)
P.O. Box 15215
Hattiesburg, MS 39402-5215
(800) 553-0304

The American Therapeutic Recreation Association is one of the newest professional organizations available to those interested in therapeutic recreation. As a nonprofit organization, its primary purpose is to promote the needs of therapeutic recreation professionals in healthcare and human service settings. ATRA was founded because of the need for recognition and accountability in medical settings. Its major publication is the *Therapeutic Recreation Annual.*

National Intramural-Recreation Sports Association (NIRSA)
850 Southwest 15th Street
Corvallis, OR 97333-4145
(503) 737-2088

NIRSA is a professional organization which has as a goal to foster the growth of quality recreational sports programs by providing for the continuing growth and development of recreational sports professionals. Membership is comprised of professionals involved in recreational sports programming at the collegiate level (intramurals, sports clubs, campus recreation), in the military, correctional facilities, and public schools. Individuals working in these settings are typically involved in informal sports, programming, fitness, recreation facility operations, fiscal and personnel management, intramurals, wellness programs, and the administration of outdoor recreation programs. Membership benefits include publications such as the *NIRSA Journal*, which is published three times a year; a newsletter; and conference proceedings. In addition NIRSA offers research grants, job listings, annual national and regional conferences, and officiating instruction and certification for recreational sports officials.

National Recreation and Park Association (NRPA)
2775 South Quincy Street, Suite 300
Arlington, VA 22206-2204
(703) 820-4940

The National Recreation and Park Association is the primary professional association of parks, recreation, and leisure services professionals. It serves professionals, volunteers, students, universities and agencies/organizations. NRPA holds an annual congress and provides a variety of services and publications for its diverse membership body. Its major publication is *Parks and Recreation Magazine*, although it also publishes *Trends*, the *Therapeutic Recreation Journal* and others. NRPA, in conjunction with AALR, implements and conducts an accreditation and certification program of colleges and universities to ensure standards commensurate with a high quality profession.

Within NRPA there are many branch affiliates designed to facilitate meeting the needs of its diverse constituencies. These include the National Student Recreation and Park Society (NSRPS), National Therapeutic Recreation Society (NTRS), Society of Park and Recreation Educators (SPRE), American Park and Recreation Society (APRS), National Society for Park Resources (NSPR), Armed Forces Recreation Society (AFRS), Citizen and/or Board Member (CBM), National Aquatics Section (NAS), and Leisure and Aging Section (LAS).

While not directly connected to NRPA, a listserv has been developed to learn more about needs and concerns of leisure services professionals to which many NRPA members belong. More information can be gained by subscribing to Leisurenet through the following process. Send a message to *listproc@gu.edu.au* with the subject line blank and typing in the message body: subscribe leisurenet.

Resort and Commercial Recreation Association (RCRA)
P.O. Box 1208
New Port Richey, FL 34656-1208
(813) 845-7373

RCRA is dedicated to promoting the interests, education, and networking of those interested in the resort and commercial recreation field. RCRA holds regional and national conferences and provides a number of services to its members including a job placement service, job fair, internship placement opportunities and a newsletter.

In addition to the organizations and associations identified above, nearly every state has its own professional organization. These organizations and associations are typically associated with a national association. For example, the Iowa Parks and Recreation Association (IPRA) is the state association linked to NRPA. It views itself as a service organization supported by membership dues and voluntary contributions. A journal, entitled *Iowa Parks and Recreation*, is published biannually. The organization offers an annual conference and workshops, scholarship program, as well as other services and opportunities to network.

As a state association linked with AAHPERD, the Iowa Association of Health, Physical Education, Recreation and Dance (IAHPERD) exists to meet the needs of physical education, dance, health, and recreation professionals within the state of Iowa. It holds an annual conference, publishes a journal biannually (*IAHPERD Journal*), and provides funding for special projects. Likewise, the Iowa Section of the American Camping Association is the state association that provides ACA services to individuals and organizations within the state. Fall and winter workshops, educational sessions, and a bimonthly newsletter are products of this association.

Summary

This chapter has addressed selected social and professional issues impacting leisure services leaders and the profession. It is easy to see how these issues impact on the profession, and the individual leadership style of leisure services professionals. An in-depth look at child abuse as a social issue impacts leisure services leaders in two ways: leisure services leaders may serve as those who intervene on behalf of an abuse victim, and leisure services leaders must take care to avoid situations in which they might be perceived as perpetrators of child maltreatment.

Leisure services leaders exhibit a commitment to the field of leisure services through their own competence and continued education. Evidence of this commitment may be seen through the various certifications one may obtain in efforts to improve leadership skills; certifications indicate that the holder has met a minimum level of standards. In addition to health and/or safety certifications and those associated with particular skill areas, another way in which leisure services leaders illustrate an interest in furthering the profession is through membership in one or more professional organizations. Ongoing practice of skills and involvement in the profession are ways in which leisure services leaders improve their professional standing and become more effective leaders.

The Front Line

Becoming a competent and effective leisure services leader is a lifelong process that takes commitment, desire, continued education, and practice. All of these elements come from within each person and each person will develop on her or his own time table and in her or his own style. However, every parks, recreation, and leisure services leader can be helped in achieving quality leadership through an early start with professional involvement and networking.

To become involved in the profession, developing leisure services leaders are encouraged to peruse professional magazines and journals to keep up with the rapid changes in social and professional issues affecting the field. By joining Internet listservs that are geared toward one's area of professional interest and searching the World Wide Web one can learn a tremendous amount about the issues and concerns facing the profession. In addition, computer listservs are quickly becoming methods of distance networking.

Personal networking may be accomplished by meeting and visiting with practitioners in the area. The more people in the field a leader knows and the more people in the field know about the individual, the greater the chance of advancement in leisure services leadership. Attending, presenting, and volunteering at professional conferences are valuable ways of becoming personally acquainted with practitioners who may later serve as mentors and teachers. Leaders who are professionally involved at the local, state, regional, national, and international levels typically are exposed to a wide variety of learning and professional opportunities.

Practicing leadership at every opportunity in a variety of situations will help improve technical, human relations, and conceptual skills of leadership. To do this students can begin by speaking up in classes; the more one becomes comfortable and practiced with speaking in front of groups, the easier and more flowing direct leadership skills become. Volunteering at a wide variety of leisure services organizations will enable a developing leader to practice skills in different situations with different types of participants. In addition to volunteering, job experiences that require standing, moving, and speaking in front of groups of people will serve to provide practice of direct leadership skills.

In addition to speaking with and leading groups, to develop and maintain effective leadership skills it is necessary to collect and utilize a breadth of resources including books, videos, audiotapes, slides, films, catalogs, photographs, computer software, and activity files. Developing a library of resources and becoming familiar with those resources will help in the many different situations a leader is likely to face in the leisure services profession.

References

Edginton, C., Jordan, D., DeGraaf, D., and Edginton, S. (1995). *Leisure and life satisfaction: Foundational perspectives.* Dubuque, IA: Brown & Benchmark Publishers.

Gustavsson, N. and Segal, E. (1994). *Critical issues in child welfare.* Newbury Park, CA: Sage Publications, Inc.

Howing, P., Wodarski, J., Kurtz, P., and Gaudin, J. (1993). *Maltreatment and the school-age child.* Binghamton, NY: Haworth Press Inc.

Land, H. (Ed.). (1992). *AIDS: A complete guide to psychosocial intervention.* Milwaukee, WI: Family Service America.

McWhirter, J., McWhirter, B., McWhirter, A., and McWhirter, E. (1993). *At-risk youth: A comprehensive response.* Pacific Grove, CA: Brooks/Cole Publishing Co.

Monteleone, J. (1994). *Recognition of child abuse for the mandated reporter.* St. Louis, MO: Mosby-Year Book, Inc.

Myers, J. (1994). *The backlash: Child protection under fire.* Newbury Park, CA: Sage Publications, Inc.

National Youth Sport Coaches Association (NYSCA). (n.d.). *National standards for youth sports.* West Palm Beach, FL: Author.

Parents and Coaches in Sports. (n.d.). *Keep child abuse out of child sports* (brochure). Author.

Rothery, M. and Cameron, G. (Eds.). (1990). *Child maltreatment: Expanding our concept of helping.* Hillsdale, NJ: Lawrence Erlbaum Associates.

Skaros, S. (1995). Blood borne pathogens: HIV and HBV contagion risks at camp. *Camping Magazine, 68*(3), 28-31.

INDEX

The A•B•Cs of Behavior Change: Skills for Working with Behavior Problems in Nursing Homes
 by Margaret D. Cohn, Michael A. Smyer and Ann L. Horgas
Activity Experiences and Programming Within Long-Term Care
 by Ted Tedrick and Elaine R. Green
The Activity Gourmet
 by Peggy Powers
Advanced Concepts for Geriatric Nursing Assistants
 by Carolyn A. McDonald
Adventure Education
 edited by John C. Miles and Simon Priest
Assessment: The Cornerstone of Activity Programs
 by Ruth Perschbacher
Behavior Modification in Therapeutic Recreation: An Introductory Learning Manual
 by John Dattilo and Milliam D. Murphy
Benefits of Leisure
 edited by B. L. Driver, Perry J. Brown and George L. Peterson
Benefits of Recreation Research Update
 by Judy M. Sefton and W. Kerry Mummery
Beyond Bingo: Innovative Programs for the New Senior
 by Sal Arrigo, Jr., Ann Lewis and Hank Mattimore
Both Gains and Gaps: Feminist Perspectives on Women's Leisure
 by Karla Henderson, M. Deborah Bialeschki, Susan M. Shaw and
  Valeria J. Freysinger
The Community Tourism Industry Imperative—The Necessity, The Opportunities, Its Potential
 by Uel Blank
Dimensions of Choice: A Qualitative Approach to Recreation, Parks, and Leisure Research
 by Karla A. Henderson
Evaluating Leisure Services: Making Enlightened Decisions
 by Karla A. Henderson with M. Deborah Bialeschki
The Evolution of Leisure: Historical and Philosophical Perspectives (Second Printing)
 by Thomas Goodale and Geoffrey Godbey
The Game Finder—A Leader's Guide to Great Activities
 by Annette C. Moore
Getting People Involved in Life and Activities: Effective Motivating Techniques
 by Jeanne Adams
Great Special Events and Activities
 by Annie Morton, Angie Prosser and Sue Spangler
Inclusive Leisure Services: Responding to the Rights of People with Disabilities
 by John Dattilo
Internships in Recreation and Leisure Services: A Practical Guide for Students
 by Edward E. Seagle, Jr., Ralph W. Smith and Lola M. Dalton
Interpretation of Cultural and Natural Resources
 by Douglas M. Knudson, Ted T. Cable and Larry Beck
Introduction to Leisure Services—7th Edition
 by H. Douglas Sessoms and Karla A. Henderson

Other Books by Venture Publishing

Leadership and Administration of Outdoor Pursuits, Second Edition
   by Phyllis Ford and James Blanchard
Leisure And Family Fun (LAFF)
   by Mary Atteberry-Rogers
The Leisure Diagnostic Battery: Users Manual and Sample Forms
   by Peter A. Witt and Gary Ellis
Leisure Diagnostic Battery Computer Software
   by Gary Ellis and Peter A. Witt
Leisure Education: A Manual of Activities and Resources
   by Norma J. Stumbo and Steven R. Thompson
Leisure Education II: More Activities and Resources
   by Norma J. Stumbo
Leisure Education Program Planning: A Systematic Approach
   by John Dattilo and William D. Murphy
Leisure in Your Life: An Exploration, Fourth Edition
   by Geoffrey Godbey
Leisure Services in Canada: An Introduction
   by Mark S. Searle and Russell E. Brayley
Marketing for Parks, Recreation, and Leisure
   by Ellen L. O'Sullivan
*Models of Change in Municipal Parks and Recreation: A Book of Innovative
   Case Studies*
      edited by Mark E. Havitz
Nature and the Human Spirit: Toward an Expanded Land Management Ethic
      edited by B. L. Driver, Daniel Dustin, Tony Baltic, Gary Elsner and
         George Peterson
Outdoor Recreation Management: Theory and Application, Third Edition
   by Alan Jubenville and Ben Twight
Planning Parks for People
   by John Hultsman, Richard L. Cottrell and Wendy Zales Hultsman
Private and Commercial Recreation
   edited by Arlin Epperson
The Process of Recreation Programming Theory and Technique, Third Edition
   by Patricia Farrell and Herberta M. Lundegren
Protocols for Recreation Therapy Programs
      edited by Jill Kelland, along with the Recreation Therapy Staff at
         Alberta Hospital Edmonton
Quality Management: Applications for Therapeutic Recreation
   edited by Bob Riley
Recreation and Leisure: Issues in an Era of Change, Third Edition
   edited by Thomas Goodale and Peter A. Witt
Recreation Programming and Activities for Older Adults
   by Jerold E. Elliott and Judith A. Sorg-Elliott
*Recreation Programs that Work for At-Risk Youth: The Challenge of Shaping
   the Future*
      edited by Peter A. Witt and John L. Crompton
Reference Manual for Writing Rehabilitation Therapy Treatment Plans
   by Penny Hogberg and Mary Johnson
Research in Therapeutic Recreation: Concepts and Methods
   edited by Marjorie J. Malkin and Christine Z. Howe

Other Books by Venture Publishing

Risk Management in Therapeutic Recreation: A Component of Quality Assurance
      by Judith Voelkl
A Social History of Leisure Since 1600
      by Gary Cross
The Sociology of Leisure
      by John R. Kelly and Geoffrey Godbey
A Study Guide for National Certification in Therapeutic Recreation
      by Gerald O'Morrow and Ron Reynolds
Therapeutic Activity Intervention with the Elderly: Foundations and Practices
      by Barbara A. Hawkins, Marti E. May and Nancy Brattain Rogers
Therapeutic Recreation: Cases and Exercises
      by Barbara C. Wilhite and M. Jean Keller
Therapeutic Recreation in the Nursing Home
      by Linda Buettner and Shelley L. Martin
Therapeutic Recreation Protocol for Treatment of Substance Addictions
      by Rozanne W. Faulkner
*A Training Manual for Americans With Disabilities Act Compliance in Parks
and Recreation Settings*
      by Carol Stensrud
Understanding Leisure and Recreation: Mapping the Past, Charting the Future
      edited by Edgar L. Jackson and Thomas L. Burton

Venture Publishing, Inc.
1999 Cato Avenue
State College, PA 16801

Phone: (814) 234-4561; FAX: (814) 234-1651